"It is notable that La Leche League started in 1956, long before it was widely recognized how much people with similar problems and loving hearts could help each other by organizing."
 —Niles Newton, PhD, professor of behavioral sciences,
  Northwestern University Medical School

"*The Womanly Art of Breastfeeding* is not a textbook. It is by itself a work of art. Every pregnant woman, every young mother should share the atmosphere this book spreads."
   —Michael Odent, MD, obstetrics, France

"The newborn baby will have only three demands. They are warmth in the arms of its mother, food from her breasts, and security in the knowledge of her presence. Breastfeeding satisfies all three." —Dr. Grantly Dick-Read

"Breastfeeding is an integral part of the reproductive process, the natural and ideal way of feeding an infant, and a unique biological and emotional basis for child development."
   —The World Health Organization

"If I had a very large, shiny, gold medal, I would like to present it to La Leche League on behalf of the hundreds of thousands of women who—like me—have learned so much about the art of breastfeeding and mothering from the combined wisdom of La Leche League mothers."
  —Dr. Penny A. Stanway, MRCS, LRCP, MBBS,
   general practice, Surrey, England

The Womanly Art of Breastfeeding

FORTIETH
ANNIVERSARY EDITION

A PLUME BOOK

PLUME
Published by the Penguin Group
Penguin Putnam Inc., 375 Hudson Street, New York, New York 10014, U.S.A.
Penguin Books Ltd, 27 Wrights Lane, London W8 5TZ, England
Penguin Books Australia Ltd, Ringwood, Victoria, Australia
Penguin Books Canada Ltd, 10 Alcorn Avenue, Toronto, Ontario, Canada M4V 3B2
Penguin Books (N.Z.) Ltd, 182–190 Wairau Road, Auckland 10, New Zealand

Penguin Books Ltd, Registered Offices: Harmondsworth, Middlesex, England

Published by Plume, an imprint of Dutton Signet,
a member of Penguin Putnam Inc.

First Plume Printing (Sixth Edition), September, 1997
10 9 8 7 6 5 4 3

Published by arrangement with La Leche League International.

Ⓟ REGISTERED TRADEMARK—MARCA REGISTRADA

La Leche League and 🤱 are registered trademarks of La Leche League International, Inc.

Library of Congress Cataloging-in-Publication Data is available.
ISBN 0-452-27908-9

Printed in the United States of America
Designed by Digital Concepts, L.L.C.
40th Anniversary Edition revised and edited by Judy Torgus and Gwen Gotsch

Photo credits are listed in the appendix.

BOOKS ARE AVAILABLE AT QUANTITY DISCOUNTS WHEN USED TO PROMOTE PRODUCTS OR
SERVICES. FOR INFORMATION PLEASE WRITE TO PREMIUM MARKETING DIVISION,
PENGUIN PUTNAM INC., 375 HUDSON STREET, NEW YORK, NEW YORK 10014.

DEDICATION

*We dedicate this book with much
love to the many caring parents who
have helped make La Leche League
what it is today, and to our patient,
loving husbands and children, all of
whom helped the seven of us learn
the womanly art of breastfeeding.*

*This book could not have been
written and the basic principles
underlying the work of La Leche
League would not have withstood
the test of time, had it not been for
the unfailing counsel of Doctors
Herbert Ratner and Gregory
White, who have wholeheartedly
supported us from the earliest days
of La Leche League. For this, we
are most grateful.*

CONTENTS

FOREWORD

I would not be alive today if not for breastfeeding.

In 1941, when I was born, the little village at the foothill of the mountain range between Thailand and Malaysia was caught madly in the battles of the start of World War II. But I was fortunate. My mother nursed me with the goodness of her milk and the love and care that came with it.

The natural power of breastfeeding is one of the greatest wonders of the world. It is about real love. It is about caring and celebrating the wondrous joy of nurturing a new life. It is about enjoying being a woman.

In a world too often dominated by materialism and greed, every act of the natural power of breastfeeding reminds us that there is another way, the natural way, the breastfeeding way.

Breastfeeding is about the power of peace, the power of goodness, and the power of responsibility.

Today, all over the world, women demonstrate this power by choosing to breastfeed. They celebrate this power and joy by helping other mothers who wish to exercise this natural choice.

Today, all over the world, the people in La Leche League International (LLLI) make breastfeeding happen. Through the partnership that LLLI forges with the World Alliance for Breastfeeding Action (WABA), groups all over the world act in unison to protect, to promote, and to support breastfeeding worldwide. And from August 1 to 7, every year, thousands of groups and millions of people celebrate this great cause through World Breastfeeding Week.

The United Nations, particularly through the United Nations Children's Fund (UNICEF), and the World Health Organization (WHO) have provided a Code that serves as a global framework to ensure that the culture of breastfeeding is not undermined.

The greatest power of all in ensuring the maintenance of the culture of breastfeeding is going to be the living example of breastfeeding mothers everywhere, demonstrating and sharing their knowledge and their wisdom about this universal heritage. This is why LLLI is so important and why this book is so necessary.

Mother-to-mother support is the warm, family, and community way and this book helps to gather the great wisdom into useful information. Don't be without it and don't forget to give a copy to a friend. It is this kind of assertive action, this linking and multiplying, that will help more and more mothers, and children, to share in the joy and power of a breastfeeding culture. It's baby-friendly, it's mother-friendly, it's family-friendly, it's community-friendly, it's eco-friendly, and good economics, too.

Enjoy!

Anwar Fazal
Chairperson
World Alliance for Breastfeeding Action (WABA)
Recipient of the Right Livelihood Award,
popularly called the "Alternative Nobel Prize"
Penang, Malaysia, May 1997

INTRODUCTION

Breastfeeding a baby—what could be more natural? Just cradle that precious newborn in your arms and offer him your breast. It sounds easy enough.

Breastfeeding a baby is simple and natural—if you know how to do it and what to expect. But it takes information and encouragement and some motherly know-how to nurse a baby, as the seven of us who founded La Leche League quickly discovered with our first breastfeeding attempts. How often should you nurse? How long on each side? How do you know if baby is getting enough to eat? What other foods does he need? And what if he seems hungry again only an hour after he has been fed?

When the seven of us found each other in 1956 and formed La Leche League, answers to such questions were as scarce as mother's milk itself. But we had breastfed a combined total of twenty-four babies, and by then had a good idea of what did and didn't work, what was and wasn't helpful. The secret of success in nursing a baby, we had discovered, was having the right information and having another breastfeeding mother to turn to for advice and reassurance.

In THE WOMANLY ART OF BREASTFEEDING we have attempted to put a philosophy about being a mother and nurturing an infant between covers. This book is our way of sharing the sense of satisfaction and fulfillment countless mothers have found through breastfeeding their babies, and the special joys that are awaiting as you embark on the great adventure of motherhood.

Our first two editions, published in 1958 and 1963, were based largely on our own personal experiences. The third edition, published in 1981, was enlarged and expanded to include the combined wisdom accumulated from thousands of breastfeeding mothers who had shared their stories and experiences with us. The fourth edition included new information, reflected current medical research, and continued the tradition of providing practical suggestions based on the experiences of breastfeeding mothers from all over the world.

The fifth edition commemorated the organization's thirty-fifth anniversary. While it was not a major revision, specific information was updated throughout the book and current research was included in the chapters on the benefits of breastfeeding.

The sixth revised edition can be considered a major revision. A great deal of new information is included, reflecting the broad range of research that has been done in recent years on breastfeeding management and the benefits of human milk. This edition celebrates La Leche League International's 40th Anniversary and is designed to reach mothers into the 21st century.

You will notice that we write from the perspective of a household consisting of husband, wife, and child or children. Some have pointed out to us that this is not a realistic approach nowadays. But we are convinced that breastfeeding and mothering progress more easily in such an environment. From personal experience, we also know that this situation does not always hold true in real life. Sometimes the father is missing from the family, and mothering then becomes a solitary endeavor. It is not an easy situation for a woman to be in. But no matter what else happens in her life, a mother can take great satisfaction in breastfeeding her baby and staying close to him. Her efforts in this regard bring a feeling of accomplishment that will increase in value as time goes by.

Our wish is that every mother anywhere in the world who wants to breastfeed her baby will have the information and support she needs to do so. Yes, breastfeeding is simple and natural—and an exquisitely beautiful way to nourish and nurture a new life.

We appreciate and applaud the fact that babies come in two genders, but in this book, we refer to baby as "he," not with sexist intent, but simply for clarity's sake, since mother is unquestionably "she."

PART ONE | *Planning to Breastfeed*

CHAPTER 1

Why Choose Breastfeeding?

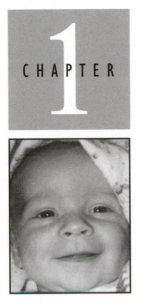

Breastfeeding is the most natural source of nourishment and security for your baby. For many mothers, breastfeeding is a fulfillment of what it means to be a woman. Pregnancy, childbirth, and breastfeeding comprise a special phase in your life—one that is bound up with an extraordinary array of emotions.

Expecting a baby brings with it a sudden realization that your life will never be the same. You recognize the need to learn more about being a mother, but you may feel doubt and uncertainty about being able to cope.

You may even share the feeling of this mother: "When I was expecting my first baby, my husband and I didn't feel comfortable about becoming parents. We had no friends or relatives living near us who had babies. We were confused by what we read, what we were told, and what we felt.... After four years and two breastfed babies, we now feel better about being parents and we also know what to listen to—our hearts."

As you watch your body grow and change to accommodate the growing child within you, you can be reassured that your own capabilities to care for your baby after he is born will also adjust to meet your baby's needs. Breastfeeding offers a beautiful transition for mother and baby alike as they learn about each other in those first hours and days following birth.

A Special JOURNEY

During early pregnancy, your baby's development is nothing short of remarkable. Eighteen days after he is conceived, his heart is beating. About the fourth month or so of your pregnancy, you feel the flutter, the unmistakable stirring that is like no other. It's the revelation of a new life. Your body changes to meet your baby's needs. There's the swelling readiness of your breasts, the expanding cradle of your womb. You are beautiful, as lovely as a tree that is heavy with fruit.

During the last trimester—the seventh, eighth, and ninth months—you may be impatient, eager to complete this stage and have the baby. Then, often when you least expect it, you feel a twinge. And another. The time is here. Mingled relief and anticipation can bring a catch in your throat. Today, sometime soon, your baby will be born!

The doctor or midwife is contacted, and the preliminary details are taken care of. You settle down to the work of giving birth. This day is like no other, and your mind, your whole body, centers on the process that is taking over inside of you.

The birth force rises, swells as a great wave, peaks, and recedes. You try to concentrate on relaxing, on willing your muscles to cooperate. In the welcome interim between contractions, there's time to rest.

The tempo quickens. Contractions are strong, they come quickly. You've probably never worked harder in your life. Labor is a fitting term! Just when you're most likely to feel exhausted and discouraged, you hear the reassurance of those who are with you—"Don't give up! We'll soon have a baby!"

And, at last, there is the moment you've been waiting for all those months, the bursting forth, the moment of blessed birth! As you catch your breath, you hear his cry. Was a sound ever before so priceless?

The umbilical cord is cut, marking the first separation. Who is to bridge this change of worlds for your newborn, who will soothe him and let him know he is again secure? Who better than his mother?

Again your body cradles him. You touch him, kiss his cheek, stroke his damp little head. Will he nurse? Perhaps. At some time within the first hour or so he will take the breast. You hold him close and he nuzzles your breast. His tiny mouth grasps your nipple. It seems no less

Your baby's first nursing is a sweet reward for both of you.

than amazing! You and your baby can relax. After the enormous effort of giving birth, this is sweet reward.

Without thought or conscious effort on your part, your milk will come. You can look beyond to the many days together as a nursing couple. The security and warmth of your arms, the ready comfort of your milk, the familiar smell and pulse of your body are all precious food to fill out your baby's body and quicken his mind and spirit. Such accomplishments take time. But is there a more awe-inspiring task? This is the age-less beauty of mother and child—a time of grace and peace.

You'll hug him to you, intensely aware of his dependence upon you. Of course he will grow, reach out, and eventually leave you. But not for a while. Give yourself time together; let there be no regrets. Together you'll begin to weave a new cord to replace the one so recently severed. This one will be plaited simply and naturally by your continuing closeness through many unhurried days. Not to be cut, it will form the first link to all human love and understanding.

The newborn baby has only three demands. They are warmth in the arms of its mother, food from her breasts, and security in the knowledge of her presence. Breastfeeding satisfies all three.

Dr. Grantly Dick-Read

But perhaps, instead of the natural birth you prepared for, you have a cesarean delivery. Or the months of waiting are not long enough, and the baby arrives prematurely, to be whisked away for specialized care. For the moment there is little sense of rapport with the baby.

These things happen. They may slow down a mother and baby's start as a nursing couple, but they need not end it. Given the right support, mothers and babies have untold levels of strength and adaptability. Mothers through the ages have happily breastfed their babies, and you can do it, too.

The groundwork is laid before your baby is born. Nothing is more important in your advance planning than your preparation for breastfeeding. There is no better time to start than now.

Best for Baby—BEST FOR YOU

When you breastfeed your baby, you're providing him with the best possible infant food. No product has ever been as time-tested as mother's milk. Human milk contains all the nutrients your newborn needs and is more easily digested and assimilated than any other infant food. As reassuring as this is, superior nutrition is only one of the many advantages you and your baby gain from breastfeeding.

Putting your newborn to the breast within minutes after delivery causes the uterus to contract and reduces the flow of blood. It also results in the uterus getting back in shape more quickly than it would if you were not breastfeeding.

With his small head pillowed against your breast and your milk warming his insides, your baby knows a special closeness to you. He is gaining a firm foundation in an important area of life—he is learning about love.

As his tiny mouth eagerly milks your breast, your baby is performing an exercise that promotes the proper development of his jaw and facial structure. Breastfeeding also encourages a normal weight gain for your particular baby, which is good insurance against a future tendency toward obesity.

There is no better safeguard for your baby against the onset of allergies than breastfeeding. A diet of your milk alone for about the first six months of his life readies his body for other foods. It protects him against infection as well as allergies. Living substances that are unique to your milk inhibit the growth of harmful bacteria and viruses in his still maturing system. With fewer health problems, you can look forward to having a happier baby.

Brain development is essential for the human infant and human milk contains all the right components to aid the development of baby's brain and nervous system. One study showed that premature infants who had been given human milk scored significantly higher on IQ tests at age 7½ and 8 years of age than children who had received formula.

Breastfeeding was meant to follow pregnancy and childbirth. The milk-producing breast represents a healthy progression in the natural sequence of reproduction that includes pregnancy, birth, and lactation. Nursing mothers find that breastfeeding is a naturally pleasurable experience.

The mother who is totally breastfeeding—not giving formula supplements or solid foods—will find that her menstrual periods will probably be delayed for six months or more after her baby's birth, especially if baby nurses often. During this time, a mother will have very little chance of becoming pregnant.

Breastfeeding uses up extra calories and a breastfeeding mother's metabolism changes, which enables most mothers to lose weight gradually without dieting.

Breastfeeding also protects a mother from certain health problems. Studies show that mothers who breastfeed for even a few months are less likely to develop breast cancer than women who have given birth but never breastfed. Breastfeeding also protects against ovarian cancer, urinary tract infections, and osteoporosis.

Breastfeeding results in an appreciable saving of time, effort, and money when compared to formula feeding. Minutes and hours of a mother's time are not diverted to the preparation of baby's milk. Feeding the baby is a time to relax. Day and night, automatically and accurately, milk is made and stored in the breasts. The temperature is always ideal; the supply is pure and practically unlimited.

Breastfeeding helps us appreciate the different yet complementary ways that men and women can participate in raising a child. If you have older children, breastfeeding the baby contributes toward their sex education. For a parent, it is an educational process itself, of a rank and value equal to a course of study at any prestigious institution of learning.

Breastfeeding is the best start in life for a baby. Unlike so much that is considered "best" and is often beyond even one's wildest dreams, in this instance the best is yours to give.

SOLID BACKING

If you had been a new mother living in Rome in the year 180 AD, there is a good possibility that you would have heard the following advice from the physician Galen, who gave public lectures on anatomy and physiology.

> *For if one places the nipple in the mouth of the newborn, they suck the milk and swallow it eagerly. And if they chance to be distressed or to cry, the best appeasement of their unhappiness is the mother's nipple put in their mouth.*

Closer to our own time, Dr. Ashley Montagu, noted anthropologist and social biologist, wrote the following in 1971 in his book, *Touching*:

> *What is established in the breastfeeding relationship constitutes the foundation for the development of all human social relationships, and the communications the infant receives through the warmth of the mother's skin constitute the first of the socializing experiences of life.*

In 1985, the late James P. Grant, who was then the Executive Director of UNICEF, wrote about the life-or-death consequences of the decision to breastfeed:

> *Almost unnoticed, many nations are now moving to preserve a vital element of child protection—breastfeeding.*
>
> *Breastfeeding is a natural "safety net" against the worst effects of poverty. If the child survives the first month of life (the most dangerous period of childhood), then for the next four months or so, exclusive breastfeeding goes a long way towards canceling out the health difference between being born into poverty and being born into affluence. Unless the mother is in extremely poor nutritional health, the breast milk of a mother in an African village is as good as the breast milk of a mother in a Manhattan apartment.... It is almost as if breastfeeding takes the infant out of poverty for those first few vital months in order to give the child a fairer start in life and compensate for the injustice of the world into which it was born....*
>
> *In many cities of the developing world, the incidence and duration of breastfeeding has begun to fall precipitously [in recent years]....The result can be a doubling or trebling of malnutrition, infection, and infant deaths.*

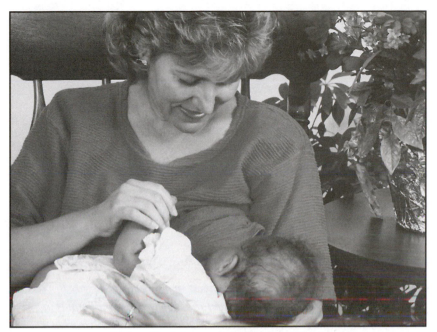

A baby receives the best start in life at his mother's breast.

An increase in the incidence and duration of breastfeeding is also one of the goals of the United States Department of Health and Human Services. C. Everett Koop, then Surgeon General of the United States, gave the following testimony before a Congressional subcommittee on nutrition in 1989:

> *Breastfeeding should be actively promoted in all maternal and child health programs. Health experts worldwide agree that breastfeeding is the optimal way to nurture infants and should be practiced whenever possible. I use the term "nurture" deliberately since it means "to feed and care for during growth."*

> *There is abundant evidence that human milk is designed to enhance optimally the growth, development, and well-being of the infant. A mother's milk provides the*

As United States Surgeon General, as a pediatrician, and as a woman, I wholeheartedly endorse breastfeeding.
The many benefits of breastfeeding to infants and mothers are well documented.

Antonia C. Novello, MD, MPH
Former United States
Surgeon General

best protection for her infant against specific infections. This cannot be duplicated in infant formula....

A decisive way to promote child health in the US in the next decade will be to implement effective breastfeeding promotion programs so that the unique and important benefits of breastfeeding can be made available to protect health, nourish, and optimally develop infants in all segments of our society.

The Paediatric Society in New Zealand recognizes that:

Breastfeeding provides optimal nutritional, immunological, and psychosocial benefits for the baby and also provides benefits for the mother.

In Germany, the National Breastfeeding Commission states that:

Breastfeeding is much more than the best and most healthy way to feed your baby, it is also nourishment for the heart and maintains in a special way the close relationship a mother and her baby develop during pregnancy.

In August 1990, participants from the World Health Organization (WHO), and UNICEF, an agency of the United Nations, met in Florence, Italy and adopted a sweeping statement in support of breast-feeding. Known as the Innocenti Declaration, it reads, in part:

As a global goal for optimal maternal and child health and nutrition, all women should be enabled to practice exclusive breastfeeding and all infants should be fed exclusively on breast milk from birth to four to six months of age. Thereafter, children should continue to be breastfed, while receiving appropriate and adequate complementary foods, for up to two years of age and beyond. This child-feeding ideal is to be achieved by creating an appropriate environment of awareness and support so that women can breastfeed in this manner.

Efforts should be made to increase women's confidence in their ability to breastfeed. Such empowerment involves the removal of constraints and influences that manipulate perceptions and behavior towards breastfeeding, often by subtle and indirect means. This requires sensitivity, continued vigilance, and a responsive and comprehensive communication strategy involving all media and addressed to all levels of society. Furthermore, obstacles to breastfeeding within the health system, the workplace, and the community must be eliminated.

This declaration was signed by 32 governments and 10 United Nations agencies and has been the springboard for a variety of programs and initiatives to support breastfeeding.

In 1991, many worldwide organizations that promote and support breastfeeding, including La Leche League International, formed a network called the World Alliance for Breastfeeding Action (WABA). To commemorate the Innocenti Declaration, WABA has established World Breastfeeding Week held the first week in August every year.

In 1991, the *Journal of Pediatrics* published an article by Allan Cunningham, Derrick Jelliffe, and Patrice Jelliffe which reviewed the research on the benefits of breastfeeding. They summarized their findings in this statement:

> *Breastfeeding has advantages for both babies and mothers, and the advantages are seen in rich and poor nations. They include the prevention of gastrointestinal and respiratory illness, and of infections as well as certain immunologic disorders. In addition to preventing illness early in life, breastfeeding appears to reduce the risk of certain chronic diseases as well. It has advantages for the premature as well as the term infant.*

In August 1994, a group of doctors representing specialties in family practice, obstetrics, pediatrics, and preventive medicine met to create a new medical society called the Academy of Breastfeeding Medicine. Their mission statement reads:

> *The Academy of Breastfeeding Medicine is a worldwide organization of physicians dedicated to the promotion, protection, and support of breastfeeding and human lactation. Its mission is to unite into one association members of the various medical specialties with this common purpose. The goals are: physician education; expansion of knowledge in both breastfeeding science and human lactation; facilitation of optimal breastfeeding practices; and encouragement of the exchange of information among organizations.*

In 1996, the American Academy of Pediatrics summarized its position on breastfeeding as follows:

> *The benefits of breastfeeding are so numerous that the Academy strongly encourages the practice during the first six to twelve months of life. Human milk is nutritionally superior to formulas for the content of fats, cholesterol, protein, and iron. In addition, there is evidence that human milk confers protection against infections and other diseases.*

The Key to Good MOTHERING

Even though your milk is important to your baby as a food and as a source of elements that protect him against infection, breastfeeding is more than a method of feeding your baby. Breastfeeding is the most natural and effective way of understanding and satisfying the needs of the baby. An experienced mother made the following observation, "Nursing the baby is the do-it-yourself kit for learning good mothering."

One explanation of breastfeeding's effect on mothering lies in the fact that a nursing mother is physically different than a non-nursing mother. She is in a different hormonal state. Because she is breastfeeding, she has a high level of prolactin—the "mothering" hormone.

We all know that motherhood can be very demanding, and breast-feeding helps balance the give-and-take of caring for a young child. It serves as a bridge from mother to child, child to mother. Lucy Waletzky, MD, a psychiatrist who breastfed her children, explains:

The more intimate bodily communication inherent to the breastfeeding situation leads to a feeling of psychological oneness with the child, which allows the mother to satisfy her own dependency needs (needs to be cared for and loved) at the same time she meets the baby's dependency needs. A mother's dependency needs may be accentuated postpartum by pain, fatigue, and the psychological stress of adjusting to new motherhood. When her dependency needs are thus met, her resentment of the child's dependency (often a very difficult problem) is alleviated, and the positive maternal feelings can flourish unencumbered.

WHAT IS MOTHERING?

Mothering is caring for your baby, communicating with him and encouraging him to communicate back. It encompasses all of the many things that you will do to keep your baby healthy and comfortable, to help him grow in body and spirit. Breastfeeding is an unequalled form of communication between mother and baby. All of the senses can be brought into play. Your baby tastes your milk. He knows you through the smell of your skin and your milk. He experiences a sense of closeness to you by feeling your skin next to his. In the nursing position, he can easily look into your eyes. He hears your voice. The many times that you nurse your baby tell him, "Yes, you are loved. You are safe. You are doing all right!" and he, of course, communicates back to you that he feels loved and is reassured. It is a learning and comforting experience for both of you.

From time immemorial, mothers have comforted their babies at the breast. They know that a few minutes of nursing can soothe an upset child's feelings of fear or anger. Nothing is more reassuring to a small one than being close to mother and tasting her warm milk.

In explaining how breastfeeding improves the interaction between a mother and her baby, Dr. William Sears, pediatrician and author, writes:

> *Breastfeeding mothers respond to their babies more intuitively and with less restraint. The baby's signals of hunger or distress trigger a biological response within the mother (a milk let-down) and she feels the urge to pick up the baby and nurse him. This responsiveness rewards both mother and baby with good feelings. If a mother is bottle-feeding, her response to her baby's hunger or distress cues is quite different. She must initially divert her attention away from the baby to an object, the bottle, and take time to find and prepare it. Research has shown that a baby's memory span in the first six months is from four to ten seconds. The time it takes to produce a non-biological response, such as bottle-feeding, is usually longer than the baby's memory span. The bottle-feeding baby does not receive the same immediate reinforcement of his cues that a breastfeeding baby does. In my practice, I have noticed that breastfeeding mothers tend to show a high degree of sensitivity to their babies, and I believe this is a result of the biological changes that occur in a mother in response to the signals of her baby.*

Good mothering means babying the baby, accepting that his wants and needs are the same. It includes holding him when he is too full to nurse, but he is not yet ready to sleep. Mothering is changing a diaper or playing peek-a-boo. It means recognizing that each child has an inexhaustible need to be loved for what he is—a person with his own individuality. As he grows, his needs will change. A toddler needs freedom and guidance, with an ever-watchful eye. The manner in which these early needs are met, or not met, has a great deal to do with a child's response to people and situations in later life. The way the child is mothered is important not only to mother and child, but to society as well. Marian Tompson, one of La Leche League's co-Founders, observes, "No matter how far our world advances technologically, the decisions of how to use that technology will still have to be made by people. And so the kind of people we produce is crucial to the direction our world takes. Raising a loving, caring child is the most important contribution any of us can make to the progress of the world."

GETTING TO KNOW YOUR BABY

Mothering is not something you can learn from a book. We can tell you, for instance, that most young babies like the secure feeling of being snugly wrapped up and cuddled. We can tell you that at about three months, most babies like company. They like to be propped up in the midst of the family. Instead of wanting to be fed or cuddled, what they often want is just to be sociable. These may be perfectly true observations for many babies—but your newborn may prefer to have his arms and legs free, or your three-month-old may be overstimulated by too much activity and end up feeling miserable. You have to be sensitive to the individual needs of your baby.

The sensitivity that helps you do the right thing at the right time comes from knowing your baby. It develops as you spend time with him, but it develops more quickly, and to a greater degree, if you are nursing your baby. The very closeness and intimacy of breastfeeding give you a quicker and surer perception of the feelings and needs of this tiny person, and help you to know how to meet them.

Ann Van Norman, a mother from Ontario, Canada, tells how breastfeeding helped her learn about her baby's needs:

> I thought I had prepared myself for mothering before Sarah's birth. I learned about diapering, bathing, and breastfeeding, but there was no way to prepare for "mothering." I found out that mothering is only learned by doing. Learning to respond flexibly to baby's needs for love, care, and stimulation, putting our own desires on temporary hold, and accepting the constancy and intensity of baby's needs are lessons only learned by living them.
>
> I believe nursing has helped make my learning relatively painless, mainly through the positive reinforcement I have received from Sarah. She showed me how much I was needed and loved. Nursing her meant that I had to take time to respond, relax, and reflect. I am a different person now. Sarah has changed me from a compulsive time-and-task-oriented tiger to a go-with-the-flow housecat.

Your joy in mothering grows as you experience the quick, strong feeling of affection so natural between a nursing mother and her baby; as you develop an understanding of your baby's needs and gain confidence in your own ability to satisfy them; and as you see the happy dividends from the good relationship as the baby grows. As one nursing mother, Shirl Butts, from Louisiana, expressed her feelings:

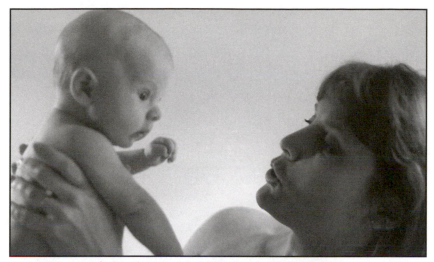

Getting to know your baby helps you learn how to meet his needs.

Those who have never nursed a child might find it hard to understand just how special a nursing relationship can be. Now as I nurse my second child, I can appreciate what I missed with my toddler, whom I did not nurse.

My favorite moments are just before bedtime, nursing my four-month-old daughter. We snuggle together in our rocking chair, her tiny mouth eagerly searching for the warmth of my milk, until at last she latches on and drifts into peaceful sleep. Her chubby little hand is outstretched on my arm, her cheek nestled against my breast. I continue to rock, lovingly studying every crease and fold of her soft body. Times like this make me look forward to the next night and the next. Sometimes she stops nursing to look up at me and give a big smile as if to say, "Thanks, Mom!" and then resumes nursing again. Those moments make me wish time would stand still.

Breastfeeding is not a guarantee of good mothering, and formula feeding does not rule it out. The most important thing is the love you give your baby and the fact that you are doing your best to be a good mother. Mary White, another of LLL's co-Founders, reminds us:

We're all learning, all the time. We're all still reaching up to the top of the ladder, and we've all got a long way to go. But for each and every one of us, the person from whom we can learn the most is our own baby; listen to him. Give to him; in the giving we are growing, as mothers and as women. As we watch him grow and thrive, we are watching an achievement we can really be proud of.

2

Plans
Are
Under Way

Planning for a new baby is one of the most exciting adventures in the life of a couple. You will dream the dreams that belong exclusively to parents. Your family's future is full of hope.

Planning usually begins with making practical arrangements. You'll select a doctor, look into childbirth education classes, and attend La Leche League meetings. Then your attention will turn to the need for rearranging the priorities in your life. Babies take time, and adjustments will have to be made. How can you change a routine here or eliminate an activity there in order to fit the new family member into your already busy life?

From long experience, we have learned that whenever a routine comes into conflict with the needs of one of the family members, it's the routine that has to give. "People before things" is a handy slogan to remember.

It should be said, too, that this change of emphasis is not a temporary interlude, with life reverting to its former style once the baby is older. Having a baby, loving a child, is forever. New experiences, endless opportunities, and depths of feelings that you can know in no other way lie ahead of you.

True, the investment in a new baby is enormous. As you are probably well aware, the financial output is a definite concern for many couples. But money is seldom the most critical or the rarest commodity that parents must provide. The coin that has greater value and is more difficult to part with is that which represents the continuous giving of one's self, emotionally and physically. Babies have no way of knowing how much it costs their parents to tend to them, worry about them, and love them day and night. They can't know, of course, until they themselves become parents someday. Then the gift is recognized and passed on as lovingly as it was given.

Plans for the BABY'S BIRTH

We learned early in La Leche League's existence that a woman's experience in giving birth affects the beginning of breastfeeding and many of her attitudes about being a mother. Alert and active participation by the mother in childbirth is a help in getting breastfeeding off to a good start.

Childbirth can be a rich, joyful, and maturing experience. Those of us who have given birth without drugs or medical intervention know that helping a baby to be born and hearing his first cry can be a crowning moment of achievement in the life of a woman. After doing a survey of women's long-term memories of their birth experiences, childbirth educator Penny Simkin reports that the women who felt the most satisfaction about their childbirth experiences "described feelings of accomplishment, control, increased self-esteem, and/or confirmation of worth. Most of those with low satisfaction expressed disappointment or anger that they were not in control." And she concludes, "a sense of maternal fulfillment and personal self-worth are hallmarks of a healthy outcome" of the birth experience.

Having a baby is a natural, normal function for which a woman's body is superbly designed. The healthiest birth situation for both mother and baby is one that is completely drug-free. Almost all mothers are physically able to deliver their babies without medical intervention. You do need a doctor or trained midwife attending the birth of your baby but this is similar to having a lifeguard on duty in case there are complications. In the natural, normal birth, it is not the doctor who delivers the baby; it is the mother.

Nursing your baby soon after birth gets breastfeeding off to a good start.

EFFECTS OF MEDICATIONS

Recent studies have shown that pain relievers and anesthesia used during labor or delivery may contribute to breastfeeding problems. In one study, babies whose mothers had received an epidural were less alert, less able to orient themselves, and had less organized movements than babies whose mothers had given birth without medication. Furthermore, these differences in behavior were measurable during the entire first month. Other medications commonly used during labor have also been found to affect baby's sucking behavior after birth.

LEARNING ABOUT CHILDBIRTH

Advance preparation can pay off for you and your baby by resulting in a safer, happier birth experience. You and your husband can begin to prepare for this event by learning as much as you can beforehand. Many of the fears, doubts, and misconceptions you may have about childbirth will disappear as you become better informed and more confident. Attending childbirth classes will help you learn about the process of giving birth as well as how to participate and cooperate in the event. In addition, childbirth options are explained in many books that are listed in the Appendix.

With concentration and practice, you can learn relaxation techniques that are invaluable in the first stage of labor. Then in the second stage of labor, by pushing with contractions, you move your baby out of the womb and into the world, perhaps even into his father's hands. The experience of seeing and holding his newborn bonds a father to his child and to the mother of his child in a special way. When you are all together—mother, father, and baby—you "claim" each other for your own.

If all goes well, you'll be able to hold your baby immediately after birth and put him to your breast. The outflow of love and warmth to your child at this time is a spontaneous continuation of the comfort and security he has known for so long before his birth. This early contact can be very soothing and satisfying for both of you. Nursing the baby soon after birth encourages your milk to come in and starts you on your way as a breastfeeding mother.

Studies have shown that if mother and baby are separated after birth and the first nursing is delayed, even by as little as twenty minutes, the baby may have difficulty latching on well. So it is definitely worthwhile to discuss this with your doctor or midwife ahead of time and be assured that you and your baby can be together soon after birth.

CHILDBIRTH OPTIONS

Nowadays, mothers are approaching the birth of their baby as the natural, normal event it really is, instead of a medical situation. They are looking into alternatives to the traditional hospital birth. Home birth and free-standing birth centers are becoming popular choices in some areas. Hospitals have responded to this by offering birthing rooms and family-centered care to replace traditional labor and delivery rooms. Many of these changes have been in response to the patients' demands.

Judy Unruh, from California, gave birth to her two daughters in the hospital. When she was expecting her third child she planned to return to the same hospital. But at her doctor's suggestion she visited the new Birthing Center. The positive atmosphere and the enthusiasm of the staff made her decide she wanted to have her baby there.

> When we arrived at the Birthing Center to have the baby, we were told to go right to the room we had chosen ahead of time. There weren't any strong hospital odors, no people rushing around, no papers for Gary to fill out while I was wheeled off down a long hall without him. We just walked together to our room.

> There is always some amount of anxiety in starting labor, but the atmosphere at the Birthing Center was so relaxing that it had a calming effect on me. The thing that meant the most to my husband was his feeling that he belonged there. No one made him feel that he was in the way. (The comfortable recliner in our room helped, too.)

I can remember how great it felt to be able to get up and shower to relieve my back labor and to take a walk out in the hall when I felt the need to walk. I wasn't confined to bed; I was in control.

Several hours later, our third daughter was born. She never left us to go to the nursery with harsh lights and lots of other crying babies. She remained in our quiet room with us. We could hold her when she wanted to be held and feed her when she wanted to be fed. Gary and I both were there when the pediatrician checked her.

Even though it was my most difficult labor and delivery, it was our happiest. My husband and I look back on our daughter's birth with good memories and love for all the wonderful people who have worked so hard to make having a baby an enriching experience for the entire family.

You'll want to find out as much as possible about the choices available as you plan for your baby's birth. Books and organizations listed in the Appendix will be helpful.

THE CESAREAN QUESTION

The cesarean birth rate in the USA was 5.5% in 1970 and increased to 24.4% of all births in 1987, according to the National Center for Health Statistics. It had not changed by 1995. This means one-fourth of all births in the USA are done by cesarean, an alarming fact that many health professionals consider to be an epidemic.

The decision to perform a cesarean is a serious one, often made at a critical point in labor when parents are not likely to question their doctor's decision. Parents will want to thoroughly discuss their doctor's views on the need for a cesarean birth early in the pregnancy. A few doctors have come to believe that cesareans are always necessary for twins, babies who are breech, and so-called "prolonged" labor. Other doctors view cesarean deliveries as only a last resort and find that in many such cases all that is needed is a little more time and patience. With proper medical support and care, most babies, even the big ones, can be successfully delivered vaginally with greater safety for both mother and baby.

The incidence of prematurity, respiratory distress syndrome, and other complications is far higher with cesarean deliveries, and the likelihood that the baby and mother will be separated from each other, often for some time, is much greater. Morbidity and mortality rates are higher for mothers who have cesarean births. The mother is more likely to experience infection, pain, and discomfort, as well as psychological effects such as depression after a cesarean birth.

If your doctor thinks it may be necessary to plan on a cesarean birth for your baby, don't hesitate to consult another doctor before making this decision.

If you have already had a previous cesarean birth you should know, too, that many mothers have had subsequent vaginal deliveries. It is not always necessary to have another cesarean. Frequently the reason for the first cesarean delivery does not apply to subsequent births. Organizations listed in the Appendix can offer further information about this.

Dottie Leach, from Oklahoma tells of her experience:

Two months ago I gave birth to Daniel, my second child. I had a vaginal birth after a cesarean (VBAC). At six months into my pregnancy, I changed obstetricians, choosing one whom I felt had a positive attitude about natural delivery and who had demonstrated success with VBACs. I prepared a birth plan stating my intentions, explaining that I wanted an unmedicated, intervention-free birth.

Probably the most important factor in having a VBAC was my labor support. My husband was there as well as a woman who was familiar with childbirth and acted as my labor assistant. They supported me through every contraction for nine hours, talking to me and praising and comforting me. Everyone was very positive and loving. I felt most comfortable standing and walking, and this was supported by the hospital staff. The last two hours of transition were intense and exhausting. I was ready to give up by the time I was ready to push, but my coaches were so incredibly positive and encouraging, they somehow gave me the energy to continue. After about forty-five minutes of pushing, my son was born weighing ten pounds and nine ounces.

My feeling about natural childbirth is that it can help build self-esteem and self-awareness that carries over to every other part of life. It has shown me how strong I really am, and that I can be courageous in other parts of my life, too. It felt right to me.

A growing number of doctors and hospitals permit fathers to be present for a cesarean birth. Mothers appreciate the comfort and support, and fathers are glad to be able to participate in the birth of their babies. Discuss these options with your doctor.

One mother, Debbie Pollock from Wisconsin, tells of some things a mother can discuss ahead of time in order to achieve a positive cesarean birth experience:

Communication with your doctor during pregnancy is as important for a cesarean birth as it is for a vaginal delivery. If a problem occurs during or after the birth, a cesarean mother is at a disadvantage and may have a difficult time handling conflict, as she is already dealing with surgery and medication.

One key factor in a positive cesarean birth and speedy recovery is to use a minimal amount of drugs, and if possible, experience some hours of healthy labor. Spinal or epidural anesthesia will allow you to be awake for your baby's birth, and your baby will be more alert than if you receive general anesthesia.

To get breastfeeding off to a good start, mother can see to it that her baby receives no supplements. Moments after birth, my husband carried our son from the operating room to the nursery, remained there for a few minutes with him, and then carried him to me in recovery. The baby nursed for the first time within an hour after birth.

If a private room is available, father, mother, and baby may be given permission to room together. In this case, baby need never be separated from mother, as dad can be there to help. Some hospitals have a form to sign, releasing them of certain responsibilities once baby and mother are rooming-in.

Mothers can experience many different emotions after a cesarean birth. It was important to me not to dwell on what happened and burden myself with guilt and regrets, but rather to absorb and cherish every moment of the present with my newborn.

Health Professionals Who CARE

There's no doubt about it—your choice of health care providers makes a difference. The doctor or trained midwife who attends you in childbirth will greatly influence how your infant is delivered, and the health care provider you choose for your baby afterward can affect the course of breastfeeding. Even the doctor who prescribes medication should you become ill must take both you and your nursing baby into consideration. A doctor who has little opportunity to learn about breastfeeding may be readily inclined to take the baby off the breast when treating either you or your baby. Such a move is rarely necessary.

Many young couples are devoting a considerable amount of time and care to finding health care professionals whose priorities are similar to their own. If you are in a situation where the choice of health care providers is limited, then it becomes even more important to dialogue with the doctor.

Attendance at La Leche League meetings and childbirth education classes is a good way to learn about other parents' experiences. As you become better informed, through reading and talking to others, you'll know the questions to ask in order to learn more about a doctor's or a hospital's practices.

Your first step will probably be to select the doctor or trained midwife who will attend the birth of your baby. Seek out a doctor who does not routinely use medications or IVs during labor, who does not routinely induce labor or use fetal monitors, who does not routinely give anesthesia or do episiotomies. Discuss whether routine procedures might interfere with breastfeeding your baby soon after birth. Ask about rooming-in policies at the hospital or other facility where your baby will be born.

You may want to meet and talk with several health care professionals before selecting one. Before the interview, write out a list of the points you want to discuss. When you make this appointment, ask what the fee will be for a consultation visit. Tell the receptionist you do not want a complete examination at this visit.

Find out, too, if the doctor or midwife is in a group practice with other doctors or midwives. You'll be interested in knowing if an associate, rather than the person you have selected, might attend the birth of your baby. Be sure to find out if the associates are also willing to respect your wishes.

After discussing your concerns with your doctor or midwife, it's a good idea to put in writing what is acceptable to all of you and ask the doctor or midwife to indicate his or her agreement by signing your list. (Of course, a health care provider must reserve the right to change procedures in any emergency.) Take this with you to the hospital. Mothers say that producing their signed list was often all the authority needed to stop someone who was ready to administer a routine procedure or medication in childbirth or give the baby the usual supplemental bottle of formula or water in the nursery.

THE BABY'S DOCTOR

In the United States, parents are usually able to choose the doctor or health care provider they want for their baby. You'll want to find someone who is knowledgeable about breastfeeding and has a positive attitude toward it. A family doctor may be caring for both you and your baby and you can discuss breastfeeding at your prenatal visits. Otherwise you may select a pediatrician or family doctor to care for the baby after birth. Make an appointment to talk to the doctor before the baby is born and let him or her know that you plan to breastfeed your baby. Ask questions. Are most of the doctor's patients breastfed? How does he or she deal with situations such as slow weight gain? A doctor who has not dealt with many breastfed babies may want to give supplementary formula or recommend that you start solid foods too early. If you are not satisfied with the answers you receive, shop around for another doctor. If this is not an option in your situation, discuss your concerns with the doctor and explain why breastfeeding is so important to you.

A NEED TO DIALOGUE

When dealing with health professionals, you may have to take the initiative in letting them know what you want. A simple, direct statement can begin a dialogue between the two of you. "Doctor, I need to discuss this with you. It's important to me." When there's a need for medication or hospitalization for the baby, you need a doctor who will treat him yet not interrupt breastfeeding—or do so as little as possible. Staying close to your baby at a time of illness, nursing him when possible, is always best.

If the doctor who is treating you or caring for your baby is not willing to discuss the options you prefer, you may want to seek another medical opinion.

Preparing to BREASTFEED

As you talk to other mothers about your plans to breastfeed your baby, you will probably hear stories about sore nipples. At one time, nipple soreness was a common reason for mothers to give up breastfeeding, so a great deal of emphasis was put on the need to "prepare your nipples" before your baby was born. In recent years, it has been found that the major cause of nipple soreness is incorrect positioning of the baby at the breast and/or improper sucking techniques. Nipple preparation is no longer considered necessary as you prepare to breastfeed.

Kittie Frantz, RN, CPNP, who is a La Leche League Leader and also the Director of the Breastfeeding Infant Clinic at the University of Southern California Medical Center, was one of the people who first emphasized the importance of correct positioning. In evaluating 300 breastfeeding mothers, she found that 57% reported nipple soreness and 43% said they were not sore. Kittie reports on her findings:

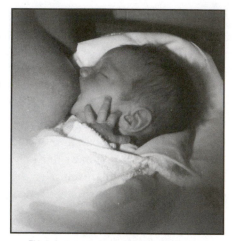

This baby is latched on well with mother's nipple far back in his mouth.

We observed a difference in the two groups—in the way mother held the baby and the way the baby accepted the breast into his mouth. When we taught the mothers with sore nipples the technique we observed the mothers without sore nipples to be using, they almost all exclaimed that the pain significantly lessened or, in most cases, vanished.

More information on correct positioning of the baby at the breast can be found in the chapter called "Your Baby Arrives."

WHAT YOU CAN DO

Some women apply a lubricant to their nipples and breasts to moisturize their skin during pregnancy. Any skin cream you normally use will do fine. One possible choice is Lansinoh for Breastfeeding Mothers®, the purest form of USP modified lanolin available. It can be used during pregnancy to moisturize the nipples. Some mothers with very dry skin who experienced nipple soreness when they breastfed a previous baby report that they were able to nurse comfortably after using Lansinoh for Breastfeeding Mothers® to moisturize their nipples during pregnancy. (See the Appendix for more information.)

Soap can be very drying so it should be avoided entirely in the nipple area. Rinsing with plain water when you bathe will keep the nipple area clean. When your baby is nursing, the Montgomery glands that surround the nipple secrete a substance that lubricates the skin and discourages the growth of bacteria. There is no need to use alcohol or other antiseptics on your nipples. If you can go without a bra for part of each day, your nipples may benefit from the air and the light friction of your outer clothing. Some women are uncomfortable going braless and instead they wear a nursing bra with flaps down.

For some couples, a normal part of their love-making includes caressing the breasts and sucking the nipples. This can be a natural way of preparing the wife's breasts for the coming work of nourishing their child.

BREAST MASSAGE

Gentle breast massage will help you feel more comfortable handling your breasts and can be useful later on if you need to express your milk. Support one breast with both hands, your thumbs above and fingers underneath. Press your fingers and thumb together gently as you slide your fingers forward from the chest wall out toward your nipple; circle the breast with this gentle massaging motion. Then switch to the other breast.

Another type of breast massage involves using your fingers to press gently on one area of your breast and moving your fingers in a circular motion on one spot. After a few seconds, move your fingers to another spot. Start at the top of your breast and spiral around the breast toward the areola using this massage.

CHECK FOR FLAT NIPPLES

In order for the baby to suck effectively, he will need to draw your nipple far back into his mouth. If you have flat nipples, the baby may have a problem latching on correctly.

To bring the nipple out, place a thumb and forefinger near the base of the nipple and gently press together. You'll be able to feel where the larger mass of the breast tissue ends and the nipple begins. Then, holding the nipple, slowly pull it out, and gently turn it up and then down. Some authorities believe doing this exercise several times a day with each nipple will increase the elasticity of your nipples and help baby grasp them more easily. Others believe it is not necessary.

If you try these nipple pulls and find that your nipples do not come out far enough for you to grasp them easily, you may have flat or inverted nipples. Squeezing or pinching gently about an inch behind the base of the nipple should cause the nipple to project away from the breast.

One method for encouraging the flat nipple to be more outgoing was developed by Dr. J. Brooks Hoffman of Connecticut. Place a thumb on each side of the nipple. Your thumbs should be directly at the base of the nipple, not at the edge of the areola. Press in firmly against the breast tissue and at the same time pull the thumbs away

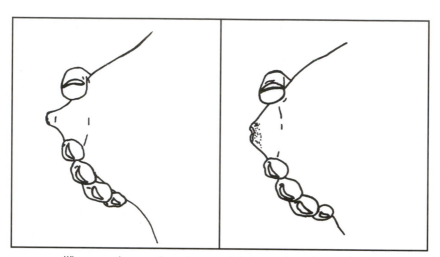

When you gently squeeze the areola, a normal nipple protrudes, as shown on the left.
A flat or inverted nipple retracts.

from each other. You'll be stretching out the nipple and loosening the tightness at the base, which will make the nipple move up and outward. Repeat this stretch five times first thing in the morning, moving your thumbs around the base of the nipple.

INVERTED NIPPLES

If you find your nipples do not come out at all when you do these exercises, then you may have inverted nipples. An inverted nipple shrinks back into the breast when the areola is squeezed. Some inverted nipples appear as though they're pushed in all the time. One mother who had this type called it "the folding model of the nipple world." A full-size nipple is there, ready and able to do the job for which it was intended, but left on its own, it folds back into the breast instead of coming out when the baby tries to nurse.

Inverted nipples may or may not require treatment. Some breast-feeding experts believe that a baby who is latched on well can draw an inverted nipple far back into his mouth to nurse. Others suggest using breast shields or shells that are designed specifically to draw the nipple out. Breast shells are comfortable to wear, lightweight, and inconspicuous under your bra. You can begin wearing them during pregnancy for a few hours a day and gradually increase the time. There are two sections to each shell, the bottom part, which has an opening for the nipple and fits directly over the breast, and the top part, which holds the bra away from the emerging nipple.

Breast shells are available from La Leche League International's Catalogue and many La Leche League Groups; complete instructions come with them.

When flat or inverted nipples are discovered after the baby is born and the baby is not able to latch on properly, breast shells can be worn between feedings to draw the nipple out.

EXPRESSING COLOSTRUM

During pregnancy, your breasts begin producing colostrum to prepare for the task of feeding your baby. You may notice a few drops leaking from your nipples during the last few weeks of pregnancy, or some may leak out if you massage your breasts.

At one time, experts recommended squeezing a few drops of colostrum from your breasts every day, but this has not been proven to be helpful in preventing engorgement or sore nipples.

What to Wear—NURSING FASHIONS

You'll probably be glad to shed your maternity garb after your baby is born and your figure changes to the smaller tummy and the temporarily fuller bust of a breastfeeding mother. Actually, you can make almost any clothes do for nursing, but a few special items can make life easier.

During pregnancy, and when the milk first comes in, the breasts often enlarge, and the support of a well-fitted bra can be most welcome. Let comfort be your guide. If you usually go braless, you may not need to wear one while breastfeeding.

You may find that you are more comfortable with a bra designed for nursing mothers. The traditional nursing bra has a flap on the cup that is opened for feedings. We suggest that you start with two to three bras and try them for fit and ease of use before purchasing more. Bras purchased during the last weeks of pregnancy should have extra room both in the cup and around the rib cage. The breasts will enlarge after the baby is born and the milk comes in, and nursing bras must be fitted with this in mind. A bra that is too tight, either around the ribs or in the cup, can cause a plugged milk duct or breast infection, and you don't want that to happen.

When trying on nursing bras in the store, be sure to note how the flap is attached in front. You'll want a fastener that you can manage with one hand so that you don't have to put the baby down every time you open or close the cup. You can also purchase washable or disposable nursing pads which fit inside your bra and absorb the milk that may leak from the nipples between feedings. A folded cotton or linen handkerchief works well, too, but avoid using the no-iron variety—the finish often retards absorbency.

If you often wear skirts or dresses, half-slips are probably the handiest while nursing, but you can adapt full slips to your needs by replacing the adjustment clip with a small piece of a Velcro-type fastener. For outer apparel, two-piece outfits—skirts, jeans, slacks, or shorts with a loose top or sweater are ideal. With your top, blouse, or sweater lifted from the waist for nursing, the baby covers any bare midriff. When wearing a blouse that buttons down the front, you can unbutton from the bottom up. If you wear a three-piece outfit, with a jacket or shawl, you will be able to nurse so unobtrusively that the person sitting next to you won't know that your baby is having lunch.

La Leche League publications often carry ads for nursing bras and clothing designed especially for nursing mothers. Today's breastfeeding mother has her choice of many fashionable and comfortable styles of clothing designed with special openings for discreet breastfeeding. Maternity shops and speciality catalogues often carry nursing fashions. The Association for Breastfeeding Fashions (listed in the Appendix) is a trade organization formed by companies who specialize in designing clothing for breastfeeding mothers. They can send you a listing of their member companies and a sample copy of their newsletter.

NURSING DISCREETLY

This brings us to a concern you may have about breastfeeding. You may worry about feeding the baby while you're away from home or when other people are around. As the American Academy of Pediatrics noted,

> *It is a curious commentary on our society that we tolerate all degrees of explicitness in our literature and mass media as regards sex and violence, but the normal act of breastfeeding is taboo.*

Embarrassment is a reason mothers sometimes give for not breastfeeding or for weaning within the early weeks. Interestingly, studies of breastfeeding mothers show that the mothers who stop early seldom know another nursing mother and have no one to help them in their new undertaking. Experienced breastfeeding mothers know how to nurse a baby so discreetly that only the mother and the baby are the wiser. Breastfeeding can be as private as a mother wishes it to be, yet it need not unduly confine her and her baby.

There may be occasions when someone is extremely sensitive to the prospect of the baby being put to mother's breast when others are present. Breastfeeding mothers note that, at such times, discretion can be the better part of valor. Some mothers find it easiest to leave the room for a few moments just to get the baby started on the breast. Then, with baby nursing contentedly, a shawl or lightweight blanket can be draped over your shoulder to cover the baby and you can return comfortably to your group of friends.

Mothers are able to breastfeed discreetly when they wear fashions designed for nursing mothers.

A mother from California, Sue Ellen Jennings Austin, tells how attending La Leche League meetings helped her learn how to nurse discreetly:

> *I have managed to feed my baby in just about every place imaginable, from teenage brother's basketball games to our church Christmas party. This came about gradually of course—after practicing in front of the mirror and becoming brave in desperate situations, but most importantly after observing other mothers nursing discreetly at LLL functions and being able to share my concerns with them.*

Don't let a concern about feeding your baby in public keep you from enjoying the advantages and convenience of breastfeeding. In Chapter 5, we offer more tips on trips and outings with your breast-fed baby.

CHAPTER 3

Your
Network
of Support

How can we adequately convey to you the tremendous value of being in touch with other nursing mothers? No book about breastfeeding can equal talking to an experienced nursing mother and seeing her happy baby. When you know a woman who enjoys being a nursing mother, you have access to a continuing source of information and inspiration. It is our hope that you can join with other mothers and together find the same reinforcement and satisfaction that we have known.

The best place we know of to receive this mother-to-mother support is your local La Leche League Group. Attending LLL meetings during your pregnancy is the ideal preparation for breastfeeding and a good way to learn what being a mother is all about. Betty McLellan, a La Leche League member from Ontario, Canada, puts it this way:

I have a background in psychology, but it was attendance at LLL meetings and the example of a wonderful Leader that showed me alternatives to many of the typical ways of handling children in our culture. The "psychology of mothering" is learned best from other mothers and comes through loud and clear at La Leche League meetings.

La Leche League MEETINGS

"Doesn't breastfeeding just come naturally? My great-grandmother never went to a La Leche League meeting, and she nursed all her babies." "Why should breastfeeding women need a worldwide organization for support?" Many who are unfamiliar with La Leche League ask these questions. More and more mothers today are choosing to breastfeed their babies, but they may not understand just how much a support group like La Leche League can help them enjoy the experience.

When La Leche League was formed more than forty years ago, breastfeeding had become a lost art. Mothers had begun seeking advice from medical professionals about caring for their babies instead of learning from the wisdom of other mothers.

Today, La Leche League gatherings are held monthly in all parts of the world. The information is divided into topics for a four-meeting series. As no two series of meetings are exactly alike, many mothers continue to attend for many months beyond the first series and even for many years.

LLL meetings are sometimes held in the home of a La Leche League member or in a convenient public meeting place. All members are encouraged to bring along their nursing babies. The meetings are conducted by an experienced breastfeeding mother who has been qualified to represent La Leche League. She presents a somewhat structured outline of information at each meeting, but these meetings are not classes; they are open, informative discussions. At the LLL Group meetings in your area, you will learn about much more than the basics of breastfeeding.

The first meeting of the series is usually about the advantages of breastfeeding. You will discover benefits of breastfeeding that may have never occurred to you—results of research on the value of human milk and mothers' own stories of breastfeeding advantages. Many mothers have remarked after this meeting, "I knew that breastfeeding was good for my baby and good for me, but I didn't know how good it was. This information makes me more confident than ever in my decision to nurse, and it makes me feel proud to know that I am doing something so wonderful for my baby."

At the next meeting, the discussion usually centers on the family and the breastfed baby. Mothers share tips on how to get off to a good

Experienced breastfeeding mothers offer information and encouragement at La Leche League meetings.

start in the hospital and at home with the new baby. Knowing what to expect in the way of procedures and routines at local area hospitals or birthing centers can be helpful to a new mother. Easing the emotional adjustment of all family members, lightening the work load, establishing a good milk supply, and preventing problems from ever beginning are all topics of discussion.

Another meeting covers basic breastfeeding techniques and problem-solving. You can receive specific advice from the best breastfeeding experts in the world: experienced nursing mothers. The overall message is that no matter what problem may arise, there is almost always a solution that does not require weaning the baby.

At another meeting, the proper diet for lactating and pregnant women is discussed, as well as starting the baby on solid foods and when and how to wean the baby. Often discipline of toddlers is also explored at this meeting.

Almost all La Leche League Groups have an extensive lending library available to their members. Current titles on breastfeeding, childbirth, parenting, and nutrition that may not be widely available can be found at LLL meetings. Most Groups also have books, booklets, and breastfeeding-aid products that LLL members can purchase.

ALL MOTHERS ARE WELCOME

All women who have an interest in breastfeeding are invited to attend La Leche League meetings. All mothers are accepted with open arms at La Leche League: mothers of all races and religions, single mothers, working mothers, and mothers whose philosophy on various aspects of infant care and childrearing may differ from La Leche League's. Each mother is encouraged to take from La Leche League's philosophy what seems sensible and helpful to her. The ideal time to begin attending is during pregnancy, because the information received in advance may prove to be vital to a mother when her baby arrives.

After her first La Leche League meeting one pregnant mother commented, "I had read all the books, and didn't think there was anything else I needed to know. I learned so much more tonight than I expected to." Another mother, Heather Karlheim from Ohio, had a similar response after attending La Leche League meetings:

As a pharmacist and avid reader, I spent the months of my first pregnancy reading everything I could find on topics related to birth, breastfeeding, and childrearing. I anticipated my child's birth with confidence.

Since I have a close friend who is a La Leche League Leader, I knew a little about LLL but I was not convinced that I "needed" such an organization.

In my fifth month of pregnancy, I was persuaded by a co-worker, who was also expecting a baby, to accompany her to a La Leche League meeting. This meeting was a real turning point for me, providing specific suggestions and lots of reassurance from other mothers.

As the months passed and my daughter and I became a happy nursing couple, I continued to benefit from La Leche League meetings and friendships made there.

As I look back now I can't believe how naive I was, thinking that I could "learn it all" from books. La Leche League has been, for me, a safe island in the tumultuous sea of first-time motherhood, and you can bet I'm not about to jump back into the water alone!

WHY IS IT NEEDED?

Though the majority of mothers today are breastfeeding when they leave the hospital, within a few months, weeks, or even days, most of them switch to formula. Why? Insufficient milk supply, breast infections, embarrassment, fear of criticism from relatives, and general confusion are some of the reasons. These problems are not the inevitable lot of the nursing mother. They can be avoided for the most part, or resolved with the correct information and support. Should a problem arise, a mother can call her La Leche League Leader for help at any time. Sometimes just being able to dial the phone number of a sympathetic, informed mother who has had breastfeeding experience is the key to the resumption of a successful breastfeeding relationship.

Ruth A. Lawrence, MD, a physician who breastfed her own children and the author of *Breastfeeding: A Guide for the Medical Profession*, agrees that mothers need information and support as they learn about breastfeeding:

> *Breastfeeding is not a reflex; it is a learned process. In our present culture, many women have never witnessed an infant at the breast. When a woman is called upon to nurse her own infant, much of her success depends on a learning process. Successful lactation depends on proper information.*

Mothers who attend LLL meetings soon find there is more involved than basic breastfeeding information. There is something very special about the sharing and companionship of other mothers. Cynthia Webb, from Montana, found this out:

> *When I was seven months pregnant and wondering if I could survive pregnancy and parenthood, I found a place that celebrates motherhood in a quiet, sustaining fashion: my first La Leche League meeting.*
>
> *I believe motherhood touches the soul of a woman in a way that nothing else can.... After being infertile for ten years, motherhood came as quite a surprise to me. Without LLL, I'd probably still be in shock. La Leche League members have helped me cope with many situations. Problem-solving and support are important, but so is having a place to share the special joys of each day's experience. An LLL meeting is a haven for all of these things.*

Sally Olson, from Nebraska, already breastfed two babies when she attended her first La Leche League meeting. Her third son was just a month old. She explains:

> *I really went to the meeting to meet some other mothers, as we had just moved to a new town and I did not know a soul. I found what I went for—friendship with other nursing mothers—but I also found much more. The mothers in my Group and the LLL information pamphlets and books found in the LLL Group library helped me to put into words and actions what I felt in my heart.*

And another LLL member, who wrote to us anonymously, told how La Leche League helped her overcome memories of her own unhappy childhood:

The reason I am so grateful to La Leche League is that it has helped me understand what "mothering" means and has given me confidence with my own children. My own upbringing was scary and chaotic. I was terribly afraid of becoming a mother. By having a stable nursing relationship I was able to tune in physically and emotionally to the needs of my baby.

At meetings I saw other mothers at peace with their infants and toddlers, learning like me and still available to be learned from. I became friends with several of these mothers and that, too, has enriched my life and my children's lives. And of course, those things that enrich us are of benefit to my husband as well.

I read your bimonthly magazine, NEW BEGINNINGS, including all the back copies in the Group's library. I am grateful I received adequate doses of support in favor of nursing to counterbalance the negative input I had received.

HOW DO I FIND LA LECHE LEAGUE?

There are several ways for you to find out the name of your local La Leche League Leader. You may find La Leche League listed in the white pages of your telephone directory, however, many LLL Groups are not able to afford such a listing. You might check at your local library to see if they have information about a nearby LLL Group. If you are attending childbirth classes, your instructor may know of an LLL Group in the area. A local newspaper may have LLL meeting notices from time to time so they may know the local Leader's phone number.

You can also write or call LLLI headquarters for the name and number of your local Leader. Our business hours are from 9 AM to 5 PM, (Central Time in the USA); the phone number is 847-519-7730. You can also use our toll-free number to find the name of a local Leader. Call 1-800-LA LECHE. The address is: P.O. Box 4079, Schaumburg IL 60168-4079 USA. In Canada, the toll-free number is 1-800-665-4324. La Leche League information can also be found on the internet at http://www.lalecheleague.org/

When you join LLL, you participate in an international mother-to-mother helping network, a valuable resource for parenting help and support. Paying your annual dues brings you six bimonthly issues of

NEW BEGINNINGS, a magazine filled with stories, hints, and inspiration from other breastfeeding families. Members in the USA receive our LLLI Catalogues by mail and they are entitled to a 10% discount on most purchases from LLLI's wide variety of outstanding books and publications on breastfeeding, childbirth, nutrition, and parenting. Your membership dues also support La Leche League activities all over the world. Additional benefits of LLL membership may also be available; they will be explained by your local Leader or in current LLL publications. Membership fees and benefits may vary in countries outside the USA.

Even mothers who cannot attend LLL Group meetings find the support they need through LLL membership. Elizabeth Hunsaker was living in Belgium, far from her family and friends, when her first baby was born. She writes:

> *I had always wanted to breastfeed because I had read it was best for the baby and that it helped to create a special bond between mother and child. I bought many books on caring for a baby, and I joined La Leche League. Our baby boy is now ten months old and is still nursing. It has been an experience I will always treasure. But it hasn't always been easy; and at times I felt very frustrated and discouraged.*

> *Receiving NEW BEGINNINGS helped me through a lot of trying times and made my nursing experience a happier one. Reading letters from other mothers who had the same experiences and the same attitudes about nursing made me feel as if I weren't alone and that it was worth the effort.*

And another mother, Elena Hannah from Newfoundland, Canada, found a friend's collection of back issues helped her get through some difficult times:

> *When I was almost overwhelmed with problems I was having with my first baby, a friend sent me her two-year collection of back issues. As soon as I starting reading them I felt I had found what I needed. Reading others' stories, many of them with problems more serious than mine, put everything back in perspective for me, and the main message seemed to be: "You can do it! You can overcome the difficulties!" By the time I finished devouring the collection I felt calmer and more confident. So today I want to say: Thank you to all the mothers who shared their stories with me and thank you, La Leche League, for having such a wonderful publication.*

Mothers enjoy the friendship and companionship of other mothers at La Leche League meetings.

Soon thereafter, Elena paid her membership dues and started receiving NEW BEGINNINGS on a regular basis.

Is La Leche League just for brand new mothers? The answer is "no." Experienced mothers provide the backbone of LLL Groups because they can offer the advice and encouragement that help a new breastfeeding mother cope. But mothers of older babies and toddlers find advantages, too, from their continued association with La Leche League. Elizabeth Hormann, who is an experienced mother and La Leche League Leader, writes:

Why would anyone want to continue with LLL once their children are weaned? It is not always easy to explain, but support is a large part of the reason. LLL addresses more than breastfeeding; there is a philosophy of mothering that grows from our experience as nursing mothers and that philosophy is not widely shared outside La Leche League circles. We need each other, especially as our children get beyond infancy and develop more facets to their personalities.

Mothers of toddlers are particularly likely to need the kind of support LLL provides. Shifting gears to care for toddlers is not easy.

Above and beyond information, La Leche League offers a special advantage to mothers summed up this way by one La Leche League Leader: "LLL gives me an opportunity to surround myself with the kind of people that I want in my life: caring, intelligent, family-oriented women who look on their children as assets, and who enjoy being mothers."

BEYOND THE BASICS

In addition to the basic meetings offered by LLL Groups all over the world, special meetings are often scheduled in response to the interest of the mothers in the Group. Toddler Meetings are held routinely for mothers who want to discuss meeting the needs of their older babies and toddlers. Employed Mothers' Meetings may be scheduled when several mothers in the Group want to discuss routines that are specifically directed to combining working and breastfeeding. Couples' Nights or Fathers' Meetings give men the opportunity to share their experiences with one another.

In addition, La Leche League periodically sponsors International and Area Conferences. These are one, two, or three day events providing information on breastfeeding and parenting that goes beyond the topics of regular LLL meetings. Doctors, health professionals, educators, and experienced parents lend their expertise to a variety of sessions throughout the day. Often luncheons are scheduled featuring a special guest speaker or allowing time for open discussion. Mothers, fathers, and babies enjoy the opportunity to spend the day together at an LLL Conference.

At International Conferences, which are held every other year, thousands of parents and professionals from all over the world meet to share their experiences and expertise. La Leche League International also sponsors annual Physicians' Seminars on Breastfeeding. Currently, these seminars are cosponsored by the American Academy of Pediatrics and the American Association of Obstetricians and Gynecologists, and accredited by other major medical associations. Lactation Specialist Workshops are also scheduled in various locations that offer continuing education credits for board certified lactation consultants.

In recent years the LLL Alumnae Association was organized. It continues to link Leaders and members together as they explore the application of LLL philosophy in new stages of their lives. It is open to all current and retired Leaders and members.

La Leche League has been a source of inspiration and encouragement for breastfeeding mothers for more than forty years. If there is an LLL Group in your community, we urge you to become a part of this mother-to-mother network.

PART TWO | *The Early Months*

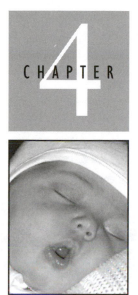

CHAPTER **4**

Your
Baby
Arrives

The newborn child is a rare and incredible sight. He seems so tiny and helpless, yet he does have certain survival skills that were not generally recognized until recently. Held up close, a newborn baby can see his mother's face clearly, and in fact has a preference for the human face. He can also hear quite well. For a period during the first hour of life, most newborns are quietly alert and receptive. A lively and intricate exchange of messages passes between the mother and the baby who are together at this time. The hours and days immediately after birth also seem to be an especially sensitive period for a mother to form an attachment to her newly arrived baby.

In their book, *The Amazing Newborn*, Marshall Klaus, MD, and his wife, Phyllis, tell about research that has changed attitudes about a newborn's capability:

> *When our own children were born, we were not aware of all their amazing talents and abilities. At that time, most everyone—*

including doctors— believed not only that infants could not see or focus their eyes, but also that they certainly would not respond to or recognize their mother's voice. No one talked about the possibility that an infant could imitate facial expressions, respond to rhythms of language, reach for objects, and start to learn at such an early age... .

Right after birth, within the first hour of life, normal infants have a prolonged period of quiet alertness, averaging forty minutes, during which they look directly at their mother's and father's face and eyes and can respond to voices. It is as though newborns have rehearsed the perfect approach to the first meeting with their parents.

Loving family attachments are formed in the first hour after birth.

Baby's First FEEDING

The sooner you put your baby to the breast, the better. Most babies are ready and even eager to breastfeed at some time within the first hour. The sucking reflex of a full-term healthy newborn is usually at a peak about twenty to thirty minutes after he is born, provided he is not drowsy from drugs or anesthesia used during labor and delivery. If this prime time to begin nursing is missed, the baby's sucking reflex may be less acute for about a day and a half.

Early breastfeeding is mutually beneficial to mother and baby. Aside from getting breastfeeding off to a good start, your newborn's immediate nursing hastens the delivery of the placenta. You will have less blood loss because the baby's sucking causes the uterus to contract. For the baby, being so close to his mother is comforting, and the first milk, the colostrum, is priceless as a source of protective immunities against disease.

When mothers are able to greet their newborns by cuddling and nursing, and infants remain with their mothers to nurse at will, breastfeeding usually progresses with few problems. Mother and baby need to be together early and often to establish a satisfying relationship and an adequate milk supply.

Your first attempt to breastfeed your baby is a learning experience, a get-acquainted effort for both of you. There are many variations in babies' responses. He may only nuzzle at your nipple or lick it a few times. You will be very emotional from the excitement of giving birth and you may feel awkward trying to position your baby at the breast. It will be hard for you to relax if there is a lot of activity going on around you.

The important thing is to hold your baby close, talk to him and comfort him. Cup your breast in your hand (as described in the sections that follow) and tickle your baby's lips with your nipple. If he opens his mouth wide, pull him in close to you so he can easily grasp the nipple and a large portion of the areola, the darker skin area that surrounds your nipple. He may take a few sucks and fall asleep. Or he may let go and prefer to look around at his new surroundings. Don't worry if he doesn't latch on right away. He will soon. This first opportunity to nurse sets the stage for the hours and days ahead when you and your baby will be getting to know each other.

If medical complications prevent you from breastfeeding immediately after your baby is born, all is not lost. You and your baby can make up for lost time once you are able to be together and begin breastfeeding. In a later chapter of this book, we discuss breastfeeding in certain medical situations or unusual circumstances. You'll also want to be in touch with your local La Leche League Leader if difficulties or special problems arise.

Getting STARTED

Getting your baby started at the breast smoothly and easily will soon be second nature to you. Breastfeeding a baby is actually much less involved than any description of the process.

One benefit of attending La Leche League meetings during your pregnancy is seeing other mothers breastfeeding their babies. This can help you more than photos or written explanations because you can observe a variety of mothers with babies of different ages and sizes who have adopted comfortable ways to breastfeed. They will probably be using pillows, cushions, footstools, and armrests to help them position their babies for nursing. Of course, no two mothers and babies are alike and as a baby gets older and nurses well, correct positioning becomes less of a concern.

Use a pillow to bring baby up to the level of your breast.

BREASTFEEDING IN SLOW MOTION

The following steps explain the correct way to position your baby at the breast in order to ensure that baby sucks well and gets plenty of milk and also to prevent nipple soreness and pain.

1. **Position yourself properly.** It's easiest to get started breast-feeding the first few times if you are sitting up. Sit up in bed, in a comfortable armchair, or rocking chair. Pillows are a must. Use them behind your back, under your elbow, and on your lap to support the baby. Use a footstool to bring your knees up or use pillows under your knees if you are sitting up in bed. You should be relaxed with none of your muscles straining.

2. **Position your baby properly.** Baby should be lying on his side with his whole body facing you and his knees pulled in close to your body. His head should rest on your forearm or in the crook of your elbow. His back should be supported by your forearm and you can hold his bottom or his upper thigh with your hand. Baby's ear, shoulder, and hip should be in a straight line. His head should be straight, in line with his body, not arched back or turned sideways.

   Baby should be held at the level of your nipple, so you are not leaning forward to reach him and he is not straining to latch on. Using a pillow on your lap will help.

3. **Offer your breast to the baby.** Cup your breast with your free hand, supporting it with your fingers underneath and your thumb on the top. Your thumb and index finger should form a "C." Be sure your fingers are well behind the areola.

4. Encourage baby to latch on properly. Tickle baby's lower lip with your nipple. If baby turns his head away, gently stroke his cheek on the side nearest you. The rooting reflex will make him turn his head toward you. Then try again to tickle his lower lip, talking to him and encouraging him to open his mouth. Wait for the baby to open his mouth wide, then quickly center your nipple in his mouth, above his tongue, and pull baby toward you with the arm that is holding him. It's important to pull baby in very close to you rather than moving forward toward the baby. It may take a few tries to coordinate your actions with baby's reactions so that all goes smoothly. If baby gets frustrated, you may have to stop and soothe him a bit before starting again.

Tickle baby's lips.

Wait for baby to open wide.

5. Effective sucking techniques. In order to suck effectively, the baby must get a large portion of your areola into his mouth along with the nipple. The milk sinuses that must be compressed in order to release the milk are located under the areola. Baby's gums should completely bypass the nipple and cover all or most of the areola behind the nipple. Be sure your nipple is centered in his mouth; it should be above his tongue. Baby

Pull baby in close to you.

should be pulled in so close that his chin is pressed into your breast and the tip of his nose lightly touches your breast. He will still be able to breathe quite well. If baby's nose does seem blocked by your breast, try lifting up your breast or pulling baby's body in closer to you rather than pressing down on the top of your breast.

6. **Nipple soreness or pain.** If your baby is latching on and sucking correctly you should not feel any painful pressure on your nipple. If baby seems to be sucking incorrectly or you feel pain as he nurses, you may have to make him stop and start over again. Break the suction by putting your finger in the side of baby's mouth and either pressing on your breast or gently pulling on baby's cheek. Don't let your baby continue to suck incorrectly because it can lead to nipple soreness; poor sucking patterns can be hard to correct later on.

    Other possible solutions:

    • Do not let baby slide onto the nipple, stopping short of the correct sucking position. Be sure he opens his mouth very wide so your nipple goes far back into his mouth.

    • If baby persistently clamps down too hard as he starts to suck, depress his lower jaw with your finger by pulling down on his chin as you tell him to "open" in a clear, commanding tone of voice. Open your mouth wide and baby may imitate you.

When baby is latched on and sucking well, a mother will not experience nipple soreness.

    • If nipple pain continues, have a helper gently pull baby's lower lip down while he is nursing and check to see if his tongue is visible between his lower lip and the breast. If his tongue is not visible, baby may be sucking it along with your nipple. Take baby off the breast and restart him, being sure his mouth is open very wide and his tongue is below the nipple and forward in his mouth when he latches on.

    • Some babies may also pull their lower lip into their mouth and suck on it, which interferes with the proper grasp of the breast and their ability to suck correctly.

    • If baby's nose and chin are not touching the breast, he is probably not sucking effectively. Take him off the breast and start again, being sure his mouth is open very wide and pulling him onto the breast chin first.

7. **Effective sucking patterns.** Many babies know exactly how to suck correctly from the moment they are born. Others take a few days to learn and need specific guidance as outlined above with lots of comfort and patience. But once baby is sucking properly you will take great satisfaction in watching him. As baby sucks vigorously, the muscles in his face work so hard that even his ears wiggle. You can see the strong action of his jaw muscles and hear him swallowing. Then once his initial hunger is satisfied, he becomes relaxed, sucking less vigorously, with fewer swallows, as he enjoys the closeness and comfort of being at his mother's breast.

Other Breastfeeding POSITIONS

It's a good idea to vary the positions you use to breastfeed your baby. When you are holding the baby at a different angle, he is putting pressure on different areas of your nipple, breast, and areola and this will help to prevent soreness. Also, it can be useful for you to know how to breastfeed your baby in different positions.

LYING DOWN TO NURSE

You may be more comfortable breastfeeding your baby in the side-lying position in the early weeks. You will need to use pillows to support yourself and the baby. At first, you may need some help getting the baby positioned properly so he can latch on correctly. Lie on your side with a pillow under your head. Have baby lying on his side facing you with his mouth in line with your nipple and his knees pulled in close to your body. Place your arm under him with his head on the crook of your

Learning how to nurse while lying down helps a mother get extra rest.

elbow. Lean back into the pillows that are behind your back and offer your breast to the baby by supporting it with your fingers underneath and your thumb above, well behind the areola. Encourage the baby to latch on properly by tickling his lower lip until he opens his mouth wide. Then quickly center your nipple in his mouth, above his tongue, and pull him in close to you so he can latch on well and suck effectively.

After you get baby started, you may want to place a pillow behind his back to hold him close and tuck your arm under the pillow supporting your head if that's more comfortable for you. Some mothers also place a pillow between their knees. To change sides, sit baby up and pat his back to see if he needs to bring up a burp, then hold him flat against your chest and roll over on your back. Lie on your other side and position baby at your other breast. This is especially good for mothers who have had a cesarean birth; while still in the hospital you can use the side rails on the bed to help you roll over.

When baby is positioned in the football hold be sure his feet don't push against the back of the mother's chair.

THE FOOTBALL HOLD

Another useful position for a baby to learn is the football or "clutch" hold. Position baby at your side with his legs under your arm and his head resting in your hand. Again, you'll need to use pillows to bring baby up to the level of your nipple. When you pull baby in close to latch on, be sure his legs are not pushing up against the back of the chair. If this seems to be happening, bend his legs upward, behind you, so his bottom is pressed against the back of the chair. This position is helpful for babies who are having trouble latching on as it gives the mother good visibility of what's going on and good control of baby's position as he latches on.

FOLLOW THESE PROCEDURES AT FIRST

Since it is important that the young baby learn to suck effectively, we recommend that you use these techniques step-by-step when you and your baby are learning. After a while, when both of you are breastfeeding experts, you can use whatever positions and procedures are comfortable for you. You will sometimes see photos of mothers using just two fingers to position their breast for the baby to latch on. At one time, this technique was recommended and some mothers do find it effective. But more recently it has been found that positioning the thumb and forefinger to form a "C" allows the mother to support her breast and avoid pressing on the areola or squeezing too hard.

THE MILK-EJECTION REFLEX (THE LET-DOWN)

After the baby has been sucking vigorously for several minutes, many mothers feel a tingling sensation and notice a strong surge of milk. This is known as the milk-ejection reflex or the let-down. It occurs several times during a feeding, and mothers sometimes notice that milk drips from the other breast when a let-down occurs. Baby usually responds to the let-down with more frequent swallowing. Even if you don't feel a tingling in your breast, you'll know a let-down has occurred by watching baby's pattern of sucking and swallowing. Sometimes, hearing your baby cry will initiate a let-down even before he starts to nurse.

Occasionally a baby will be caught off-guard by mother's strong let-down and will choke and sputter a bit. It's a good idea to keep a towel or clean diaper handy to mop up the drips as you sit baby up and let him catch his breath.

Some mothers do not feel the milk-ejection reflex at all, but it is still occurring if their babies are nursing well. For other mothers, the tingling sensation may be very strong, especially in the early weeks.

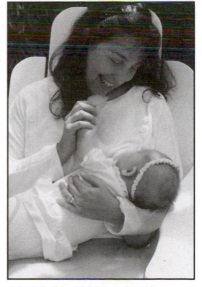

Breastfeeding offers rewards for mothers, too.

Engorgement—
When the Milk "COMES IN"

Your milk will become more plentiful, or "come in," at some time between the second to the sixth day after delivery. Before that time, your baby will get colostrum, which will provide him with all the nourishment he needs, plus important elements to protect him against infections. It takes about two weeks for the colostrum to gradually change into mature milk.

A combination of factors influences when a mother's milk becomes more plentiful. Nursing the baby soon and often after birth encourages milk production. An unmedicated delivery and having your baby with you make an important difference. It also helps if you are reasonably at ease. For most mothers, being in the familiar surroundings of home, with the freedom that gives you to cuddle and nurse your baby frequently, is all that is needed to bring in the milk.

When the milk becomes plentiful, your breasts may seem fairly bursting. You feel as though you could satisfy twins—or triplets! This fullness comes about because additional blood has rushed to the breasts in order to assure that there will be adequate nourishment for the new baby. It is like the marshaling of the grand army—all the forces come to the fore to get things in good working order. The extra blood, along with some swelling of tissues, produces the fullness. Some mothers notice only moderate or little fullness, while other mothers become engorged with each of their babies.

In the usual course of events, this feeling of fullness subsides in a matter of days. It is especially important to continue to nurse the baby frequently, at least every two hours, since removing milk from the breasts relieves the congestion. A comfortably warm shower, followed by a nursing, often reduces any discomfort. For some women, the normal feeling of fullness develops into engorgement with the breasts becoming hard and painful. The mother may even develop a low-grade fever. Some mothers find applying warm moist compresses and expressing some milk before feedings help to relieve engorgement. Ice packs can be used between feedings to reduce swelling.

A gentle breast massage may also help to relieve engorgement. Sometimes the engorged area is mainly in one part of the breast, perhaps high up toward the arm. With the palm of your hand, gently stroke the breast downward toward the nipple. This is most effective when done under the shower or while leaning over a bowl of warm water and sloshing the water over the breasts.

An effective home remedy to relieve engorgement is the use of cabbage leaves. They can be refrigerated or room temperature. Rinse the cabbage leaves, remove the hard vein, and cut a hole for the nipple. Apply directly to your breasts, inside your bra. In two to four hours, the cabbage leaves will become soft and wilted. Reapply, between feedings, until your breasts feel comfortable.

Cynthia Webb, from Montana, tells how her La Leche League Leader helped her to overcome the problem of engorgement and get off to a good start breastfeeding her daughter:

The day after we got home from the hospital was the day my breasts became engorged. With the baby crying in the background and the sample bottle of formula from the hospital looking temptingly easy, my LLL Leader gave me advice and solutions that had us back on the right track in half an hour.

It took Kelli and me a little longer to really get the hang of nursing. Then one day everything seemed to fall into place. The reward for perseverance has been tremendous. Kelli has shown me the gentle joys and subtle pleasures of motherhood. More than the baby at the breast, it's the first smile of recognition, little arms around my neck, a sleepy head on my shoulder, or snuggling under the covers during an early morning feeding.

Engorgement can present a problem if the fullness causes the nipples to flatten making it difficult for the baby to latch on properly. It may be helpful to massage your breasts and pump or hand-express some milk first to relieve the fullness. Some mothers worry that expressing even a small amount of milk will increase their milk supply and make their breasts even more engorged. This is not the case. Enabling the baby to latch on effectively will help to soften the breasts and eventually eliminate the problem. Sometimes briefly holding a cold washcloth or ice pack on your nipple will help to bring it out. Breast shells, made of hard plastic, can also be worn for thirty minutes before feedings to draw out flat nipples. (Do not confuse these with nipple shields which are worn over a mother's nipples during feedings. These are sometimes recommended for flat nipples but they are seldom helpful and often contribute to nipple confusion and sucking problems. They should be avoided.)

How Long to NURSE?

At one time new mothers were often told to limit nursings in the first few days to three to five minutes on each side at each feeding. Such advice does not take into account the fact that it may take two to three minutes for the milk to let down, especially in the early days. Nursing for less than five minutes could mean that the feeding would end almost before it started. And once the milk is flowing, the slight soreness that may be felt when the baby starts to nurse subsides. Keep in mind that, in the beginning, nursing frequently—every two hours or so from the beginning of one feeding to the beginning of the next—is easier on the nipples and at the same time stimulates the production of milk. Frequent nursing can also help to prevent exaggerated levels of jaundice in your newborn.

We also know that correct positioning of the baby at the breast and proper sucking techniques are the best protection against nipple soreness, so limiting baby's time at the breast is not necessary to prevent sore nipples.

The length of a breastfeeding session should be determined by the baby's interest and response. He will usually suck eagerly, swallowing often, for the first ten to twenty minutes. Then the flow of milk decreases and he begins to doze or lose interest. That's the time to switch him over to the other breast. You may want to stop at this point to burp him or change his diaper, and then get him started on the other side. As long as he is sucking correctly, you can let him nurse as long as he wants on the second side.

TAKING BABY OFF THE BREAST

If you must end a nursing session while baby still has a firm grip on your nipple, you can comfortably remove your baby either by gently pressing the breast away from the corner of his mouth or by pulling back on his cheek near the corner of his mouth. Pulling your baby off the breast without releasing the suction may be painful, and it can also be damaging to your nipples.

ONE SIDE OR BOTH?

Most mothers find it best to offer both breasts to the baby at each feeding in the early days. The baby's sucking stimulates milk production and offering both breasts at each feeding will help keep the breasts from becoming overfull.

At each feeding, alternate starting sides. For instance, if at one feeding you start nursing on the right and then switch to the left, reverse the order for the next feeding. You'll be using the last-used side first and the first, last. To help remember the starting order, mothers have come up with all kinds of ideas from fastening a small safety pin on the bra on the side used last to transferring a small ring from hand to hand.

If you do forget, your baby and your own full breast will probably soon let you know you've offered the "wrong" side. No harm is done if this happens from time to time; there's no need for you to worry about it.

"EMPTYING THE BREAST"

Sometimes mothers are told to empty their breasts completely after each feeding by pumping out whatever milk the baby may leave. This is not really practical because, first of all, the lactating breast is never empty; there will always be another drop of milk, and yet another. Secondly, we have yet to find a mother of a normal, healthy baby who found such emptying to be necessary in order to build up a good milk supply.

If you should have a baby who does not suck well at first, as might be the case with most premies or an occasional full-term baby, you will want to pump after each feeding in order to provide sufficient stimulation to keep up your supply and to provide your own milk for your baby.

KEEPING YOUR NIPPLES CLEAN

There is no need for special cleansing techniques for your nipples either before or after nursing. The Montgomery glands that surround the nipple secrete a substance that lubricates the skin and discourages the growth of bacteria. When you bathe or shower, use only plain water on the breasts and nipples as soap can be drying. It is important to wash your hands before a nursing session, especially while you are in the hospital.

BURPING THE BABY

During a feeding a baby sometimes swallows air that needs to be expelled or burped if the little one is to be comfortable. Your experience with your own baby will be your best guide as to when and if he needs burping. Some breastfed babies never seem to need burping, while others will swallow air when mother's breast is very full and the milk comes quickly. The baby who by nature is a "gulper" is always a likely candidate for burping. Burping is one of the things to try whenever the baby is fussy.

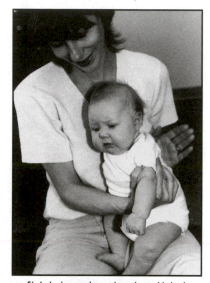

Sit baby in your lap and gently pat his back to bring up a burp.

There are any number of ways to burp a baby. You can try placing your baby on your shoulder and gently patting his back. A clean cloth diaper, small towel or blanket tossed over the shoulder will absorb any milk that comes up. Just holding your baby in a more or less upright position will bring up most air bubbles in an easy and relaxed way. Another tried and true method is to sit baby in your lap and slowly lean him forward, bending at the hips, while patting or rubbing his back. When he is very small, take care to support his head and back, and hold him in this position for only a few seconds. Some mothers rest the baby, tummy down, across their knees and rub or pat his back. Try burping the baby when you switch from one breast to the other during a feeding and again when your baby is through nursing. If there is no burp after a few moments, you can forget the idea—unless, of course, he is fussy.

Anytime your baby burps especially heartily, see if he wants a little more milk. The big bubble may have made him feel full when he really wasn't. But if baby falls asleep at the breast while nursing, you don't need to disturb him with the burping routine.

HICCUPS

We'd also like to mention hiccups here. Little babies seem to be prone to them, often hiccupping after every feeding. Don't worry about them; they're perfectly normal and more upsetting to the parents than the baby. If you like, you can let the baby nurse for a few more minutes. This may stop the hiccups.

Hospital ROUTINES

Hospitals want what is best for the patients, but often their size and bureaucracy come between their good intentions and the kind of care you need. Be prepared to speak up for what you want. Often, getting what you want is simply a matter of persistence. One mother said that whenever she was told "I'm sorry, we can't do that" in answer to a request, she would say that she did not want anyone to go against hospital policy, but that she would like to talk to someone who had the authority to alter the policy. Carrying her appeal up the line did at times result in a happy resolution of the problem.

YOU MAY ALSO NEED HELP

Assertiveness takes energy, of course, and may be an effort that you aren't up to at the time. Your husband can be your partner in helping to bend or bypass routines that hamper your breastfeeding efforts. You concentrate on caring for the baby, and he can take the position of running interference against red tape and regulations that get in your way. After all, this is your baby, a fact that is sometimes obscured in the delicate balance between institutional and parental authority.

Susan and Larry Kaseman of Virginia tell of their experience when their son Peter was born:

As my husband, Larry, and I planned for the birth of our second child, one major concern was that our family be together as much as possible. When a cesarean became necessary, we quickly changed plans, but not priorities. With a combination of diplomacy and determination, Larry communicated our wishes and began a dialogue with the hospital staff. They would state hospital policy, we would offer an alternative, and they would consider and sometimes cooperate.

"May I please have my baby?" became my theme throughout my hospital stay. I had been reluctant to refer to our first child as "my baby" for fear of being thought an over-possessive mother. I have since decided it is an effective way of emphasizing to myself and the staff exactly who has the primary responsibility.

Again and again I found that exceptions could be made to many of the rules. Peter was brought to us in the recovery room, two hours old and sleepy, but eager and able to nurse. What a tremendous help that contact was! When a nurse said an injection of painkiller would make me too woozy to be trusted with Peter, I declined the injection and she found a milder, oral drug that worked well enough.

Through my hospital stay, I had to keep asking for Peter. If one person refused to bring him, I'd ask someone else. Staff members were generally cooperative in responding, but seldom offered to bring him. I felt like a minority of one because of my "unusual" ideas, and was grateful for the reassurance of those who agreed with me.

My initial concern had been that Peter be with me so I could meet his needs, but I was continually amazed at the strength of my need for him—how much better I felt, physically and emotionally, when he was in my arms, and how difficult it was when he was in the nursery.

Father, mother, and baby become a nursing trio.

NO SUPPLEMENTS— FREQUENT NURSING

In the hospital your constant refrain should be that you do not want your baby to be given any artificial nipples, especially bottles of water or formula and you do want to be able to breastfeed him often. This is very important because artificial nipples and supplementary formula are the greatest deterrents to establishing a good milk supply. Frequent nursing will also help to prevent jaundice in your newborn. Your milk is regulated by what your baby takes, and the more he nurses, the more milk your breasts produce. If your baby is given formula, he will take less from the breast. Also, your baby will be confused if he is given an artificial nipple.

A baby is particularly vulnerable to nipple confusion in the first few days because he is learning how to suck properly. A baby uses his tongue, jaws, and mouth differently when sucking on an artificial nipple. If he is given bottles or other artificial nipples at this point, it may be a long hard struggle before he learns to breastfeed effectively.

If you do not have rooming-in, be sure to let everyone know that you want your baby brought to you as often as he wants to be fed. This should be at least every two hours during the day and whenever he wakes at night. Babies need to be fed at night and if your newborn is not brought to you, he may be receiving a bottle of water or formula in the nursery.

ROOMING-IN

Problems caused by hospital routines can often be avoided if it is possible for you to room-in with your baby. Rooming-in allows you to have your baby in your room for all or most of the time. You care for the baby, and others care for you. Connie Horenhamp of Illinois tells of her experience:

> *My first two children were totally breastfed, but they were forced to live those first precious days behind the glass wall of the hospital nursery. I spent many hours standing at the window making sure everything was all right. When Marissa was born, hospital policy was more relaxed and I was more determined; we roomed-in together. We nursed frequently, napped together, and just cuddled. The first day she slept very little as she adjusted to her new life, but I was able to phone a Leader for the reassurance I needed. Now I keep remembering (three months later) how Marissa slept in my arms and in the arms of my husband. Those first days were ours in which to grow together. I went home confidently knowing my baby.*

Laurel Cohen of New Jersey planned on having rooming-in when her daughter, Debbie Sue, was born, but she was informed that the required private room was not available. The baby would have to be in the nursery, and feedings could be only every four hours. Laurel was in a double room with another patient, but when the woman left soon afterward, Laurel went immediately to the supervisor's desk. Could she pay the private room charge and have her baby with her? A call to the business office procured the needed permission, and a delighted Laurel reported, "I had my dear little baby with me all day."

SLEEPING OR SCREAMING?

If you are able to have rooming-in or at least nurse your baby on demand, you won't be bothered with problems that can be caused by hospital feeding schedules. Still, there may be times when baby is not waking up to be fed as often as he should. A newborn needs to nurse at least 8-12 times in twenty-four hours.

If your baby has been sleeping for more than two or three hours, try gently to awaken him. Rough handling is very disturbing to a newborn, but you can jiggle him a bit, rub his head, talk to him, stroke his cheek with your nipple; try rubbing his feet or blowing on them.

One suggestion is to sit baby on your lap with his chin in your hand and bend him forward at the hips. Usually he awakens in just a few seconds. If not, try walking your fingers up and down his spine. Or gently bring him from a horizontal to a vertical position, one hand supporting his head, the other holding his bottom.

You can also try undressing him or changing his diaper. If nothing works to awaken him, you may have to give it another half hour or so and then try again. If the nurse comes to take him back to the nursery, be sure to let her know the baby did not wake up to nurse, and should be brought back for a feeding as soon as he wakes up. Make it clear that you do not want your baby to be given a bottle in the nursery.

If for some reason your baby is crying very hard before you get a chance to start feeding him, a little patience may be needed to calm him down before he's ready to nurse. Try rocking him or putting him over your shoulder and patting his back. Sing a soothing melody—baby will be calmed by hearing your familiar voice. Then try offering him your breast and see if he calms down and starts to suck. If he's not ready yet, try a few more minutes of calm mothering to help him relax.

With either the sleeping or screaming baby, squeeze a few drops of your milk onto his lips to give him a taste of what he's missing. We do not advise putting anything else, such as honey, on the nipple to entice the baby to take it. Anything other than your milk can cause a reaction in a sensitive baby. Also, these products may have impurities in them which could cause problems for baby—a certain type of botulism spores, for example, has been found in honey and can be very dangerous. Honey should not be given to babies under one year old.

Breastfeeding-Aid PRODUCTS

Experience has taught us that breastfeeding proceeds most smoothly when kept as simple and natural as possible. But there are some circumstances when a product designed to aid breastfeeding can be helpful. Breast pumps and other breastfeeding-aid products may be available from your local LLL Leader. Some are also sold through the La Leche League International Catalogue. See the Appendix for details.

BREAST PUMPS

Not every breastfeeding mother will need a breast pump. If a mother needs to remove milk from her breasts on a short-term basis, she can usually learn to use the techniques explained for hand-expression in Chapter 7. But there are situations when a breast pump is useful, for example, when a mother is saving her milk for a premature or sick baby, when a mother plans to return to work, or when a mother and baby must be separated for other reasons. More information on breast pumps can also be found in Chapter 7.

In the hospital, you may be advised to use a breast pump to relieve engorgement. If used for this purpose, be sure to pump only enough to soften the breast for baby to grasp the nipple. You will probably not need to do this for more than one or two feedings.

BREAST SHELLS OR BREAST SHIELDS

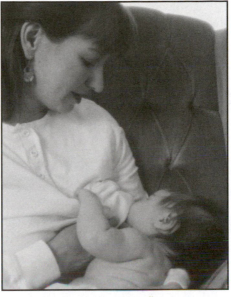

The relaxed atmosphere at home allows you to get to know your baby.

These two-piece hard plastic shells are the same ones recommended for use during pregnancy to correct flat or inverted nipples. They can be used for thirty minues or so before feedings to draw out flat or inverted nipples that were not treated during pregnancy. One type of breast shell has large holes that allow air to circulate around the nipples. Milk often collects in these breast shells but it should not be saved or fed to the baby. It should be discarded.

NIPPLE SHIELDS

A nipple shield looks like a regular nipple and is worn over the mother's own nipple during a feeding. From our years of experience, we know that nipple shields are often an invitation to trouble. Their use is almost never justified, and they usually create more problems than they solve. The impulses to the mother's brain that normally come from a baby sucking directly on his mother's nipple are fewer, and the secretion and let-down of the milk are slowed.

A baby who has been accustomed to sucking on a nipple shield is usually upset when his mother tries to take it away. With patience and understanding, a baby can be weaned from the rubber nipple but it is no easy task. You may be tempted to continue using the nipple shield since the baby is used to it, but the sooner you eliminate it the better. Once the baby is accustomed to the real thing, the shield can be thrown away.

If you are given a nipple shield to use in the hospital, we suggest that you refuse it. If your baby has already become accustomed to nursing with a nipple shield it may be difficult to convince him that it's better to nurse without it. Some mothers trim away a bit of the nipple shield around the nipple area every day so baby becomes accustomed to feeling skin in his mouth instead of the rubber nipple shield. (This cannot be done with a silicone nipple shield as cutting it will leave sharp edges.) Other mothers start a feeding on the nipple shield and wait for their milk to let down then take baby off and restart him on the breast without the shield. Your LLL Leader may be able to offer specific suggestions that will help your baby learn to suck effectively without the use of a nipple shield.

Leaving the HOSPITAL

Nowadays, there is a lot of controversy in the United States about how long new mothers should stay in the hospital after giving birth. Some mothers have been forced to leave sooner than they were ready. Some believe the mother needs to stay in the hospital for two or three days to get breastfeeding well established. Others believe nothing can duplicate the relaxed atmosphere at home that allows you to get to know your baby.

The mother who leaves the hospital in twelve to twenty-four hours needs to realize she is not fully recovered from the birth. She needs help at home so she can rest and breastfeed her baby. Also, she should be in touch with a La Leche League Leader or other breastfeeding specialist if she has questions or problems.

Karen Stange of Nebraska went home from the hospital twelve hours after her baby's birth. Karen explains how it worked out:

The doctor said the baby should be observed for twelve hours, but after that we were allowed to go home. Thus began three of the best days in eleven years of marriage. All of us got to know each other better than ever, and Clay seemed to thrive on the added love of five-year-old Sean and three-year-old Eric. The evening of Clay's birth all five of us sat in our home and, I'm sure, glowed with the love we felt.

Larry took three days off and we did nothing but be a family. We had few visitors as no one realized we were home. I was free to rest as I chose, and needless to add, breastfeeding went very well. For us it was a time that will be remembered fondly all our lives.

You can do yourself and your baby a favor by not taking any formula home from the hospital. You won't need it, and if it isn't in the house you won't be tempted to use it at one of those moments of doubt that most mothers have. The take-home packs of formula are simply advertising, a promotion for artificial infant feeding. Research has shown that these formula gift-packs interfere with a mother's determination to breastfeed.

Hospitals have become much more consumer-conscious in recent years and want to know what patients like or dislike about their hospital stay. By taking a few minutes to write a personal letter or fill out a patient questionnaire stating your preferences, you can support the practices you found helpful and point out the ones you'd like to see changed. Your suggestions could make it easier for the next breastfeeding mother giving birth in that hospital and, who knows?—you may find a delightfully improved atmosphere during your next visit.

If for some reason your breastfeeding experience in the hospital has not been the best or if you could not relax, don't fret. The hospital stay is now in the past. When you are at home with your baby, you will be able to breastfeed him. Thousands of mothers have done so and you can, too.

5

CHAPTER

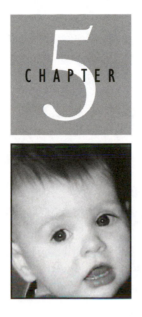

At Home with Your Baby

There is a sense of joy and satisfaction on everyone's part when your newborn is settled at home, in the heart of the family. Things are as they should be—you are all together. You'll find your mothering skills improving every day. But don't be surprised if you feel unsure of yourself and even a bit panicky at times. The care of this tiny baby is yours day and night, and the realization can seem overwhelming at times.

Many of us can say that we've been there; we know the feeling. One of La Leche League's co-Founders thinks back with amazement at her own ineptness when she and her husband brought their first-born home:

> *The picture is vivid in my mind. Baby was lying in her basket, which was beautifully done up with a frilly, ruffled liner that I had made before she was born. She was crying her heart out, oblivious to this finery. She had been fed and changed and was supposed to sleep.*

The early weeks are a time of adjustment.

The first six weeks were rough but well worth it. It took a while for me to recover from my daughter's long, difficult birth. We made it through together—Tiffany receiving the best through my milk and her nursing helping me to get back into shape. Six weeks, I had been told, was the magic number. I was told not to give up the idea of nursing until after that period, as both mother and child need time to adjust to one another. We had problems in the beginning, but nothing that a phone call to one of my LLL Leaders could not resolve.

**Diane McAleer
Florida, USA**

I remember thinking, "If only she were old enough to talk. She could tell me what is bothering her." Unfortunately, I was not yet aware of a far more basic form of communication with a little baby—a caring touch. How much more effective than speech! How simple if only I had picked her up! Instead I was feeling somewhat put out at the turn of events, disappointed in myself and my baby.

Think of the baby's first four to six weeks as an adjustment period for both of you, a time of getting to know each other. Your baby is mastering the skill of nursing to bring in milk, and your body is fine-tuning the system for producing it. It's not unusual for a new mother to feel as though her breasts are "bursting" with milk one day, and then be frantic a few days later because she thinks "there's nothing there."

Is the baby getting enough? Why is he crying? Haven't we all asked ourselves these questions and more? A good many of us announced firmly at some point in those early weeks that breastfeeding was "impossible." But at the urging of a supportive husband or with the help of another nursing mother, we decided to keep going for just a few more days.

Nowadays, new mothers have the advantage of being able to call an LLL Leader when questions or problems arise. She can give you reassuring answers and mother-to-mother encouragement.

Babies Are to LOVE

Through doubts and anxious moments, remember—babies are to love. The task of caring for your new baby will not seem nearly so awesome if you keep this thought in mind. "Tender loving care" is what the very best authorities recognize as the prime need of babies. Look to your own baby. Is he happiest when snuggled close to you, nursing very often, perhaps even every hour? Or does he respond best when laid down after a nursing and patted to sleep? Your baby's well-being, comfort, and security are your guides.

> *The needs of the infant are urgent. They are necessary for survival. When adults meet these needs day after day and week after week with reasonable consistency and promptness, the infant gradually develops a sense of trust.*
>
> James Kenny
> Clinical Psychologist

There is a beautiful simplicity about the care of the young baby that does not apply at any other stage of childrearing. With sureness we can say that a baby's wants are a baby's needs. The wants of a two- or three-year-old, however, may not always be what he needs. Parents will not respond any less lovingly then, but their approach will adjust to the changing world of the mobile child.

Mary Ann Cahill, one of La Leche League's co-Founders, talks about the needs of a newborn:

> *From living in the womb with the umbilical cord supplying all his needs, he has progressed to a position outside of, but near, mother's body. He is meant to be within close proximity of her warm breast and the sound of her voice. It is nature's careful way of providing a transition from the infant's old world to his new one. The little newcomer has the freedom needed to grow, yet is assured of continuous, loving support. The all-important mother-child bond replaces the umbilical cord.*

With your newborn, "giving in" to him is good parenting. Feed him according to his own time schedule. Comfort him when he is upset. But you may ask, won't such permissiveness spoil the baby? This question is asked by many parents who are sincerely concerned about their children and want to do what is best.

A mother, grandmother, and La Leche League Leader, Marion Blackshear, had this to say on the matter of spoiling and babies. "When you think of a piece of fruit as spoiled, you think of it as bruised, left on the shelf to rot, handled roughly, neglected. But meeting needs, giving lots of loving care, handling gently, is not spoiling. I could carry this one step further and say that a piece of fruit is at its best when left to ripen on the tree, its source of nourishment—and a baby is at his best when held close to his source of physical and emotional nourishment—his mother."

And others agree, Dr. William Sears, pediatrician and author of numerous child care books says, "Spoiling is a word that should be forever stricken from parenting books....Babies do not get spoiled by being held. Babies 'spoil' when they are not held."

And in his classic book, *How to Really Love Your Child*, Dr. Ross Campbell explains:

> *We cannot start too early in giving a child continuous, warm,*
> *consistent affection. He simply must have this unconditional love to*
> *cope most effectively in today's world.*

How Many Times Do I Feed the BABY?

Throughout this book, we refer repeatedly to feedings "every two or three hours" since it is a common time span for babies' appetites. And it is a fact that when baby's tummy is filled often enough, and mother's breasts are emptied regularly enough, most breastfeeding problems are avoided. But no timetable can tell you how often you should nurse your baby. Some babies, some of the time, will nurse more often than every two hours. Others will nurse less often, or perhaps go for one longer stretch at night.

Some people are more comfortable with the explanation that a newborn usually breastfeeds 10-12 times in twenty-four hours. This way, a mother is not watching the clock to see if two hours have passed since baby's last feeding.

Mothers who live in a world that is not as mechanized and scheduled as ours would be aghast at the thought of regulating the comfort their babies receive at their breasts. In a study of New Guinea tribeswomen, it was found that infants nursed about once every twenty-four minutes. The babies were carried close to their mother's body all the time and an average feeding lasted about three minutes.

NURSING MANNERS

As parents soon learn, babies have distinct personalities, and nowhere is this more apparent than in the way each little person approaches the important matter of eating. With our first babies some of us had preconceived ideas of how babies should nurse—beautifully mannered, of course, with no starts and stops or spitting up. With later babies, we found it much more revealing and entertaining to relax and observe each new stylist. You may find that your baby will fit one of the following descriptions. On the other hand, he may create a style that is strictly his own.

You will spend a great deal of time nursing your baby in the early weeks.

THE LEISURELY DINER

This young miss or mister thoroughly enjoys mealtime, which may be just about all of the time, especially in the early weeks. Intervals between nursings will lengthen as he grows older, and while he will probably always enjoy unhurried dining, he'll become much more efficient about drinking his fill. Once you are sure that he is gaining well, you can on occasion end a nursing after twenty minutes or so, feeling confident that he will not go hungry. A bonus with this type of baby is the opportunity to take it easy and cuddle lots.

Sometimes the leisurely diner can be encouraged to suck more effectively with some "switch nursing." After he has been nursing on one breast for about ten minutes you'll probably notice his sucking and swallowing slow down. It's time, then, to

Successful lactation is an expression of a woman's femininity and she doesn't need to count how often she feeds the baby any more than she counts how often she kisses the baby.

Babette Francis
Guest Editor,
Journal of Tropical Pediatrics

switch him to the other side. A new supply of milk may encourage him to finish his meal a bit more efficiently. If he slows down again, but still wants to suck, switch him back again to the first side.

THE NIP AND NAPPER

The nip and napper has much in common with the leisurely diner, although he tends to drop off to sleep (nap) after a few minutes of nursing (nip) and repeats this sequence rather often.

This is another instance when switch nursing can encourage more efficiency. As soon as baby starts to doze, switch him to the other breast. If he's really sleeping soundly, but you know he hasn't nursed enough to be full, try burping him or changing his diaper before switching to the other breast.

A baby who spends too much time sleeping at the breast instead of sucking well could be headed for a problem with slow weight gain. You'll want to work at encouraging him to suck well and watch for wet and soiled diapers to be sure he's getting enough to eat. (See the information in the next section under "Is Baby Getting Enough?")

THE NO-NONSENSE NURSER

Feedings are a down-to-business operation with this youngster. Once beyond the early stages of learning about breastfeeding, nursing time may be over in ten or fifteen minutes or less. He may be a baby who is only willing to nurse from one breast at each feeding. There is little opportunity for a dinner time tête-à-tête with the no-nonsense nurser. But look for a big smile, sometimes with milk trickling from the side of his mouth, at the end of a nursing before he moves on to the next challenge.

You may want to be sure that a baby who only nurses for short periods of time is given the opportunity to breastfeed often enough. There may be a question about whether he is getting enough to eat at these short, quick feedings, so again, you'll want to watch for wet and soiled diapers to be sure he's getting enough milk.

THE WHAT-GOES-DOWN-TENDS-TO-COME-UP TYKE

Is this a personality type or a physical trait? No matter, it is unmistakable. While almost all babies bring up a little milk occasionally after a feeding, this little one spits up regularly after feedings and in-between time. He is happy enough and gains weight, but you wonder whether he's keeping enough milk in his tummy to keep on gaining. The information in the next section will help you determine if he's getting enough to eat.

He may or may not speed through nursings. Some babies spit up because they're getting too much milk too quickly. If your baby gulps and gasps just after you have a let-down, try taking him off the breast for a moment or two as the milk rushes down. Have a diaper handy to catch the overflow. Let baby start nursing again as the milk flow slows to a rate he can handle. Some babies may even let the overflow trickle out of their mouths, which is a nice way of alleviating the problem. Your main response to this characteristic should be very gentle handling, with no sudden movements. Too vigorous burping can bring up milk that would otherwise stay in the baby's stomach. Gentle handling after a feeding will help your baby keep down his lunch. It may help to raise the pad or mattress in baby's bed or basket by an inch or two at the head end as laying baby flat is sometimes what triggers the spitting up.

Occasionally a baby will finish nursing as usual and promptly bring up what seems to be the entire feeding, perhaps even with jet-like force. If the baby does not show any signs of illness—no fever or unusual crying—it is probably just one of those things. After things calm down a bit and you've cleaned up the mess, go ahead and nurse the baby again. Of course, you'd want to check with your doctor if this happens often. (For more information on frequent spitting up or vomiting, see Chapter 17.)

A handy supply of diapers or small towels is a help in protecting your clothing with a spitter in the family. And along with diapers, take extra changes of clothing for baby (and maybe for yourself!) when going out. As Dr. Gregory White has observed, "in a healthy baby, spitting up is a laundry problem, not a medical problem."

Getting bigger is a sure cure for this tendency in a baby. While spitting up is a nuisance at the time, there is less odor and staining with human milk than there would be if baby were formula-fed. And really, what's a little milk between a mother and her bosom buddy?

ABOUT THE PACIFIER

Be forewarned that the pacifier can create more problems than it solves, often because it works too well. Pop it into a crying baby's mouth, and the room is suddenly blanketed with silence. What could be handier? But therein lies trouble. The use of a pacifier has a way of sneaking up on you by making it so simple to take the easy way out. While a pacifier can sometimes substitute for mother's breast, it is never a substitute for mother. A La Leche League Leader from Great Britain, Christine Blissett, explains that the British term for pacifier is "dummy." "This is exactly what it is!" she adds.

Used judiciously, however, for a short period of time and in a limited number of circumstances, a pacifier can be a help to the breastfeeding mother. Sucking can be very soothing to a newborn, and a pacifier may be convenient when you find yourself in a situation where you absolutely can't nurse him. A pacifier may satisfy him briefly until you can. Sometimes a baby with colic will find it soothing to suck on a pacifier between feedings.

The "pacifier habit" develops when it's used routinely, for instance, as a way to put the baby to sleep. Ordinarily, if your baby likes to fall asleep sucking, let it be at the breast. You have the best pacifier in the world from baby's point of view. And more nursing at the breast means more milk for the baby.

If your baby sucks on a pacifier regularly every day, your milk supply could be adversely affected and the baby may not gain well. One study showed that mothers who gave their babies pacifiers regularly tended to wean sooner than those who did not.

Is Baby Getting ENOUGH?

How will you know if your baby is getting enough milk? He is probably getting enough to eat if he nurses every two or three hours. Is he "filling out" and putting on weight? Growing in length? Active and alert? A "yes" to these questions is an indication that your baby is thriving.

A quick, easy way to reassure yourself that your infant is getting enough milk is to check the number of wet diapers. If he has six to eight really wet cloth diapers a day (five to six disposable diapers), you can be sure he is getting plenty of milk. Frequent bowel movements are also a sign that baby is getting enough to eat. For the first six weeks or so, a breastfed baby will usually have two to five bowel movements a day.

From time to time, your doctor will weigh the baby as a way of measuring his physical progress. Some babies never lose an ounce from the day they're born, and put on weight with the greatest of ease. Most babies lose some weight during the first week but get back to birth weight by two to three weeks of age. After that, a pound a month (453 grams), or four to eight ounces (113-226 grams) a week, is usually considered an acceptable gain, although some babies gain as much as a pound a week in the early months. Family characteristics and the baby's individual makeup need to be considered. Remember—healthy, happy babies come in all shapes and sizes. Both the quite fat and the very slim baby can be normal and healthy. Neither bigness nor smallness is a reason for concern as long as the baby's food is human milk and nursings are according to his needs. If you feed your baby in the way that is naturally intended for the human infant, his weight gain will be what is natural for your particular child.

With regard to baby's size and appetite, Malinda Sawyer of Missouri observes, "Mothers who give birth to large babies and mothers who give birth to small babies have at least one thing in common: They can expect to have their ability to totally breastfeed the baby questioned."

Marian Tompson, one of La Leche League's co-Founders, remembers when two of her nieces had identical weights of seventeen pounds—but one baby was six months old and the other was one and one-half years old. Yet the doctor for each was satisfied that the baby was healthy.

If you are having any problems with your milk supply, or if your baby is not gaining at least four ounces a week, see the section later in this book on "Increasing Your Milk Supply" (in Chapter 7) and "Slow Weight Gain" (in Chapter 17).

LEAKING

A common occurrence while you are breastfeeding is for milk to drip from one breast when baby starts to nurse on the other. If your breasts are very full or engorged, there is good reason to let the milk come out rather than hold it back. It's a great way to relieve that full feeling. To catch the overflow and keep yourself dry, hold a diaper or something equally absorbent under your breast.

Sometimes a breastfeeding mother will find her milk is leaking at inopportune moments. This is most likely to occur during the first weeks of nursing. Suddenly, to your dismay, you realize that milk is leaking from your breasts. Often, it is nearly time for a feeding and the sight, sound, or even the thought of your baby triggers the let-down reflex.

Nursing mothers have learned that pressure applied directly against the nipples will keep the milk from dripping out. If you notice the tingly, stinging sensation of the let-down—or if you feel milk starting to leak—fold your arms across your chest and apply pressure with the heels of your hands directly on your nipples. Another unobtrusive way to stop leaking is to rest your chin on your hands and press against your breasts with your forearms.

There are nursing pads available in drug stores, discount stores, and maternity shops that are designed to absorb leakage. Some are disposable; others can be washed and used over and over again. You'll want to avoid pads that have a plastic liner as they can keep air from getting at your nipples. Some mothers make their own pads by stitching together circular pieces cut from old diapers or other absorbent material. The pads can be washed along with baby's other things and reused. A folded cotton or linen handkerchief works well, too, but avoid the no-iron variety as they are less absorbent.

The possibility of your milk leaking when you least expect it can lead to a certain amount of embarrassment, as Sue Ellen Jennings Austin, from California, recalls:

> *I remember an early outing with our first nursing baby. I had carefully planned to be out between his every-two-hour nursings and was even armed with a water bottle in case (heaven forbid!) he should want to nurse in public. We were strolling down the aisle of a grocery store when a woman approached me and whispered, "Excuse me, Miss, your milk is leaking."*
>
> *Glancing down at the floor, I was horrified to see a trail of milk all around me and my shopping cart. Panicked, I clasped both arms across my chest. It was only then I realized that the milk had not come from me but from a milk carton in my shopping cart that had overturned.*

BUT WHERE HAS ALL THE MILK GONE?

When the milk comes in and your breasts feel quite full, you are overjoyed and supremely confident that you will have plenty of milk for your baby. Then the fullness goes away, and you may find yourself thinking that the milk must be gone, too. At this point you may feel discouraged. You begin to wonder, "Have I lost my milk?"

You haven't, we can assure you. The absence of that full feeling and dripping is no indication that the amount of milk you have for your baby has been diminished. The making of milk is an almost continuous process. As the baby takes some out, more comes in. Just keep nursing, and your eager eater will be rewarded with milk, even though you do not feel "full."

The more often your baby takes milk, the more milk you will have. When a mother has twins, there is twice the stimulation to the breasts to produce milk, and so she has enough for two babies. When your baby nurses less often or with less vigor, the amount of milk you produce decreases accordingly. If it drops too low to suit his needs, he will want to nurse more often. With added nursings, your breasts will respond by making more milk.

As you will see, breastfeeding is an excellent example of the law of supply and demand in operation. Problems arise when rigid feeding schedules, bottles of water, or supplementary feedings hamper the natural balance. It takes a little while to establish a good balance between baby's appetite and your milk supply, so be patient. The first six weeks are sometimes the most challenging. This is the time when you'll really want to be in touch with other breastfeeding mothers, especially your La Leche League Group.

Breastfeeding becomes easier as it continues. As your baby's personality emerges, the fun increases. There are smiles and love pats. The time you spend with baby at your breast helps you get to know each other in a very special way. The concerns of the early weeks will soon give way to the enjoyment awaiting you in the months ahead.

BABY'S BOWEL MOVEMENTS

For the first few days after birth, baby's stool will be very dark—greenish-black—and sticky. It may be a nuisance to wipe off his little bottom, but it's a reassuring sign that all is well with baby's digestive system. This first stool is called meconium. Nursing the baby soon after birth assures that your baby will get the colostrum he needs to help get rid of the meconium.

Once the meconium is cleared out, the stool of the baby who is receiving only mother's milk differs a good deal from that of the formula-fed infant. The stool of the breastfed baby is usually quite loose and unformed, often of a pea-soup consistency, and may be yellow to yellow-green to tan in color. The odor, unlike that of the formula-fed baby's stool, is mild and not unpleasant.

Frequency of bowel movements varies from baby to baby and even from week to week with the same baby. Some babies may have very frequent bowel movements that are little more than a stain on the diaper. At first, your baby may have a bowel movement with every nursing. This is definitely not diarrhea in the breastfed baby. It is a sign that he is getting plenty of milk. As he gets older, past six weeks or so, he may have only two to three large bowel movements a week, sometimes only one a week; even less often is normal for some babies. As his bowel movements decrease in frequency, they will increase in volume. There is room for considerable variation among perfectly normal breastfed babies. Even an occasional green, watery stool is not a cause for worry in the otherwise healthy baby. Bowel movements can also change in color after exposure to the air.

Happily enough, because human milk contains enough water for his needs, your breastfed baby does not get constipated. Constipation (hard, dry stools) has nothing to do with the time interval between bowel movements. Some older breastfed babies go five to seven or more days between bowel movements and have perfectly normal, though very profuse, stools.

Many babies love to be carried in a sling.

Babies sometimes fuss just before or at the time they have a bowel movement, and a change of position may help them. Some can get down to business more easily when in a semi-reclining position, either in your lap or in an infant seat. Others want to brace their feet against something. If you hold the baby against your shoulder, hold one hand under his feet. If your baby is one who seems to have a difficult time with this, you might try helping him by sponging the rectal area gently with warm water. If that doesn't help, some doctors suggest inserting a small glycerin suppository. This is seldom necessary, and there's no need to bother unless your baby has a real struggle and seems very uncomfortable. Be assured that your baby will outgrow this problem.

Caring for Your BABY

As a very new little person, your baby continues to need many of the same conditions that helped him to grow in the womb. He needs to be close to you most of the time, whether awake or sleeping. Being close to you is very reassuring to your newborn. The rhythms of your breathing and heartbeat are familiar to him. In addition, he has been hearing your voice since about five months before he was born, so talking to him in soft, loving tones is especially soothing. For the time being, you are his world.

As Herbert Ratner, MD, philosopher and long time friend and advisor to La Leche League, states, "It is a wise and providential nature that gives each newborn his or her private caretaker and tutor—the mother."

Viola Lennon, one of La Leche League's co-Founders, tells a story of a young mother who had what seemed to her a hundred and one problems. Vi recalls: "I invited her over for a visit. As she sat down in the living room with me, she immediately began asking questions. Soon I noticed she was not listening to my answers but was watching me handle my baby, Marty, who was rather fussy that day. I nursed him, walked him, bounced him, rocked him, and carried him with me to the kitchen while I made a pot of tea. Finally, she blurted out, 'Does he often act this way?' When I said yes, she smiled and said, 'I don't think I have any real problems. I just didn't know that babies needed all that attention.'"

KEEP YOUR BABY CLOSE

Along with whatever else you are doing during the day, you will want to have your baby close to you as a matter of course. You don't have to have him in your arms every minute, although you will be holding him often, both when you are nursing and between times (as he needs this contact). But you will just want to be there because what your baby needs most of all is you. No one else can take your place. To him, there is nobody quite like his mother.

In many cultures it is the custom for mothers to be practically inseparable from their babies during their first years, with the baby either strapped to his mother's body or sleeping cuddled next to her. In these cultures, it is unusual to hear a baby cry.

> *In the biological program of mother and baby there are built-in guarantees for the satisfaction of the baby's needs that ensure the formation of human bonds in the first eighteen months of life. The mother is the primary "need satisfier," and that need satisfaction should lead the infant through a series of stages in the first year in which the mother is loved more than any other person in his small world.*
>
> Selma Fraiberg
> **Author and Psychologist**

So it is not surprising that a recent study found that more human contact makes for a happier baby. Those babies who spent more time being held or carried either in mother's arms or in a baby carrier—even while contented or asleep—cried less. The younger the baby, the more dramatic were the results. Three extra hours of carrying a day reduced the amount of crying in a four-week-old infant by forty-five percent.

These findings confirm what our mothering instincts tell us—that plenty of loving contact does not "spoil" a baby or make him more demanding, but instead helps him feel more comfortable and happy in his new world.

For many mothers, owning some type of a sling or baby carrier is essential. Helen Nichols of Massachusetts can't say enough "in praise of the baby carrier." She writes: "As with breastfeeding itself, the benefits of the baby carrier are not entirely for the baby. In fact, as I discovered, mother receives a generous portion of them. I could cook, clean house, wash dishes, care for the older children, even sew while Benjamin slept blissfully in his cozy nest. It was, purely and simply, the very easiest thing to do."

When you are considering what kinds of equipment you'll need for your new baby, remember that very little specialized baby equipment is really necessary; more important to the baby are mother's sweet milk and loving arms. Lee Stewart of Missouri sums up the subject well: "Children's natural values are very human and simple. They want to be held and loved. They want to be with those who care for them. They want to be comfortable. Given a choice between the warmth of human values and material values, babies will almost always choose the human."

Taking Care of MOTHER

As a brand new mother, you may find yourself concentrating so completely on your baby that you forget about taking care of yourself, so a quick review of the basics of "mother care" is worthwhile here. Mother care isn't elaborate or demanding; it involves mostly common sense things that are important to any new mother, breastfeeding or not.

Good food, plenty of fluids, and adequate rest come quickly to mind. We also include in our list the need for plenty of loving exchanges—if only a hug or a quick squeeze of a hand—between the new baby's parents. Such shared moments will help keep you going during this demanding time in your life.

Choose between-meal snacks carefully. A nursing mother gets hungry almost as often as her baby, and there's the temptation to nibble on sweets. Choose instead nutritious snacks such as fresh fruit, raw veg-

Good food, plenty of fluid, and lots of rest help a new mother cope with the challenges of caring for a new baby.

etables, whole wheat crackers, or cheese. Getting enough to drink can be taken care of by keeping unsweetened juice or water handy at all times.

Sufficient rest is right up there with the most important recommendations for a new mother. In the days immediately following your baby's birth you will want to spend a good part of your day relaxing. A certain amount of being up and about provides needed exercise, but this is the time to enjoy being pampered. "Mothering the mother" is an integral part of the care of a new mother and baby in many cultures.

A handy rule of thumb for a new mother is to sleep, or at least rest, whenever baby dozes. Even the baby who "never sleeps" catnaps more often than parents may realize. True, the times when the baby sleeps are probably not when you are accustomed to sleeping, and it will take some discipline on your part to put aside what interests you at the moment, close your eyes, and think "sleep." When baby's eyes close at the breast, settle back in your chair with your feet up, your little bundle still in your arms, and try to drop off to sleep. And

I want to thank La Leche League, not only for the breastfeeding information, but for their outlook on babies and mothering. There are many baby gadgets and gimmicks around these days to substitute for mother's time and closeness. I don't think our society is really comfortable with babies and their simple needs: security in mother's presence and the best possible food, mother's milk.

**Michele Acerra
New York, USA**

even if you can't sleep, just closing your eyes, forgetting work that needs to be done, and relaxing can be refreshing.

Other times, mothers find that lying down, closing their eyes, and listening to soft music for ten minutes or so is refreshing. Try it! Think of tension draining away as water drains from a basin. Or snuggle with baby and a book. The important part is to forget about those things which "must be done." Remember, "people before things," and that includes you!

Every so often take a moment to think through the ways to make the most of this time in your life. Use your own good judgment as to what is or is not important. Your baby and the rest of the family, too, need and appreciate a mother who is relaxed and feels good about herself.

A NURSING CORNER

Many breastfeeding mothers find it convenient to set up a comfortable spot for their nursing sessions. Since you'll be spending a lot of time there in the early weeks you'll want everything as handy as possible to save time and effort.

You'll probably start with a comfortable armchair or rocker. We'd go so far as to say that a rocking chair is one of the most essential items you'll need for your new baby. A footstool is another handy item as it helps to lift your knees when positioning your baby for breastfeeding. There's nothing like putting up your feet to help you relax!

Lots of cushions or pillows are another essential aspect of our nursing corner. You need these to properly support yourself and your baby for comfortable feedings.

A good reading lamp should be nearby, as there will be occasions when you'll want to lean back and enjoy reading a book or magazine as baby nurses the time away. A small table allows you to keep a large glass of water or juice within easy reach—something you should bring along every time you sit down to nurse the baby.

You might want to keep a stack of diapers, a wastebasket or diaper container, and other baby items (wipes, undershirts, and a few small blankets) close at hand. With these essential supplies always nearby, you can feed and change baby with a minimum of effort.

VISITORS—A HELP OR HINDRANCE?

Friends or relatives may offer to help out when you have a new baby. While an extra pair of hands is always welcome, some well-wishers may bring advice and comments that are not at all helpful. Be specific about the kind of help you would appreciate—a nice hearty casserole or a nutritious dessert perhaps. Don't be afraid to ask your mother or mother-in-law to stop at the grocery store if you need supplies—

or to throw a load of laundry in the washer when they stop by to see the baby.

It may seem unusual for you to sit back and be waited on by your guests—but that's very much the way it should be for a new mother. If you enjoy visiting with friends, then welcome them but let them know you won't be up to the role of "perfect hostess" for a few weeks. One way to reinforce this message is what one mother calls "robe play." Slip into your robe when the company knocks on the door, even if you have been wearing daytime clothes. Without saying a word, the message is conveyed that you are not yet up to entertaining as usual.

In general, a new mother can be as active as she wants to be, provided that she stops whatever she is doing the instant she begins to feel tired. You will find that this little reminder covers a multitude of new-mother indiscretions. By taking care of yourself in the early weeks, you will feel better in the months ahead.

WHEN RELAXING ISN'T ENOUGH

If your baby happens to be one of those fussy, active babies who is always looking for mother's attention and who thrives on change, you may find it hard to follow our advice to relax and take it easy. If this is the case, you have our sympathy, because we've had this kind of baby too, and we know how trying it can be. The very busy, alert baby is almost always more contented as he gets older and can do more for himself. He can't wait to conquer the world on his own!

If you find that you just can't relax, ask yourself if you are trying to pack too much into your day. We hope you have taken to heart our remarks about the baby being more important than housework or other commitments. But if you do find yourself tense and jittery and you know the baby will want to nurse again soon, take a breather for a minute or two. An exercise break can do wonders. The activity will loosen tight muscles and perk up the blood circulation. There are new books and videotapes available that explain exercise routines that include your baby. (See Appendix.)

Weather permitting, look forward to a walk outdoors each day. Take baby with you, of course, in his carriage or baby carrier. The fresh air, sunshine, and change of scenery will do both of you a world of good.

It may be that, when you begin to feel on edge, you could be hungry. How long has it been since your last good meal? Why not eat a piece of fresh fruit or nibble on a tasty piece of cheese? A hard-cooked egg, ready in the refrigerator, will furnish you with the staying power of protein. A slice of whole-grain bread with peanut butter is also quick and good. Or brew a fragrant cup of hot tea to enjoy as baby nurses.

The end of the day is often a troublesome time for mothers and babies. Clare Vetter of Kentucky tells of one particularly trying evening that worked out well in the end:

After a very busy day, my son, Isaac, was too "wired-up" to nurse. Of course, I was worn out also and perhaps a bit low on milk supply. Each time Issac would start to nurse, he would stop suddenly, sit up, and fuss loudly.

My husband, Tom, came in and put on some lovely, relaxing music, Pachelbel's Kanon. It seemed to be just what our family needed. I stood up with Isaac in one arm and the three of us began a lively yet soothing waltz. Our dance was spontaneous and improvised, and our aching muscles seemed to work out their pains. Gazing into Tom's eyes I remembered our first dance at a college waltz party ten years ago. There is so much more to our lives now than then!

The canon ended too soon. Bathtime, storytime, then bed and lights out. Isaac and I lay nursing and the melody played itself again inside me, and there was plenty of milk. Sometimes a little romance helps.

NEW BABY BLUES

Occasionally, a woman feels down or depressed for no particular reason following the birth of her baby. "There I was, holding my beautiful new daughter in my arms, knowing that I had everything to be thankful for, yet I was dissolved in tears," one mother remembers. Another mother described the feeling as "combat fatigue following delivery." Dr. James Good, a wise family doctor, once pointed out the similarities between the depression a mother may feel following the delivery of her baby and that which often sets in the day after a special occasion. The anticipation and planning that filled the months before have come to an end. A high point of participation is over, and a period of adjustment follows.

This emotional seesaw may also arise as a result of the change of hormones in your body from a pregnant to a nonpregnant state. It is usually short-lived, but if the feeling persists, you may want to check with your doctor. Breastfeeding and having your baby close to you will help you to deal with this transition. The hormonal changes are more gradual when you breastfeed. The old standbys, eating well and getting enough rest, are important in helping you feel well, both physiologically and emotionally.

Marlane Edelman of New Jersey stresses the benefits of being in touch with La Leche League:

At our last La Leche League meeting our Leader asked all of the mothers to share what they liked most about breastfeeding. One mother said that she considered La Leche League meetings to be one of the advantages of breastfeeding. Her answer caused me to look back on the influence La Leche League has had in my life.

I became pregnant shortly after we moved to a new state. During my pregnancy I had no friends in our new hometown and I was very lonely.

I attended my first LLL meeting because after three months of breastfeeding I was still having considerable difficulty with sore nipples and breast infections. I was looking for information and consolation that things would get better. I went home from that first meeting with some helpful information and returned for the next three meetings.

It hadn't occurred to me to continue past those first meetings, but the Leader called to invite me, so I went. Now, sixteen months later, I am still attending LLL meetings. I have found they are more than just a place to learn about breastfeeding. I've learned about the nutritional, emotional, and physical needs of growing babies and ways of coping with people who ask, "Are you still nursing?" I've found a place where people understand why my career is my family. And, I've finally found friends. Friends who have joined together with their children to form a playgroup. Friends who understand how frustrating it is to be housebound on a long winter day.

LLL has meant so very much to me. I hope someday to be able to give other mothers what I have found there—a warm accepting environment where I'm encouraged to love and nurture my child in the way I feel is best, beginning with breastfeeding.

Going Out? Take Baby ALONG

You don't have to be a stay-at-home with a breastfed baby. Baby can go right along with you almost everywhere you want to go. In the early weeks, it's a good idea to pace yourself—take things easy—for your own sake. A brief shopping trip or a visit to see proud grandparents would be good to start with and can be a refreshing break in the everyday routine. When you're ready to go, baby and a diaper bag are easy bundles to take along.

Feeding your baby or comforting him at the breast is not a problem, since it is possible to nurse inconspicuously almost anywhere. In most parts of the world no one gives a second thought to the sight of a nursing mother. But if you feel more comfortable nursing your baby without drawing attention to the fact, this can be easily accomplished.

Two-piece outfits are probably the most convenient for nursing away from home. A loose-fitting sweater or overblouse can be lifted from the waist for easy nursing. You remain covered on top, and a diaper or small blanket can be a casual cover-up. The never-out-of-fashion shawl also lends itself to discreet nursing. Maternity shops and specialty catalogues now feature special tops and dresses for nursing mothers with concealed openings for breastfeeding. Many La Leche League publications carry advertising from companies that specialize in fashionable clothing designed for discreet nursing.

It's a simple matter to conceal the whole operation. You will need only a minute or so of privacy to get baby started at the breast. Once he's nursing, your baby could be sleeping in your arms for all anyone knows. Many large stores, airports, train stations, and shopping malls have rooms set aside for mothers and small babies. Another possibility when shopping in a large store or shopping center is a visit to the women's clothing department. If it isn't too crowded, you can relax in a fitting room while you nurse the baby. If you sew or just enjoy looking at fashions, take a nursing break in the fabric department—one with comfortable stools at the pattern-book counter.

You will soon be able to devise a way to nurse inconspicuously to suit any occasion. At the beach, a large beach towel thrown casually over your shoulders and arms can serve as a kind of private tent for your nursing baby.

As a new breastfeeding mother, you may feel more at ease about nursing in different situations if you practice inconspicuous nursing at home first, with your husband or a good friend as critic. Mothers find that it doesn't take long to smooth out their performance.

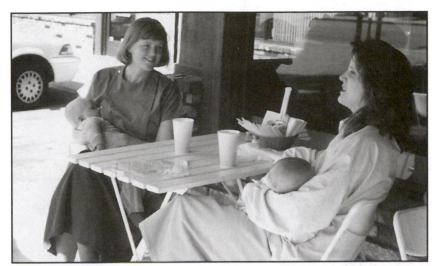

It is possible to nurse your baby so inconspicuously that no one will know he is having lunch, too.

BREASTFED BABIES GO EVERYWHERE

A little advance planning or innovative thinking will often keep a young one and his mother together and happy. When Mary White, one of LLL's co-Founders, was the matron of honor at her sister's wedding, she brought a babysitter along for the specific purpose of holding her three-month-old baby during the ceremony. Between the ceremony and the reception, Mary slipped off, nursed the baby, and was back in the receiving line in time to shake a few hundred hands.

The women in the La Leche League Group in Hull, England, drew up a list of places they had gone with their nursing babies. In many of the situations, they felt it would be difficult to feed or comfort a bottle-fed baby. Lynne Emerson wrote the following account:

Bridget said that she's nursed in restaurants, doctors' and dentists' offices, and in church. Christina took the minimum of equipment on a canalling holiday compared with another bottle-feeding mum on another

After the birth of our daughter, Dawn Michelle, Fred and I were invited to speak about our experience at a childbirth class. Toward the end, Dawn decided that she wanted to nurse. I continued answering questions as I put her blanket over her head and my shoulder, and she took the breast. One of the expectant mothers commented that I certainly had a unique way of quieting my baby—throwing a blanket over her head! I explained that the baby was nursing. Fred later said that I was getting to be such a pro, I didn't even pause in mid-sentence.

Charlene Brown
Nevada, USA

boat. She has also nursed baby Sarah in the changing room at the local sports centre. Lynne said she had nursed at a wedding reception, in a snow blizzard while stuck in her car when her ten-minute car trip turned to all day after the car broke down, while football spectating, and on the beach.

I nursed Lucy, when only three months old, at a one-day yoga seminar. The yoga teacher was skeptical at first, but I assured her Lucy wouldn't distract the class. Our last excursion (to see the local pantomime) was really exciting. The whole family went, and there were a few raised eyebrows when we walked in, but afterward people remarked how good the baby had been. We hope this will help dispel the myth that breastfeeding the baby is confining.

TRAVEL PLANS

On longer excursions, babies make good travelers if some thought is given ahead of time to their special needs. Breastfed babies have logged a phenomenal number of hours in the air. Judy Sanders of Washington flew halfway around the world to New Zealand with her daughter, Maria. Judy reports that it was easy to travel with Maria because she was breastfed. Wearing a caftan-type dress with hidden zippers was comfortable and convenient for discreet nursing.

You'll want to check with your specific air carrier for their regulations before planning a trip by plane. They may provide special infant safety seats or suggest you bring your own. Reserving a bulkhead seat will give you some extra room. Pack your tote bag with baby's diapers, soft toys, and a change of outfits—just in case your luggage does not land at the same time or place that you do. Nursing your baby at take-off and landing will lessen the pressure on his ears, but this may not be possible if baby is restrained in a seat belt. This may be a time when a pacifier would be useful.

Kay McFerrin of Texas tells of her family vacation:

Last summer we traveled to Acapulco, Mexico, with our infant daughter, Monica. Thanks to breastfeeding, our little girl was a delightful travel companion. Monica was six months old then, and still on just mother's milk. All she needed for the trip was her mother, some diapers, and a bathing suit. We all had such a marvelous time. I had no worries such as what to do if the room doesn't have a refrigerator, or what if I don't take enough formula, or how will I warm the bottles, or how to take formula and feed baby away from the hotel, or any other problems a bottle-fed baby and mother might

*face. No matter where we were—beach, sightseeing, poolside,
or plane—wherever Monica got hungry, she just did what came
naturally.*

*At night we never had to bother with baby beds, we just tucked our
baby in with us as we do at home. She didn't care where she was—
no insecurity for her! She was happy just being with her mother and
daddy. It never even occurred to us to leave her out of this
adventure.*

Lisa Gehring from Ohio tells about bicycling with her daughter.
She and her husband ride a tandem bike, and they fastened the baby's
car seat to a special trailer that attached behind their bike. She writes:

*My husband and I, being avid bicyclists, decided that we didn't want
to give up our favorite hobby just because we had a baby—we would
take her along!*

*Since Heidi is totally breastfed, going bicycling with her couldn't be
any easier. We just put her in the trailer with her diaper bag, and off
we go. It's great not having to pack bottles and formula.*

*When Heidi was four months old, we participated in a two-day tour
along the south shore of Lake Erie. Whenever Heidi would get
hungry, we would take a break. She had her lunch at a park on the
shore of Lake Erie. We did attract quite a bit of attention, and at
rest stops Rich would answer questions regarding our tandem and
trailer. Meanwhile Heidi would nurse inconspicuously, oblivious to
the crowd gathered around our bike.*

*We believe that a happy family is one that enjoys going places and
doing things together. Taking Heidi with us is so easy that we would
never dream of leaving her with a sitter. We're planning a cross-
country ski vacation this winter, and guess who's going with us?
That's right, have baby—will travel!*

IF YOU MUST LEAVE YOUR BABY

If you must leave your tiny baby for a short time—and the shorter the
time the better—leave him with someone he is happy with when you
are around. Be sure to leave the baby well fed and contented. Don't
rush—babies can sense when mother is in a hurry to get away. When he
is happy and settled, then go off. For some time you won't leave him

longer than an hour or two, and then only occasionally. Since you don't want your little one to miss you or go hungry, you'll want to be back soon.

Some mothers like to have the added security of leaving a container of their own expressed milk stored in the freezer in case it's needed while they're gone. (Information on expressing and storing human milk is found in Chapter 7.)

Mothers often ask about leaving a bottle of formula when they're gone. We cannot recommend that you do that. Leaving your own milk assures that your baby will continue to receive his favorite food. Does one bottle of formula make that much difference? We wish we could say that it doesn't, but we can't. Even one bottle of formula can be a problem for some babies because of the risk of allergy. Animal studies have also shown that introducing formula may upset the balance of enzymes and nutrients in the digestive system and interfere with the protective qualities your milk provides.

ALONE IS LONELY

You won't want to leave your baby any more than you have to because babies need their mothers. It's a need that is as basic and intense as his need for food. "That's all well and good," you may be thinking, "but what about me? I have needs, too."

Of course a mother has needs, and sometimes other responsibilities and obligations cause a mother to be away from her baby more than she wants to be. But you may be surprised to find how strong the bond is that develops between you and your baby. A mother often finds that when she does leave her baby for that long-awaited "night out," she worries so much about how the baby is getting along that she doesn't really enjoy the occasion!

Dr. William Sears, pediatrician and author, explains how this can happen:

> *When mother and baby are separated, both of them miss out on the full benefits of a continuous mother-infant attachment. When mother and baby spend most of their time with each other, responding positively to each other's cues, they get in harmony with each other....not only does the mother help the baby develop, but the baby also helps the mother develop.*

Mothers do grow along with their children. Judy Kahrl from Ohio, tells of her experience in gaining an understanding of her baby's need for her:

One thing that helped me when I wanted to leave the baby was to remember that a baby has no sense of time. When he is left, he thinks it is forever. He can't understand that his mother will be back later tonight or whenever. Also, what seems like a short time to parents, for instance a weekend, is proportionately speaking, a long time in the baby's life. It has helped me to try to look at this from the baby's perspective, his sense of time, his understanding of the world. Of course, we mothers have needs, too, but because of our maturity, we are better equipped to cope with ours, to postpone them for a bit. A baby's needs are immediate.

CHAPTER 6

A Time to Learn

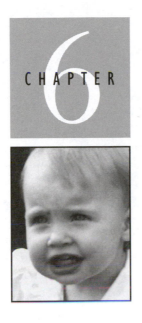

The early weeks of caring for your new baby are a time of adjustment for both of you. Mothering is a learned skill and your baby is the best teacher you could have. As you learn to respond to your baby's needs, your baby learns to trust that his needs will be met.

Why Is My Baby CRYING?

The sound of a baby crying is not easy to ignore. It is not intended to be. Your baby's cry is meant to be disturbing, for it is his most important means of communication. Only by crying can he let you know that he needs you to help him—to come to his rescue. Something is bothering him or frightening him. It may be that he is hungry, or he may be lonesome for you. He only knows the security of your presence when his body is next to yours; as far as your baby is concerned, you might as well be on Mars as on the other side of the house. Vi Lennon, one of LLL's co-Founders, recalls that she once asked an older child to pick up the crying baby and hold him while she finished frying

As a mother learns to respond to her baby's needs, the baby learns that his needs will be met.

chicken. Her helper responded, "I already tried that, but it's no use. He's having an attack of loneliness for you."

RESPONDING TO YOUR CRYING BABY

When a baby cries, a nursing mother's immediate instinctive response is to offer her breast. Whether it's been ten minutes or two hours since baby was fed, a few minutes of sucking may be all he needs to settle down. Baby's appetite can vary from day to day, so he may really be crying because he's hungry. Or perhaps he just wants the comfort of being close to you. Either way, nursing him may be the answer.

But what if that's not what he wants after all? Then you need to check into other possible causes. Perhaps he's too warm, or maybe he's too cold. Perhaps something he is wearing is causing the problem. Try removing all of his clothes. Look for a pin or rough label, or something binding around his leg or arm—sometimes a hair from a mother's head can wrap tightly around baby's toe. Look him over carefully from top to bottom, just to be sure that nothing is hurting or irritating his tender skin.

> *Parents are led to believe that if they pick up their baby every time he cries, he will not learn to settle himself and will become more demanding as time goes on. This is not true. A baby whose cries have been promptly responded to early on learns to trust and to anticipate that a response will be forthcoming.*
>
> Dr. William Sears
> Pediatrician and Author

If he seems too warm, try leaving him in just a shirt and diaper. If the room is chilly, try wrapping him in a soft blanket. Some babies feel more secure if they are wrapped up snugly, or swaddled.

Once he is snug and dry, offer him the breast again. This time, he just may drift off to sleep. But sometimes the baby doesn't want to nurse, or has downed so much milk he repeatedly spits it up, and still he cries. What then? Try holding him against your shoulder and with a background of soft music or your own lullaby, glide through the house doing the "baby waltz." Some mothers put the baby in a baby carrier and vacuum the rugs. The droning noise of the vacuum cleaner and the accompanying body movements often lull the baby to sleep. How about a drive in the car? Or a stroll outdoors? A warm bath may soothe and relax both of you—try taking baby into the tub with you.

A time-honored way of soothing a crying baby is time spent in a trusty rocking chair together. A steady rocking rhythm, some gentle patting on his back, and perhaps a soothing lullaby can work their magic on the fussiest of little ones. In fact, Becky Conley from Illinois swears by her "magic rocker":

> No matter how hectic the day or how frantic the world may seem, we can retreat to the arms of our rocker and be suddenly oblivious to it all. Peace descends on us; tensions float away; and love surrounds us like a cloud. We can go anywhere we please in our rocker. Over the years since Eli was born, we've been to desert islands, mountain ranges, endless beaches, and on a few, very special occasions, to what surely must have been heaven.

Some babies cry because they are overtired, but they aren't happy being held as they fall asleep. Try laying your baby in his cradle or on a blanket on the floor and talk or sing to him softly as you pat him gently. He may continue to fuss for a few minutes, then close his eyes and drift off to sleep. You'll soon know if he is truly tired and ready to sleep or not. If he becomes increasingly more anxious (even five minutes is a long time for a baby to cry), pick him up again.

Babies are sometimes fretful for reasons that no one, not even a mother, can understand. If you can't calm your baby right away, try not to let it upset you. "Don't take it as a personal rejection of you," a mother who has gone through the experience advises. Your baby will always benefit from a calm, loving mother. In handling any tiny baby, you have to move slowly and gently. Fast, jerky motions and loud noises may startle him. If he is already upset for some reason, accept the fact and work from there—slow and easy.

You can't spoil a baby; a baby's wants are his needs.

The baby whose cries are answered now will later be the child confident enough to show his independence and curiosity. But the baby who is left to cry it out may develop a sense of isolation and distrust, and may turn inward by tuning out the world that will not answer its cry. And later on in life, this child may continue to cope with stress by trying to shut out reality.

Dr. Lee Salk
Pediatric Psychologist

SHOULD BABY CRY IT OUT?

While holding and carrying the baby may comfort him, it may also elicit some stern advice from friends and relatives. The notion still persists that the baby who cries when put down, but is soothed when held, should be laid down gently but firmly to "cry it out."

Sometimes a mother wonders if it really makes a difference if the baby cries in her arms or in a crib. It makes a considerable difference. Jan Wojcik of Florida puts the matter in a different light by asking how any of us would feel if we were the ones who were upset. "If we were crying, wouldn't we feel better if someone were around to reassure us? To care that we were upset? Wouldn't we wives feel rejected if our husbands were to say, 'Go into the bedroom. I don't want to be around you until you regain control of yourself.' Don't we want to be loved in times of stress as well as in times of happiness?"

Our suggestion to the mother of a fussy baby is: Don't let your baby cry alone. The comfort and security extended by your loving arms is never wasted. Love begets love. Then, too, the next thing you try may be just the right thing to ease baby's discomfort and restore peace and serenity to the house.

97

A TIME TO LEARN

BABY THE BABY

You can't spoil a baby; his wants are his needs. His need to be lovingly held when he is upset is as strong and important as his need to be fed and kept warm and dry. So, if your infant stops his crying when you pick him up and hold him, just keep on holding him and be happy that you are there to satisfy this important emotional need. By all means, "baby" the baby. As for crying being good exercise for baby's lungs, the late Dr. Lee Salk, who was a pediatric psychologist, said, "If crying is good for the lungs, then bleeding is good for the veins!"

A FUSSY TIME OF DAY

Some babies have a regular fussy period, often late in the afternoon, that occurs predictably day after day. At other times, the baby is good-natured, and there doesn't seem to be any particular cause for these fussy spells. The baby is not uncomfortable, as with colic, but is not happy either. Folklore refers to this time as the "Granny Hour," meaning that a loving grandmother is needed who has nothing more urgent to do than rock and cuddle the baby.

Your husband may not always be home at baby's fussy time but it can be a great comfort if he can take over for a spell. The change of loving arms and voice often relaxes an upset child. While your husband and baby watch the fish swimming in the fish tank or the cars passing by, you may want to take a refreshing shower—it can really help wash the tension away.

> *I suspect that colic is the result of many causes, temperamental, physiological, and environmental, that overwhelm a baby's immature coping skills.... In light of present knowledge about colic, the best anyone can do is to comfort the baby and minimize the factors that may contribute to the baby's fussiness.*
>
> **Dr. William Sears**
> **Pediatrician and Author**

Babies Who Are COLICKY

When a tiny baby has long periods of hard crying and seems to be in some sort of physical discomfort for which there is no apparent reason that you or your doctor can discover, he is often said to be colicky.

"Colic" is a catchall word meaning essentially "loud, persistent screaming for undetermined reasons." As many causes of colic are put forth as there are doctors who have studied it. As far back as the turn of the last century, colic was referred to in one widely used pediatric text as "a scientifically inaccurate and unsatisfactory term which serves such a useful purpose in practice and covers so well a multitude of abdominal pains that it maintains its place in our medical books." The same loose definition could apply today; doctors still seem to know little or nothing about the true cause of this kind of crying.

So what can a mother do about colic? Calm, gentle handling is essential. Many doctors feel that frequent, shorter feedings are easier for baby to handle than long feedings. But a colicky baby may be soothed by lots of sucking, plus the extra cuddling that comes with nursing, so what do you do then? Try feeding him from one breast only during a two- to three-hour period. He may want to nurse a number of times during that time span; just keep to the "empty" breast. After two hours or so, switch to the other breast and again limit nursings to one side.

If your baby shows signs of colic, you'll want to be sure he gets nothing else but your milk. Avoid giving formula, juice, or water. Some babies also react to vitamins, especially those with added fluoride.

Occasionally, something the mother eats might be a possible cause of colicky symptoms in her baby. Some possibilities include certain vitamins, food supplements such as brewer's yeast, large amounts of caffeine, or foods or drinks with artificial sweeteners. In some instances, a food such as milk (or foods containing milk) in the mother's diet can make her baby uncomfortable. (This is more likely to occur if there is a history of allergy in the family. It is explained later in Chapter 18.) Mothers who smoke cigarettes seem to have more instances of colicky babies.

Mothers of colicky babies have come up with a variety of ways to comfort and soothe them. Sue Nobriga Buckley of California talks about a "colic hold" that helped her daughter feel better:

> Although Lara gained weight quickly and proved to be alert and healthy, every evening found us rocking or walking her back and forth for hours before her crying and wailing gave way to sleep. After five weeks of steady evening and occasional daytime crying sessions, we were hesitant to visit her grandparents. When we did visit, Lara typically acted pleasant during most of the day, only to start in loud and long in the early evening. As usual no one could comfort her until her grandfather picked her up, laid her astraddle his arm with her head slightly higher than her feet, and proceeded to

immediately rock her to sleep. Amazed, we imitated his way of holding her whenever Lara began to act colicky, and almost every time the new way of holding her quieted and comforted her.

A soothing, pleasant bath proved to be a refuge for Judy Wesockes and her baby daughter, who live in Florida:

The colic hold often works wonders to settle a fussy baby.

When Amy has an attack of colic, usually between eight and ten in the evening, we go into a warm, deep tub and stay there for the duration of her attack. The moist heat, holding her, and relaxing all help. She gets almost immediate relief, but if we get out of the tub, the symptoms return. So we stay in, and I add more hot water as needed.

Knowing that your milk is the best possible food for your baby will help you to be relaxed and calm. It's one less thing to worry about, and baby will be spared the risks that come with changing formulas. The warm closeness of the nursing relationship and your gentle, loving ministrations will help ease your baby through this trying time.

HIGH NEED BABIES

As you read through this section you may be saying to yourself, "But I've tried all those things and my baby is still fussy." It may be that you have the kind of baby that Dr. William Sears talks about in his book, THE FUSSY BABY. He explains it this way:

In the first few days or weeks, parents begin to pick up on clues as to the temperament of their baby. Some parents are blessed with so-called easy babies. Others are blessed with babies who are not so easy...the term "fussy baby" is a bit unfair....I prefer to call this special type of baby the high need baby. This is not only a kinder term, but it more accurately describes why these babies act the way they do and what level of parenting they need.

Dr. Sears assures parents that having a high need baby can be a blessing. He points out that high need babies bring out the best in their parents. He says, "Those same qualities which at first seemed to be such an exhausting liability have a good chance of turning out to be an asset for the child and the family."

If you want to find out more, you can buy a copy of THE FUSSY BABY from your local bookstore or your La Leche League Group. For details, see the Appendix.

Growth SPURTS

Some time after the first week or two the baby who has been peacefully nursing every three hours may suddenly want to dramatically increase the number of times a day he is fed. No sooner does he drift off to sleep than he is up again, nuzzling the bedding or his fist, looking for something to eat. You may hear comments to the effect that it was a nice try, but breastfeeding isn't working.

Tune out such remarks. This increase in the number of nursings is normal. Medical writers in old textbooks referred to such periods as "frequency days." They recognized that more frequent nursing builds up the milk supply to meet the growing baby's increasing need. So settle in with baby for a few "frequency days." Even the skeptics would be hard-pressed to think of anything else you could be doing that is more important than giving your baby the best possible nourishment.

Twenty minutes of fairly vigorous nursing every hour or so is more effective in building up your milk supply than less frequent, longer sessions at the breast. Most babies eventually settle into a fairly consistent pattern of nursing, one that is right for each particular child. These increases in frequency usually show up in relation to growth spurts. Like the rest of us, babies are hungrier at some times than others. Rather than check out the refrigerator, baby looks to mom. Baby's appetite temporarily gets ahead of his mother's milk supply.

Mothers commonly report such a fussy period coinciding with a growth spurt around the third week and again around six weeks. If this happens, put baby to the breast as often as he wants to nurse. With extra nursings, it isn't long before your milk production steps up to meet his need. The interval between nursings will soon lengthen, and baby will be his old self again. The extra rest that comes to you with more frequent nursing may be exactly what the doctor would order. It may be that the tempo of all you are doing has picked up a little faster than is good for a new mother. Nature and your baby combine forces to help you get much needed rest.

When your baby is three months old, more or less, there is often another fussy period. It is probably due partly to a jump in appetite, and again, increased nursings will generally take care of this part of the difficulty. It is still too early for solids for most healthy babies, so don't risk an allergy to new foods by introducing solids too early.

Another factor in the three-month fussy period, which you may or may not experience with your baby, is that he stays awake longer and is taking a greater interest in the world around him. Fussing may also indicate a need for company and action. Keep him in the center of activity. Settle him near you in a safe spot on a blanket on the floor where he can really stretch out. He will enjoy music, movement, and people going by. As he gets older, he thrives on change and variety. As he becomes more aware of the world around him, the sights and sounds of the family group are wonderful stimulation for his senses. People often notice and comment on the early alertness and responsiveness of the baby who is part of the family group, who is talked to and sung to and smiled at often.

Nighttime NEEDS

During the early months, it is especially desirable for the baby to nurse at least once during the night. Your young baby is growing at a phenomenal rate and has a physical need to be fed during the night. Also, your breasts can become engorged and uncomfortable if you go for five, six, or more hours without a feeding, and in the morning your baby might have trouble getting started at the breast because of the fullness.

A study of nursing mothers in West Nigeria by Derrick and Patrice Jelliffe revealed that babies as old as ten months received at least twenty-five percent of their mother's milk at night. So it is not at all unusual for your baby to want to nurse at night.

In his book, NIGHTTIME PARENTING, Dr. William Sears points out that babies sleep differently than adults and he says that babies aren't designed to sleep through the night. Dr. Sears goes on to say, "Sleep problems occur when your child's night-waking exceeds your ability to cope."

One secret of coping with your baby's need for night feedings is to develop your skill at nursing the baby lying down. If you feel awkward when you first try to nurse in bed, continue to experiment with different positions and lots of pillows. Once you can feed the baby while comfortably stretched out, you've eliminated much of the work of mothering for about eight of the twenty-four hours in a day. In order to see what you are doing in the early weeks without turning on a bright light, consider keeping a small flashlight on the nightstand or under your pillow. Or leave the light on in the closet with the door ajar. To change sides with a minimum of strain when nursing while lying down, simply hold baby close to you with both arms and roll over.

When your baby wakes at night, just tuck him into bed with you, start nursing him, and the two of you can drop off to sleep again together. It is quite safe—we have all done it, and so have mothers all over the world for centuries. The babies love the warm closeness, and mothers say that they quickly develop a sixth sense about allowing room for the baby.

Nighttime nursings in bed allow for greater skin contact and touching. Mother and baby are not encumbered by layers of clothing. In his book on the importance of touching to the development of the person, anthropologist Ashley Montagu states, "The infant's need for body contact is compelling."

You may have heard stories of a parent rolling over on the baby in bed. Don't worry; your healthy, normal baby, even when very small, can move his head and in some way let you know if a blanket is over his face or if he is feeling closed in. Baby should sleep on his back or side to avoid getting his face buried in the bedding. Studies have shown that the risk of Sudden Infant Death Syndrome (SIDS) is reduced when babies sleep on their backs or sides. Of course, parents should not sleep with their baby if they are under the influence of drugs, alcohol, or tranquilizers that may diminish their awareness of the baby's presence.

If parents sleep on a water bed, keep it very full so it is firm and be sure there is no crevice between the mattress and frame. A free-floating water bed, without internal baffles, is not safe for baby.

Recent research on SIDS shows that sleeping with your baby, along with breastfeeding, actually decreases the risk of SIDS. In his book about SIDS, Dr. William Sears summarizes his conclusions:

> *I believe that in most cases SIDS is a sleep disorder, primarily a disorder of arousal and breathing control during sleep. All the elements of natural mothering, especially breastfeeding and sharing sleep, benefit the infant's breathing control and increase the mutual awareness between mother and infant so that their arousability is increased and the risk of SIDS is decreased.*

There are a number of ways to avoid the possibility that baby could fall off the bed. Pull his cradle or bassinet next to your bed. When close by, it's convenient to scoop him into your bed when he cries, and if it is high enough it serves as a guardrail to keep baby from falling when he's in your bed. Or you can purchase a guardrail that fits along the side of your bed to keep baby safe.

A resourceful mother in Pennsylvania, Pat Muschamp, uses a blanket to keep her baby from moving away from her after she has drifted back to sleep. Place baby's blanket diagonally on the bed, like a kite. You lie down with the inner corner under you and baby next to you on the blanket. Pull the outer corner of the blanket across baby's body and tuck it under your body. Your baby is wrapped snugly against you, and there is no worry about falling.

Some mothers wear a bra to bed at night. This is not necessary, but if you find you're more comfortable with some kind of support, choose a bra that is big enough or stretchy enough to allow for expansion if your breasts fill during the night hours.

When mother and baby sleep together, they develop harmonious sleep cycles.

WHEN WILL HE SLEEP THROUGH THE NIGHT?

Probably the reason this question ever assumed the proportions it has is because of the inconvenience of nighttime bottle-feeding—getting up with the baby into what may be a chilly house, waiting while the bottle warms, fighting sleep, and being fearful that baby or bottle may be dropped. As a nursing mother, you are spared such inconvenience, so when you hear that a neighbor's baby sleeps through the night and yours doesn't, ask yourself, "Is it really that important?" Isn't the important thing that your baby is content and happy and you can satisfy his needs at night as well as during the day? To a baby, it makes no difference whether the sun is up or the world is hushed in darkness. His need for mothering remains. It is no less important at night than during the day.

As to when he will sleep through the night, it's impossible to say. Babies are human beings, and each and every human being in the world is different from every other. Some babies will sleep through the night at an early age, and some will not. And not infrequently, the little one who sleeps through the night one week is waking the next.

Getting up in the night is never a favorite part of parenting. But there are ways to cope, to come to terms with the situation. How you react can make a considerable difference in how it affects you. We know the truth of this because many of us learned it the hard way. Pat Yearian of Washington says she gradually came to the realization that she could change the up-at-night syndrome by changing her attitude. After all, a mother's reaction to interrupted sleep is up to her. Pat writes:

> If you resent the interruptions to your sleep—and haven't we all come to believe we need a full night's rest?—you will face each day more frustrated and trying harder and harder to fit the baby into your sleep pattern. On the other hand, if you can adjust your mental attitude to one of greater acceptance, you will find yourself able to enjoy those quite moments in the night with your infant who needs to be held and nursed, or with your toddler who just needs to be with someone. Acceptance of interrupted sleep doesn't come right away. In fact, for many of us it has taken a baby or two to fully appreciate their needs. When you begin to notice that your sleep can be interrupted many times a night, and yet you are able to face the next day with a smile, your attitudes are changing.

Dr. Gregory White, an experienced family practice physician, once commented on the subject of sleep in a talk he gave to parents:

> A lot of people think they are entitled to a night's sleep. Nobody's entitled to a full night's sleep and very few mothers get one. Many people do at one time or another during their lives, and I'm all for it. But no one's entitled to it, whether she's a new mother or not, if someone needs her. If a lazy, self-indulgent old man like me can get out in the middle of the night to help people he hardly knows, certainly a mother can do this for her own child.

NIGHT WAKING GOES ON

Even if your baby begins sleeping almost all night when he's a few months old, that may not be the end of your nighttime parenting role. Toddlers often wake up at night for a variety of reasons. Many one-year-olds have erratic eating habits and may wake up really hungry during the night. If you think that this could be the reason your toddler is waking at night, be sure there are nutritious foods available to him frequently during the day and offer him a good bedtime snack. Perhaps he is thirsty. Offer your toddler water often, especially in warm weather.

The older baby or toddler who wakes a number of times at night may be bothered by teething. Even though there doesn't seem to be much of a problem during the day, his gums may hurt more at night when he isn't distracted by a busy daytime world. Have you ever had a mild toothache that started throbbing madly just as you were dropping off to sleep? A toddler cannot express what he is feeling in words, but since frequent waking during the night is so common in children during their second year, teething might have something to do with it.

Fatigue or aching muscles might cause a busy toddler to be wakeful. There are other possibilities. Is he getting enough fresh air and exercise? Was there tension during the day caused by such things as long shopping trips or visiting? A frightening experience? Were there enough hugs and kisses? Too many restrictions? If your answers to these questions satisfy you, and your toddler is still waking at night, blame it on whatever you like and remember that it will pass. Whatever the reason, nursing seems to offer special comfort in satisfying nighttime needs.

Sharing SLEEP

Rather than try to change their children's needs for parenting at night, many families have decided to change sleeping arrangements. After all, what babies and young children are seeking is not all that strange—they just want to be closer to those who love them.

The custom of mother, father, and young child sleeping together at night is "an age old concept in childrearing which has been practiced throughout the ages, throughout the world," Tine Thevenin writes in her book, *The Family Bed*. She addresses the fears and questions that some parents have on the subject, and she probably touches the heart of the matter when she comments, "I have been asked numerous times if it is not bothersome to have our children sleep with us. To this I reply that it is no more bothersome than their presence in our family."

Learning to breastfeed comfortably while lying down helps night feedings go more smoothly.

Dr. Herbert Ratner, former editor of *Child and Family Magazine* and longtime Professional Advisor for La Leche League, has encouraged the use of the family bed for a long time. And Dr. Hugh Jolly of London says, "Psychoanalysts may be firm in their advice that parents must never allow their children into their beds, but those who have practiced it know better and have not had any dire consequences to face—just the opposite."

Dr. William Sears uses the term "sharing sleep" because he emphasizes the fact that physical closeness causes mother and baby to share sleep cycles. But he doesn't leave out fathers. He points out that fathers report they feel closer to their babies when they sleep together.

Dr. Penny Stanway, a noted British doctor, had this to say about sleeping with her children. Penny and her husband, Andrew, also a physician, have two daughters and a son:

> *Ben and Amy slept in our bed. Amy stayed in our bed till she was about one and then she moved in with Susie in a double bed. It was similar with Ben. He stayed in with us until he was about sixteen months and then went into a double bed with his sisters. I think nighttime is very hard with our built-in belief that we should be able to have our own beds and sleep with our husbands. It is fairly rooted in our culture, and any departure is met with quite a lot of criticism from friends and relatives. But I wouldn't give up that first year or so with a baby in bed. It is so much easier.*

The beauty of bedding down as a family is that it can be customized to suit each individual family's needs. Some mothers choose to return the baby to his own bed once he is fed and settled. In other households, the crib and separate room for the baby are abandoned, and an all-night family bed is adopted. Sleeping arrangements are as varied as families, and we share only a few of the many experiences of couples who have tried this innovation.

Ann Parker's story is rather typical. This Indiana mother explains that for the first six months after birth, baby Bryan slept in his parents' room, but in his own bed. Ann writes:

> *I kept going back and forth every few hours to nurse him, and one time I caught myself asleep, sitting on the side of the bed, with baby in arms. I could have dropped him, and that really scared me! From then on I nursed him in bed lying down, but as soon as he stopped nursing, I would take him back to his bed. That plan didn't work all the time, since I kept falling asleep while he was nursing. But in the morning, I felt better. I had slept longer and without as many interruptions. My husband's sleep wasn't disturbed either, and so Bryan began sleeping with us.*

Quite often one parent is enthusiastic about bringing the new baby into bed, but the other has reservations. In the Zavari household in Michigan, husband Hassan was born in the Middle East, where a baby sleeping with his parents is a natural part of life. Joan Zavari tells of her reaction to some of her husband's ideas.

> *When Hassan suggested breastfeeding, I didn't hesitate. However, being of a conservative nature, I put my foot down when he suggested putting two beds together and sleeping family style. How would I make the beds? I found lots of excuses. When Stevie was born, I soon found out that some babies wake up five or six times at night. Hassan didn't even say, "I told you so," when I suggested putting two beds together so he could sleep with us.*

By age two or so, many youngsters will proudly take to a conventional bed of their own, although it will be easier for short legs to reach if the spring and mattress are placed directly on the floor. With a full-size mattress you can lie down next to your little one if he wakes up. It's less disturbing for you to then move back to your own bed than it would be to move him. For the child who is ready for his own bed, but still wants to be near you once in a while, a sleeping bag or air mattress and blanket can be stowed under your bed and pulled out to make a cozy spot.

Are there other children in the family? If your little one has outgrown sleeping with you but he has an older brother or sister, consider some night pairing—two sharing one bed. Young children have probably slept together throughout time, and the arrangement has been beneficial. Before establishing the little one in the older one's bed, discuss the prospect with each, stressing the positive aspects of having a night-time buddy. Then make the move with great fanfare. On more than one night, you'll probably find your two youngsters soundly sleeping, like little puppies, a tangle of arms and legs. They don't mind in the least. Is there reason to worry about how you'll eventually discontinue the arrangement when the children grow older? Not really. They manage this on their own when they no longer need—or want—the companionship. Usually one unceremoniously moves the other out of the bed, but by that time, they are older and quite ready to be on their own. It just means you'll have to get another bed.

PRACTICAL ARRANGEMENTS

Many couples find that they can accommodate a baby and, perhaps, other little night visitors in the ready-made spaciousness of a king-size or queen-size bed. Those who do not have such a large bed can create one by fastening two twin-size beds or a double and a twin together with a heavy-duty cord or wire. The space between the two mattresses is filled in with a blanket.

Once the baby is moving well on his own, there is the fear that he may fall off. There are guardrails you can buy that slide into place between the mattress and box spring. Taking the spring and mattress off the frame and placing them directly on the floor reduces the danger of a fall.

If you have a standard double bed and a crib, you may want to try the solution used by a Wisconsin family. Judy Haugen describes their sleeping arrangement:

At the point of investing in a king-size bed, or building a trundle, we came upon what we feel is a better method of enlarging our sleeping area. We have an adjustable crib. By raising its mattress to dressing-table height, flipping the side rail down, and lowering the legs to playpen level, we can make it the same height as our bed. When the crack between the beds is covered with an extra blanket, we have the perfect bed for our one-year-old who needs early morning snacks and pats.

Since the beds are separate, we do not disturb him, and most of the time he does not disturb us. If he whimpers during the night I only need to reach out and rock his crib (the casters have been replaced by springs) without even opening my eyes. If he is hungry I can pull him to me and, after nursing him, push him back to his bed without sitting up.

When the big bed seems crowded (even though it may be almost the size of the room) because everyone is huddled over in one spot (yours), you may wonder if this time of intense togetherness will ever come to an end. It does, and your reaction at the time may not be what you thought it would be. Ann Backhurst of Michigan tells of her experience:

Amy, age four, sleeps alone willingly all night. When Emily was about eighteen months old, she indicated an interest in sleeping in the crib. She now sleeps all night in it. Ken and I have our queen-size bed to ourselves again; to my surprise, I find that I really miss having the little girls sleep with us. While living through a difficult time with sleeping arrangements, I thought we would never see the end of this "family bed"—I couldn't wait. Now that it's over, we have cherished memories of a little person snuggling up on a cold winter night, or reaching out and putting an arm around one of us and knowing that all was secure.

Parents will find many practical suggestions on meeting their children's nighttime needs in the book we have referred to several times in this chapter—NIGHTTIME PARENTING by William Sears, MD. Copies are available from your local LLL Group, La Leche League International, or a bookstore. See the Appendix for details.

Babies, Beds, and SEX

You may be wondering—if baby's going to be sleeping in your bed, what happens to your marriage? Is there a survival plan for new parents?

We can offer some suggestions, but in the final analysis you and your husband are your own best authorities on what is the most loving, satisfying sexual relationship for you. Sex, like breastfeeding, is ninety percent mental attitude and ten percent technique. Both sex and breastfeeding flourish on the power of positive thinking. Needless worries can be counterproductive. The joy that you experience with the arrival of your baby will spill over into other areas of your life.

COMMON MYTHS AND QUESTIONS

With the baby nursing so often and possibly sleeping in our bed, will there be any time for my husband and me to be alone together? Absolutely. We have all found opportunities. You will have to outwit the baby, but there are two of you. Consider a change of time and place. Where there is a will, there is a way.

Babies usually have one fairly long period of deep sleep. Take advantage of it. If your baby is easily disturbed, leave your bed (carefully) for the spare bedroom or the floor in the living room.

If baby is awake, you might try combining romance and distraction by lining up an array of lighted candles. Little babies are fascinated by the flickering lights. Some soft music is another possibility.

Few married couples can expect complete freedom all the time, without interruptions, to make love. There are the everyday outside demands from a job and from others who have needs. Restrictions do not go away as the children grow older and leave the parental bed. Ask any couple with teenagers. But you have a lifetime together to share your love. Tomorrow can be even better than today.

My breasts are tender, and it's uncomfortable when my husband touches them. Also, I'm concerned. Can sexual foreplay affect the milk? No. Your milk will be fine. Don't worry about passing germs from your husband to the baby on your nipples. Your baby is already exposed to family germs and there are special glands that keep your nipples free of germs when baby nurses. Nursing does not make your breasts off limits to your husband. The feeling of fullness and tenderness comes mostly in the early days of nursing and is temporary. You will notice it less if you nurse the baby just prior to making love. Your breasts will not be as full, and the baby will be more apt to sleep. But as one husband says, "Engorgement is gorgeous!"

At the time of a sexual climax, some women also have a milk letdown. The husband is often as surprised as his wife the first time it occurs, since the milk literally sprays out. The hormones that produce the let-down are also present at the time of an orgasm. Not all women experience this at a climax, and it lessens as the let-down reflex is better established. Keep a towel nearby for drying off in case it happens.

When breastfeeding, a woman has a greater interest in sex; OR: When breastfeeding, a woman feels less desire for sexual relations. The response to both of the above is "yes" some of the time and "no" at other times. There are no pat answers.

After childbirth one woman may enjoy a feeling of great responsiveness. Giving milk and making love are very natural and exciting parts of her life. Another woman may notice the opposite. Her desire for sexual relations could be better described as understated, although she loves her husband as much as ever and wants to be close to him; in fact, she needs the reassurance of his affection. Such different reactions are not unusual or abnormal. All men and women have highs and lows in sexual desire at different times in life.

As a breastfeeding mother, it can probably be said that you feel good about being a woman and are at ease with the way your body functions. Breastfeeding is the completion of a woman's sexual cycle. There are marked similarities in the way a woman's body responds during breastfeeding and intercourse. It is a fulfilling time in a woman's life.

Fatigue, it must be said, is probably the greatest deterrent to sex for any new mother. Fit in a nap after dinner, if you can. Sometimes, even when you're feeling more tired than sexy, an extra output of loving effort on your part at the right moment could produce results that are a delight to both you and your husband.

What about feeling "touched out"? A mother once wrote to us, "After having my baby or toddler in my arms most of the day, I feel as though I don't want one more person touching me. I'm annoyed when my husband approaches me. Is this unusual? Can you help me?" We replied to this mother by telling her she was not alone. Many a mother, after spending a good part of the day holding the baby and having little hands cling and pat, finds herself thinking that the last thing she needs is more body contact. She's "touched out."

Our cultural heritage probably shapes this response at least to some extent. The person who grows up in a society where people maintain a certain physical distance from each other, and even family members seldom hug, may find the almost constant contact with a baby a new experience, one that takes some getting used to. Add to this the fatigue that comes at the end of the day for most mothers and young children, and there may not be the energy or inclination to feel romantic.

The low estrogen level present during breastfeeding is often the cause of vaginal dryness. There is some truth to this as estrogen is low when breastfeeding, but the solution to dryness is simple enough—a little more lovemaking ahead of time, supplemented, if need be, by a little lubrication such as KY jelly. An episiotomy can also cause painful intercourse, sometimes for many months.

You were a wife before you were a mother, so your husband should come before the children. This is very misleading. It isn't fair to put your husband and children in competition with each other for your time and affection. Whoever has the greatest need for love and attention at the time receives it. With maturity, gratification of want can be postponed for a time. Adults who are hungry can wait a while or find something to eat on their own. Babies cannot. With a little understanding, there needn't be a conflict. There is more than enough love to go around.

A new baby can bring out the best in husband and
wife and love abounds.

Dr. William Sears, pediatrician and author, reminds parents of the
importance of their commitment to one another:

> *For mother-baby attachment to work in the way it was designed to
> work, it must be practiced within the structure of a stable and
> fulfilled marriage....The whole family works together—mother-baby,
> father-baby, and husband-wife....You should not make an either-or
> choice among these relationships. You need to work at all of them
> because they complement each other.*

This brings us back to the basic relationship. Loving husbands and
wives want to please each other. They each try to respond to cues from
the other. On one occasion, the wife puts forth an extra effort to
respond to her husband's embrace, and on another, he puts her feelings and needs ahead of his own.

There's a time to give and a time to take. With mutual good will
and good humor, it all works out. One word of caution: don't keep
score. Once you do, you're sure to lose.

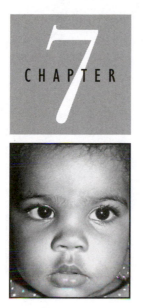

CHAPTER 7

Common
Concerns

The early weeks of breastfeeding are a time of learning for both you and your baby. Most of the time the process goes smoothly, but once in awhile, problems develop that threaten to interfere with or interrupt breastfeeding. Some of those problems are covered here, along with information to help you overcome any difficulties and continue to enjoy breastfeeding.

Additional information on special circumstances will be found in later chapters. If you still have questions or concerns, we encourage you to contact your La Leche League Leader. More than likely she can offer suggestions and encouragement based on your specific situation that will help solve your problem and allow you and your baby to continue enjoying the benefits of breastfeeding. We can assure you that it is rarely necessary for a baby to be weaned because of a breastfeeding problem.

Avoiding and Treating SORE NIPPLES

Even though sore nipples can be very uncomfortable, they are

Hold the baby with his whole body facing you and his head at the level of your nipple.

certainly no reason for you or your baby to miss out on the advantages and pleasures of breastfeeding. It is normal to experience slight tenderness when baby latches on in the first three to five days after birth. After that, if proper positioning and latch-on techniques are used, you can expect little or no nipple soreness. If your nipples are sore or cracked, check the earlier sections of this book that explain the positioning and latch-on sequence.

POSITIONING BABY

While studying breastfeeding difficulties encountered by mothers in the early postpartum period, Kittie Frantz, RN, CPNP, Director of the Breastfeeding Infant Clinic at the University of Southern California Medical Center, concluded that the most significant cause of sore nipples was the incorrect positioning of the baby at the breast.

There are two aspects to proper positioning: the position of the nipple in your baby's mouth and the position of your baby's body in relation to yours. When using the cradle hold, baby's head should be in the crook of your arm with your hand holding his buttocks or thigh. Baby's body should be turned on his side, with his whole body facing you, and your nipple directly in front of his mouth so that he doesn't have to turn his head to reach it. Your other hand should support the breast with your thumb on top, behind the outer edge of the areola (the dark area around the nipple) and your index and second fingers below the breast, behind the outer edge of the areola. Tickle your baby's lower lip gently with your nipple so that he opens his mouth very wide. Center the nipple quickly in the portion of his mouth above his tongue and pull baby in very close. His mouth should be positioned as far back on the areola as possible before he begins to suck. His jaws must compress the milk sinuses which are located beneath the areola.

Have someone check once he is latched on to be sure he hasn't pulled in his lower lip along with the nipple. If he has, it should be gently pulled out. Check also to be sure baby is taking a large portion of the areola under the nipple. It may help to pull him onto the breast chin first, as his lower jaw does most of the work.

Many mothers experience immediate relief from nipple discomfort when they begin positioning the baby properly. It is worth taking the time to reposition yourself and your baby until he is able to latch on correctly. If your nipples are very sore, it may also help to change positions each time you nurse the baby. Sit up for one feeding, lie down for the next. You can try holding the baby in a "football hold" for some feedings. Hold his head in the palm of your hand and tuck his legs under your arm, close to your body. Changing positions puts the pressure on a different part of the nipple.

The way your baby grasps and releases the nipple is also very important in avoiding sore nipples. The nipple should not be sucked in, but rather placed far back in baby's mouth when his mouth is open very wide. When removing him from the breast, always break the suction first using a finger to press down on your breast or pull baby's cheek close to his mouth.

LIMITING FEEDINGS

If your baby is positioned properly at the breast, there is no need to limit the length of his feedings. It can take several minutes before the "let-down" occurs and the milk begins to flow, so by taking him off after three or five minutes, as some recommend, the feeding could end even before it starts. If soreness persists throughout the feeding, your baby is probably not sucking correctly.

Allowing your baby to nurse frequently, as often as he seems to be hungry, will actually minimize soreness; he will tend to suck with more vigor if he is ravenously hungry. Babies should nurse at least every two to three hours during the day in the early months. Breastfeeding is a learned art and it is not supposed to hurt. Once you and your baby develop your own way to nurse effectively, the soreness will heal.

When baby is latched on correctly, his chin is pressed into the breast with his nose resting on the breast.

My daughter Katie nurses beautifully. We are truly a happy nursing couple now. But the first four months I suffered terribly from sore and cracked nipples. I hope I can offer some encouragement to other women who may be experiencing a similar situation.

First of all, in my genetic makeup, no provision was made for protruding nipples. Before the baby came, I didn't even realize that this was unusual; I thought they would magically pop out when the baby was born. My next mistake was not attending La Leche League meetings ahead of time to see other mothers care for their babies.

We had several problems following Katie's birth. She had a hard time grasping my nipple in her mouth; this combined with a weak sucking reflex caused much frustration for us both. A week later, extremely sore nipples became the main issue. I now know that I was not positioning her properly at the breast. Because of the way I was holding her, she was stretching the areola around the nipple causing me pain and reducing the amount of milk she was getting. I dreaded each moment of nursing and cried through most of them because of the pain.

After learning to position her correctly at an LLL meeting, the pain totally disappeared. Now I can't wait for each nursing moment. Love does conquer all, but sometimes the right information is needed, too.

Karen Price
British Columbia, Canada

FLAT NIPPLES

Positioning the baby properly can be very important if your nipples are flat and difficult for the baby to grasp. If the problem is caused by engorgement, the swelling that may occur when the milk comes in, it may help to hand-express a little milk ahead of time to bring the nipple out. (See other ways to treat engorgement in Chapter 4.) Be especially careful to wait for baby to open his mouth very wide before latching on.

Many experts believe that a baby who is latched on well can nurse effectively and draw out a flat or inverted nipple.

OINTMENTS

Most ointments sold for the treatment of sore nipples are not useful and some may even be harmful. Avoid any product that needs to be wiped off before the baby nurses. Ointments containing antibiotics, steroids, astringents, or anesthetic agents are *not* recommended because they are potentially harmful to both mother and baby. In addition, numbing the nipples with ice may inhibit the let-down reflex. Antiseptic nipple sprays should also be avoided. Ointment can worsen soreness if it prevents the baby from grasping the nipple and areola properly.

Expressing a few drops of your milk after baby is finished nursing and rubbing it gently into your nipples will take advantage of the healing effects of human milk.

Moist Wound HEALING

Drying sore nipples with a hair dryer and using a sun lamp are no longer recommended treatments. It has been shown that moist wound healing is more effective in treating nipple soreness as it allows healing to occur without the formation of a scab. Moist wound healing involves maintaining the internal moisture of the skin. It should not be confused with surface wetness which can cause chapping and further irritate the skin.

One way to retain this internal moisture and promote the healing of sore nipples is to apply a specially formulated type of lanolin, called modified lanolin.

Lansinoh for Breastfeeding Mothers® has been endorsed by La Leche League International for use in treating sore nipples. It is the purest and safest brand of modified lanolin. Other modified lanolin products may contain high levels of pesticides, along with free lanolin alcohols and detergent residues which have been identified as the cause of lanolin allergies.

Lansinoh for Breastfeeding Mothers® does not have to be removed before feeding the baby.

To treat sore or cracked nipples, gently pat nipples dry after feedings and take a pea-sized portion of Lansinoh for Breastfeeding Mothers®, soften between clean fingers, and apply to each nipple. Use enough to maintain the moisture barrier and apply after every feeding. Gently pat it on; do not rub it in.

The use of Lansinoh for Breastfeeding Mothers® may also relieve pain as it protects the nerve endings that signal pain. If the pressure of your clothing causes discomfort, apply Lansinoh for Breastfeeding Mothers® and then use breast shells with large air holes, tea strainers with the handles removed, or even a ring of Styrofoam from a disposable cup to keep your clothing away from sore nipples.

Lansinoh for Breastfeeding Mothers® is available from many drug or discount stores in the USA and is also sold through LLLI's Catalogue and many La Leche League Groups.

NIPPLE CLEANSING

Bathing with plain water is all that is necessary for your nipples. Avoid using soap on the nipples as it can remove the natural protective oils and predispose the nipples to cracking. Be careful, too, not to apply cologne, deodorant, hair spray, or powder near the nipples to avoid irritating the tender skin.

Avoid any kind of plastic lining in your bra or nursing pads. A plastic lining can cause trouble by keeping the nipples wet and causing chapping. Wearing a bra that is too tight can also put pressure on your nipples and cause soreness. Avoid using nipple shields which are worn during feedings as they will not prevent soreness and their use almost always leads to further difficulties.

SORE NIPPLES DO HEAL

Frequent opportunities to nurse and cuddle your little one will help you cope until your nipples heal. Try napping during the day, eating nourishing foods, and drinking plenty of liquids. Limit visitors, especially those who may discourage or upset you, and accept offers of help with the household while you and the baby rest. Fortunately, sore nipples rarely last more than a few days, especially if you are following the suggestions given here.

If soreness persists, you'll want to check with someone who is knowledgeable about correct positioning and latch-on. A La Leche League Leader or a lactation consultant may need to observe your baby as he is nursing. If your baby is not taking your nipple into his mouth correctly, there are techniques that can be used to help him learn to nurse more effectively. Be sure that your baby is opening his mouth very wide and taking a large portion of breast tissue into his mouth, not holding the tip of your nipple between his gums. If baby is not latched on well, remove him from your breast by using your finger to break the suction and start over.

There may be a relationship between apprehension on the part of the mother and sore nipples. Tender nipples may cause enough tension to hold back the let-down reflex. The delay in the milk may cause frustration for the baby and create greater concern on your part. What can you do about this? You can hand-express a little milk to start the flow, and you can make a deliberate effort to relax before nursing. You may want to ask your doctor to prescribe an analgesic to relieve the pain while your nipples are very sore.

Some mothers have given up breastfeeding because of sore nipples. This is unfortunate because it isn't necessary. In a few very rare cases of extremely sore nipples, which might occur if baby has been sucking incorrectly for some time, it may be necessary to discontinue breastfeeding temporarily while the nipples are healing. During this time the mother may have to hand-express or pump her milk and give it to the baby from a cup, dropper, or spoon. As soon as the nipples respond to treatment, the baby can be put back on the breast, paying careful attention to positioning and latch-on.

Baby's mouth should be opened very wide before he latches on to your breast.

THRUSH

If you suddenly get sore nipples after several weeks or months of comfortable nursing, you and/or your baby may have contracted thrush. (Thrush can also occur in the newborn period.) If the nipple area gets itchy and feels very tender, or if the skin becomes pink and flaky, you may have thrush. Thrush is a fungus infection that thrives on milk. It's not really serious, although it is a nuisance for you. It rarely bothers the baby at all. It may appear as white spots on the inside of your baby's cheeks, or on his gums. Your baby may also have a persistent diaper rash in connection with thrush, and you may have a vaginal yeast infection. Thrush can be related to taking oral contraceptive pills or an antibiotic. Mothers with diabetes may have greater susceptibility to thrush. It is more common in warm, humid climates. You may have it on your nipples even when there is no sign of it in the baby's mouth.

Thrush may take several weeks to cure. Your doctor may prescribe medication or other forms of treatment. Be sure to treat both the baby's mouth and your nipples. Others in the family may also require treatment.

Wash your hands thoroughly after using the bathroom, as this will help keep thrush from spreading. You must be persistent about treating thrush but it is no reason to discontinue breastfeeding.

Sore Nipples In LATER MONTHS

Another possible cause of sore nipples in later months is teething. Some babies' sucking pattern changes when their gums are sore, and this can temporarily cause nipple soreness. Try being more careful of baby's position at the breast and the way he is grasping your nipple. A change of nursing positions may help. Using Lansinoh for Breastfeeding Mothers® can also help.

On occasion, mothers have developed sore nipples due to eczema. This most often happens when a baby who has started solids nurses while there are still particles of food in his mouth. When food particles come in contact with the sensitive skin of your nipples, eczema can result. This can be avoided by being sure that your baby's or toddler's mouth is empty when he begins to nurse.

Sometimes a mother will notice a small painful blister on the tip of her nipple. This is called a "milk blister" and could be caused by a plugged milk duct. Soak the nipple area in warm water several times a day and keep the area very clean. Try varying nursing positions so baby's mouth puts the least pressure on the blister. It may take a few days to heal completely, but resist the temptation to pop the blister yourself as this can lead to infection.

If you are nursing an older baby or toddler and suddenly notice that your nipples are sore, but none of the above reasons seem to be the cause, then there are some other questions that you can ask yourself. Has your little one been nursing more often, perhaps due to illness or a major change such as moving? Has he been experimenting with unusual nursing positions which might cause nipple strain and abrasion? When he grasps or releases the breast, has he been sucking the nipple in or pulling off without first breaking the suction? Is it possible that you might be pregnant? One or more of these situations might cause sore nipples in even a veteran nursing mother.

When you are experiencing sore nipples or any kind of problem it can be helpful to share your experience with another nursing mother, especially an LLL Leader. She may have additional insight into the situation. Sometimes, all you really need is support and encouragement to help you work through your problem or difficulty and see the brighter side of nursing your baby.

Pumping and Storing Your MILK

When situations or circumstances occur that cause a mother to be separated from her breastfed baby, she'll need to know how to remove milk from her breasts by hand or by using a breast pump. She may also need information on how to safely store the milk she pumps so it can later be fed to her baby.

Some of the situations in which pumping will be needed include having a premature or sick baby who is unable to nurse, a mother planning to return to work, a need to relieve engorged or overfull breasts, or a situation where added stimulation is needed to increase a mother's milk supply.

HAND OR MANUAL EXPRESSION

One of the best techniques to learn is hand or manual expression. This is the least expensive and most portable method you can use. It may require some practice in order to make it work for you. In some cases, watching another mother hand-express her milk is the best way to learn how to do it.

With practice, many mothers are able to express several ounces of milk very quickly. Wash your hands before you begin. The basic technique is to place your fingers on your breast with your thumb above and fingers below so they form a "C." Push back toward the chest wall while squeezing your thumb and fingers together rhythmically just behind the areola (dark area of skin that surrounds the nipple). In the case of a very large areola, fingers should be positioned about 1 to 1½ inches (2½ to 4 cm.) behind the nipple.

Hand-expressing your milk is a skill that may take some practice.

Do not slide your fingers along the skin. Rotate your hand around the breast in order to reach all the milk ducts. Do this for three to five minutes on one breast; then switch to the other breast. Switching back and forth at least twice helps to increase the flow of milk.

You may find it more comfortable to use your right hand, but it's better to alternate, using both hands on each breast in order to reach more of the milk ducts.

Have a clean container ready to collect the milk. A Hand-Expression Funnel that fits on top of a baby bottle can be used to collect milk without spills or splashes. See the Appendix for details.

THE MARMET TECHNIQUE OF MANUAL EXPRESSION

(© 1978, 1979, 1981, 1988 Chele Marmet. Used with permission.)

Another hand-expression technique has been developed by Chele Marmet, a La Leche League Leader and lactation consultant who is the Director of the Lactation Institute in Encino, California. Many mothers who have been previously unsuccessful at hand-expression have found this method effective.

The key to the success of this technique is the combination of the method of manual expression and the use of massage to stimulate the milk ejection reflex. This technique can be learned by following this step-by-step guide. As with any manual skill, practice is important.

DRAINING THE MILK RESERVOIRS

1. Position the thumb and first two
fingers about 1 to 1½ inches
(2½ to 4 cm.) behind the nipple.
    - Use this measurement, which is
      not necessarily the outer edge of
      the areola, as a guide. The areola
      varies in size from one woman to
      another.
    - Place the thumb pad above the
      nipple and the finger pads below
      to form a "C."
    - Note that the fingers are
      positioned so that the milk reser-
      voirs lie beneath them.
    - Avoid cupping the breast.

2. Push straight into the chest wall.
    - Avoid spreading the fingers apart.
    - For large breasts, first lift and
      then push into the chest wall.

3. Roll thumb and fingers forward as if
making thumb and fingerprints
at the same time.
    - The rolling motion of the thumb
      and fingers compresses and emp-
      ties the milk reservoirs without
      hurting sensitive breast tissue.

4. Repeat rhythmically to drain
the reservoirs.
    - Position, push, roll; position,
      push, roll.

5. Rotate the thumb and finger
position to milk the other
reservoirs. Use both hands on each
breast.

Push into
chest wall

Roll

Finish Roll

Right Hand

Left Hand

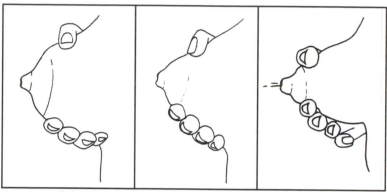

Notice how the thumb and fingers rotate to press in on the milk reservoirs.

AVOID THESE MOTIONS

- Avoid squeezing the breast. This can cause bruising.
- Avoid pulling on the nipple and breast. This can cause nipple damage.
- Avoid sliding fingers on the breast. This can cause skin burns.

STIMULATING THE FLOW OF MILK

1. Massage the milk producing cells and ducts.
   - Start at the top of the breast. Press firmly into the chest wall. Move fingers in a circular motion on one spot on the skin.
   - After a few seconds move the fingers to the next area of the breast.
   - Spiral around the breast toward the areola using this massage.
   - The motion is similar to that used in a breast examination.

2. Next, stroke the breast area from the top of the breast to the nipple with a light tickle-like stroke.
   - Continue this stroking motion from the chest wall to the nipple around the whole breast.
   - This will help with relaxation and will help stimulate the milk ejection reflex.

3. Shake the breast, leaning forward so that gravity will help the milk eject.

FOLLOW THIS PROCEDURE

This procedure should be followed by mothers who are expressing in place of a full feeding and those who need to establish, increase, or maintain their milk supply when the baby cannot breastfeed.

- Express each breast until the flow of milk slows down.
- Assist the milk ejection reflex (massage, stroke, shake) on both breasts. This can be done simultaneously.

- Repeat the whole process of expressing each breast and assisting the milk ejection reflex once or twice more. The flow of milk usually slows down sooner the second and third time as the reservoirs are drained.

The entire procedure should take about 20-30 minutes.

- Express each breast 5-7 minutes.
- Massage, stroke, shake.
- Express each breast 3-5 minutes.
- Massage, stroke, shake.
- Express each breast 3-5 minutes.

Note: If the milk supply is established, use the times given only as a guide. Watch the flow of milk and change breasts when the flow gets small. If little or no milk is present yet, follow these suggested times closely.

Breast PUMPS

Many breastfeeding mothers do just fine without ever owning or using a breast pump. When mother and baby are together most of the time, right from the beginning, and the baby is able to nurse often, a mother may have no reason to pump her breasts. If you learn hand-expression, it can be used for the occasional times when you might need to save your milk or to empty your breasts. Before investing your money in a breast pump, you may want to consider whether it is something you will really need.

There are several types of circumstances in which a mother will want to use a pump. Mothers who plan to return to work when their babies are still very young can continue breastfeeding by pumping their breasts during their lunch hour and/or at midmorning and midafternoon breaks while at work. They can save their milk for feeding to the baby later on.

A working mother will be looking for a breast pump that offers both ease and convenience. She probably needs to carry the pump back and forth to work with her and she needs to be able to use it quickly and efficiently. She also wants a pump that is easy to clean, perhaps even dishwasher-safe, to save time in her already busy day.

The mother who is pumping milk for a premature baby is in a situation where she needs both to establish her milk supply for the future and possibly to provide a specific number of ounces per day to meet her baby's present needs. However, she may not have the opportunity to actually nurse her baby for many weeks. She needs a pump that will closely simulate a baby's sucking action and initiate a good let-down reflex.

Some nursing mothers may decide they want to have a breast pump on hand just in case of a family emergency or other situation where they'll need to be temporarily separated from their baby. These mothers want to buy an inexpensive pump that just gives them the security of knowing it will be available even though it may never be needed. Breast pumps and other breastfeeding-aid products are available from most La Leche League Groups and from La Leche League International. See the Appendix for details.

CHOOSING A BREAST PUMP

"Bicycle Horn" Pumps. At one time, this was the only type of breast pump available and it is still the least expensive. Suction is created by squeezing a rubber bulb, but sensitive breast tissue can be damaged as the suction cannot be regulated. In addition, these pumps cannot be adequately sterilized. They are not recommended.

Cylinder Pumps. Several different manufacturers offer piston-type cylinder pumps with a wide variety of adaptations. All consist of basically two glass or plastic cylinders. The outer cylinder usually doubles as a storage container and feeding bottle. Suction in these pumps is created by pulling the outer cylinder away from the breast. Many women report that this pump is comfortable to use and works effectively. Most of these pumps are small and lightweight, making them easy to fit into a purse, so they are convenient for the working mother. Most are also dishwasher-safe.

The Loyd-B Pump. This pump is an old standby, and for many years it was the only truly effective manual breast pump on the market. It is bulkier than most cylinder pumps, but it comes apart easily and is still small enough to be carried to and from work in a large purse or tote bag. This pump works with a trigger-like mechanism (similar to the triggers on many household cleaning products), and many women report that it is both comfortable and effective.

Handle Squeeze Pump. A squeeze pump designed to be operated with one hand can be convenient to use when a mother wants to pump her milk from one breast while baby nurses on the other side. These pumps are lightweight, very portable, and relatively inexpensive. Most women report they are comfortable and effective.

The Ora'Lac Pump. This pump is unique in the method used to extract milk. Two tubes extend from the top of the collection bottle. One attaches to the breast flange, the other goes into the mother's mouth. The mother provides the suction which draws the milk from her breast directly into the collection bottle. The pump is small enough to fit into a purse and can be used while the mother is lying down.

Small Motorized Pumps. Small motorized pumps provide a combination of convenience and portability. They are small, lightweight, and relatively inexpensive. Suction is provided by a small motor that operates on electricity or batteries, saving mother the effort involved in using a hand pump. When a battery-operated pump is used regularly, the batteries need to be replaced often. A small motorized pump can be operated with one hand which is important in some situations.

Semi-Automatic Electric Pumps. These small electric pumps require the mother to regulate the suction and release but offer the advantage of an electric motor to provide the power. The new models are small enough to be very portable and moderately priced. A working mother who plans to pump her milk for several months could decide that buying one of these pumps would be a good investment.

Full-Size Automatic Electric Pumps. An automatic electric pump usually provides the most effective pumping action. Electric breast pumps are designed to provide an alternating pull and release suction which most closely resembles the sucking action of a nursing baby. Most mothers find these pumps to be gentle and efficient. Most can be used for double-pumping (pumping both breasts at the same time). These are the pumps of choice for the mother who is pumping her milk for a premature or sick baby who is unable to nurse at the breast. Because electric pumps are the fastest and easiest way to pump your milk, they provide the best stimulation for building and maintaining a good milk supply. This can be particularly important in a stressful situation.

Full-size automatic electric pumps are expensive, but they are widely available on a rental basis. In the case of a sick or hospitalized baby (or mother), health insurance will often cover the rental fees when the use of the pump is prescribed by a doctor. A working mother will find the cost of renting a pump less per month than the cost of buying formula for her baby.

No pump can match the effectiveness of a baby at his mother's breast.

BABY IS BEST

No breast pump can match the effectiveness of a baby in stimulating a mother's milk supply and extracting milk. This is partly because mechanical suction cannot duplicate the synchronized action of the baby's tongue, jaw, and palate, but it is mainly because the mother's emotional response to her baby is an important factor.

TECHNIQUES FOR PUMPING

Learning the techniques of effective pumping requires patience and practice. But the rewards can be well worth your while if you are in a situation where you must be separated from your baby. Here are some tips that will help in any situation that requires you to pump your milk.

1. Follow the manufacturer's directions for any pump you use.

2. When using any kind of pump it's a good idea to moisten your breast before applying the breast flange. This improves suction.

3. Be sure to go easy at first and use the lowest setting or the least amount of suction to get started. It is possible to damage sensitive breast tissue, so heed the first signs of discomfort. Pumping should not be uncomfortable and never painful. Reduce the strength of the suction or the amount of time spent pumping. If discomfort occurs, check to be sure you are using the pump correctly. If necessary, switch to a different brand or type of pump.

4. Pumping in a quiet, relaxed setting will usually help the milk to flow more easily. Although this is not always possible in an office setting or a hospital nursery, it is worth the effort to try to find a secluded spot where you can pump undisturbed. Thinking about the baby or looking at a picture of him can do wonders to encourage the milk to flow.

5. If you are planning to save the expressed milk to be given to the baby later on, be sure that your hands and the container you use to collect the milk are clean. Follow the pump manufacturer's direc-

tions for cleaning the pump. Bacteria can accumulate if dried particles of milk are left in the breast flange, tubing, or collection bottle.
If you are pumping for a hospitalized baby, there may be more specific precautions you need to take. Check with the nurses who are
caring for the baby.

6. Research has shown that human milk can safely be kept for up to 24
hours if it is stored at 60 degrees F (15 degrees C), just below room
temperature. An insulated cooler with ice packs will keep milk at
this temperature. At 66 to 72 degrees F (19 to 22 degrees C), human
milk can be stored for 10 hours. At 79 degrees F (25 degrees C),
milk is safe from harmful bacteria for 4-6 hours. Human milk has a
remarkable ability to retard bacterial growth. You may need to be
more cautious if you are expressing milk for a hospitalized baby.

7. Milk can be refrigerated for up to 8 days at 32 to 39 degrees F (0 to
4 degrees C) with no increase in harmful bacteria.

8. For longer storage, milk can be frozen and kept in a refrigerator-
freezer for up to two weeks. In a separate door freezer it can be kept
for three to four months. In a separate deep freeze that stays at a
constant 0 degrees F (-19 degrees C) it can be kept six months
or longer. Be sure to label and date frozen milk and use the oldest
milk first.

9. It's a good idea to freeze your milk in small amounts varying from
two to four ounces (60-120 ml.). You can always thaw more milk if
your baby needs it. Once thawed, human milk can be refrigerated for
up to twenty-four hours but should never be refrozen. Do not let
milk stand at room temperature to thaw. Instead, thaw it quickly by
putting the container under running water, first cold, then gradually
getting warmer until the milk is warm. Do not heat the milk on the
stove or in a microwave oven. More information on storing your milk
and feeding it to your baby can be found in Chapter 8.

TO EXPRESS MILK FOR A MILK BANK

Because human milk has been found to be so important for sick or premature babies, nursing mothers are sometimes asked to donate their
extra milk for these babies. In many hospitals, special milk banks have
been established for this purpose. If you are asked to donate your milk,
you will naturally consider your own baby's needs first, and you will
probably pump or hand-express milk to donate only after feedings. If
your baby is a little older, you might be able to express milk from one
breast while the baby nurses at the other. This is less time-consuming,
and can usually be done if you are using a pump that can be operated
with one hand.

The milk bank will probably have its own set of instructions and may even provide you with a breast pump to use. If you are donating your milk for a sick or premature baby, you must be scrupulously clean in your techniques for expressing and storing your milk. If you, your baby, or any other member of your household has been ill, you should not donate milk until everyone has been well for twenty-four hours.

When the time comes that you are no longer donating milk, cut down gradually on the pumping. If you have built up a milk supply much greater than your own baby's needs, the sudden drop in demand might cause engorgement, just as sudden weaning would. Taper off gradually by pumping out some of the milk whenever your breasts feel overly full and uncomfortable. Or, see if your baby will help out with an extra nursing when you are feeling full. He'll probably be happy to oblige.

Breast Problems: SORE BREASTS, PLUGGED DUCTS, AND BREAST INFECTIONS

It sometimes happens that a nursing mother notices a very tender spot or sore lump in her breast. This can be a plugged duct or a breast infection. Knowing what to do about it can clear things up quickly and avoid further difficulty.

Whatever the cause of a sore breast, there are three basic steps involved in treatment:

Apply Heat; Get Plenty of Rest; and keep the breast comfortably empty by **Frequent Nursing.** These procedures may sound deceptively simple, but immediate action can mean the difference between a few hours of discomfort and several days in bed.

PLUGGED DUCTS

If a breastfeeding mother notices a very tender spot, redness, or a sore lump in her breast, this may very likely be caused by a plugged milk duct. What this means is that a milk duct has become inflamed because the milk is unable to flow through it freely.

Plugged ducts may be caused by any of the following—improper positioning of the baby at the breast, prolonged periods of time between nursings, giving supplementary bottles or overusing a pacifier, wearing a too-tight nursing bra or other clothing that constricts the breasts. If an older baby suddenly starts sleeping through the night, or nurses often one day and cuts way back the next day, a plugged milk duct may occur. Occasionally a plugged duct is caused by dried milk secretions covering one of the nipple openings.

Rest is essential at the first sign of a problem. If at all possible, you should climb into bed with the baby tucked in beside you for the remainder of the day. At the very least you should eliminate all extra activities and spend an hour or two relaxing with your baby at your breast and feet off the floor. A plugged duct or a sore spot on your breast may be the first sign that you are trying to do too much. You would be well-advised to heed this warning and get lots of extra rest for a few days after you've experienced a plugged duct.

In addition to rest, there are some other things you can do to treat a plugged duct:

- **Apply wet or dry heat to the affected area, and remove any dried milk secretions on the nipple** by soaking with plain warm water. Lean over a basin of warm water and soak your breasts for ten minutes or so three times a day, take warm showers, use hot wet packs, a heating pad, or a hot water bottle. Massage the affected area gently while it is warm, and nurse the baby or hand-express some milk immediately after treating the area with warmth. Getting the milk to flow while the breast is warm will help unplug the affected duct.

- **Nurse the baby on the affected side frequently.** Nurse at least every two hours including during the night, as long as the breast is tender or warm to the touch. Nurse first on the affected side at each feeding. Frequent nursings will keep the breast fairly empty so the milk flows more freely. Try positioning the baby so his chin is pointed toward the plugged duct.

- **Loosen constrictive clothing, especially your bra.** If possible, you may even want to discontinue wearing a bra for a few days. If you are more comfortable with a bra, try wearing one that is a size larger or a least change to one that has a different cut or style. This should relieve any pressure that the bra you usually wear may have been putting on the milk ducts. Some mothers try to get by without a regular nursing bra by wearing a stretchy type of bra and pulling the cup up or down for feedings. This could be causing pressure on the milk ducts with the result that they are not emptied properly. Some nursing bras with stretchy cups that pull down or to the side for nursing can have the same effect, putting too much pressure on some milk ducts.

- **Check the baby's position at the breast.** He should be on his side with his whole body facing you, and he should be able to grasp your nipple without having to turn his head. A large portion of the areola should be in his mouth. It is important for the baby to be positioned properly so that all the milk ducts are emptied at every feeding.

- **Try changing nursing positions from time to time.** Lie down, sit up, switch from the rocking chair to the sofa to a lounge chair. Try nursing with baby in the football hold. A variety of nursing positions will give the baby a better chance to reach all of the milk ducts and keep them emptied. (See Chapter 4 for details on various nursing positions.) One position that may be particularly helpful in clearing up a plugged duct is to place the baby in the middle of a bed or a quilt on the floor or in your lap while you sit with legs crossed, yoga-style, (or get up on your hands and knees) and lean over him to nurse, with the breast hanging freely from the rib cage. This position may not be the most comfortable for you, but it can allow a plugged milk duct to be opened more easily.

BREAST INFECTIONS

Prompt and proper treatment of a plugged duct will usually keep a breast infection from developing. However, if you notice the type of soreness or lump that is usually associated with a plugged duct, and it is accompanied by a fever or flu-like symptoms (feeling tired, achy, or run-down), you probably have a breast infection. A breastfeeding mother will sometimes find herself developing a breast infection when other family members suffer from colds or other types of flu.

It is important that you begin treating a breast infection immediately. The treatment for a breast infection is the same as for a plugged duct: **Apply Heat, Get Plenty of Rest,** and **Nurse Often.** If this course of action is begun quickly, you may not need further treatment for a breast infection. However, if you still have a fever after 24 hours, and other symptoms persist, you'll want to get in touch with your doctor. In this case, your doctor may prescribe medication. You'll want to continue getting lots of rest and nursing often while you take the medication.

It will not harm your baby to continue nursing when you have a breast infection. At one time it was standard procedure to recommend weaning if the mother had a breast infection. However, studies have shown that the infection clears up more quickly when the breast is kept empty. Also, the mother is much more comfortable than she would be after a sudden weaning. Antibodies in mother's milk protect the baby from the bacteria that may be causing infection. Even temporary weaning is an unnecessary hardship at a time when you aren't feeling well in the first place.

If your doctor prescribes an antibiotic, be sure to take all of the medication that is prescribed. People sometimes stop taking a medication as soon as they start to feel better, only to have the infection reoc-

Getting extra rest is an important part of the treatment for a breast infection.

cur in a few days. In the case of a breast infection, this would be hard on both you and your baby, so it's important to take the medication that is prescribed for you until it is gone. Antibiotics in general do not usually cause a problem for a nursing baby. If a doctor is wary about certain antibiotics, he can usually prescribe one that has been found to be safe to take while a mother is nursing.

If you find yourself with a second breast infection within a few days or weeks of the first one, chances are good that the original infection didn't clear up completely. Repeated breast infections do occasionally happen, but they are almost always a recurrence of the first infection rather than a brand new infection.

If you do find that plugged ducts or breast infections seem to occur frequently, you may want to look into your general health, being sure you are eating a balanced diet and limiting extra activities so you have enough time to relax and enjoy nursing your baby.

Donna Sutton, a mother from Iowa, found that the advice she received from her La Leche League Leader helped her recover when she had a breast infection:

After being home from the hospital one week, I found myself with a sore breast and other symptoms of a breast infection. A consultation with a local physician produced the advice to stop nursing on the infected breast for at least four to five days, and express the milk by hand or breast pump. I knew that this was the wrong course to take, so after much deliberation I continued to nurse on both sides. My infection did not abate, and I could still feel a lump in my breast.

*I finally called my local La Leche League Leader. Her advice soon
made all the difference in the world. After applying warm packs,
nursing often (especially on the affected side), and resting, the lump in
my breast began to disappear. I still remember my Leader telling me
that nothing should be more important at this time than nursing my
baby. I realize now that if I had consulted her initially, the infection
would have cleared up more quickly and been less frustrating for
Sarah and me. How many mothers have received the wrong advice
and been forced to quit nursing?*

*I am grateful to my LLL Leader for her advice, and I'm a firm
believer that breast is best!*

BREAST ABSCESS

In very rare cases, a breast infection may develop into an abscess. This
usually does not occur if prompt treatment is initiated at the first sign
of a problem. An abscess is a localized infection that may need to be sur-
gically opened and drained. Usually your doctor can do this in his office
or perhaps he'll want to do it at the hospital on an outpatient basis. If
this procedure should be necessary, you can continue to nurse on the
unaffected breast with no problem, but you may need to pump or hand-
express your milk from the abscessed breast for a day or so. Keeping that
breast empty will promote healing, but the incision may be too close to
the areola for the baby to nurse without causing discomfort.

Remember that any of these breast problems can be an indication
that you should carefully evaluate other things that are going on in your
life. These symptoms are often a nursing mother's first clue that she
should be taking better care of herself. Conserve your energy by keeping extra activities to a minimum and spend as much time as possible
just relaxing and enjoying your baby without regard to schedules and
deadlines.

Breast Lumps and BREAST SURGERY

Most lumps in a nursing mother's breast are inflammatory, due to
plugged ducts or a breast infection. Some are due to benign tumors
(fibromas), a milk retention cyst (galactocele), and only in the very
rarest of cases are they due to cancer.

If you have a lump that does not go away in a week with careful
treatment for a plugged duct, we suggest that you consult a physician.
Weaning is not necessary either for diagnosis or treatment of breast
lumps. Mammograms, x-rays, and ultrasound tests will not interfere

with breastfeeding. Mothers have had cysts removed, biopsied, and aspirated, without finding it necessary to wean. If your doctor is not familiar with the lactating breast, you may need to call his attention to this fact. It may be advisable to empty the breast by nursing the baby immediately prior to examination and/or whatever procedure the doctor may want to undertake. Nursing may be resumed again right after most diagnostic procedures, except after a radioactive breast scan.

If surgery is needed, care must be taken so that the fewest milk ducts and major nerves are damaged. Barbara Ann Paster of New Hampshire worked closely with her surgeon to be sure she would be able to continue breastfeeding after surgery:

Shortly after our second child, Sara, was born I noticed a lump in my breast just to the left of my nipple. I arranged to go in for the removal of the breast lump soon thereafter. Before the scheduled date of surgery, I sat down with my surgeon to discuss the nursing breast and how he could help me make my return to nursing go smoothly as soon as possible after the operation. While the surgeon had known I was nursing, he had never considered the problem of operating on a nursing breast. After discussion he agreed to be especially careful during the surgery to cut as few milk ducts as possible.

Because my lump was deep within the breast, my surgeon ruled out anything less than general anesthesia, claiming that it was too tender an area to manage otherwise. To minimize engorgement, we worked out a plan for me to nurse Sara immediately prior to surgery. We also decided on dissolvable stitches, which would absorb after healing.

Sara was put to breast on my unaffected side as soon as I regained consciousness. The incisional area was dressed with as small a dressing as possible so as not to alarm her. Within twelve hours of the surgery I was able to nurse on the affected side.

I won't say it was comfortable. I found that putting some pressure on the dressing helped allay the feeling that she would pull the incision or my breast apart. By the second or third day it was quite tolerable. Putting my baby to the breast was more comfortable than trying to hand-express or use a pump. My surgeon was amazed at how well the breast healed.

My incision line follows the curve of the outer edge of the areola. The surgeon went in from there and excised the lump from almost directly under the nipple. Luckily it was fibrocystic in nature which meant it was not life-threatening.

Another mother, Beverly Scott from Washington, found that surgery was not needed for her breast lump. She learned that the lump that formed in her breast when her son was ten days old was a galactocele, a milk-retention cyst. Fortunately, her doctor was familiar with this uncommon phenomenon and advised her to continue nursing and ignore the lump. However, by the time her son was twenty-one months old, the lump had enlarged to twice its original size and the doctor became concerned and suggested weaning. Beverly goes on to explain what happened:

I was determined to continue with baby-led weaning. I decided to learn all I could about available options and then ask my doctor to proceed with treatment without waiting for Jesse to wean.

I talked to my LLL Leader and received helpful information regarding surgery during lactation. I contacted my obstetrician, summarizing my conclusions in a letter and then calling him. We agreed that he would go ahead and remove the fluid from the cyst immediately for diagnostic purposes. If surgical removal of the cyst was indicated, I would arrange with a general surgeon to have the procedure done on an outpatient basis under local anesthetic with minimal interruption of breastfeeding. However, that did not become necessary, as a laboratory analysis of the fluid confirmed the original diagnosis: The cyst contained only milk.

A woman who suddenly finds a large breast lump soon after giving birth should ask her doctor about the possibility of a galactocele before submitting to invasive treatment such as surgery. Ultrasound and/or aspiration could confirm the diagnosis if there was any uncertainty.

Breastfeeding has been shown to reduce the incidence of breast cancer; nevertheless, there have been rare instances of a mother developing breast cancer while she is still nursing a baby. It is a good idea to learn how to do a monthly breast self-exam, and do it regularly. Any mother who discovers a lump in her breast that does not change or go away should have it checked by her doctor.

PREVIOUS BREAST SURGERY

Previous breast surgery usually need not stop a mother from nursing her baby even if she has had a breast removed because of cancer. Breastfeeding will not expose the mother to any greater risk of malignancy; nor will it harm the baby. And since milk production works on the basis of supply and demand, one breast can supply plenty of milk for the baby.

If a biopsy was done or a lump or cyst removed from the breast, a mother may be uncertain whether or not milk ducts or major nerves have been damaged. She will need to monitor her baby's wet and soiled diapers as well as his weight gain to be sure he is getting enough milk.

BREAST IMPLANTS OR BREAST REDUCTION SURGERY

If a mother has previously had breast implants or breast reduction surgery, there is always concern about how the surgery will affect her plans to breastfeed. If the majority of milk ducts and major nerves have not been cut, breastfeeding may proceed smoothly. In some cases, even milk ducts that were cut have been found to "recanalize" or grow back.

It is not always possible to know ahead of time whether or not a mother who has had breast augmentation or reduction surgery can fully breastfeed her baby. The best recommendation is to try breastfeeding and watch carefully for signs of baby getting enough milk. If there is a problem, and baby is not gaining well, a mother can continue to breast-feed along with offering supplements with a cup, spoon, bottle, or nursing supplementer.

Some concerns have been raised about silicone leakage when a mother breastfeeds with silicone breast implants. There is no evidence that silicone used in breast implants can leak into a mother's milk.

Is Your Baby Getting Enough MILK?

There is nothing quite like the delight that comes from seeing your baby thrive and grow on your milk. As his arms and legs fill out and his cheeks turn plump and rosy, you can't help but glow with pride ... and marvel at how perfectly your body is continuing to provide for all of his nutritional needs.

A baby's need for milk and his mother's ability to produce it in just the right quantity have been said to be one of nature's most perfect examples of the law of supply and demand. Until the advent of mass produced artificial formula, the very survival of the human race depended largely on a mother's ability to produce a sufficient quantity of milk to adequately nourish her baby.

There is nothing mystical or magical about producing enough milk to satisfy your baby's needs. Establishing and maintaining an ample milk supply is easy when you understand how the milk supply is regulated and what kinds of things are likely to upset the balance between the amount of milk the baby needs and the amount of milk that is produced.

The more the baby nurses effectively, the more milk there will be. Understanding this "golden rule" of breastfeeding is the key to an abundant milk supply and a contented baby. Years ago, mothers were often told to wait four hours between feedings so that their breasts would "fill up." Many a mother and baby had a short-lived breastfeeding experience due to this well-intentioned but erroneous advice.

It is now well understood that milk is produced almost continuously, and that the more often and effectively the baby nurses, the more milk there will be. Thus, the mother of a baby who is nursing every two hours will have a bountiful milk supply, while the mother who is trying to "hold off" the baby and nurse only every four hours will have considerably less milk. Frequent and effective sucking at the breast signals the mother's body to produce a correspondingly increased amount of milk.

In the first two days after birth, your baby will have only one or two wet diapers per day. After that, you can be confident that your baby is getting enough milk if:

- He has six to eight really wet cloth diapers (five to six disposable diapers) and two to five bowel movements per day and is receiving nothing but your milk—no supplemental water or formula. (A baby older than six weeks or so may have fewer bowel movements and still be getting enough to eat.)

- He is gaining weight at an average of four to eight ounces (113 to 227 grams) a week or about one to two pounds (453 to 906 grams) per month in the first three to four months. From four to six months, average weight gain for the breastfed baby is three to five ounces (85 to 142 grams) per week; from six to twelve months, average gain is one and one-half to three ounces (42 to 85 grams) per week.

At your baby's first checkup, weight gain should be determined from the lowest weight the baby reached rather than his birth weight. Most babies lose five to seven percent of their birth weight and may take two to three weeks to regain their birth weight.

- In the first six months, growth in length of approximately one inch (2.5 centimeters) per month and growth in head circumference of one-half inch (1.25 centimeters) per month also show that baby is getting enough to eat.

- He is nursing frequently and is satisfied after each feeding. Most newborns nurse every two to three hours or eight to twelve times in a twenty-four hour period. This is an average, and some babies may nurse less frequently while others nurse more often.

- He appears healthy—has good color and resilient skin, is "filling out" and growing in length, and is alert and active with good muscle tone.

A baby who is alert and active with good muscle tone is getting plenty of milk even if he is gaining weight slowly.

FALSE ALARMS

Some mothers think they do not have enough milk when actually there is no problem with their milk supply. They worry about symptoms which have other causes or they're unfamiliar with the variety of patterns that are normal in breastfed babies. If your baby is gaining well and has plenty of wet and soiled diapers, there is no need to worry if:

Your baby nurses very often. Wanting to nurse frequently does not mean baby is hungry. Many babies have a strong need to suck and a need for a continuous contact with their mothers. Frequent nursing assures that your baby is getting enough milk.

Human milk digests more quickly than formula and places less strain on a baby's immature digestive system, so that the breastfed baby needs to be fed more frequently.

Your baby's nursing habits, weight gain, or sleep patterns don't compare with other babies you know. Each baby is an individual, and there are wide variations within the normal range.

Your baby suddenly increases the frequency and/or length of his nursings. Babies who are very sleepy as newborns often suddenly "wake up" and begin nursing more frequently. Babies also go through occasional growth spurts (frequently around three weeks, six weeks, and three months). During these times they nurse more often than usual to bring in more milk for their expanding needs.

Your baby suddenly decreases his nursing time, perhaps down to five to ten minutes per breast. He may simply be able to extract the milk more quickly now that he is more experienced at nursing.

Your baby is fussy. Many babies have a fussy period each day, often at about the same time of the day. Some babies are fussy much of the time. Fussiness can be caused by many things other than hunger, but often there is no discernible reason.

Your breasts leak only a little or not at all. Leaking has no relationship to the amount of milk you produce and often stops after your supply becomes established and regulated to your baby's needs.

Your breasts suddenly seem softer. This happens as your milk production adjusts to your baby's demand and the initial fullness or engorgement subsides.

You never feel the let-down sensation or it does not seem as strong as it did before. This may occur as time goes on. (Some mothers do not feel it at all; it does not mean that they do not have a let-down.)

IF YOUR MILK SUPPLY IS LOW

If it seems that your supply is not meeting your baby's needs, then it is important to determine what is interfering with your production of milk. The following factors can cause or contribute to a lessened milk supply:

- **Supplementing.** Supplementing with even an occasional bottle of formula, juice, or water can interfere with a mother's milk supply. Supplements fill up the baby and cause him to wait longer for the next feeding, thereby decreasing his sucking at the breast. The more formula he gets one day, the less milk the mother's body will make the following day. Supplementing causes a mother's breasts to produce less, not more.

- **Nipple Confusion.** A baby can become confused by the use of any artificial nipple, as it requires a different type of sucking. If your baby is not sucking properly at the breast, he will not be able to stimulate your breasts to produce enough milk.

- **Pacifiers.** Some babies are willing to meet their sucking needs with a pacifier, which may significantly reduce their sucking time at the breast. Pacifiers can also lead to nipple confusion.

- **Using Nipple Shields.** Nipple shields worn during feedings interfere with the impulses to the brain that normally come from a baby sucking directly on his mother's nipples. The milk secretion and let-down of the milk is slowed down—directly affecting the amount of milk the baby receives. Nipple shields can also lead to nipple confusion.

- **Scheduled Feedings.** Delaying the baby's feedings until the clock dictates a certain amount of time has passed can interfere with the supply and demand system of milk production. Feeding on demand usually assures an adequate supply.

- **Placid, Sleepy Baby.** Some babies sleep most of the time and nurse only infrequently and for short periods. If this describes your baby, and if he is having few wet or soiled diapers and not gaining weight, it is important for you to awaken him regularly, stimulate him with gentle handling, and encourage him to nurse at least every two hours. You'll need to decide how often he should nurse, until he learns for himself how to get enough to eat.

- **Cutting Back on the Length of Feedings.** Long nursings can help assure an adequate milk supply. Cutting them short can prevent your supply from increasing as your baby's needs increase. Also, the fat content of the milk increases later in a feeding. On the other hand, a baby who nurses almost continually and never seems satisfied may not be sucking correctly. A baby who is satisfied will end the feeding when he is full.

- **Offering Only One Breast per Feeding.** After the milk is established, some mothers prefer to nurse at only one breast per feeding if baby is gaining well. If you are working to increase your supply, use both breasts, but don't limit baby's sucking time at the first breast.

MOTHER CARE

A breastfeeding mother needs to take good care of herself in order to provide a good milk supply for her baby. Fatigue and tension can interfere with your let-down and contribute to an inadequate milk supply. Take the time to really relax every so often during the course of the day.

A poor diet can contribute to tension and fatigue and detract from your general well-being. Many mothers feel better when they eat five or six small meals every day rather than three big ones. Good nutritional intake, and eating more often, may be the answer for you. Eat fresh fruits and salads, whole-grain crackers, meats, cheese, nuts, and fish. Avoid poor quality foods such as cookies, pastries, candy, fried snack foods, and the like.

Breastfeeding increases your need for fluids, as your body needs more fluids to make milk. Take a glass of water or juice with you each time you sit down to nurse the baby. If your urine is dark yellow in color and small in amount, you are not drinking enough liquids. What you drink is equally important. Water and unsweetened fruit juice are your best choices. Avoid excessive amounts of caffeine in coffee, tea, and colas.

Sometimes problems with a mother's health can affect her milk supply and her baby's weight gain. If you are having any health problems, check with your doctor about them. Most medications are safe for nursing mothers, but some can adversely affect your milk production. If a doctor prescribes any medication for you, be sure to mention that you're breastfeeding.

The use of hormonal contraceptives too early in the course of lactation can reduce milk production and affect baby's weight gain. There are no conclusive studies on potential long-term effects of hormones that are passed on to the baby through the mother's milk. Non-hormonal methods of contraception do not have any potential effects on the baby or your milk supply. Breastfeeding delays the return of fertility for several months. (See Chapter 19.)

Smoking has been found to have a detrimental effect on your milk supply and your baby's health. Mothers who smoke may find that their babies gain better, are healthier, and less fussy when they cut down or stop smoking.

INCREASING YOUR MILK SUPPLY

If you do find that some or all of the above factors have caused your milk supply to decrease, there are some positive steps you can follow to increase your supply of milk. If you are in a situation where you are concerned about your milk supply, it will be very helpful to get in touch with an LLL Leader or a board certified lactation consultant. While we can offer you basic information here, she can supply additional insight based on your specific situation.

If your baby is not gaining weight, or is losing weight, you'll want to be sure to keep in close touch with your doctor. There is always a possibility that a health problem is causing baby's slow weight gain. A baby who is losing weight may need to receive a supplement until your milk supply increases. In addition to going over the points listed here to improve your milk supply, be sure to read the section in Chapter 17 on "Slow Weight Gain."

Nurse Frequently for as long as your baby will nurse. Plan to spend twenty-four to forty-eight hours (or longer if your supply is quite low) doing little else but nursing and resting. A sleepy baby may need to be awakened and encouraged to nurse more frequently.

Offer Both Breasts at Each Feeding. This will ensure that your baby gets all the milk available and that both breasts are stimulated frequently.

Try Switch Nursing. Switching breasts two or three times throughout each feeding may help to keep a sleepy baby interested in nursing. Watch baby's sucking and swallowing as he nurses, and switch to the other breast as soon as the sucking slows down and he swallows less often. For some babies, this will be about ten minutes on each side, for others it could be as little as two to three minutes. Use both breasts at least twice at each feeding.

All Your Baby's Sucking Should Be at the Breast. Avoid bottles and pacifiers as they can confuse the baby. Drinking from an artificial nipple requires a different type of sucking than nursing at mother's breast. If some supplement is necessary temporarily, it can be given with a nursing supplementer while baby nurses or by spoon, cup, or dropper. (See the Appendix for information about the nursing supplementer.) Pacifiers can interfere with the extra nursing that is needed when you are trying to build up your milk.

Give Your Baby Only Human Milk. Avoid all solids, water, and juice. If your baby has been receiving formula supplements you will not want to cut these out abruptly. You can gradually cut back on the amount of supplement as your milk supply increases, but you need to watch baby's wet and soiled diapers to be sure he is getting enough to eat. You need to be in touch with your doctor to monitor your baby's weight gain as you are cutting back on formula supplements.

Drink Plenty of Liquids and Eat a Well-Balanced Diet. Eat a wide variety of foods in as close to their natural state as possible. Try to have a glass of water or juice with you each time you nurse.

Get Plenty of Rest and Relaxation. Your milk supply will increase faster if you are relaxed and rested. Plan to do as little as possible for a while. Cut out all non-essential tasks. Take naps with your baby as often as possible. For relaxation, try a warm bath, soft music, exercise, or whatever works best for you. Try to spend at least a few minutes each day doing something special to pamper yourself.

After reading through this section, if you have any further questions or concerns be sure to get in touch with your La Leche League Leader. Being in touch with other breastfeeding mothers through your La Leche League Group will offer you the support and encouragement you need. Your happy, healthy breastfed baby will soon provide the reward for your efforts.

The Baby Who Is PLEASINGLY PLUMP

If your breastfed baby is a round little fatty, some may say he's gaining too much. While he may weigh more than the average shown on the doctor's charts, the baby on human milk alone will not be overweight. A totally breastfed baby who is "overweight" is not necessarily overfat or obese. Still, in a weight-conscious world, even baby fat is suspect, and the mother of a plump, fully breastfed baby may be told that her child should be put on a diet.

Heredity plays a definite role in determining a child's growth pattern, as became obvious in the Nixon family in Florida. Baby Alena weighed almost eighteen pounds at three and a half months, and her mother, Janice, was told that the development of a large number of fat cells in infancy would cause Alena problems later in life. This was Janice's first child and she was understandably upset. "But I thought back over all I had read or heard at the LLL meetings I had been going to since my eighth month of pregnancy," Janice recounted. "Was Alena happy and alert most of the time? Yes. Was she developing well in all other aspects? Yes."

Janice also remembered her mother telling her that she herself had been a very large baby, and she and her mother searched the family album for baby pictures. "A picture of my mother when she was a baby also showed her to be extremely chubby, and she was completely breastfed." Their findings were meaningful because neither has had a weight problem as an adult.

At the four-month checkup, Alena weighed in at almost nineteen pounds and was twenty-five inches long—way above the norms. Janice showed the doctor the family pictures:

When the doctor saw the pictures, he was so impressed that he called in another doctor to look at them. They talked about the loopholes in the "fat cell" theory, and the obvious fact that fat babies do not always become fat adults. They both agreed that there was no reason for me to alter Alena's present care in any way. Absolutely no diet!

There are hazards in limiting growth by putting a baby on a diet. The young child is a dynamic body builder, producing cells of all kinds, brain and nerve cells as well as fat cells. Researchers have observed that the flesh of the breastfed baby is firmer than that of a formula-fed infant. There are no "empty" calories in human milk, as there are in highly processed foods.

It must be remembered here that fat accumulated in the relatively inactive pre-toddler state is preparatory for the highly active time when the busy toddler hardly has time to eat. It is not unlike the extra weight that a woman puts on during pregnancy in preparation for the extra demands of motherhood. We have found that by age two or three, the heavyweights among the tiny tots usually slim down beautifully.

Mothers need not worry that their fully breastfed baby will get too plump.

Some babies who start out tiny and petite at birth surprise everyone with their rapid gain. Ann Tutor from Japan tells how she handled critics with the comment, "We grow them big at our house!" She writes:

Although Melanie weighed in at six pounds ten ounces at birth, by the time we left the hospital she was six pounds even and seemed to me the tiniest, prettiest little baby girl I had ever seen.

We attended our first La Leche League meeting when Melanie was one month old. She weighed nine pounds at her two-month checkup, and by the second LLL meeting we attended I began to notice that while Melanie had started out smaller than some of the other babies, she had caught up and even passed a few of her little friends. When she was about three months old, people began to casually mention how big my "dainty little girl" was getting, and at her four-month checkup I was surprised to find out that she weighed eighteen pounds.

When at six months Melanie weighed twenty-four pounds, she became a real conversation piece. While I was proud to have a healthy, happy baby, I began to worry about and even resent some of the comments about my baby's weight. Thank goodness my La Leche

League friends and my wonderful doctor kept assuring me that as long as Melanie was totally breastfed we were doing great! My doctor even paraded Melanie around to his colleagues at one visit to show them this lovably round, totally breastfed baby.

Melanie is seventeen months old now and weighs thirty-one pounds, and while she doesn't yet have to worry about being called skinny, she has slimmed down considerably. We still get comments and questions about her once in a while, some of which still aggravate me, but I don't worry about Melanie's weight anymore. We're in no hurry to end our nursing days. While I hope that Melanie doesn't keep that cute round tummy and those dimpled thighs forever, I know she has had a wonderful start in being breastfed.

WEIGHT PROBLEMS IN LATER YEARS

While some people may be concerned that too much weight gained in infancy will lead to obesity later on, the truth is that many factors contribute to weight problems in adults. Some aspects that are related to eating habits in childhood are automatically avoided when you breastfeed your baby and follow the guidelines included in this book.

As a breastfeeding mother, you are not going to fall into the anxiety trap of monitoring how many ounces of milk your baby takes. You will not get into the habit of coaxing him to finish the last few ounces in a bottle. When you start solids, your child will probably be at least six months old. You will have bypassed the unnatural situation that comes when solids are given to the younger child, who automatically pushes out whatever is spooned into his mouth, making it difficult for a mother to know if her baby is hungry or not.

Breastfeeding is the first preventive measure against obesity in adult life. In fact, one study showed that breastfeeding protects against later obesity. Children who were breastfed were found to be less likely to be overweight in adolescence.

Good eating habits do start early, and you can be assured that your baby is receiving the very best nutrition available if he is breastfed.

Did You Ever Hear of a NURSING STRIKE?

Occasionally a young baby will suddenly refuse to breastfeed for no apparent reason. This can be a real puzzle, especially if the baby is under a year old and probably not at all ready to be weaned.

A situation like this is called a nursing strike. It's a baby's way of communicating the fact that something's wrong. It usually lasts from two to four days and requires some motherly ingenuity to figure out exactly what the problem is.

How can you tell whether your baby has gone on a nursing strike or has just decided to wean himself? A baby who is really ready to wean will usually be well over a year old, will be eating lots of solid food and drinking liquids from a cup, and will gradually lose interest in one nursing at a time. A baby who is on a nursing strike may not be eating much or drinking from a cup at all. He nurses fine one day and abruptly refuses to nurse at all the next day. He also shows signs of being obviously unhappy about the whole situation. He wants you to figure out what's wrong and solve the problem for him.

Consider the following possibilities: Is your baby teething? Does he have a cold, sore throat, or stuffy nose that prevents him from nursing easily? Does he have an earache that makes it painful to nurse? Are you anxious or upset about something? Babies respond to their mothers' feelings.

Has nursing become a stressful time, with too many outside interruptions or distractions? Have you been deciding when the baby should nurse and when he should stop, instead of letting him lead the way? Has the baby become dependent on a pacifier or his thumb, so that he routinely sucks quite a bit on either?

Has some recent change in your nursing pattern confused the baby? Has he had too many bottles? Been left with a sitter? Been repeatedly put off when he cries to nurse? Have you gone back to work, or are you worrying about what will happen when and if you do have to leave the baby?

Sometimes a nursing strike occurs after baby bites mother a time or two, and your understandable reaction has upset him. He bites, you jump or let out a startled cry. Baby is frightened, cries, and won't resume nursing for fear of another jolt or yell.

Sometimes the unexpected can cause a baby to refuse to nurse. Mary Shumeyko of New Jersey writes:

> *The other day our twenty-month-old, Jonathan, bumped his chin. His mouth seemed to be bleeding a bit, so we wiped it off, I nursed him, and he continued playing. I went back to what I was doing. Several hours later, after happily nursing to sleep, Jonathan awoke crying in obvious pain. I offered him my breast. He tried to nurse, then drew away, crying harder. This continued all night, with Jonathan waking every half hour or so, and my husband or I walking the floor with him since he wouldn't nurse.*

The next morning he seemed to feel better and tentatively asked to nurse. When he opened his mouth I discovered the problem: he had cut his tongue when he bumped his chin, and (after the initial numbness wore off) nursing obviously had been quite painful. My heart went out to him. Not only had he injured himself, but his standard "cure-all" hurt even more. Fortunately the mouth heals quickly, and he's once again nursing regularly. The episode was a good reinforcement for me, though. After one night of not nursing, I'm more aware than ever of how precious this beautiful relationship is.

Even if you are not sure why the baby has gone on a nursing strike, you will want to help him get back to regular nursing as soon and easily as possible. Try nursing him when he is very sleepy, or already asleep. Many babies who refuse to nurse while awake will nurse when they are drowsy or asleep. Some babies are more likely to nurse if mother is walking about rather than sitting still. In any case, plan to devote yourself almost entirely to the baby for a few days. Lots of cuddling, stroking, and skin-to-skin contact may help. Maybe some relaxing time spent just with mom away from the hubbub of the rest of the family will calm the baby and encourage him to start nursing again. Rethink your priorities. You will both be better off and happier when things get back to normal again.

A mother from Guam, Becky Hallowell, found that calling her La Leche League Leader helped get to the bottom of her problem:

We were on our third day of six-month-old Todd's refusing to nurse when I decided that something had to change. We were at wits' end, and I was in pain from engorgement. My husband had been very supportive but was finding the situation increasingly difficult as I became more and more upset. He begged me to call Linda, our La Leche League Leader: "She'll be able to help you," he said.

Linda and I talked it over, and she suggested the possibility of a nursing strike. I had been too close to the situation to recognize the problem, but soon realized we had all the usual causes and then some.

1) We all had bad colds.

2) Solids had been introduced on a trial basis and seemed to upset him.

*3) We were all very tired and in a new situation with extra stress.
Todd's grandparents, whom we hadn't seen in a year, were visiting
us for a month. During their visit, Grandpa ended up in the
hospital. There had also been two recent deaths in our family.*

4) Todd had been biting me due to teething, and I had reacted strongly.

*Our solutions were to relax and try to nurse him as often as possible,
especially when he was sleeping. We also kept in close physical touch
by my carrying him around the house in his usual nursing position.*

*After we began to try these solutions, the strike continued one more
day (a total of four) and then nursing became easier. But it did take
time to get back to normal. We found during this transition time that
the swimming pool was perfect for relaxed nursing. Todd is a
swimmer and loves the water. It took another week, but thanks to La
Leche League and Linda, we're a happy nursing family once again.*

HOLIDAY WEANING

Another disruption in the normal course of breastfeeding that sometimes catches mothers by surprise is the "holiday weaning syndrome."
It occurs when holidays or other especially hectic times, such as moving, result in our getting so busy that we overlook our baby's needs. It's
easy to put off that nice quiet moment of nursing when there are so
many other demands on our time. In the midst of cooking, entertaining, shopping, and such, the leisurely closeness of the nursing relationship is temporarily or even permanently lost. Solids or bottles may be
tried to tide baby over, or perhaps he's "good" and consents to wait—
and wait—for nursing time to come around. And then suddenly, no one
knows quite how, baby is weaned. Toni Pepe from Connecticut
describes holiday weaning:

*A unique season in the private life of the baby has been cut short, and
later, in the long days at home, come the regrets. Guard against
holiday weaning. In the seasons of the world, these days of celebration
return again and again—but the special season of nursing comes only
once in the life of a child.*

CHAPTER 8

Breastfeeding and Working

If you plan to return to your job soon after your baby is born, you may be wondering if you should even consider breastfeeding your baby. By all means, you can look forward to being a nursing mother. Not only is breastfeeding possible, many working mothers consider it easier than bottle-feeding. Breastfeeding is a joy for both mother and baby. Usually, a quiet time with baby at the breast is the last thing on the agenda before mother goes off to work and the first thing she does when she returns home.

You may even be able to furnish your baby with all the milk he needs while you are gone. You may be thinking, "All right, but isn't breastfeeding difficult when a mother has to miss feedings?" It does take some extra effort, and it requires that you plan ahead, but isn't that true of most worthwhile things in life?

The Benefits of BREASTFEEDING

In many ways breastfeeding simplifies life with a baby. When at home there are no bottles to

Breastfeeding is worth the effort even if mother must return to work.

prepare, disruption of sleep can be minimized, and the one-on-one attention every baby needs is practically guaranteed despite the other demands of the household. The protection from illness that human milk provides is an advantage that is especially important to a working mother.

The breastfeeding relationship may be particularly precious to the mother who is regularly separated from her baby. The emotional closeness can contribute to the special bond between mother and baby, helping to compensate for their time apart. As one working mother said, "I love being able to make the shift from the workaday world to the world of family with the closeness of breastfeeding." Another mother added, "I wish I could tell all working mothers how much easier, special, and joyful it is to breastfeed. I am surprised to find that some people seem sorry for me and others think it is so courageous to do the perfectly natural thing."

Charlotte Lee Carrihill from New York works full time as a stock broker but she was able to breastfeed her son Colin and is now nursing her daughter Laura. She writes: "The bond that we have built through these nursing experiences will be with us always. Through breastfeeding, I have learned more about mothering. I have learned to put 'people before things.' Nursing isn't only a way to feed your baby; it's a way to comfort and love your baby, too."

Gale Pryor, co-author of the popular *Nursing Your Baby* and author of *Nursing Mother, Working Mother*, writes:

> *Looking back, I realize that continuing to breastfeed while working tied the two halves of my life together and helped me make sense of myself as a mother.*

SURVEY FINDINGS

To find out more specific information about how employment affects breastfeeding, Kathleen Auerbach, PhD, a lactation consultant, La Leche League Leader, and former editor of the *Journal of Human Lactation,* surveyed 567 married and single employed nursing mothers.

When these women's responses were tabulated, certain patterns emerged. Of the factors Dr. Auerbach analyzed, how soon after the baby's birth a mother returned to work seemed to have the most influence on the course of breastfeeding. This affected breastfeeding even more than the number of hours a week the mother worked. Mothers who rejoined the workforce when their babies were at least sixteen weeks old typically nursed longer than those who returned to work sooner. This may be because their milk supplies were solidly established and they had had more experience breastfeeding.

Whether the mothers worked full-time or part-time also affected how long breastfeeding continued. A greater percentage of the mothers working part-time nursed their babies for at least a year. The longer a mother waited to return to work and the fewer hours per day she worked, the longer she was likely to nurse.

Another variable that influenced the course of breastfeeding was whether or not the mothers expressed their milk when they missed a feeding. Eighty-six percent of the mothers surveyed expressed milk by hand or pump while they were away from their babies and forty-nine percent fed their babies only human milk until they were ready for solids at about six months. Mothers who chose to express their milk were more likely to nurse longer than those who did not.

Expressing milk offered five main advantages: 1) It helped keep up the mothers' milk supplies; 2) It provided human milk for their babies, lessening the risk of sensitizing them to allergies through formula; 3) It prevented or relieved uncomfortable fullness; 4) It minimized leaking; and 5) It helped prevent plugged ducts or breast infections, which may develop if the breasts remain overly full.

Pumping or expressing seemed to accomplish its purpose best when it was done every three hours or so. For the mother who was away from her baby for six hours, two pumping sessions were usually sufficient. If mother and baby were apart for eight to ten hours, three pumping sessions seemed to be needed.

When mothers experienced breastfeeding problems such as leaking, engorgement, and breast infections they were often able to solve them by expressing milk at work if they were not already doing so, or expressing their milk more often. Some mothers solved their problems by revising their priorities—making more time to be with their families and learning to leave work at the workplace.

When asked if they would combine breastfeeding and working with future babies, the responses were overwhelmingly in favor of breast-feeding. Eighty-two percent of the mothers said they would again choose to combine breastfeeding and working; eighteen percent said that with future children there was no doubt they would breastfeed, but they would make other choices regarding work, such as giving it up entirely, delaying their return until their children were older, or reducing their work hours.

Proceed SLOWLY

The length of time a mother is able to spend at home with her baby before returning to work is an important factor in assuring success at breastfeeding. Also, a mother and baby have a great need to be together in the early months. Once you hold your baby in your arms you'll probably decide you want to delay returning to your job for as long as you can so you and your baby can enjoy this precious time together.

Bargain for as long a maternity leave as you can possibly manage. If at all possible, arrange to be home at least six to eight weeks after your baby is born. One study found that women who returned to work before their babies were two months old had more breastfeeding problems and weaned earlier than women who returned to work later. Three months at home with your baby is better yet. If you can stretch the time to six months, you will probably have seen him to the time when he begins to take other foods. The longer you can stay home with your baby, the longer both of you will enjoy the benefits of being together.

Stretching your maternity leave may mean using vacation time or accumulated sick or personal leave. Sometimes this leave will be paid, other times it will be an unpaid leave with an understanding that your job will only be held for a certain number of weeks or months. Some companies are willing to add an unpaid leave of six months or so onto a standard maternity leave. Policies are changing as more and more people, both men and women, request provisions for extended leaves for a variety of reasons. It is worth your while to look into the company's past treatment of employees who have received personal time off for whatever reasons.

Mothers and babies need time to be together in the early days and weeks. This is a special season in the life of a child, a time when mother and baby establish a relationship meant to last a lifetime. Whatever your plans for the future months, take time now to nurture this new being.

In *The Baby Book*, Dr. William Sears discusses the importance of making the most of your maternity leave:

> *Don't dwell upon the day you will return to work, lest the preoccupation rob you of those precious weeks of connecting with your baby. During the weeks or months at home with baby, let your baby develop your nurturing skills. Enjoy the time spent with your baby as you let mutual giving bring out the best in both of you.*

Take the opportunity to enjoy the time you are able to spend at home with your baby.

DELAY INTRODUCING THE BOTTLE

Many mothers who are planning to return to work may be tempted to begin using bottles early "to get the baby used to them." But there are several reasons why this can bring a quick end to breastfeeding. If the bottles contain formula, this can interfere with a new mother's milk supply. The amount of milk a mother produces is determined by how often her baby nurses and how much her baby takes from the breast. Giving formula during the adjustment period sometimes short-circuits this "demand-and-supply" process, reducing the amount of milk produced.

Even if the mother pumps her own milk, giving bottles too soon can cause nipple confusion. Nursing at the breast requires more active participation from a baby than taking liquid from a bottle. If both breast and bottle are given during the impressionable early weeks, a baby may try to suck the breast as he sucks the artificial nipple. Babies who become nipple confused suck less efficiently at the breast and may not gain well or may refuse to nurse altogether. A pacifier sometimes produces this same effect. Once a baby is three to four weeks old and has had lots of practice nursing, nipple confusion is less of a problem.

Remember, too, that if baby does refuse the bottle, feedings can be given by cup or spoon until baby gets used to the change.

TRY WORKING "MOTHER HOURS"

When the time comes that you can no longer postpone making a decision about returning to work, try to begin with a part-time schedule. Returning to work for three days a week will be easier on you and your baby than five days a week. Being separated for just six hours a day can make it easier to continue breastfeeding than being gone for eight or nine hours a day. Keep an open mind about such options. If you have specialized skills or years of training, your employer may be willing to make adjustments rather than losing you entirely.

Some Practical HINTS

If you plan to combine breastfeeding and working, you'll want to learn how to pump or express your milk. The milk you collect while separated from your baby can be given to him the next day. Expressing your milk will continue to stimulate your milk supply and avoid overly full breasts. Some women are reluctant to ask their employers for time to pump during their work hours. Studies have shown that breastfeeding provides benefits to employers because working mothers who breastfeed have healthier babies and take less time off. Because of this, several large US corporations have begun corporate lactation programs.

SAVING YOUR MILK FOR YOUR BABY

No other milk or formula is as good for your baby as your own milk. Many mothers are able to provide enough milk to satisfy all their baby's needs while they are away. This involves knowing how to pump your milk as well as how to store it. You'll want to be sure your sitter is aware of how to handle the milk you leave for your baby.

New research has shown that human milk can safely be kept at room temperature (66 to 72 degrees F [19-22° C]) for up to ten hours because of its remarkable ability to retard the growth of bacteria. Milk can be kept refrigerated for eight days. For longer storage, it can be frozen. Frozen milk can be kept up to two weeks in the freezer compartment of your refrigerator, three to four months in a separate door freezer that is opened frequently. It can be kept six months or longer in a separate freezer that stays at a constant 0 degrees F (-19 degrees C). Once the milk is thawed, it cannot be refrozen; if the freezer defrosts for any reason, the milk must be discarded.

After pumping or expressing your milk into a clean container, transfer it into a glass or plastic storage container, baby bottle, or plastic milk storage bag. Use a separate container to refrigerate the milk each time you pump or express. These cooled batches can later be combined for a feeding or for freezing. You can add refrigerated milk to milk that is already frozen, just be sure the amount you are adding is smaller than the amount already frozen so it does not thaw the frozen milk. Allow room for expansion when filling containers for freezing. Do not tighten caps until milk is completely frozen.

Freeze the milk in small amounts varying from two to four ounces(60-120 ml.). There will be less waste this way as the sitter can choose the amount according to a baby's hunger or usual feeding pattern. Always label each container with the month, date, and year. If your milk will be used in a situation where more than one baby is being fed, you'll want to add baby's name on each container.

You can freeze your milk in either glass or plastic storage containers. Some mothers store their milk in plastic nurser bags designed for feeding babies. Freezing milk in these less-durable bags can be risky. It is a good idea to use them doubled to avoid tearing. Squeeze out the air at the top, roll down to one inch above the milk, fasten, and place the bag into a container which will hold it upright until it is frozen solid. These bottle liners are not recommended for long-term storage.

COLLECTING YOUR MILK

There are a number of inexpensive manual breast pumps available today, but many mothers find that hand-expressing their milk is easy and convenient. (See Chapter 7 for more information on pumping or hand-expressing your milk.)

Don't be discouraged if the amount of milk obtained is small at first. With practice many mothers are able to pump three or four ounces (90-120 ml.) in fifteen or twenty minutes. Some pumps allow you to pump both breasts at once which saves pumping time. It is normal for the amount to vary from one pumping session to the next.

Follow the manufacturer's directions in caring for any type of pump. Usually it is necessary to clean the parts carefully after each use and sterilize the pump occasionally. Talk to other mothers about the types of pump they find effective. LLL does not recommend the type of pump which requires squeezing a rubber bulb to draw out the milk, as the mother has little control over the amount of suction and these are usually not very effective.

WHEN AND WHERE TO PUMP

Some mothers start pumping and storing their milk ahead of the time they will be returning to work in order to have a reserve supply available. Others pump only while they are away and have enough for the baby's feedings on the following day. Some mothers pump once or twice a day in the morning or evening to be sure baby has enough to eat when they are gone. It is easy for some mothers to pump some milk after baby has nursed in the evening or early morning.

The number of times you'll need to pump or express your milk while you are away from home will depend on the total length of time you are away from the baby as well as baby's age. It's usually best not to go more than three or four hours without removing milk from your breasts. If you are leaving a very young baby who has been nursing more often, you may need to pump or express your milk more frequently at first so your breasts do not get uncomfortably full or start to leak.

If your breasts start to leak at an inopportune time, apply firm pressure directly on the nipple for a minute or two. This can be done discreetly by folding your arms across your breasts. You don't want to do this too often, though, as it is better to relieve the fullness by removing some milk. You can purchase nursing pads to wear inside your bra to absorb this leakage. After a while, your breasts will adjust to your new schedule and you will have fewer problems with leaking.

Finding a suitable location for pumping or expressing your milk will depend on each individual situation. You may be able to use a private office, an isolated storeroom, or the women's lounge. If you'll be using an electric pump you'll need access to an electrical outlet. You'll want someplace where you can relax and have some privacy. Some mothers find leaning over a sink helps avoid milk dripping on their clothes and makes use of gravity in removing the milk. Wearing two-piece outfits will make your pumping sessions easier.

As you prepare to pump or express your milk, think about your baby and visualize an outpouring of milk. It's a special gift that only you can give your baby.

If you prefer to keep your milk cool and no refrigerator is available where you work, you can use an insulated thermos or small cooler. Put ice into the thermos in the morning to get it cold, then pour out the ice and add your milk. You can keep ice packs in the cooler and add the containers of your milk throughout the day. You can also use one of these methods to keep your milk cool on your way home.

GIVING YOUR MILK TO THE BABY

Your milk can be given to the baby by spoon, cup, eyedropper, or bottle. You don't need to introduce the bottle in baby's first few weeks just because you'll be returning to work later on. Some babies refuse to take a bottle from mother when they know the breast is right nearby, but they soon become accustomed to taking a bottle from the sitter. Explain to the sitter that your baby may need some persuasion in learning to accept a bottle. Since you'll want the baby and the sitter to get to know each other before you actually return to work, these get-acquainted visits can be a good time for the sitter to get the baby used to taking a bottle.

The sitter needs to know that you plan to leave your own milk for the baby and what to do with it. Also be sure to emphasize that you do not want the baby given formula or other foods without your permission and that your baby should be held while he is being fed. Stress that you don't want your baby left to cry.

Mothers sometimes wonder how much milk they need to pump for each feeding they will miss. Breastfed babies normally take between two and four ounces (60-120 ml.) of milk eight to twelve times a day. No one can predict ahead of time how much milk an individual baby will take, but it is unlikely that a breastfed baby would consume an eight-ounce (240 ml.) bottle of human milk at one feeding. Storing your milk in two to four ounce (60-120 ml.) quantities allows the sitter to prepare just enough to satisfy your baby without wasting any milk.

OTHER SUPPLEMENTS

Mothers usually instruct the sitter to give only human milk if it is available. Any other supplement, if needed, should be prescribed by the baby's doctor. If your baby is older than three or four months, and seems to need more milk than you can pump, consider asking your doctor if you could start some mashed banana as a supplement instead of introducing formula.

Feeding Tips for the SITTER

Refrigerated human milk will separate as it is not homogenized. Shake gently to mix. If milk has been refrigerated in small batches, you can mix these together for a feeding. To warm the cold milk, hold it under warm running water for several minutes until it reaches room temperature or immerse the container of milk into a pan of water that has been heated on the stove. Do not heat the milk itself directly on the stove or in a microwave oven as valuable components of the milk can be destroyed if it gets too hot.

To thaw frozen milk, hold the container under cool running water and gradually add warmer water until milk is thawed and warmed to room temperature. If hot running water is not available, heat a pan of water on the stove and immerse the container of frozen milk into the warm water. If necessary, remove the container of milk and reheat the water. If more than one container is being thawed, you can combine the milk for a feeding.

An unopened container of human milk that has been frozen and thawed can safely be kept refrigerated for up to twenty-four hours. It is not known whether or not leftover milk should be discarded after baby has taken some of it from the bottle. Recent studies have shown that human milk actually retards the growth of bacteria so it may be safe to refrigerate unused milk for later use. Thawed milk should not be refrozen.

If baby seems hungry just before mother is due home, try to keep him satisfied with just a small amount of milk as mother will want to nurse the baby as soon as she arrives.

Be sure all bottles, nipples, cups, or spoons used to feed the baby are kept clean. Washing your hands is important before feeding the baby and after changing his diaper.

ENCOURAGING BABY TO TAKE A BOTTLE

Most babies take a bottle easily no matter when it is first introduced; others take a while to get used to a new way of feeding. Some ways that have worked to encourage a baby to take a bottle include:

- Try running warm water over the bottle nipple to bring it up to room temperature.
- Instead of pushing the bottle nipple into the baby's mouth, try tickling baby's lips with it and allow him to draw the nipple into his mouth.
- Try different types of nipples and different sizes of holes.
- Try feeding the bottle in different positions, such as, with baby sitting on the caregiver's lap, facing outward, or try feeding the baby while walking or swaying from side to side.
- Remember that baby can be fed in other ways. Try using a cup, spoon, or eyedropper if baby is reluctant to take a bottle.

Establish A ROUTINE

Time will be a most precious commodity in your life. When a woman combines mothering and working, she must be a miser with her time. Don't overlook the trusty baby carrier or sling to help you catch up with household work and keep the baby close to you. It has proved a blessing to all of us at times. And don't be surprised if your baby becomes something of a "night owl," wide awake, bright-eyed, and busy in the center of family activities during the evening hours. Some working mothers tell us that they deliberately encourage an up-at-night, down-during-the-day sleeping pattern for the baby. If the baby sleeps for longer periods while mother is away, he will need fewer feedings during the day and be more eager to nurse in the evenings.

Try setting your alarm for at least twenty minutes before you have to get up. Nurse the baby during this time (even if he's still half asleep) so that he's more likely to be contented while you dress and prepare for the day. Then nurse again just before you leave. It'll calm you both and make separation a bit smoother.

If you and your baby are separated for a considerable length of time, give special attention to your homecoming. Plan on sitting (or lying) down and nursing or playing with the baby for the first thirty minutes after

Usually baby enjoys one last nursing session before mother leaves for work.

you arrive home. Everyone will be more relaxed and dinner preparation won't be so chaotic. Plan ahead and keep nutritious snacks on hand for both you and the family.

Drink plenty of fluids and eat a nutritious diet of simple wholesome foods. Get most of your daily liquid in water or juice. The biggest problem mothers face is fatigue. This is especially true for employed breastfeeding mothers. Adequate rest will make life smoother and alleviate many problems.

Starting a new job, or even taking up where you left off in the old one, is very tiring for a new mother. One suggestion is to start back to work on a Thursday instead of a Monday so you'll have the weekend to recuperate before facing a full workweek.

Many working nursing mothers are able to nurse their babies full time on their days off or on weekends with no problem making the adjustment. If you have been pumping regularly while at work, your milk production will be about the same. (You can refrigerate or freeze the milk you pump on Friday for the sitter to give the baby on Monday.) Even if baby needs a supplement during your absence, frequent nursing on the weekend will supply him with plenty of milk, probably much more than you can remove by pumping. In this case, you may experience some fullness on Monday because of the increased stimulation over the weekend. It will make your pumping efforts easier.

A mother from Indiana, Leslie Koczan, tells this story of her experience as a working breastfeeding mother:

I knew that I had no choice but to return to work shortly after Laura's birth, although I would have dearly loved to stay home with her. I returned to work when Laura was only seven weeks old. She was so tiny and precious, and so very difficult to leave.

Our nursing relationship sustained us and strengthened our bond, despite the daily separation. For mothers who must work, I would strongly encourage breastfeeding. For me the major advantage was this: It was the one thing that I could do for my baby that the sitter could not do. It was a special bond between my baby and myself.

By seven weeks of age, Laura's need to nurse followed a fairly regular three-hour pattern. So, depending upon when she had last nursed in the morning, the sitter gave Laura a bottle of my milk about three hours later. I took my lunch hour to coincide with her next feeding and nursed her while eating my sack lunch. The sitter gave her another bottle three hours later, and I nursed her immediately after work. For each missed feeding, I pumped my breasts, I collected the milk in disposable bags, marked them with the amount and date, and stored them in a refrigerator at work. Each evening, I took the day's milk to the sitter's to be stored in her refrigerator or deep freeze until needed.

There were several important factors contributing to our success.

- *I found a sitter close to my workplace, so I could be with Laura each noon. This also gave us an extra hour together driving to and from work. My sitter, coincidentally, had been very active in LLL and therefore was very supportive of my nursing.*

- *Laura was given a bottle only by the sitter. No bottles were ever given at home.*

- *My job was sufficiently flexible to allow me time to pump twice a day and to take my lunch hour beginning anywhere from 11:00 AM to 2:00 PM. Knowing that the need to pump would end as Laura got older made it more acceptable to my supervisor. It also helped keep up my morale when I became tired of pumping. After about three months, I was pumping only once a day and in another month, not at all.*

- *I became active in my local LLL Group and its members were very supportive and encouraging.*

- *Last, but definitely not least, I had lots of help from my older daughter and husband, who fixed sack lunches every morning, started dinner in the evening, changed diapers, and entertained the baby.*

NIGHTTIME NURSING

Be prepared for more evening, nighttime, and early morning nursings. Bringing the baby to bed with you is a definite plus.

Lori Brewster, a mother of two from Michigan, found nighttime nursings very special. She and her husband worked opposite shifts in the automotive industry so one of them was home while the other was at work:

The first time I was pregnant, I was sure that I wanted to nurse. I breastfed Matthew for eight weeks but weaned him when I had to return to work. I found out later that weaning was not necessary.

When I was pregnant for the second time, I knew that I wanted to breastfeed once again. This time instead of just turning to books, I contacted my local La Leche League Leader. That turned out to be the best phone call of my family's life.

Since the birth of Amy Rose five months ago, she and I have nursed happily. I returned to work after eight short weeks of leave, but brought to work my breast pump and cooler. While I am at work, I pump my breasts three times a day. On Friday I freeze bottles for Monday. While at home, I nurse on demand and love it.

The nights are very special for Amy and me. People think I am crazy when I tell them she nurses four or five times during the night. They wonder how in the world I can survive. They do not understand that she sleeps right next to me. Nighttime is my favorite time of the day.

After breastfeeding Matt and then going to bottles, I knew that I did not want to do that again. Bottles are such a hassle. Now when I get home, I just have to clean my pump and a few bottles and I am done and have the rest of the evening for my family. If you have never breastfed, you can't appreciate the convenience. Take it from one who has done both, "breast is best."

I would encourage any mother to read all she can but also contact La Leche League for the support needed. If you are working full time, don't let that stop you from nursing your baby.

Who Will Take Care of the BABY?

The most important task you will face before you go back to work is finding the best person possible to care for your baby while you are gone. Can you arrange for a family member to take over this responsibility? The baby's father is an obvious first choice, if he is available. The element of change for the baby will be minimized. A loving grandmother or an aunt who is already familiar to the baby are also high on the list of choices. A motherly neighbor may be interested in caring for your little one during the day.

Most people, though, are not fortunate enough to have a family member or friendly neighbor available as a caregiver and must look further. They must then concern themselves with references and interviews. If the caregiver is new to the baby, by all means have her come to your home or visit hers a few times with the baby so the two of them can get acquainted before you begin working. Be sure to tell her that you are breastfeeding and explain in detail how you want the baby fed, what his likes and dislikes are, what his sleeping pattern is, and, most important, the fact that you do not want your baby to be left to cry. Let her observe your interaction with the baby so she can see how he is accustomed to being handled. And you can watch how the caregiver and the baby relate to one another to be sure she is the right person to care for your baby.

Think about finding a caregiver who lives close to your place of work rather than close to where you live. This would make it possible for you to visit the baby at lunch time or have the caregiver bring the baby to you.

When choosing a caregiver, look for someone who will give your baby as nearly as possible the same single-minded devotion and care that you give him yourself—someone who knows babies—who understands their needs. Will she sing to him? Talk to him? Rock him gently to sleep? Keep him dry and comfortable and always close by?

Constancy in nurturing is the means by which a child learns to trust others. A baby needs a loving, nurturing person, and this person should be the same someone, not an often changing parade of new faces and personalities. While a working mother naturally hopes to find such a reliable, loving substitute, she should also be aware that over a period of time, her baby will inevitably grow to love this "other mother."

You must also face the possibility that the patient, kind caregiver you have this morning may announce at nightfall that she is moving away or taking another job. Such a disruption can be a serious loss for a young child.

Because of the unpredictability of finding and keeping a private caregiver, working mothers may consider a day-care center as a solution. While there is a degree of permanence in using a day-care center, day-care workers may come and go. And while the decorations may be charming, chil-

Continuing to breastfeed after mother returns to work helps to compensate for the time spent apart.

dren under the age of three may not adjust well to a group situation. A young child was not meant to compete for attention with a large number of children of similar ages. Often a child will enjoy short play sessions in a preschool setting, but all-day care may become a threatening situation. Group care in a day-care center falls far short of meeting a baby's or toddler's needs to relate to one person, to count on one person for loving attention at any time. The chances of illness and infection are also considerably greater when children are in a group setting. If your child is in a day-care setting, providing your milk will help to protect him from such illnesses.

In the *New York Times Magazine*, Sally E. Shaywitz, MD, had this to say about mother substitutes:

> *We do not know enough about nurturing to be able to tell mothers that if they find a person or an institution that meets such-and-such standards that this will be an adequate mother substitute. We can list people's credentials, pinpoint the standards for a day-care center, but just as human milk cannot be duplicated, neither can a mother. We cannot put mothering into a formula and come up with a person who has the special feeling for your child that you do.... Just as everyone but a mother is excluded from nursing a baby, so they are also excluded from those immense feelings of satisfaction and inner unity with the child.*

COPING WITH THE SEPARATION

For many mothers, separation from the baby turns out to be the hardest part of returning to work. Lisa Bicknell Casey of Oklahoma tells what happened to her:

I was allowed only two short months off after Jason was born. I spent most of those two months recovering from his cesarean birth. It seemed I was no sooner on my feet being the kind of mother I wanted to be, when it came time to return to work.

After contacting my LLL Leader, I purchased a breast pump, and the week before I went back to work, I dutifully pumped my breasts. It seemed so slow and awkward. I doubted I could ever pump enough to feed my beautiful boy. Thank goodness it got easier.

That first week of work I cried every day after leaving Jason at the sitter's, but I was blessed with an excellent sitter whom Jason took to immediately. This only upset me more. After all, every day I was replaced by a bottle and a sitter. Would my baby need me?

Things proceeded well in spite of my fears. Then one day the sitter had to give Jason almost eighteen ounces of my milk. I was ready to give up. How could I possibly keep up with his demand? Fortunately, this only happened once. Before long Jason had adjusted his nursing so he was taking only eight to ten ounces during the day and nursing frequently at night. I did not hesitate to take Jason in bed with us from the start, so I slept through many feedings and was never really sure just how frequently he nursed at night.

Jason refuses his bottle if he knows I am around, which reinforces my confidence as a mother. I know now that my baby does need me. Jason and I are able to share this kind of physical closeness that working might have denied us. For a mother who reluctantly returned to work, breastfeeding has been a godsend.

A mother who plans to combine breastfeeding and working would do well to find the time to attend La Leche League meetings. Breastfeeding mothers who are separated from their babies regularly need the important support that comes from being with other nursing mothers. Your baby is welcome at LLL meetings.

Is it all worth it? Would it be easier to give up breastfeeding if you plan to return to your job? One working mother who had bottle-fed a previous baby and is now breastfeeding puts it this way. "Breastfeeding simplifies many things for me, plus it helps to ensure that when I am home, I am spending time with my children." Another mother says: "My child benefited both physically and emotionally from the time we spent as a nursing couple!" And many others add: "I didn't want my baby to miss out on the benefits of breastfeeding just because I had to return to work."

CHAPTER 9

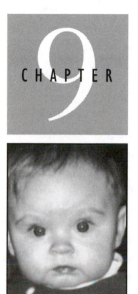

Making
a Choice

Choosing whether or not to work
outside your home after your
baby is born is a complex decision. You'll want to take your
time and evaluate your options
before you reach a conclusion.
Author Kaye Lowman talks
about making this choice in her
popular book, OF CRADLES AND
CAREERS:

> *A woman today is able to
> choose to be single or
> married, to pursue a
> career or to stay at home,
> to raise a family or to
> remain childless, to
> combine motherhood with
> a career or to make raising
> her children a full-time
> commitment.*

> *But make no mistake: the
> availability of so many
> options is a mixed
> blessing....Implicit in the
> freedom to choose is the
> obligation to choose wisely.*

I realize that the economic necessities of life often force us to do things differently than we would like. But when it comes to child raising, I am convinced that a woman should make every possible effort to spend the first three years with her child. It does make a tremendous difference.

Dr. Joyce Brothers
Psychologist

The Mother-Child RELATIONSHIP

There are many important factors to be considered when you make the decision about returning to work after your baby is born. Let's take a look first at the mother-child relationship. This subject has fascinated the scientific community for a long time. A child's early years hold the clues to his future behavior as an adult. Society stands to gain or lose, depending on the soundness of mother-baby attachment.

La Leche League is strongly committed to the belief that babies and mothers need to be together in the early years. We are convinced that a baby's need for his mother's loving presence is as basic as his need for food. Mary Ann Cahill, one of La Leche League's co-Founders, writes:

> *No one can replace you as mother. From all evidence, from all that is known about how babies grow and learn to live and to be competent adults, it can be said that a mother is the one most perfectly suited to be nurturer in the early years.*

Scientists hold that a child's initial one-to-one relationship with his mother is the foundation for emotional growth. From the security of the baby's ties to his mother he learns to relate to others. "The only true basis for the relationship of a child to mother and father, to other children, and eventually to society," Dr. W. Winnicott, a pediatrician from Great Britain, says, "is the first successful relationship between mother and baby."

SEPARATION BRINGS ANXIETY

In her book *Oneness and Separateness*, Dr. Louise Kaplan, psychologist and Director of the Mother-Infant Research Nursery of New York University, explains that an infant does not have an identity of his own at birth. Based on her work in mother-infant research, Dr. Kaplan states, "From the

Before the baby is born a mother cannot know how strongly attached she will be to her baby.

infant's point of view, there are no boundaries between himself and mother. They are one." The child must negotiate the move from oneness with his mother into separateness and a sense of individuality. It is a second birth that unfolds gradually in the first three years of life. Maintaining the early mother-baby relationship is extremely important to the successful completion of this journey.

And Selma Fraiberg, a professor of child psychoanalysis who wrote *Every Child's Birthright: In Defense of Mothering*, states her views very emphatically:

> *It has been determined that children who do not have the benefit of a single, sustained contact with a loving mother or mother-figure for at least the first three years of their lives, will—depending upon the degree of deprivation—manifest a diminished capacity to love others, impaired intellectual powers, and an inability to control their impulses, particularly in the area of aggression.*

Donna K. Kontos, PhD, a consultant psychologist from Canada, comments, "There is at present no known substitute for a family environment for childrearing....Prolonged maternal separations cause distress to the child. All the research and all of the literature tell us that the best thing for an infant is to have a consistent good mother around most of the time."

The young child who is separated from his mother exhibits all of the classic symptoms of grief. He may cry unconsolably or withdraw into unnatural quietness. Regarding this separation anxiety, Humberto Nagera, Professor of Psychiatry at the University of Montana, points out:

When the child is confronted with the mother's absence his automatic response is an anxiety state that on many occasions reaches overwhelming proportions. Repeated traumas of this type in especially susceptible children will not fail to have serious consequences for their later development.... No other animal species will subject their infants to experiences that they are not endowed to cope with, except the human animal.

STAYING AT HOME—FOR NOW

How does a mother reconcile her own need for a healthy sense of self-esteem, achievement, and self-confidence with the needs of her baby? Many young women today are opting to put their careers "on hold" when the baby arrives. They see motherhood as a special season in their lives, one that they do not want to miss. The working world will still be there two or three, five or ten years from now. Stay-at-home mothers of young children often see themselves resuming their working careers once their children are older. They view the time at home as a short period, "a sliver of time" when gauged against the many years that they can, and probably will, work outside the home.

Mary Ann Kerwin, one of LLL's co-Founders, is a good example of this. After spending more than twenty years as a mother at home, deeply involved in caring for her large family, she found there was still "plenty of time for another career." Mary Ann began attending law school when her youngest child started high school. She adds:

Our children teach us much more than we realize. Being a mother taught me patience, perseverance, self-discipline, and hard work. After coping for twenty-four hours a day with children, no task seemed too hard.

Judy Kahrl of Ohio appreciates the fact that it takes courage for a woman to stand in the face of society's pressure and say, "At this time in my life, and with this new person as my responsibility, I am going to use my resources of time and physical and emotional energy in the most effective way possible for the nurturing of that new life."

DOES IT PAY TO WORK?

Perhaps you would like to stay home with your baby, but you can't see how your family can manage without your paycheck. Home is where your heart is, but a job is where the money is—or is it?

Many women discover that it is not realistic to think of one's take-home pay as "pure profit." Often the costs involved in working are overlooked. Some quick calculations of expenses versus income yield surprising results. There is the cost of a working wardrobe and transportation expenses getting to and from work each day. When you spend the day on the job, you probably prepare more convenience foods or eat out more often. And then there's the cost of child care. Sit down and estimate how much money these things add up to and subtract this amount from your income. You may very well find that there will be little net gain if you continue to work after the baby arrives.

When tallying up the funds that will be available to you if you stay home, consider the likelihood that you may drop into a lower tax bracket (in the United States) after you stop working. The tax savings alone may be substantial. Many mothers find that it doesn't "pay" for them to work outside the home.

Some mothers find a way to work from home so they can be with their babies.

EARNING EXTRA MONEY

What if your family's financial situation is such that you feel you absolutely have to bring in some extra income? Happily more and more mothers have been able to combine working and keeping their babies with them.

Many kinds of work can be done just as well at home, so you might be able to interest your employer in having you do part-time work at home, coming into the office just for planning or meetings. With computers, modems, faxes, and email, this kind of flexibility in the working world is becoming more available to families.

If you have a computer, get in touch with several different companies or secretarial services about free-lance computer work from home, or run an ad in the newspaper. If you have a specialty like art, writing, photography, or public relations, you can develop a free-lance clientele and work out of your home. Giving music lessons is another good option. Or, if you are a teacher, contact local schools about tutoring in your home. Taking care of other mothers' children is another way to bring in extra income.

Another possibility is to take baby along with you to your job. Given the right circumstances, an increasing number of women find that mothering the baby is compatible with their jobs. They may not spend as much time in the office as they would if they left the baby behind, but the bottom line compares favorably to full-time work and paying for child care.

A mother from Mississippi, Melissa McLain, tells about her work situation: "When Megan was three months old, I returned to work. Luckily we have a family-owned business. My parents, brothers, and my husband, John, all work there, so it seemed only natural to take Megan along. We just work mornings. We don't always get a lot of work done, but everyone has fun." And Debi Drecksler from Florida adds, "I've been able to take my children along with me whenever I needed to work outside the home. My most recent job was a Youth Director. I ran a day camp, and, during the school year, an after-school enrichment program."

Jo Montgomery, from Washington, tells how she found a way to stay at home after her baby was born:

Elizabeth was born on leap year day. I had planned on returning to work full time when she was three months old. By the time she was six weeks old, we had developed a solid nursing relationship. When I investigated day-care options, I became depressed. I felt cheated at the thought of leaving my precious baby.

I talked to my husband about my feelings. He was very supportive, and we both decided that I wouldn't return to work in June. I told my employer that I thought I might possibly return in September, but I couldn't make any promises.

I had been working in the graphics field for six years, so I entertained the idea of putting my skills to work for myself at home. On July 1st I started my own business retailing wedding and baby announcements. Through referrals, my business has blossomed to include some commercial accounts, too.

Taking your business home won't work for everyone, but it's worth thinking about. I am so glad I have gotten to know my daughter, Elizabeth, "full time."

In the practical context of mothering a young child day after day, of changing and feeding him, returning his smiles, applauding his efforts to reach a toy, distracting him at times, or consoling him when tears appear, the mothers we have talked to make no distinction between the quantity and quality of time they spend with their babies. Mary Ann Kerwin, a co-Founder of La Leche League, has observed, "Babies need quantities of quality time."

Take One Step at a TIME

If you are awaiting the arrival of your baby, you are probably thinking about what you should tell your employer regarding your future plans. From experience, many mothers insist: "Do not make any commitments before your baby is born." If at all possible, keep your options open.

You do not want the specter hanging over your head of having to return to a job by a certain date because of an agreement you made while still pregnant. Most businesses offer a maternity leave, and will hold your job for you for a specified period of time after the baby is born. By all means take advantage of whatever leave is available to you, and give yourself that time to assess how you will feel about leaving your baby. For someone to expect you to promise away your future and that of your baby before you even have a chance to meet is tantamount to signing a blank check— no, it is worse.

I really didn't know what to expect of motherhood or how I would feel, and it's hard to describe the feelings that flowed through me those first few days, weeks, and months of my daughter's life. I was needed by this tiny person; I knew I could not leave her with someone else, no matter how loving.

Shirley Callanan
Utah, USA

EXPLORING OPTIONS

In OF CRADLES AND CAREERS, Kaye Lowman explores many aspects that are available to women who refuse to make an "all-or-nothing choice" between their careers and their families. Her book includes stories of women who have "reshaped the workplace in order to make it more responsive to their need to work and their desire to have a family." She goes on to explain:

> *Whether a woman's need to work is financial, social, or emotional, the desire to be a parent may be equally strong....The career woman today understands her baby's need for her and the importance of being a meaningful part of her baby's life. And she realizes how much she herself will lose if she misses out on the opportunity to mother her own children....Careers can be put on hold; babies grow up and are gone. It was a wise and thoughtful Mother Nature who brought babies into the world needing to be breastfed and cared for, reminding us that mother and baby are very much a unit for many months after birth and that they need to be together. To try to ignore or circumvent this physical and psychological need is to tamper with one of the most fundamental and basic elements of human nature.*

Some women make one decision before their babies are born and find their attitudes change once they become mothers. Such was the case with Joy Cohen of New York:

> *I have worked with children for eleven years: as an early childhood teacher, as a teacher and therapist in a therapeutic nursery, and as a psychotherapist caring for seriously disturbed children and their families.*

> *When I was pregnant, I believed that I would be ready to resume my part-time psychotherapy practice after three or four months. I couldn't have known then the power and intensity of my baby's and my need for each other. I wanted to give myself totally to this new and wonderful adventure called mothering. Slowly but surely I did just that.*

> *Those first few months passed quickly, and I began to feel pressure to resume my practice. The children and families with whom I had been working were anxious to continue. My friends and family encouraged me not to give up my career.*

My own cultural stereotype of the woman who can easily manage family and career during her children's early years was being challenged. The only stimulation I felt I needed was the stimulation of my baby nursing at my breast. I wanted to savor every minute of my new life and this delicately unfolding new relationship. I felt a crisis of the heart upon me.

Fortunately, I did not have to work for economic reasons, and my husband said that he had confidence in me and that he would be supportive of any decision that I made.

I had previously arranged to have my mother care for Michael during my sessions. When I told her that I didn't want to go back to work and felt the baby strongly needed me, she told me that I was making a big mistake. I was pained that my mother couldn't be as supportive as I would have liked, but if I have learned anything from helping people know their feelings, it was to acknowledge and trust my own.

After much soul-searching, I decided to stop working with my clients. The separations were difficult and sad for everyone. I tried hard to stay connected to my own heart and knew that what was best for me would ultimately be best for all concerned. When I knew I would no longer have to be away from Michael, I breathed a long, deep sigh of relief. The internal and external work had been difficult, but as I nestled in to nurse my baby with the knowledge that I would not have to be away from him until we were both ready, I knew that it had been necessary work from which I had grown deeply as a mother and as a person. I knew that I had made absolutely the right decision.

For some mothers, even working part-time interferes with their ability to mother their child. Elizabeth Golestaani, from Iran, is one such mother:

Until recently, I had always thought part-time work—say two hours three times a week—was the ideal for the mother of a small child. Add to this the great demand for my English-teaching skills here in Iran, and I was under a lot of pressure to return to work. So I did—and what a mistake. It took me a long time to accept the fact that I'm not Superwoman and that in my case working even part-time is too much. I kept thinking that soon I would get more organized or my toddler, Sa'id, would need me less, and then all would be well.

The idea of "giving up my career" was so scary! I kept wrestling with my thoughts and emotions. Then I received the January-February issue of NEW BEGINNINGS. In it, I read an article by a mother who had been in exactly the same situation. She wrote about how important it is for one to acknowledge and trust one's feelings, and that helped me enormously.

I was finally able to decide to do what I believed was right for me, which was to stop accepting teaching commitments while I have a small child. I still had to finish out the university semester, but just having made the decision changed my attitude so much.

After just two days, I realized my feelings and behavior towards Sa'id had changed. I was less irritable, more loving, and the angry scoldings were replaced by hugs and listening and eye contact. Life seemed so good again.

I hadn't realized my teaching had such a bad effect on my mothering until my decision to stop. It was hard telling everybody "no more," but I kept reminding myself "Sa'id first." For me, staying home allows me to be the kind of mother I want to be.

Choosing to Stay HOME

"Becoming a mother is unlike almost any other experience, and it is impossible for a woman to know beforehand how deeply the experience will affect her. Until your baby is born and in your arms, nursing at your breast, you cannot know what it means to have a child, and then to leave a child." These words reflect the thoughts and emotions of mothers who have decided to stay at home full-time while their children are small.

One mother, Pat Smith from Pennsylvania, was faced with a difficult choice during pregnancy:

Of course I would return to work after having our baby! This was a foregone conclusion during the several years my husband, Skip, and I tried to conceive a child. We had rarely, if ever, considered otherwise, because the reasons for my continuing to work were so compelling: finances, lifestyles, careers.

In many ways we followed the young suburban working couple lifestyle. As happy consumers, we weren't quite ready to relinquish some of our material well-being. Among our peers, a mother's right to work after childbirth wasn't questioned.

Then there was the matter of careers. I had a promising future with a fine corporation owned by the major stock exchanges. In fact, I was due for a promotion into middle management that would mean relocation to New York at the company's expense.

Five months into my pregnancy, the New York promotion offer came, and it proved to be the undoing of my finances, career, and lifestyle. The offer was a fork in the road, because it brought into focus the commitment the new job demanded. Although the rewards were positively tantalizing, it didn't take me long to realize that I'd have little time or energy left for anything but part-time mothering if I were to pursue this career path.

Did I want to be a future vice-president of this corporation, or did I want to be a full-time mother? This was the question I had to answer once I accepted the premise that I couldn't be both. As I considered the question, images of the baby started invading my thoughts. They were fleeting, fragmented images at first, but when the images formed this scenario, I stopped cold: I saw myself wrapping the baby in blankets, taking him to the babysitter's house, holding him in my arms, then handing him over to someone else for the day. I knew right then and there that I would not go back to work after he was born.

For me, this was an irrational way to make a decision. I had a list of every rational reason to work, and at one single thought—separation from my little one—I tossed the list right out the window. I resolved that I would do whatever was necessary to stay home with the baby.

Colin was born three years ago, and we have been almost inseparable ever since. In retrospect, my worries at the time seem trivial now. After all, we now own a home in a friendly, family-oriented town, a car, and all the comforts we really need. A real worry, as I see it now, is how I would ever had made it through a working day without my baby.

My ex-boss called me about a year ago and offered me my old job. I was delighted to decline. I told him I wouldn't even consider it.

A SENSE OF WORTH

The value of good parenting is never denied, but all too often it is unsung. Jobs in the marketplace have a highly visible rating system; usually, the higher the pay, the greater the prestige. The at-home mother has only one title, and there are no periodic raises telling her that she is doing a good job. But the rewards are there, right in the family, though they are much more subtle. A California mother, Emily Holt, discovered unexpected enjoyment in mothering. She reflects on the changes in her life that came with the birth of her baby. "I sit holding our five-month-old daughter, who is nursing so sweetly at my breast. I watch my husband's face light up with joy as she grabs his beard, laughing aloud. Oh yes, my job was wonderful as jobs go, but in these five short months, I have seen myself grow in a hundred ways, reaching for what is best in me to greet this beautiful new life. Sharing every delightful moment of Sarah's discovery of our world, I realize how blessed I am to be a mother."

Carolyn Keiler Paul of New York doesn't think she's wasting her time by staying home with her children. She says "I think it's time we stop apologizing for being 'just a mother.' Childrearing is not a menial job. It calls for all our talents and resources. My college education isn't going to waste, because it has enriched me so that I may in turn enrich the lives of my children."

A MAJOR INVESTMENT

Other mothers' stories can be inspiring and informative, but no one else can tell you what is the best course of action for you and your family. We can tell you about a baby's needs, we can tell you what works best to ensure successful breastfeeding, we can tell you how mothers have combined breastfeeding and working. And we can tell you about mothers who have discovered unexpected personal growth and fulfillment in staying home. But only you can make the decision that best reflects your own family's needs.

We encourage you to learn as much as you can, explore all the options that are available to you, and discuss these questions with others who have been faced with similar decisions and choices.

Attending La Leche League meetings can be a helpful source of information and encouragement. Talking with other mothers who are in situations similar to your own can reinforce the choices you make. Whether you are an employed or at-home mother, you can look to La Leche League for support in breastfeeding your baby. We will not hesitate to answer your questions, delight in your progress, and stand by you in your decision to breastfeed whether or not you return to work.

Mothers who stay home to care for their babies need support and encouragement from other at-home mothers.

Be as cautious in your decision-making about returning to work as you would be with a major investment—the investment here is a critical period in your life and that of your baby. The early months and years set the course for the rest of your child's life, and they can never be recaptured. And as Dr. Marilyn Bonham, a psychiatrist who wrote *The Laughter and Tears of Children*, reminds us, "The outflow of (a mother's) love and affection for the very young child is pure gold in the bank."

PART FOUR | *Life as a Family*

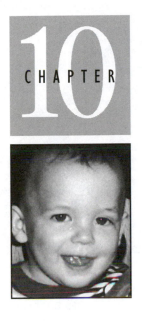

CHAPTER 10

The Manly Art of Fathering

A father's unique relationship with his baby is an important element in the child's development from early infancy. From our experience, we know without a doubt that breastfeeding is enhanced and the nursing couple sustained by the loving support, help, and companionship of the baby's father.

Nowadays, men no longer fit the stereotyped image of the father in the waiting room of the hospital, pacing the floor, while his wife delivers their baby surrounded by strangers. A father today is more often next to his wife during childbirth, supporting her and sharing the unforgettable emotions of this event. From the moment of birth, father and baby begin to get acquainted. The more a man can participate in the birth of his son or daughter, the more powerful and meaningful it will be. Just ask a new father who was at the birth of his child and be prepared to listen!

The metamorphosis that makes a man a father does not happen overnight. He usually acquires the title "father" much more quickly than he captures

Fathers find special ways to develop a loving relationship with their babies.

the spirit of fathering. In fact, men can't even count on the natural assistance of hormones that aid the mother. It has been said that when a baby is born, so is a mother. Fathers emerge more gradually.

Sue LaLeike, from Florida, tells how father and daughter developed a special relationship:

> There is no way a father can take over a mother's role or vice versa—breastfeeding sees to that. But a nursing mother needs the baby's father to do his part by giving love to them both. The baby may not experience the closeness of nursing with Dad, but going for walks in the front-pack carrier, laughter and nuzzlings, the family bed, and even burping and diapering can all contribute to very intimate relationships at a very early age. Charlie's role has been important since our baby's conception. He has helped all along— he didn't wait. He caught and prepared fresh Rocky Mountain trout for me in the first weeks of pregnancy. He supported my views on birthing and nursing. He read and discussed and went with me to doctor's appointments and birthing classes. And then he held and cradled our beautiful daughter moments after her birth in a way that made me know that he was the only person in the world I trusted her with.
>
> He made all the first moves, and it sure does show in the way our daughter cries, "Daddy—home—happy!" when she hears him opening the gate at the end of our driveway.

Fathers Get INVOLVED

While more and more men are recognizing that breastfeeding is the natural and ideal way to feed the baby, some first-time fathers don't realize how much they can be involved during the breastfeeding period.

After birth, the intimate relationship between mother and baby continues. They are still a unit, and for some time mother will be the baby's sole source of nourishment. In language that is irrefutable, biology makes it clear that the mother-baby relationship is primary and should not be set aside. This relationship is unique and the prototype of all other relationships throughout life. A father's contribution is equally important, but it is different. Babies thrive on both.

Chris Phillips, from New Jersey, describes one way a father can spend time with his child:

> *Although mothers do indeed have a hormonal head start on developing their intuition, I believe that fathers also have natural nurturing abilities, and, if given the opportunity to develop these abilities, fathers can indeed participate in the care and comforting of their babies.*
>
> **Dr. William Sears**
> **Pediatrician, Author**

A lot of new nursing mothers seem to worry that Daddy will feel left out if he can't help feed the new baby. Not so! Actually, I think just the opposite is true. The lack of bottles seems to encourage a father to become more active in other areas of an infant's care and upbringing. My husband, Ronny, took on the job (or should I say joy?) of bathing our firstborn son, Nicholas, starting with his very first bath.

Everything went smoothly until Nicholas was about five months old and began to outgrow the kitchen sink. We discovered that bending over the tub was too much of a back strain for Ronny. He missed his special time with Nicholas. Thankfully, we came across a solution when someone told me about her husband taking their kids in the shower with him. What a terrific idea! It had never occurred to me that a baby would enjoy a shower, but why not? Nicholas had always loved the water; we would give it a try.

That was over a year ago and Nicholas still loves the shower. Of course, there are a few adjustments to make when showering with a baby, but all in all, bathtime became a joy again and Ronny enjoys being an important part of his baby's life.

In BECOMING A FATHER, a book written especially for dads, Dr. Sears encourages them to get involved with their children:

Speaking as one father to another, let me share a secret with you: Babies are fun, kids are a joy, and fatherhood is the only profession where you're guaranteed that the more effort you put into it the more enjoyment you will get out of it.

Some fathers take a while to grow into a nurturing relationship with their baby. Sally Thomas from Wisconsin writes about the changes as her husband developed more interest in their son:

During my pregnancy, Eric, my husband, had surprised me with his interest and delight in my diet, exercise, and our growing baby. He was so supportive and interested in making our birth the kind of experience we wanted.

However, after we got home with our son, Eric didn't seem as involved. He'd hold Joseph only with my prompting and only for a very short time. He kept saying "He doesn't do anything."

When Joseph was a couple of weeks old I was talking to a friend about my concerns, and she told me that her husband had had a hard time relating to a tiny baby, too. She suggested I let Eric blossom as a father in whatever way that he felt comfortable.

As the months went by and Joseph became more alert, Eric began to take more and more of an interest in his son. When Joseph became mobile and learned to like roughhousing, there was no holding Eric back. Soon Joseph seemed to prefer his daddy, and his face would light up at Eric's appearance.

I am thankful every day for our now fourteen-month-old toddler and his wonderful and supportive father. And I love to watch my two favorite fellows playing as Eric—the tough-guy father—leans over and whispers in Joseph's ears, "I love you so much. What would we ever do without you?"

Fathers and BREASTFEEDING

Of all the sources of encouragement a woman may receive in breastfeeding, the support of her baby's father is the most meaningful to her. But for some women, support from the baby's father is not easy to come by. Perhaps a mother is a single parent and she is alone with her

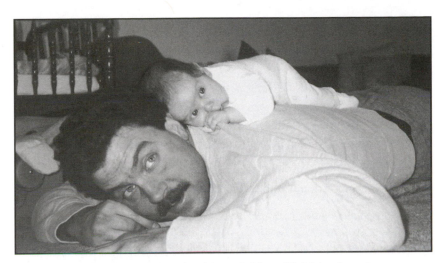

The father of a breastfed baby doesn't have to be left out of his baby's early months.

baby. She may need to look for support from friends or relatives. Or it may be that a married woman has a husband who is uncomfortable with the idea of his wife breastfeeding. A mother who faces these situations can still have a satisfying breastfeeding experience.

Sometimes a father who has misgivings before the baby was born learns to accept breastfeeding as he sees his baby thrive on mother's milk. A mother's enthusiasm for breastfeeding often sparks a father's interest. A father who is hesitant can only begin to support your decision to nurse the baby if he understands what it means to you.

Dr. Sears encourages fathers to support their wife's decision to breastfeed. He writes:

I am absolutely convinced of the superiority of human milk for human babies. I want to convey to new fathers a feeling from the bottom of my heart: Do everything within your power to encourage and support the healthy breastfeeding relationship between your wife and your baby. Breastfeeding is a lifestyle, not just a method of feeding. Providing understanding and support for the breastfeeding pair is one of the most valuable investments you can make in the future health and well-being of your family.

Men are sometimes surprised at the intensity of their reaction to seeing their wives breastfeed their babies. Archie Smith, a father from Texas, recalls his first impression:

Before becoming an expectant father, I had never given much thought to breastfeeding. When my wife, Sheri, asked me what I thought about it, without hesitation I said I thought it was a good idea. It seemed to be the natural way. We talked more about it, and Sheri was eager to try breastfeeding.

After Angie was born the nurse handed her to Sheri and she began to nurse. Standing a few feet away I could feel the emotions flowing from one to another. Then seeing the smile of satisfaction on my wife's face, I knew we were a family. It was an experience I will long remember.

And another father, Dean Cook, also from Texas, adds his thoughts:

Before our baby was born, my wife, Kathy, and I discussed breastfeeding, and we agreed our baby would be breastfed for at least six months, preferably as long as he needed it. I have long felt that there is no better way to nurture a child. However, I soon discovered after reading the materials that Kathy brought home from her LLL meetings that I knew only a few of the benefits of breastfeeding. And after gaining some experience as an active father of a nursing baby, I became amazed at my own intense emotional involvement with nursing.

What Can Fathers DO?

Though mother is the only one who can nurse the baby, there are a number of things that no one else can do quite as well as a loving father. Have you ever watched a mother try to soothe a fussy baby by nursing and rocking and patting, and just about everything else she can think of, and then watched in amazement as the baby's father lifts the little one out of her arms, hoists him onto his shoulder, and promptly puts the baby to sleep! It is a trade secret known only to fathers; we don't know if it's the broad shoulders, the large, strong hands, or the deep baritone voice that does the trick. But no matter—we know that it works, and clever nursing mothers are the first to take advantage of it.

Babies are often their fussiest late in the day, mother is tired after a full day of baby care, and perhaps there is the added pressure of hungry children awaiting dinner. When dad arrives home, even though he may have had a hard day at work, he can often approach the baby in a more relaxed way than mother can at that point. Many fathers take advantage of this to establish their own special relationship with their babies.

In BECOMING A FATHER, Dr. Sears describes a special form of baby-soothing that only works for dads—he calls it "the neck nestle." Dad puts baby in a sling or baby carrier on his chest and lifts him up a bit so baby's head nestles under dad's chin. Dr. Sears explains:

The "neck nestle" is a unique way for fathers to comfort babies.

In the neck nestle, father has a slight edge over mother. Babies hear not only through their ears, but also through the vibration of their skull bones. By placing baby's skull against your voice box in the front of your neck and humming or singing to your baby, the slower, more easily felt vibrations of the lower-pitched male voice will often lull baby right to sleep. An added attraction of the neck nestle is that baby feels the warm air from your nose on his scalp. Experienced mothers have long known that sometimes just breathing onto their babies' faces or heads will calm them. They call this "magic breath." My children have enjoyed the neck nestle more than any of the other holding positions.

What do fathers most enjoy doing with their babies? There are probably almost as many answers as there are fathers, but over the years we have observed that fathers seem to have a special gift for playing with even very young babies. While mother is often preoccupied with cuddling and feeding, father is likely to tickle baby under his chin, hoist him into the air, or bounce him on his knee. A caution may be needed about shaking a baby as this can be harmful, but movement and exercise are important to the baby's overall development. Babies thrive when provided with both gentle nurturing and lively activity. As Louise Kaplan, PhD, explains in her book *Oneness and Separateness,* "Fathers have a special excitement about them that babies find intriguing.... Fathers embody a delicious mixture of familiarity and novelty."

Fathers need to spend time with their babies in order to get to know them better and get "tuned in" to their needs. Watch for cues that baby is ready for some fathering interaction. A hungry baby won't be at all interested in playing. But once baby has nursed his fill, dad can take over the burping, diaper-changing, singing, rocking, and cud-

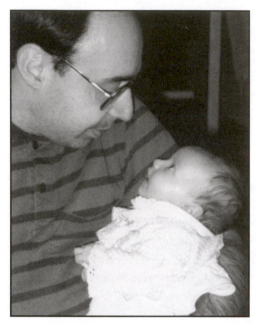

Even young babies respond to a father's deep voice and gentle touch.

dling. Some fathers enjoy bathing the baby—or bathing with the baby, soaking together in a warm tub. A gentle massage can be another form of interaction between father and infant and don't overlook the sling or baby carrier. It's not just for mothers.

Learning about the usual stages of a baby's development in the first year can help a father enjoy his baby more. It's important for him to know when his son or daughter is ready to play peek-a-boo, when to expect reaching and grasping, and when to encourage crawling and climbing. A father can play an important role in these stages of development and proudly watch his child's growth and advancement. Another book by Dr. William Sears, GROWING TOGETHER: A PARENT'S GUIDE TO BABY'S FIRST YEAR, explains baby's stages of growth and development. See the Appendix for details.

Husband and Wife—A PARENTING TEAM

A husband and wife are a parenting team—each has an important and unique contribution to make to their child's development. They need to trust each other, respect each other's unique role, and help each other in times of stress. The most important thing you and your husband can do for your baby is to love one another.

The fact is that babies both expand horizons and rock boats. Your marriage will never again be the same. But it can be even more loving and it need never be dull. The silver and gold of future anniversaries are waiting. A prerequisite to attaining that treasure is putting your heads together now to chart your course.

There's a need to talk through the feelings that come with any important junction in life. We have referred to the emotions that a new mother often experiences, and it is just as reasonable to expect the father to react emotionally to his new responsibilities. A father and pediatrician, Jerald Davitz of California, tells fathers: "A very difficult feeling that most fathers have shortly after the new baby arrives home from the hospital is the unsettling sensation, 'Am I sure this is really what I want?' or 'Things were better before.' You need to understand you've got some reason to feel jealous and threatened at first, but these feelings will soon go away."

COMMUNICATE YOUR FEELINGS

While talking with other young mothers, Martha Hartzell of Georgia found that communication between husband and wife about what is important to each can go a long way toward improving their relationship.

Mothers often find themselves totally immersed in nurturing and caring for their tiny baby. Some women have described their feelings about having a newborn as "like falling in love all over again." As one mother recalled, "I found everything about her endlessly exciting and fascinating. I could hardly think about anything else. My feelings were so intense for several weeks that there seemed to be little room in my life for anything else."

Such a new and powerful emotion could well upset the equilibrium in a marriage. A husband may find himself feeling like a jilted lover and, to make matters worse, his wife is too preoccupied with the baby to even notice!

It helps to remember that today's intense involvement will become tomorrow's comfortable, easygoing relationship. A baby must be loved and cared for in order to survive, and this initial intensity between mother and baby is designed to assure that the baby's needs will be met. With plenty of time, and ongoing communication about their needs and feelings, mother, father, and baby will eventually settle into a new relationship that is comfortable and satisfying for all three of them.

First-time parents are often preoccupied with their new responsibilities. Both husband and wife are putting out a tremendous effort. They must be careful not to let their concentration on these new responsibilities isolate them from each other.

Psychiatrist Lucy Waletzky of Georgetown University, Washington, DC, found that husbands often experience some jealousy because of the closeness of the nursing mother and baby. She advises: "Effective communication between husband and wife should be encouraged before, during, and after birth." Motherhood and fatherhood are new roles that need to be talked over and learned together. Time spent together during the first few weeks after the baby's birth can add a new dimension to a husband and wife's love for each other.

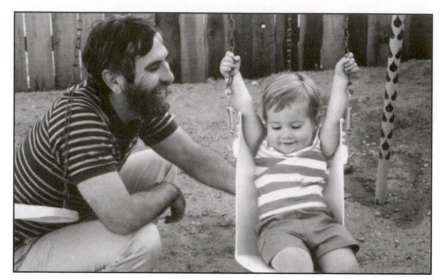

Fathers and little ones have great times together.

THE REWARDS ARE GREAT

Being a parent is not easy, but it can be extremely rewarding. Dr. David Stewart, father of five from Missouri, has this to say:

Parenting is not easy. It can try us to the point of frustration. But this frustration can be productive because it is the symptom of growth and expansion. I sometimes think that nature gives us children to force us to grow up ourselves....

Parenting is the greatest opportunity we normally receive to make good in this world. Your job may be important. Your volunteer activities may be important. But few of us do anything so important as to make much difference in society a hundred years from now. But the way you treat your children will matter a hundred years from now. The attitudes you pass on to them will be passed on to their children, who will pass them on to theirs....

Parenthood works in two directions: good parenting makes for happy children; but it also makes for happy, fulfilled parents. It is not possible to give happiness without receiving it.

Men seldom have the opportunity to get together and share their ideas about being fathers. This can be just as important for them as it is for mothers. La Leche League Groups are not just for mothers—activities are often scheduled when fathers can get together and compare notes about their role. Couples' Meetings and Area Conferences provide these opportunities. In some local areas, fathers are invited to attend regular LLL Group Meetings. Check with your La Leche League Leader for details.

The book we've quoted throughout this chapter, BECOMING A FATHER, by William Sears, MD is also a source of encouragement for fathers. Copies are available from La Leche League Groups and La Leche League International. See the Appendix.

To quote David Stewart, "Ever uncertain, ever unreliable, ever unpredictable—most of life's offerings are fickle. Fatherhood is forever."

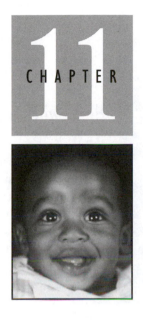

CHAPTER 11

Meeting Family Needs

Throughout this book we talk about a mother meeting her baby's needs as though she and her baby were alone on a desert island. In reality, there are probably other family members whose needs must be met as well as household tasks that somehow must be accomplished. Faced with these responsibilities, you may be wondering just how you can keep things running smoothly while breastfeeding and caring for a newborn.

Over the years, La Leche League mothers have developed some techniques and tips that may help you. A basic recommendation is to always put people before things. Meeting the needs of family members should always come before immaculate housekeeping or caring for material possessions. Along with this, you'll want to remember that your family's priorities may not be the same as those of your next door neighbor or your favorite cousin (who doesn't have any children). Other people's standards or values may not be the ones that work out best for you and your family. Babies are small for such a short time. It

Breastfeeding gives you one arm free to hug an older child.

would be a shame to waste those precious months trying to please others instead of enjoying your baby and meeting his needs.

Housework and a NEW BABY

Top household efficiency and a new baby mix about as well as oil and water. Meeting baby's unscheduled needs makes a strict household schedule pretty much a thing of the past. This is not to say that a well-ordered life automatically becomes chaos at the moment of birth, but it is fair warning that you may want to reorganize your approach to household chores.

The key to survival is to simplify. Pick an afternoon to take a walking tour of your home, critically examining each room for items that should be removed, rearranged, or discarded. Do you hate to see the knickknacks on the bookshelf covered with dust? Then put them away and replace them with a fresh new plant that will brighten both the room and your spirits. How about that overstuffed closet where everything from ski gear to broken lamp shades seems to end up? If you take the time to clean it out while you are pregnant, it won't get on your nerves later. Discard the things that are beyond repair or that you no longer need—don't just move them somewhere else or they will soon be in your way again. Box up the things you want to keep and store in the attic or basement.

Whatever the season, do as much "spring cleaning" as you can before the baby is born. Light household chores are good exercise, and having them done will be a godsend later when you'll want to devote your time and energy to the baby. This sudden zeal for cleaning and readying the house so often felt by mothers during the last months of pregnancy is referred to as the "nesting instinct."

Give some thought to rearranging your cleaning supplies so that they are readily accessible (but stored in a high, child-proof cupboard). You'll want your supplies to be handy so you can quickly clean a bathroom mirror or scour a sink if you have a moment before stepping into your shower or while keeping an eye on a three-year-old in the tub. Your bathroom will be clean in minutes following bathtime if you quickly wipe a mirror (already fogged), take a swipe over the sink and counter, and wipe up the water on the floor with a large towel, one that was already consigned to the laundry hamper.

In households where there is a baby, housework is nearly always done in quick snatches—a series of mini-cleaning sprints. Five to ten minutes at full speed in the kitchen, devoted to whatever is most both-ersome to you—perhaps the breakfast dishes on the table or the grubby floor in front of the sink or refrigerator—will improve the looks of the house and give you a sense of accomplishment. Throughout the day, center your attention on what you have accomplished, beginning with the all-important work of nurturing your baby, rather than dwelling on the tasks that still need doing.

Make your bed or not, as it pleases you. Plumping up the pillows and tossing the covers back to air is a time-honored custom. Without a spread in place, you'll probably lie down to nurse the baby more often during the day. Keeping up with the dishes is about as easy as keeping up with the Joneses. If baby is not agreeable to having you do the whole job when the meal is over, fill the sink with hot soapy water and let everything soak until you can get back to it later on or the next morning. If you have a dishwasher, reload it during those times when baby is wakeful and wants to be held in your arms or snug-gled in his baby carrier. Babies usually love the con-stant up-and-down and back-and-forth motions that accompany the loading and unloading process. Don't rush it. Some babies are soothed by the sound of running water. And many a fussy baby has fallen asleep in a baby carrier while his mother vacuums.

Little people and clut-ter seem to be inseparable. But clutter can be picked

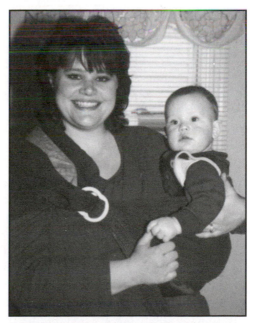

Using a sling or baby carrier keeps baby close while mother gets some basic housekeeping done.

up and put out of sight quickly if you are equipped with a clutter-catcher—a cardboard box or other suitable container to carry with you as you whiz through each room depositing all the odds and ends that have been scattered about. This system enables you to de-clutter an entire house in fifteen minutes or so. The contents of the box can be sorted later when you have more time, but for now the house looks fairly straightened, and a visitor will be able to walk in the door without fear of skidding on a stray truck. Concentrate on immediately putting away the especially important items such as car keys, which will drive you frantic when misplaced. Always putting your keys on a handy hook just inside the door could be one of the best habits you could get into. For safeguarding other small, valuable items picked up around the house during the day, the pockets in your jeans or an apron are indispensable.

Early in the morning, perhaps while you're relaxing with your baby for an after-breakfast nursing, make a list of the "must do" tasks for that day. Further refine your choices by selecting one, or possibly two, of the most important. Box off these top-priority items and plan on getting to them at the first opportunity, before you get caught up in another project or just the everyday chores. If it's something you can't do until later in the day, set your alarm clock or oven timer to ring at the appropriate time. Getting just one "top-priority" item crossed off your list every day will give you a feeling of accomplishment no matter how many things are left undone. Beware of going all out for cleaning, cooking, and scrubbing whenever the baby is taking a nap. Give some of that time to the other children, take a nap yourself, or relax with a project you enjoy.

MEAL PLANNING

When there is a new baby in your life, mastering the art of advance meal preparation is as vital as knowing how to relax in a rocking chair. Many women prepare double recipes of stews, casseroles, spaghetti sauce, chili, and the like during the last weeks of pregnancy and put the extra portions in the freezer. We've heard of thoughtful friends giving the mother-to-be a "casserole shower," presenting her with meals which they have prepared and frozen in disposable pans, complete with instructions for cooking or reheating. And the lovely practice of bringing a meal to the new baby's family has certainly not lost its appeal.

After the baby arrives, let simplicity in menu-planning be your watchword. Make a list of your favorite one-step, no-fuss meals and be sure to keep the necessary ingredients on hand. A dessert or snack of fresh fruit is always quick and nutritious.

If you don't already have a slow cooker or crock pot, put it at the top of your list for the next gift-giving occasion. These marvelous cookers allow you to prepare your meat, potatoes, and vegetables at any convenient time during the day, and it's all ready to eat at suppertime with no fuss or bother when you're tired and the baby is most likely to need your undivided attention. If you have a microwave oven, foods can be prepared quickly or cooked ahead of time and reheated when everyone is ready to eat. An inexpensive item that is helpful for a mother whose attention is often distracted from cooking is a metal plate that fits between a cooking pot and the stove burner and keeps the food from burning.

For help in meal planning, you will find many ideas in La Leche League's cookbooks, WHOLE FOODS FOR THE WHOLE FAMILY and WHOLE FOODS FROM THE WHOLE WORLD. Both are collections of mother-tested recipes with an emphasis on good nutrition and easy preparation. For details, see the Appendix.

One last thought on meal preparation: Now is the time to reinforce safety rules! When using the stove, turn in the handles of all pans so the children cannot grab them. Even babies still in their mothers' arms can reach surprisingly far. Keep knives and other sharp utensils where children cannot reach them.

POWER SNACKS

Nursing mothers should eat at regular intervals, and active children also need to eat often. To keep young temperaments soothed and tummies satisfied until mealtime, consider introducing salad snacks. Simply assemble an assortment of fresh, raw vegetables and fruits. (Note that raw carrots and nuts should not be given to toddlers because small chunks can be aspirated instead of swallowed.) Preschoolers can be happily occupied in the preparations by washing and tearing greens, pulling the strings from celery stalks, breaking the cauliflower or broccoli florets, shining the apples, and arranging them all on a platter. Prepare these early in the day and keep in the refrigerator for quick munching later on. The addition of cheese, slices of hard-cooked eggs, or strips of cooked meat will add protein and staying power.

Sitting down for a few minutes for a snack is a positive measure to divert youngsters when they're tired and hungry and perhaps getting irritable. You can create a happy atmosphere with music—a favorite recording, or better yet, a sing-along with mom. The songs from your childhood are fresh and dear to your children and can become a part of their heritage.

LAUNDRY

We are all amazed at how much laundry a new baby can generate and how quickly laundry stacks up once a baby joins the family. Before the baby arrives, try to be sure that all of you have the most ample supply of clothing that your budget will permit, particularly underwear and socks, so that you won't have to do laundry every day or two. Another item mothers like to stock up on is a dozen or more lightweight, inexpensive washcloths ("seconds") that often come packaged in bundles. They're handy for all kinds of mop-ups and since they are thinner than regular washcloths, they are convenient to use when washing behind delicate, small ears and in the creases of chunky arms and legs.

Eventually the laundry has to be done, of course, and your own approach undoubtedly will depend on the kind of facilities available to you. Whether you depend on the neighborhood laundromat or have your own equipment, enlist your husband's help. If your husband isn't already familiar with the intricacies of a washer and dryer, the hour is at hand for him to learn! When you are doing the laundry, you can use a sling or baby carrier to good advantage. Whether it involves trips to the laundromat or doing the laundry right at home, baby will be held and comforted, and you'll get clean clothes!

Consider using two to three inexpensive plastic buckets to soak clothing that might stain. Then you can run it through the washer at a time that is convenient. Some system of pre-sorting laundry is a great help, too. As a container fills, you can quickly see when you have a load of white or colored items, and you can drop them into the washer as time permits.

Your toddler will love to be in on the action of transferring laundry from the dryer to the basket and then helping sort the clothes. Long ago, many of us decided that a considerable amount of laundry is just as serviceable when left unfolded. Undergarments, in particular, can be sorted—tops and bottoms—and put away in a drawer, in plastic bins, or on a shelf. Clean socks can be sorted into two baskets—one for white and the other for colors—and the older members of the family can each match their own pairs.

If you're in the habit of ironing some things, now would be the time to give it a second thought. Try the ten-minute test. Wear an ironed piece of clothing for ten minutes and notice how it takes on a more lived-in, rumpled look before too long. The same item, left as it is straight from the dryer or line, often "shakes out" or folds smooth, and looks just as good after a ten-minute wearing. You'll wonder if it's worth the time and energy (your own and the electrical power) to take to the ironing board.

As you make plans for keeping up with the laundry, concentrate on ways to lessen it. To start, you may find that the large bath towels that are used for drying when jumping out of the tub can be recycled if they're spread out and hung to dry instead of bunched on a small towel rack. A towel can be fastened around a towel bar with a large safety pin or gripper snaps, so children can use it to dry their hands without having it end up on the floor and then inevitably in the hamper.

Popular speakers at one of La Leche League's Conferences were Peggy Jones and Pam Young, authors of the book, *Side-Tracked Home Executives*. They explained how they developed a system of organizing household tasks in order to accomplish necessary chores in the shortest amount of time. You might find their suggestions helpful. Other books are also available that can help you get your household organized.

SAFETY TIPS

As you try to get some housework done or care for your other little ones, there will be times when you need a safe place to put the baby. The safest place for the baby is on a small rug or blanket on the floor. He can stretch and kick and look around to his heart's content.

Never leave your baby unattended in an infant seat on a table or counter. An active baby can easily scoot the seat across the smooth surface until, crash! baby and seat are on the floor. A changing table can also be dangerous. Fasten your young baby securely or take him with you if you go for a forgotten item or to answer the phone or door. In just a few seconds, the baby who supposedly does not roll over can fall and be seriously injured.

A word of warning is in order, too, regarding walkers. Too many babies have fallen down the stairs in them. A walker also restricts the baby and denies him the opportunity to naturally develop the coordination of arms, legs, and eyes that comes with crawling. Safer and more comfortable for the baby is a type of infant seat that rests on the floor and has a cloth back and seat on a slightly springy, metal-tubing frame.

Most mothers do not find playpens useful or necessary. By the time baby can crawl, he wants and needs his freedom to explore. A high chair can be a convenience when baby is older and ready to be eating solid foods, but a high chair can also be dangerous. Be sure the one you select has a wide base to prevent tipping over as well as a safety strap to ensure that baby can't climb or fall out. Fasten the safety strap faithfully—it takes only a few seconds.

Time for the OTHER LITTLE ONES

You will find that generous portions of love and reassurance will go a long way toward helping your older child, the ex-baby, accept the demands that the new baby is making on your time. When the baby is fussy you can remind an older child, "Mary, when you were little and hungry, I always asked Elizabeth to be patient and wait because you needed to be fed (or rocked, or held, or whatever)." The child loves the idea of once having been the "star," and it's a happy thought that can be reinforced with a hug. When feeding the baby, a nursing mother usually has an arm free for quick hugs or other important tasks.

There's peace of mind in keeping your older child near you when you're nursing the baby, rather than having him off somewhere on his own. A popular suggestion is to arrange a nursing corner that accommodates at least three—mother, baby, and an older brother or sister. Have an extra chair or stool next to your rocker, with some interesting play items nearby. Change the assortment regularly; surprises are always fun. One creative mom, Marge Bazemore of Georgia, added a small table for a work surface, and she and son Russ enjoy a variety of activities while the baby nurses. Marge describes their favorite choices:

- *A cassette tape recorder. It's easy to operate and Russ enjoys hearing his voice as well as Phil's cooing.*

- *Simple puzzles.*

- *Playdough. I also keep a cookie cutter handy.*

- *Finger puppets.*

- *Crayons, paper, pencil, and coloring book.*

- *Pegboard. I made one out of a piece of ceiling board and used golf tees for the pegs.*

- *Viewmaster and slides.*

- *Books and family photo albums.*

- *Spools and a cord for stringing.*

From time to time, sit on the floor while nursing. You'll be at eye level with your toddler, and the whole floor is the play area. It's great for building with blocks or rolling a soft ball. This is especially helpful when the ex-baby is looking for extra attention. Jealousy toward the new baby often shows up when the baby is three or six months old, if it hasn't happened sooner.

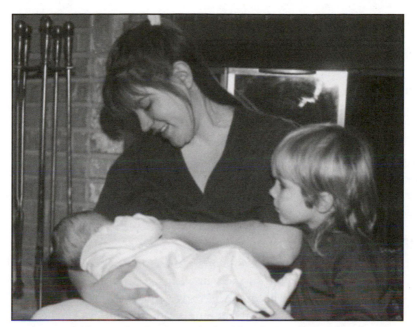

Toddlers are safest when they are close by while mother is nursing the baby.

The mother who is expecting her second child sometimes finds it hard to imagine that she will feel as close to the new baby as she does to the little one who is already here. Can there be the same strong love the second time around? The miracle of mother love is that it increases with each new birth. It is not diminished, not limited. It is not a pie that must be sliced into smaller pieces to accommodate extra plates at the table. With the new baby comes a resurgence of love for all of the family.

LITTLE HELPERS

Toddlers love to help, and clever mothers find lots of things for their little ones to help with. If you use nonbreakable dishes, your little one may enjoy setting the table, carrying one item at a time from the stack of dishes set out. Young ones never tire of the repetition of walking back and forth, especially when a smile and "thank you" accompany each dish that is delivered to the table. Shining the glass in a low window that has been sprayed with cleaner (or plain water) is another enjoyable pastime for budding artisans (a task that is often signed by the young polisher pressing a small nose against the pane!).

Many toddlers seem to be fascinated with a hand brush or whisk broom and dustpan, so put yours to work under the kitchen table or some other open area. Old mittens and socks make great dusting mitts for little hands. If mother helps, too, even children who are barely walking will learn to put toys back in the toy box when it's time to clean up.

Preschoolers need lots of stimulating learning activities to keep them happy and out of mischief. A wonderful resource book is PLAYFUL LEARNING, by Anne Engelhardt and Cheryl Sullivan. Written for parents who want to organize an at-home preschool for their little ones, it can also be used on an individual basis. Craft projects, simple recipes, music and number activities, story-telling, and reading readiness are all included. The information about a preschooler's development can help you better understand your child's needs. For details, see the Appendix.

DADS CAN HELP

An understanding husband is one of a nursing mother's most treasured assets. He can step in to provide you with a welcome respite when he is home, and your older children will thrive on the extra attention.

Dads are often masters at keeping toddler minds and hands busy when mother needs some time alone with the baby, or when she decides to take advantage of baby's nap time for a relaxing bath or some much needed rest. Father and toddler will both enjoy some toddler-size roughhousing, and who but daddy can add such excitement to stories by putting in all those low, rumbling noises?

Fathers and their little ones often develop a new and very special relationship when a new baby joins the family. Let your husband know how much he is needed and appreciated, encourage him to spend some extra time with your toddler or preschooler, and be prepared to watch the two of them become the best of friends.

OLDER CHILDREN

If you have older children, you're also probably wondering, "How can I possibly have enough time for them after the new baby arrives?" You ask if there won't be times when an older child will want your attention, and the baby will also need you. More than likely there will be, and this is when—and how—the mutual love and understanding that cement good human relationships are fostered. Learning to consider the needs of someone who is helpless before one's own needs is a valuable lesson for the older children. It is something that you will want to help them understand as much as you can.

In discussions about the arrival of the new member of the family, ask your older children to help you think of ways of managing and helping each other. Encourage them to remember that the new baby will be

Older children can be a great asset when a new baby arrives.

the only member of the family who is completely dependent on you—just as they were at that age. When thought of in this way, it's easier for a young person to recognize (if not always accept) that baby's needs must certainly come first.

The period before your new baby arrives is an excellent time to teach the older ones some new household skills. Select chores that match each one's ability and continue to work along with your child whenever possible. The children will learn from you, and humdrum chores, such as doing the dishes, can be transformed into special moments for sharing youthful hopes and problems. Children do not make appointments with their parents to talk over their deeply felt concerns. Such sharing takes place in the context of normal activities, during times when parent's and child's hands are busy, but their minds and hearts are in touch with each other.

Don't be surprised if your young helpers are less than enthusiastic at times. That's normal. Pour on the praise and be patient with your apprentice. We all need to feel needed, and children benefit from knowing that the family is depending on them to carry out their assigned jobs. We parents overlook a golden opportunity if we don't help our children learn to accept responsibility and to enjoy the self-esteem that comes with being expected to do a job and doing it well.

School-age youngsters in the family are generally very accepting of a new baby. They enjoy babies, and vice versa. Potential problems usually come from a variety of outside activities in which this age group is often involved and which demand a parent's participation. These often include driving to and from games or lessons, attending programs, or working together on special projects. Such a pace can be hectic for a mother who also has a new baby.

You will have to be realistic and firm in setting limits for the time being. Do only those extras that you and the baby can honestly manage. Your husband can be a big help here, spending extra time with the older children's activities whenever possible. If a particular program is very special to an older child, and neither you nor your husband can participate, be assertive in asking another parent to help you. For instance, a friend or neighbor could drive to and from functions for a few weeks; you can reciprocate later.

If you will be driving with the baby along, an infant auto safety seat is a must. If you use it faithfully, beginning with baby's first ride (possibly the trip home from the hospital), you and your baby will soon accept the procedure as a matter of course. The safest place in the car for baby or toddler is the back seat. Plan to nurse the baby before starting out in the car, so you and baby will be more relaxed. If baby does need to nurse before you arrive at your destination, pull over in a safe location and tend to his needs. What better excuse could you have for being late?

When it comes to getting your husband and older children off to work or school on time, advance planning can save the day. Betty Wagner, one of the LLL co-Founders, managed by setting her alarm for about twenty minutes earlier than usual. Still resting in bed, she'd reset the clock for the regular time and nurse the baby. When she had to get breakfast and help the older children, she at least knew the baby would not be hungry in the midst of the morning rush.

You will be proud of your older children as they grow to understand the helplessness of the baby and accept the sacrifices they are asked to make. It has been gratifying to many of us to find that a crying baby is almost always disturbing to older children. They sense that something is not right, and they are happy again only when baby is happy. Looking ahead, you'll find that cheerfully putting the needs of the baby first, as a matter of course, is an example of caring for others that benefits everyone. It's a good way to educate your children for their future roles as loving parents.

Developing a PARENTING STYLE

Parents find themselves making many decisions as their children grow and family needs change. We all grow up with some idea of what it means to be a parent and raise children. Perhaps we were brought up in a loving, caring family and we choose our own parents as role models when we have children. Or possibly, our childhood was not a happy one and we want to offer a more secure environment to our children.

Either way you'll want to make an effort to learn as much as you can about parenting, child care, meeting children's needs, and child development. You'll find books listed in the Appendix that offer practical information on these topics. Also, discussing these matters with other parents with values and concerns similar to your own can prove invaluable. La Leche League Groups offer this opportunity. Although the basic meeting topics are related to breastfeeding and young babies, additional topics are often discussed at Couples' Nights, Chapter Meetings, or informal get-togethers that are planned.

La Leche League Area and International Conferences offer further opportunities to expand your understanding of parenthood. Check with your local La Leche League Leader or LLLI for details of upcoming events you may be interested in attending.

CHAPTER 12

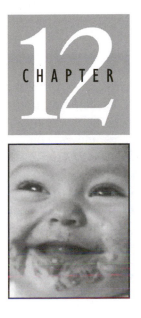

Nutritional Know-How

If you already have good eating habits, there is no reason for you to make any major changes while you are breastfeeding. On the other hand, if you know that your eating habits need improvement, pregnancy and breastfeeding are good incentives to do this. Your baby's development during pregnancy depends to a great extent on good nutrition; your own health and well-being are also at stake. Your investment in your baby's welfare should provide strong motivation that will make it easier for you to change your eating habits.

Your baby will get off to a fine start on your milk. You will want him to build on this good start by giving him healthful foods when he is ready for them and by teaching him nutritionally sound eating habits that will become lifelong practices. The best way to accomplish this is by being a family in which everyone has good eating habits.

In this chapter, we include some general principles of food selection to help you learn how to choose the foods you and your family need to maintain good health. We urge you to pursue this topic further, reading other books on good nutrition and keeping up-to-date on current dietary recommendations from knowledgeable sources.

La Leche League's basic approach to good nutrition is to recommend eating a well-balanced and varied diet of foods in as close to their natural state as possible. With few exceptions, the more a food is processed the more nutrients are lost. To help you prepare tasty and nutritious meals for your family, La Leche League publishes two cookbooks that include mother-tested recipes and tips on good nutrition. WHOLE FOODS FOR THE WHOLE FAMILY is a complete cookbook that can be used by beginning cooks as well as experienced family chefs. The recipes use only whole unprocessed foods with minimal amounts of salt and sweeteners. WHOLE FOODS FROM THE WHOLE WORLD is a collection of family-tested recipes from La Leche League families all over the world. Both cookbooks are available from La Leche League Groups and La Leche League International. WHOLE FOODS FOR THE WHOLE FAMILY is also available in bookstores. See the Appendix for details.

The Basic APPROACH

Some of the following suggestions have come from Dr. Herbert Ratner whose sensible approach to good nutrition is based on selecting foods in proper balance in order to meet all of our nutritional needs. He suggests the following:

- Eat a variety of foods,
- Eat a variety of animals and plants,
- Eat a variety of the parts of animals and plants.

People instinctively seek a variety of styles and colors to decorate their homes and their bodies. The inner body also thrives on a diversity of foods with a wide range of flavors, colors, even textures—chewy, soft, firm, juicy, crisp. All the different textures, colors, and flavors of food reflect different food elements and values needed for the body.

In selecting foods, don't concentrate on four-legged animals, like the cow, to the exclusion of two-legged animals; or land animals to the exclusion of water animals. In fact, don't limit yourself to animal sources of protein. When you think "main dish" think also of beans and other legumes (lentils, peanuts), nuts, seeds, and grains. Many wonderful traditional recipes feature these healthful foods, either by themselves or combined with small amounts of meat or cheese. Your family—and your food budget—will benefit.

In the plant kingdom, don't restrict yourself to the tried-and-true vegetables and fruits. Besides green vegetables look for orange and yellow vegetables—squashes, sweet potatoes or yams, varieties of peppers. There are different parts of plants, too, that are edible. The parts don't have to belong to the same plant. There are leaves, including greens that go into a salad, as well as Swiss chard, collards, beet greens, kale, and cabbage. There are roots, like carrots, beets, yams, turnips, and onions. There are stems and tubers, including asparagus and potatoes, and the fruits of a plant, such as corn, beans, and tomatoes, as well as apples, oranges, grapes, bananas, and melons.

Fats are needed in the cooking and preparation of some foods and they supply us with energy. There are animal fats and vegetable fats, solid fats and liquid fats, saturated fats and unsaturated fats. Animal fats include butter, cream, lard, and chicken fat. Vegetable fats include margarine and vegetable oils. Research has linked high-fat diets to heart disease and other ills, and nutritionists tell us that many people today consume too much fat in their daily diets. Some fats are better for health than others. Any fat that is solid at room temperature (butter, margarine, vegetable shortening) should be eaten in moderation. Olive oil and fish oils from certain fish (tuna, salmon, whitefish) are better for you and will add variety and flavor to your family's diet. Safflower oil, canola oil, and soybean oil also contain the kind of fats that are important for your health.

You can lower the fat content of your favorite ground beef recipes by substituting ground turkey for all or most of the ground beef. When seasonings and other ingredients are added, there is little difference in appearance or taste. Another way to cut back on animal fat is to decrease the amount of foods you eat that come from animals and to rely more on plant sources for protein.

VARY YOUR MEALS

As you plan your family's meals, you'll want to provide a variety of foods. You can respect your own likes and dislikes as long as your dislikes aren't too numerous and as long as you do not impose your likes and dislikes on the rest of the family. After all, you don't want your children to grow up with restricted eating habits.

If there is a particular food you or other members of your family dislike, there is always a substitute. Cheese and yogurt are good substitutes for milk. Eggs are a good alternative to meat and fish, as are combinations of whole grains, nuts, dried peas, beans, and lentils. This demonstrates one rule of nature. There are so many different kinds of foods that every culture in every age on every continent has had a varied selection of foodstuffs available to eat. This has resulted in a wondrous variety of national cuisines. Modern transportation and mechanization make possible a varied selection of foods throughout the

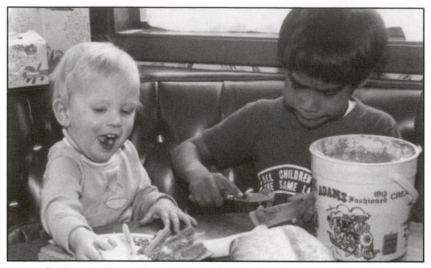

Creative approaches to wholesome foods make them more appealing to everyone in the family.

year by sharing the productive seasons and rich bounty of other parts of the world with all of us.

EAT NATURAL FOODS

Generally speaking, the further one gets away from the natural state of food, the less nutritional value the food is left with. Fresh foods are usually better than frozen and frozen foods are preferable to canned. Since cooking is one step removed from the natural state, some foods are better raw than cooked. This is especially true of fruits and vegetables, with a few exceptions. For example, vitamin A is more available in cooked carrots. Most protein foods need to be cooked. Under-cooked foods, with due allowance for digestibility, are better than over-cooked foods. The stir-fry method permits food to be cooked quickly and to retain many of the nutrients and flavor found in uncooked foods.

By partaking of the many digestible parts of the living whole, and by concentrating on natural foods, you will get all of the known nutrients in proper and natural proportions. You will get all of the essential nutrients that have been discovered by science, and you should get those that have yet to be discovered; not only the vitamins and minerals of today, but the vitamins and minerals and other nutritional factors still undiscovered. If you eat a wide variety of foods daily, you don't need to worry about taking vitamins and other supplements. This approach to nutrition is more economical, and doesn't require a science course. It will protect you against ill health and at the same time supply you with a variety of choices to please everyone in your family.

WHAT TO AVOID

Chemical additives. The fewer the additives the better! Civilization, although it has brought much progress, has also created some real problems in nutrition. In common use today in the food industry are a large number of chemicals that are added to enhance color or prolong shelf life. Much more study needs to be done to determine just how safe these chemicals are. In the meantime, since some of the chemicals have not been properly tested and their safety is uncertain, it seems wisest to avoid them. Read the labels on bottles, cans, and packages and choose those items that have the fewest artificial flavors, colors, and preservatives. Better still, whenever possible, prepare your own food from the freshest products available.

Sugar. One of the chief offenders in confusing our appetites is sugar. Used excessively it can dull the palate for the delicate flavors of fresh, natural food. Sugar can be easily misused and is especially bad for infants and young children, primarily because it satisfies hunger and displaces healthful, natural food. Sugar is obvious in many desserts, candies, and soft drinks. But there is also an amazing amount of "hidden" sugar found in many other commonly used packaged and/or bottled foods. It is very important to your good health that you acquire the habit of reading the label on every packaged or bottled food item you buy. Corn syrup, corn sweeteners, fructose, sucrose, and dextrose are other names for sugar.

Many of the best cooks in La Leche League have learned to cut out sugar entirely or greatly reduce it in as many recipes as they can. They have found that even in dessert recipes a sharp reduction in the amount of sugar called for works equally as well, and does not detract from the flavor. If your family is fond of gelatin desserts, for example, prepare your own using unflavored gelatin. Let ripe fruit be the only sweetener. If your little ones are served fresh fruit gelatin from the beginning, they'll love it. As you and your husband wean yourselves from too much sugar, your taste buds will begin to appreciate the flavor of natural sweetness.

Salt. Salt (sodium chloride) can be another offender in our diet. Like sugar, it is often overused in an attempt to enhance the flavor of our food. This may result in an excessive intake of salt, which can be harmful. Overuse of salt is linked to high blood pressure in some individuals. (Hypertension can lead to stroke—a leading cause of death in many parts of the world.)

Salt was originally added to foods as a preservative and to cover up the unpleasant taste of foods that were spoiling because of lack of refrigeration. We are better off if we reduce the amount of salt we use.

Many excellent cooks have found other ways to enhance flavor; they use lemon and/or a variety of herbs, spices, and other seasonings.

Highly processed cereals and grains. These products provide another source of confusion to our appetites. Processing robs cereals and grains of important minerals and vitamins. To make up for the loss of natural nutrients they must be enriched. This prevents obvious nutritional deficiencies that can develop when people eat nothing but refined foods (white flour instead of whole-wheat, white rice instead of brown, etc.). But the enrichment is only an enrichment of an inferior product; many other valuable nutrients are lost, including fiber.

Whole grains and cereals are excellent sources of fiber, as are many fruits and vegetables. In the long term, a high-fiber diet may help prevent certain kinds of cancers. For the short term, fiber is important in preventing constipation, a problem for many women during pregnancy and postpartum. Processing removes fiber from foods, along with flavor and texture. Serving whole-grain breads, whole-grain cereals, both hot and cold, and other grains such as brown rice or barley will boost the fiber in your family's diet and add interest to your meals.

How to EAT WELL

By following the basic approach we have outlined so far, and adding the art of making foods tasty and attractive, you'll bring the joy of eating to the family table and you and your family will benefit nutritionally. Here are some practical tips to help you and your family eat well.

READ THE LABELS

Acquiring the habit of reading the list of ingredients on food packages, cans, and bottles is most important. This will help you select foods that provide the most wholesome ingredients and avoid those that contain too much sugar, salt, fat, chemical additives, or ingredients to which you or other family members may be allergic.

It is important to read the list of ingredients because other information on the label can often be misleading. A can labeled "fruit juice drink," for example, turns out to be a fruit-flavored drink, with lots of sugar. It is not pure fruit juice. By calling it a "drink" the company has stayed within acceptable labeling standards and has probably led some people to believe the product is better for them than it really is. Another confusing term is "fortified." Sometimes the company lists the vitamins they've added, but these "fortified" foods usually offer less food value than the real thing—and at a greater cost.

Don't be deceived by the term "wheat flour" in a list of ingredients on a bread label. "Wheat flour" refers to white flour. It must say "whole wheat" to mean that. You should also know that ingredients are listed in descending order of amounts found in the product. For example, if flour is the first ingredient listed, it means there's more flour in the product than anything else. If the second item is sugar, dextrose, or corn syrup, that means that next to flour there is more sweetener than anything else, and so on down the line. (Of course, when several types of sweetener are listed separately, it might be that sugar is really the main ingredient when you add them all up.) The chemicals are usually listed last, but some highly processed items may have more chemicals than food: for example, coffee-cream substitutes, some pudding desserts, and some ice creams contain more chemicals than any other ingredient.

CHANGING FOOD HABITS

Food habits don't change overnight. Introducing new foods requires tact, patience, and imagination. In the beginning you'll want to choose alternatives that resemble familiar foods. When you are shopping and reading labels, don't even bring home the foods you don't want your family to eat. If the adults in the family continue to snack on cookies and chips, the children will want to follow their example.

Creative approaches can make new foods more appealing. Melted cheese on whole-grain bread may look better to a toddler if it is in the shape of a triangle or a butterfly. A melon slice on salad greens can be a sailboat salad. Tickle your toddler's imagination by calling the crunchy inside slice of an apple an apple "cookie." Colorful sliced vegetables with dip have eye appeal. Even unusual containers can pique children's interest. Serve snacks on toy dishes, in special cups, or in a toddler's very own lunch box. Try a blender drink of bananas, milk, some ice, and a little vanilla. If it's served in a fancy glass with a straw, what child could resist?

USING WHOLE GRAINS

Introducing whole grains to your family can be an enjoyable change because there are hundreds of ways to use them. If your family doesn't like oatmeal for breakfast, try cornmeal, either as a cereal, good old-fashioned fried cornmeal mush, or nice hot corn bread. Some recipes use a combination of cornmeal and whole-wheat flour, others use corn-meal only. Kasha is an old standby from people whose origins are in the Middle East and Eastern Europe. It is both nutritious and easy to cook. It can be used hot or cold, much like rice. The smell of spicy raisin-bran muffins baking will draw people to the table. A hot muffin is hard to resist, and muffin recipes are easily changed to include whatever

Little ones enjoy being involved in preparing nutritious meals.

ingredients you have on hand—apples, nuts, blueberries, grated carrots, etc. What a pleasant way to get your family off to a good, energetic start for the day! Try using granola, too. Granola recipes abound and it's fun to make your own, since the commercial varieties are often heavy on sweeteners and fats.

Husbands and older children have been known to balk at the introduction of whole-wheat bread. One suggestion is to offer them "half and half" sandwiches for a while—using one slice of whole-wheat bread and one slice of white. Very young children whose tastes have not had time to become conditioned usually like the whole grain bread right away.

If you do a lot of baking, you can introduce whole-wheat flour gradually into your baked goods. Just substitute whole-wheat flour for part of the white flour you usually use in the recipe. This is especially easy to do in homemade breads and muffins. Many mothers have found that baking their own bread is great fun and a lot easier than they expected. If you gradually increase the amount of whole-wheat flour to the white flour over a period of months, eventually you'll be making a one hundred percent whole-wheat bread that no longer tastes "strange" to your family. It may even become more desirable than the white bread they used to like, especially when it's hot from the oven!

If you do use white flour in your recipes, be sure to use unbleached flour, so as to avoid the extra chemicals used for bleaching. For extra nutrition, place one tablespoon of soy flour in each cup of white flour. Soy is high in protein, so it will add to the food value of the baked goods and will not be noticed in the final product. Dried skim-milk powder is also a nutritious supplement if milk allergy is not a problem. A tablespoon or two can be added to various cake, bread, muffin, or pancake recipes without changing texture or flavor.

USE NUTS AND SEEDS IN RECIPES

Plain raw nuts and seeds are too full of goodness to overlook. Even when roasted they are still nutritious, though less so than when raw. You can increase the food value in your potato salad, or chicken or tuna salad, by adding a tablespoon or two of hulled raw, unroasted sesame seeds. They are so tiny and bland in flavor that even the pickiest member of your family won't notice them. A sprinkle of raw sunflower or hulled raw sesame seeds over breakfast cereal or yogurt also will increase food value and add both flavor and a bit of crunch. In just about any kind of batter you make, you can add sesame seeds or finely ground nuts, and no one will be the wiser. Nuts and seeds are delicious in waffles, pancakes, muffins, and breads.

Nuts and seeds packaged by the ounce and sold in the grocery store are relatively expensive, as well as often stale. Look for one of the new, "old-fashioned" stores where you can scoop nuts, seeds, and dried fruits from big bins and buy them by the pound. These usually offer considerable savings over the packaged variety, and they are likely to be fresher and better flavored. Store them in the freezer to keep them fresh longer.

A caution is needed about giving nuts to children under three or so. The young child may not chew them well and there is a danger of small chunks being inhaled into the lungs instead of going down the throat.

EAT LESS MEAT

If your family is accustomed to eating only beef and chicken, try this easy way to prepare fish. Start with fillets, about one-inch thick, completely boned, either fresh or frozen. Broiling is the easiest and quickest way to cook them, and the shorter the cooking time the more nutrition is retained. Spread a thin coating of melted butter or olive oil on the fillet and broil about five minutes on each side, longer if frozen or if fillet is more than an inch thick. Before serving, sprinkle with dill weed, paprika, curry power, or whatever spice you prefer, then squeeze on some fresh lemon juice or place lemon slices on the serving plate as a finishing touch.

BETWEEN-MEAL SNACKS

Make between-meal snacks nutritious and not just something to fill up on. If you or the children are ravenous and supper isn't ready, try raw vegetables or fresh fruit. If the apple or orange you offer a hungry little one is sliced, peeled, and cut into small portions, even the most finicky little eater is unlikely to refuse. Even if a light eater's appetite is somewhat lessened by the before-meal snack, it really doesn't matter as long as the snack is nutritious. Just consider it part of his meal. Many times a nutritious morsel is gobbled avidly when handed out beforehand when it might have been scorned had it appeared cooked on a dinner plate. This reminds us of a mother who routinely cooks only half of the vegetables for a meal, serving the remainder raw at the table so each child can take his choice. You'll have to be careful of raw carrots, though, for the child under three. They may not be chewed properly, and can be inhaled rather than swallowed. Young children can usually handle other raw vegetables and fruits quite well.

Frozen snacks have special appeal in hot weather. While toddlers are teething, frozen foods can also be soothing to sore gums. Some nutritious frozen snacks are: yogurt and fruit juice popsicles, frozen blueberries, strawberries, slices of peach or pear, and even frozen green peas. Frozen bananas on a stick are much better for your children than ice cream bars.

Dried fruits, including raisins, are nutritious, but should not be eaten as a daily snack. They are hard on the teeth because of the high natural sugar content. Because of their sticky texture they also tend to stick in the crevices of the teeth, evading the toothbrush and thereby contributing to tooth decay. In addition, many dried fruits have been dipped needlessly in honey or rolled in sugar, which you don't need. Sun-dried fruits with no sugar or honey added, make excellent sweeteners for cakes, cookies, or muffins made from whole-grain flour. Used in baking they less harmful to the teeth.

QUENCHING YOUR THIRST

Unsweetened fruit and vegetable juices provide food value as well as quench your thirst. There are many varieties of canned or bottled apple, grape, tomato, grapefruit, and pineapple juices that are unsweetened, with no chemical additives. Mixed flavors of juices are popular now, too. But you have to read the labels and avoid any that are called "fruit drinks," which have added sugar. Frozen orange, apple, grape, and mixed juice concentrates are also available in unsweetened brands. Freshly squeezed orange or grapefruit juice is delicious when available. Try adding carbonated mineral water to fruit juice for a bubbly treat.

If you begin having these juices on hand, chilled and ready, your family will learn to enjoy their natural sweetness. Of course, you'll want to completely avoid buying colas and other soft drinks or sodas. If they aren't even in the house, the natural drinks will be more appealing.

Don't forget water! To really quench one's thirst there is nothing like it! Sometimes when it comes from the refrigerator it is more appealing to the younger set. Water will seem more attractive poured from a brightly colored container than if it is just "plain old water from the faucet." A slice of fresh lime in a glass of ice water on a hot summer day both looks and tastes refreshing. Because of the pressure to serve soft drinks, parents have to be patient and persistent in resisting, and imaginative in providing substitutes.

GROW IT YOURSELF

One of the best suggestions we can offer is to plant your own vegetable garden. If you have space in your yard, so much the better. If not, see if your local park district offers small plots of land to would-be gardeners. Or see if a friend or neighbor would like to lend you space in return for a few fresh fruits and vegetables.

There is something very special about the smell of a garden growing—the pungent scent of tomatoes, the sweet-sharp smell of carrot tops, and the rich warm smell of good dirt.

An advantage of growing your own vegetables is that they will be free of the chemicals commercial growers use in the soil, as well as free of the pesticides that are sprayed on the plants during various stages of growth. Unfortunately, some of these chemicals remain on the skin of the fruit or vegetables and cannot be washed off. When you peel them to get rid of the chemicals, you also lose some valuable nutrients. With homegrown produce, it's a choice you don't have to make.

Special Hints for NURSING MOTHERS

We stated earlier that if you have good eating habits, there is no reason for you to make any major changes when you are breastfeeding. You do have to remember to eat enough to keep yourself in good health. Eating well is part of being a good mother.

A FEW REMINDERS

Nursing mothers just naturally feel the need for extra liquids and should drink enough to satisfy their thirst. You can drink water, fruit and vegetable juices, milk, soup, or other liquids. In the excitement and bustle of caring for a new baby, you may not always notice that you are dry and thirsty. Some mothers take a drink of water whenever they

Eating well keeps you feeling good so you can enjoy nursing your baby.

sit down to nurse the baby. If you are producing large amounts of pale yellow urine, you are probably drinking all you need.

Constipation (hard, dry stools) may be a sign of inadequate fluid intake. If you get constipated, increase your liquid intake as well as your consumption of fresh fruits and raw vegetables. And be sure you're getting enough whole grains (breads and cereals). Avoid commercial remedies. In fact, it is better to try to prevent the problem by starting during pregnancy to see that your kitchen is well stocked with high-fiber foods and fruits and vegetables so that it is easy to eat the right foods. Many new mothers have found that raw pears are especially effective for keeping bowels loose. Prunes, raw or cooked, and prune juice are also helpful.

MILK PRODUCTS AND OTHER SOURCES OF CALCIUM

You don't have to drink lots of milk in order to make milk for your baby. If you are allergic to milk, you don't have to drink it at all. Cow's milk is a good source of calcium but it is also a very common allergen. If there is a history of allergy in your family you might want to cut down on milk during your pregnancy as this is when some babies become sensitized to it. The reaction shows up after the baby is born.

Even if you are not sensitive to cow's milk, you may not care for it. It is good to realize there are other products that will provide the calcium you and your baby need. Yogurt, hard cheeses (such as cheddar, Swiss, and parmesan), and cottage cheese are good sources of calcium. Many people with milk allergies can tolerate at least small amounts of these. Blackstrap molasses and tofu, a soybean product that is becoming more widely available, are also good sources of calcium, as are bok choy, spinach, collards, and kale. Sesame seeds are especially rich in calcium. They can be added to baked goods, muffin or pancake batter, or sprinkled on salads or cereal.

Generally, meat and nuts are not good calcium sources, but three exceptions worth noting are liver, almonds, and Brazil nuts. In the fish family, very high calcium is found in canned sardines and canned sockeye red salmon, both of which are normally eaten with bones. These bones, unlike the thin sharp bones found in most fish, are usually round and soft enough to eat. They provide a nice crunchy contrast to the softer consistency of the fish.

CAFFEINE AND SOFT DRINKS

If you are accustomed to drinking lots of coffee, tea, or cola, you may wonder how the caffeine will affect your baby.

Excessive caffeine intake by the nursing mother may cause a reaction in her baby. The amount of caffeine in five or fewer five-ounce cups of coffee (less than 750 ml.) will not cause a problem for most mothers and babies. You may be getting additional caffeine from tea or colas. Caffeine is also found in some over-the-counter medications. If you suspect that caffeine may be causing fussiness or slow weight gain in your baby, cut down for a week or two and see if it helps. Since people do become addicted to caffeine, cutting it out abruptly may give you a headache for a day or so. Some mothers use herbal teas without caffeine and most brands of herbal tea are safe to use in moderation. However, certain herbs can be potent if taken in large amounts. In general, it's best to get most of your daily liquids in water, juice, or milk and limit your intake of coffee or tea.

Remember that in addition to caffeine, soft drinks contain lots of sugar and no food value. Sugarless soft drinks are not good either. Sugar substitutes, like aspartame and saccharine, may be easier on the teeth but could be hazardous to your health and they don't really satisfy your appetite. These artificial sweeteners should not be given to children. Remember—if you as a parent consume soft drinks daily, you can be sure your children will want to follow your example.

SUPPLEMENTS

Many people today report good results in preventing or eliminating certain deficiencies by taking vitamin or mineral supplements. Of course they are only supplements—they do not substitute for good food.

Your doctor may advise supplementary vitamins and minerals for you during pregnancy, particularly iron, to replenish and build up the stores from which your baby is building up his own supply of iron to carry him through at least his first half year of life. During the time you are breastfeeding, your doctor may suggest that you continue taking them.

A mother who is on a vegan or macrobiotic diet that includes no animal protein may need to take a vitamin B_{12} supplement in order to avoid a vitamin B_{12} deficiency in her baby.

Many mothers report good results from taking brewer's yeast, a natural vitamin B-complex concentrate. Some feel that it definitely helps increase their milk supply; others report that it is a help in combating fatigue, depression, and irritability. Of course, the best way to avoid these problems is by improving your daily diet and getting enough rest. But if you feel you need extra help, brewer's yeast might be right for you. It contains not only the B-complex vitamins but also large amounts of iron and protein.

There are some mothers who report fussiness in their babies when they take brewer's yeast.

Weight Loss and EXERCISE

Mothers often wonder if it's possible to lose weight while breastfeeding. The answer is yes. In fact, breastfeeding makes it easier to shed the extra pounds put on during pregnancy. Those pounds were put there, after all, to store energy for producing milk. New mothers who do not breastfeed have to depend on diet and exercise for weight loss. Breastfeeding women have a head start, because the caloric demands of milk production are already using up extra energy. Studies have shown that breastfeeding mothers tend to lose more weight when their babies are three to six months old than formula-feeding mothers who consume fewer calories. Of course, patterns of weight loss are highly individual and depend on diet and activity level as well as whether you are breastfeeding.

According to Dr. Judith Roepke, a nutritionist at Ball State University in Indiana, and a member of LLLI's Health Advisory Council, lactation may be an ideal time to lose weight. Lactation seems to mobilize even fat accumulated before pregnancy. But it's important to go slowly. Dr. Roepke suggests that nursing mothers do nothing to consciously bring about weight loss during the first two months postpartum. Your body needs that time to recover from childbirth and to establish a good milk supply, and most breastfeeding mothers will lose a few pounds anyway while eating to appetite. If after two months you haven't lost any weight, you probably need to increase your activity level as well as decrease your caloric intake by cutting back on fats and sweets. Put the baby in a stroller or baby carrier and head out of doors for a two-mile walk five times a week. At the same time, eliminate just 100 calories from your daily diet (the equivalent of one tablespoon of butter or oil) and you can expect to lose two or three pounds in a month. Not a dramatic weight loss, but one that guarantees that you and your baby will both stay well nourished. And the exercise has benefits that go beyond pounds and inches.

Some questions have been raised about the effects of exercise on a mother's milk. One widely publicized study suggested that mothers should avoid nursing right after exercising because of changes in the composition of their milk. Other studies did not show this same effect; in fact, one study showed that breastfeeding mothers who exercised regularly had a higher milk volume than those who did not exercise. After reviewing many studies of breastfeeding mothers who exercise, researchers concluded that moderate exercise during breastfeeding is safe and beneficial for most women.

Crash diets, fad diets, and quick weight loss present problems for nursing mothers. For some time there has been concern that losing weight too quickly would release environmental contaminants into your blood and increase the levels in your milk. However, more recent research shows that this may not be a significant increase. Exceptionally high protein/low-carbohydrate diets are potentially harmful for breastfeeding mothers because of substances released into the milk by the mother's altered metabolism. Any kind of drastic weight loss carries the risk of a drop in milk supply.

Many mothers find that weight loss takes care of itself while breastfeeding. Steering clear of sweets and "junk foods" (high-calorie foods with little nutritious value) and concentrating on good nutrition are often all it takes. Good nutrition will also help you combat the fatigue and emotional ups and downs that are an inevitable part of new motherhood.

PART FIVE | *As Your Baby Grows*

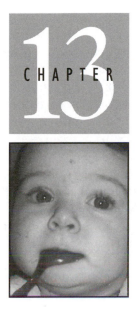

CHAPTER 13

Ready for Solids

Hand in hand with formula feeding of babies, a trend toward feeding solids earlier and earlier in infancy developed and took hold in the United States. A spirit of rivalry and competition arose among mothers (and sometimes doctors) to have the biggest baby who ate the most foods in the largest quantities at the earliest possible age. The baby food industry promoted and encouraged this trend. Mothers were led to believe that there was an advantage in giving early solids.

Today medical scientists have verified that human milk gives the best assurance of proper nourishment because it is nature's complete food for the baby. Young babies do best without the early addition of solids to their diet. Human milk is the perfect food for at least the first six months for the healthy, full-term infant, and there is usually no reason for adding any foods to the breastfed baby's diet before that time. In its recommendations, The American Academy of Pediatrics Committee on Nutrition advocates only human milk until four to six months of age and does not routinely advise vitamin, mineral, or fluoride supplements for the full-term breastfed infant.

There are at least two good reasons for waiting. First, you want to maintain your milk supply, and the more solids the baby takes, the less milk he will want; the less he takes from the breast, the less milk there will be. Research has confirmed that babies who start solids early balance their energy intake by reducing the amount of mother's milk they consume. When solid foods replace human milk in a baby's diet, it decreases the protective antibodies the baby receives. Starting solids too early substitutes an inferior food for a superior food

The second reason for waiting is that the younger the baby, the more likely it is that any foods other than mother's milk will cause food allergies. Most solid foods are poorly digested by a young baby, and may cause an unpleasant reaction in a two-month-old, but are readily assimilated by the same child if they are delayed until he is six months or older.

Until his immature digestive system develops to the point where it can utilize other foods without upsets, it is both kind and wise to give the baby the benefit of a few extra months of the food that is perfectly suited to meet his needs.

Some babies with a tendency to allergies will refuse solids even at seven or eight months. This could be nature's way of protecting that baby from foods that will cause him problems. Such babies can continue to do well on human milk alone until their systems are ready to tolerate other foods.

At some point around six or seven months, most babies start to teethe, and your baby's natural urge to chew and bite begins to develop. His mouth and tongue are ready for the new skills he will need, and his digestive system is probably ready to handle new foods.

Your baby will let you know when he is ready; watch him, not the calendar. If he suddenly increases his demand to be fed at some time around six months of age, and this increased demand continues for four or five days in spite of more frequent nursings, you can assume the time has come to start him on solids. If he is much younger than six months, however, don't get excited at these first signs and rush the start of solids, because his behavior might be due to other causes. A cold coming on might make him want the solace of nursing more often. If he is ill, this is not the time to begin new foods. Stepped-up activity on your part may be making you feel rushed and tense, and he is calling for needed attention. If he is fussy for some reason other than hunger, he will have enough to cope with. So play it safe and nurse more often for a few days before deciding it is really hunger that is responsible for his behavior change.

VITAMIN SUPPLEMENTS

First, a word about vitamin supplements. If the nursing mother gets an adequate supply of vitamins from her diet, her milk will have an adequate supply of vitamins, in just the right proportions for her baby. Research continues to bear this out. Your physician may suggest that you continue taking prenatal vitamins while you are breastfeeding. Vitamin supplements for babies got their impetus as a supplement to formula, which is still not the perfect food for your baby. As long as your baby is thriving on your milk alone, he has no need for additional vitamins, iron, fluoride, or other supplements in the early months.

Questions have been raised about a baby's need for vitamin D supplements since the amount of vitamin D in human milk is small. Exposure of a small patch of skin to sunlight for just a few minutes per day provides plenty of vitamin D for most babies. In severe climates, where mother and baby both go without sunlight for months or wear protective clothing that does not allow exposure of the skin to sunlight, a vitamin D supplement may be indicated.

Watch your baby, not the calendar, for signs of readiness to begin solids.

BABY'S FIRST FOODS

By the time babies are ready for solids, they are also ready and able to sit up with support and they just naturally want to put everything in their mouths. The simplest way to begin solids is to sit baby in his chair or, if he prefers, on your lap, and let him experiment with a tiny taste or so of his first food.

These first feedings of solid food usually go more smoothly if you nurse your baby first, to take the edge off his appetite. Otherwise he will be in no mood to try something new. With practice and patience on your part, he will catch on soon enough. These first few attempts are merely to introduce the idea of solids to him, not to fill him up. At first, use a small spoon and place just a small amount of food on it, about a teaspoon or less. If you have an independent baby who balks at spoon feeding, provide him with finger food, small bites of food he can pick up and put in his mouth by himself. Learning to grasp small finger food like cooked peas or beans will help him gain finger control and coordination. By the time he is one year old, he will probably be feeding himself with very little help from you.

A word of warning is in order here. Most babies have an excellent gag reflex and manage to get up anything that goes down the wrong way. But while your little one is learning to handle food all by himself, you don't want to leave him alone and walk away. Also be sure your baby is not given any foods to teethe on while he is lying down, as these could go too far back into his throat and cause him to choke.

Go Slowly at FIRST

New foods should be introduced one at a time. This means a single food, not a mixed food like stew or soup, or even a mixed-grain cereal. The reason for this precaution is that although the baby of six or seven months is not nearly as likely to have an allergic reaction as a younger child, it is still possible. If you introduce foods one at a time and he develops a rash or a sore bottom, potential indications of allergy, you will know what the most likely cause is and can eliminate the food temporarily. Wait until baby is at least a year old before introducing foods that cause allergic reactions in other family members.

It is a good plan to allow a week between each new food introduced. There is no advantage to be gained by striving for the widest variety of foods in the shortest time possible. Rather it is good for the baby to be given the opportunity to experience each new food thoroughly before going on to another. Start with a teaspoon or so of a new food once the first day. Increase the amount little by little until by the end of a week he is getting as much as he wants two or three times a day. He will probably let you know when he has had enough by turning his head, clamping his mouth shut, spitting the food back out, or some other unmistakable gesture. Take his word for it. Don't start feeding problems by coaxing, pushing, or forcing. Give him only as much as he wants, not what you think he should have.

Babies have likes and dislikes about foods, as we all do. So if your baby turns away from any particular food, don't panic. Just skip it and try something else. Even if he has happily consumed three bananas a

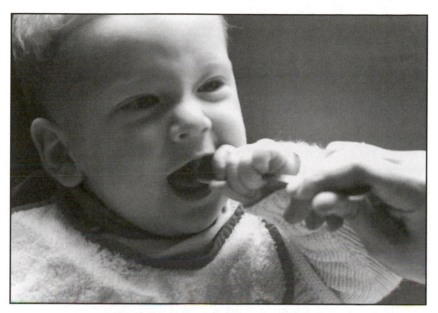

Some babies grab the spoon and try to feed themselves.

day for a week, and suddenly he won't look at one, go along with him. He's not sick—just sick of bananas.

Once a food has been started, try to keep at least a bit of it on his menu once a week or so thereafter, to avoid the possibility of an allergic reaction on its reintroduction after a lapse of time. This precaution should be kept up during the baby's first year.

NEATNESS DOESN'T COUNT

Now is not the time to worry about neatness. A hungry baby is easily frustrated when he is suddenly attacked by a wet washcloth instead of another tasty bite of food. Squelch your tidy impulses for the time being. Your baby is just learning the basics of eating and isn't ready for lessons in manners yet. Put a big bib on him and move his chair off the rug or put a sheet of plastic under it. (A hungry dog is handy for cleaning up under the high chair!)

You will avoid some messes, though, and make the learning process easier for him, if you have only one thing at a time on his tray—one piece of the finger food, later one unbreakable dish with a not-too-large serving of one food, and (not at the same time) a small unbreakable cup, half full. Keep servings small.

What Foods to CHOOSE

Most of us find it unnecessary to use commercial baby foods at all. They are relatively expensive, and some varieties contain undesirable fillers and preservatives. If you do use commercial foods, read the labels to determine exactly what is in them. Though improvements have been made in recent years, for most babies, starting with table foods is easiest and best. If you understand good nutrition and your family's eating habits are pretty good, then the food from your table will be fine for your baby, too. This also makes the transition to family meals easier. (See Chapter 12, "Nutritional Know-How.")

A blender, baby food grinder, or food processor can be used to make some table foods easier for baby to manage. However, a fork works nicely for most things you'll be giving him. If baby is six months or older when he's starting solids, he does not need foods pureed or liquified.

A SUGGESTED GUIDE FOR INTRODUCING SOLIDS

Raw, Mashed Banana. This is a good food to start with, since it is fresh and wholesome and contains more food value than cereals. Babies usually love the smooth consistency of a ripe banana. After you've given your baby a small taste the first time and gradually increased the amount, you can offer the baby a whole piece of banana to handle himself, thus quickly eliminating one mashed food as well as pleasing the baby who likes to feed himself, and mash it himself, too...between his fingers!

If your baby doesn't care for banana, sweet potato (yam) and avocado are good alternatives. It is preferable to bake the sweet potato whole to preserve the nutrients. Sweet potato has a fine flavor and maximum food value. Avocado has the same smooth consistency as banana and is high in vitamins and iron. You can slice off a piece and refrigerate the rest for another day. Most babies love it.

Meat. Meat is introduced early among solid foods because of its high iron and protein content. In vegetarian families, other foods high in protein may be substituted for meat. It is not difficult to reduce table meats to a consistency right for baby. Chopped beef, stew meats, or tender pieces of chicken can easily be cut up into small pieces or mashed with a fork. Better yet, scrape across a piece of raw meat with a knife. Tough connecting fibers will remain behind while the tender portions can be gently cooked for baby to eat.

When baby has had a week or so on one meat, try handing him a good-sized bone with no splinters or sharp corners, but with a few fragments of meat still on it. A chicken drumstick is good, and just about the right size for his grasp. (Be sure to remove the needle thin splint bone and gristle cap on the end.) Chances are he will chomp away on the bone with great relish, especially if he has the urge to chew and bite. He'll be developing muscle coordination in the process, too.

To make sure you have on hand the kind of meat your baby can handle, keep individual portions of cooked, chopped, or scraped beef or chicken, wrapped and frozen. When you have meat at the table that might be too difficult for the baby, you can quickly prepare a small portion of frozen meat for him.

Fish is another excellent protein food and quite easy for baby to eat, but it is a common source of allergy. If allergies are not common in your family, and your menu often includes fish, you can introduce it carefully to your baby. Watch out for bones. Check each piece between your fingers before giving it to baby. And wait until baby is older to introduce smoked and pickled fish or shellfish.

Whole-Grain Breads and Cereals. Finger-sized pieces of dried or toasted whole-wheat bread are good chewing foods for your baby and handy to offer him, perhaps between meals or while you are preparing dinner. Whole-wheat bread is the type most commonly available, but other whole-grain breads are also good. If you regularly serve a cooked whole-grain cereal you might want to introduce this; but be sure there is no sugar or other sweetener added, and cook it with water, not milk. Avoid mixed-grain cereals until baby has been introduced to each one. Baby cereals do not have quite as much food value as your own freshly cooked whole-grain cereals because they are more highly processed. They are an additional expense as well.

Another nice thing about whole-wheat toast (or a day-old heel of the loaf) is that it's good for spreading things on. A very thin layer of smooth peanut butter, for instance, is a popular spread, once baby is old enough to handle it without choking. (Be cautious of peanut butter in families with a history of allergy.) Be sure to buy the natural peanut butter, without added sweeteners and preservatives. Babies love it. Later on, cheese and homemade nutritious spreads can be used on the bread.

Fresh Fruits. Raw, peeled apple or pear can be grated, or scraped with the edge of a spoon, and put in a little mound on baby's high-chair tray. It won't be long before you can hand him a piece of peeled apple, ripe pear, or peach to munch on. Apricots, plums, and melons are good, too. If baby is eight months or older, other fresh fruits in season may be offered, but with caution. Some berries have seeds that babies are not old enough to handle well.

Frozen blueberries make wonderful finger food; baby will love the cold, crunchy taste, especially if he's teething. Citrus fruits can cause allergy, so wait with those until baby is about a year. Tangerine segments are good to start with, but be sure to take the seeds out.

Avoid canned fruits that contain sugar. They have less food value than fresh fruits, but unsweetened canned fruits are better than no fruit at all. Dried fruits such as raisins, dates, or figs should not be given at all in the first year, and later only on a limited basis. Although they are nutritious, they are very sweet and tend to stick between the teeth which can cause tooth decay.

Vegetables. Sweet potato, as we suggested earlier, and white potato are both good choices for baby. Don't add butter or margarine to baby's portion. He'll enjoy the natural flavor of the food without these enhancements.

Finely grated raw carrot can be mixed with grated apple or some of the other foods baby is getting. Cooked carrots are good, too. Other cooked vegetables may be offered from your table one at a time, just as you do with any new food. Some little ones enjoy frozen vegetables right from the package—especially frozen peas they can pick up and pop into their mouths one at a time. Wait until baby is about a year old before offering corn or tomatoes, as these are potential sources of allergy.

Don't be concerned if, in the beginning, you find little bits of vegetable, virtually unchanged, in the diaper. Even cooked vegetables are harder to digest than many other foods.

Raw vegetables have more food value than cooked vegetables, but most of them are too hard for a little one to chew and digest. Some raw vegetables—particularly carrots and celery—can be dangerous as small chunks can be inhaled rather than swallowed.

Eggs. Since eggs, especially the whites, seem to be a common cause of allergies, it might be best to wait until the baby is about a year old before introducing them. At first the egg should be hard-boiled. Place the egg in water and bring to a boil. Remove from heat, cover, and let stand twenty minutes. Peel under cool water. Feed baby only the yolk at first, mashed and moistened to suit his preferences. Start with no more than a quarter-teaspoon and increase gradually, a quarter-teaspoon at a time. After baby has been eating eggs well for a month or so you can give him scrambled eggs. Babies usually love to eat them as a finger food. Or cook an egg in with his cereal for extra nutrition.

Cow's Milk and Other Dairy Products. If there is a history of allergy in the family, or baby has already shown signs of it, avoid cow's milk entirely. The only milk your baby needs is yours. In some parts of the world, adults do not drink milk at all, but eat well otherwise, and the people are healthy and well-nourished.

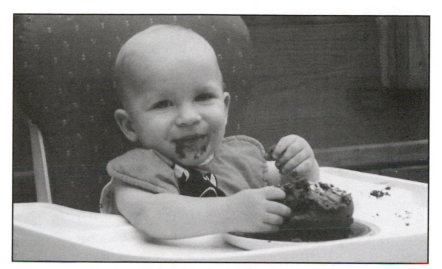

Let baby dig in and enjoy his own special cake, made with nutritious ingredients, when he celebrates his first birthday.

Cottage cheese, yogurt, and natural cheeses can be introduced when baby is nine or ten months old. These dairy products provide calcium and other nutrients and they are much less likely to cause allergies than cow's milk.

INTRODUCING THE CUP

At some point during baby's first year, you can start offering water or juice from a cup once a day at mealtime or in between, whichever suits you best. There's no need to rush. A tip on getting the baby started with a cup comes from Betty Wagner: let him drink through a short straw. (The bendable kind works well.) The sucking comes easily to him, and it's neater too—no drips or dribbles. Or, try the kind of plastic cup that comes with a tight-fitting lid and a spout.

Baby's beverages should consist mainly of your milk, water, homemade soups (canned soups may contain a lot of salt and preservatives), and unsweetened fruit or vegetable juice. You may want to dilute the juice with water so it is not so concentrated. Giving babies or toddlers too much fruit juice has been found to contribute to malnutrition by decreasing their appetite for wholesome foods. Limit fruit juice to four ounces or less per day. No soft drinks or colas please—these are heavy on sugar or sugar substitutes and sometimes caffeine, and are lacking in anything worthwhile. Soft drinks with artificial sweeteners such as aspartame or saccharine should also be avoided. There is still no substitute for a good drink of water.

WHAT TO AVOID

You will notice that from the beginning we are suggesting you feed your baby wholesome, nutritious foods. We would strongly urge you to avoid processed foods that are full of sugar, salt, dyes, preservatives, and chemicals.

Once you have given your baby the best start by breastfeeding him, we are sure you'll want to continue along those lines when he starts to eat other foods. Your baby will do just fine without cookies, pretzels, teething biscuits, puddings, cakes, and ice cream. Let him first develop a taste for the natural sweetness of fresh fruits and the natural goodness of whole grains. Now is the best time to start developing habits of good nutrition that will last a lifetime.

The whole process of starting your baby on solid foods may take from three to six months. Once he's eating a variety of foods without any signs of allergy or distress, you can be less concerned about mixing foods or introducing something new. As long as what you offer him is good, nourishing food, you can let his appetite be your guide as to what he wants to eat and when he wants to eat it.

As you are getting your little one well launched in the eating department, you'll want to learn as much as you can about good nutrition for your whole family. LLLI's cookbooks— WHOLE FOODS FOR THE WHOLE FAMILY and WHOLE FOODS FROM THE WHOLE WORLD— will give you good suggestions for keeping baby, and everyone else in the family, deliciously well-fed. For details, see the Appendix.

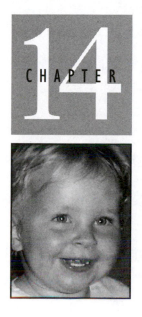

CHAPTER 14

Weaning Gradually, with Love

"When shall I wean my baby? How shall I go about it? How long will it take?" Some mothers begin to worry about weaning when their infant is only a few weeks old.

Why do mothers begin worrying about ending breastfeeding almost as soon as they've started? No doubt there are many reasons, but we suspect that not the least among them is the fact that society often expects babies to be weaned early. Mothers are uneasy about the thought that their babies might still be nursing after society expects them to be weaned from the breast.

We don't agree with society's attitudes about early weaning. We believe that ideally the breastfeeding relationship should continue until the baby outgrows the need.

One mother who had weaned because of criticism from others, had this to say about her decision: "I let pressure from people prematurely end one of the most meaningful experiences I have had with my son....I wish I had it to do all over again now that I am more sure of myself."

More Than MILK

Your milk continues to provide special benefits for
your baby as long as you
nurse him. It doesn't lose
its goodness with the passing of time. Research has
shown that the immunolog-
ical benefits of human milk
that protect your baby from
illness in the early months
continue to offer significant protection as your
baby gets older.

If we consider breast-
feeding only as a means of
nourishing the infant, then
we can see why it might be
feasible to bring nursing to

Your milk continues to offer significant benefits
as your baby gets older.

an end as soon as the baby can handle a variety of solid foods and drink
from a cup—perhaps even before his first birthday.

It is when we view the breastfeeding experience as a whole, when
we understand that the baby has emotional needs which can easily be
satisfied through the closeness of breastfeeding, that it is hard to
understand why we must set a specific time for ending this important,
intimate relationship. If we do not satisfy these needs when our children are small, they may be as undernourished emotionally as they
would be physically if they were deprived of an important nutrient in
their diet.

EMOTIONAL NEEDS

The breastfeeding mother and her baby build a relationship based on
their mutual needs, and the relationship changes gradually as the
needs change. One of the most urgent needs of the tiny baby is food,
and during this period of infancy the mother's physical need is to be
relieved of the milk that fills her breasts for the sake of the baby.
However, the mother and baby depend upon each other for many other
things. The baby needs affection, and the mother enjoys responding to
his need to be loved. The mother has a strong desire to be truly
needed by this tiny one. But at some point, usually gradually, the
baby's dependence on mother lessens. He begins to broaden his hori-

zons, to try his wings. But nursing is still important, for it is a secure haven in a sometimes difficult world.

When the baby does not wean by a year or so, a mother may wonder if this means he is too dependent on her. She may fear that letting him continue to nurse will prevent him from growing toward independence. But weaning is a step toward growing up and, like walking or talking, a child takes these steps according to his own timetable. All children stop nursing sooner or later. Some have the need to continue the nursing relationship longer than others—but they do grow out of it eventually. And still they do not become overly dependent. We have been reassured on this point many times over because we have observed first-hand hundreds of babies who were considered "late weaners." Independence, not dependence, is one outstanding trait they seem to have in common as they grow up.

Remember, too, that at a year or so your baby will not be nursing as often as he was at two weeks or six months. By the time he's nine months old or so he has probably cut down considerably, and the toddler who is "still nursing" may be only enjoying a bedtime snack or a "pick-me-up" when he bumps his head or has caught a cold. Nursing is so comforting to him when he's ill. It makes his recovery much smoother if he can nurse away his troubles.

Some of the most physically and emotionally healthy children in my practice are those who have been breastfed in terms of years.

Dr. William Sears
Pediatrician and Author

STILL NURSING?

It helps to keep in mind that all children wean eventually. Young children have a tremendous desire to move on to the next stage of development. They want so much to be like the older members of the family that you can be sure they will stop nursing when they are able to do so. You are certainly not out to set a record for prolonged nursing. Late nursing is not something you strive for, but it is a very special relationship between mother and child.

One mother, Susan Redge from Michigan, tells how she and her son grew into and out of this special relationship:

When my son was a newborn and he and I were at our first LLL meeting, the mother sitting next to me was nursing her two-year-old. I assumed that she came to get help with weaning. I was surprised to hear that instead she was there to learn more about toddler nursing. I was sure I would never need to learn about toddler nursing!

When my baby was about eight months old, my mother-in-law couldn't understand why he didn't eat solid foods. Although I had offered him solids, he didn't seem too interested and I knew he was thriving on "mother's best." I was savoring our nursing time because I knew it couldn't last forever.

By the time he was a year old, my husband said "Don't you think he ought to quit? After all, it's been a year." I was ready for that and told him all about baby-led weaning and its benefits to both mother and baby. "Why some even nurse until three years old!" I said. "But, of course, our child will certainly wean before then!"

By the time he was two, I couldn't imagine not nursing him. I didn't think he would ever go to sleep without it. I was pleased that out of our chaotic life I could take time to relax and nurse knowing that I could close my eyes and the plants would be safe, he wouldn't be cracking eggs on my living room rug, or having a tantrum, or doing any of the other things two-year-olds might do. I felt real sympathy for mothers of two-year-olds who did not nurse.

By that time, no one asked me about nursing anymore. Most people assumed that he was weaned. I never dreamed I'd be nursing this long! He nurses at night to go to sleep, maybe once more in the wee hours, and usually once during the day.

The most important thing I have learned from La Leche League is to meet my child's needs. As a baby, he needed to be held close and nursed often. As he has grown, his needs have changed. He needs to know I am there for him and there are still times when nothing else but nursing can calm him. I've had the thought countless times that it is nursing that soothes the savage beast. It has many times turned a kicking, screaming, out-of-control toddler into a calm, smiling, confident, and contented young man, bravely ready to face the world.

Now he's been telling me that only babies nurse, and he is a big boy. Sometimes he even falls asleep without being nursed. I probably will not have a nursing toddler much longer. I just hope I can continue to satisfy his needs as easily and with as much joy when breastfeeding is no longer a part of our lives.

NATURAL WEANING

"But when will he wean?" you ask, as your two-year-old holds up his arms to be picked up and nursed again. Actually, he's been weaning himself ever since his first bite of solid food. "To wean," says the *Concise Oxford Dictionary*, is "to teach the sucking child to feed otherwise than from the breast." While most people see weaning as the end of something—a taking away or deprivation—it's really a positive thing, a beginning, a wider experience. It's a broadening of the child's horizons, an expansion of his universe. It's moving slowly ahead one careful step at a time. It's full of exciting but sometimes frightening new experiences. It's another step in growing up.

In MOTHERING YOUR NURSING TODDLER, Norma Jane Bumgarner talks about the "unpredictable course of natural weaning." She says there will come a time when "your child will not find nursing so absolutely essential to her well-being. She may stop asking so often. Or she may be distracted sometimes from nursing....You will very naturally and with hardly a thought respond a little less quickly to her requests to nurse....In time—how much time no one can say—your child will abandon all but a few favorite nursing times."

Norma Jane goes on to describe how some children will continue to enjoy one or more of these special nursing times for a while, dropping them ever so slowly until eventually they are weaned. She concludes: "Every natural weaning is unique so that it is impossible to guarantee anything about it except that it will happen."

What If I Want to Wean My BABY?

Each of us must make decisions about breastfeeding and weaning in keeping with our family situations and personal circumstances. Perhaps you do not agree with the concept of natural weaning or you don't think it will work out for you. Before you decide that circumstances will make it necessary for you to wean your baby, think over all possible alternatives. Perhaps there are some compromises that could be made in order to allow the baby to nurse at least once or twice a day. Stop and think about whether weaning your baby will really improve matters. Norma Jane Bumgarner says, "Nursing makes the job of mothering easier, not harder." Remember that illness, medications, surgery, or returning to work do not necessarily mean you must wean before you and your baby are ready.

If at all possible, you'll want to take your time with weaning and proceed slowly. We talk about weaning as something to be done "gradually and with love." You'll need to step up the loving attention you give your baby in other ways during the time that you cut back on nursing him. Dr. William Sears encourages the same thing when a baby is being weaned. He points out: "A wise baby who enjoys a happy nursing relationship is not likely to give it up willingly unless some other form of emotional nourishment is provided which is equally attractive or at least interestingly different."

Basically, weaning is accomplished by substituting other kinds of loving care for nursing. You'll want to cut out one nursing at a time, distracting your little one with a cup of juice or water, a story, or a walk around the block at the time he would usually nurse. Wait a few days to allow him to get used to this change and to avoid feeling uncomfortable yourself from overfull breasts, and then tackle another nursing time. This may take up to two weeks or so depending on how many times a day your baby has been nursing. It is not a good idea to rush things. Weaning is a big change for both of you and it takes time to adjust.

You may need to be flexible, too. If your little one reacts strongly to the idea of not nursing at naptime or bedtime or whenever, you may decide to let him continue with that one nursing for a while. Weaning doesn't have to be an "all or nothing" situation.

If you decide to wean when your baby is under a year old and perhaps not drinking well from a cup, you'll probably want to talk to your doctor about giving him a bottle and ask the doctor what to put in it. If you are weaning from breast to bottle, you'll be substituting a bottle for some of the times you used to nurse the baby. Remember that your baby was nursing for comfort some of the time and will probably not need as many bottles per day as the number of times he was nursing per day. You'll need to double up on cuddling, rocking, hugs, and kisses throughout the day to make up for this. Instead of holding your little one in the familiar nursing position, bring his face close to yours and hold him cheek to cheek as you rock or comfort him.

With an older baby or toddler who is eating well and drinking from a cup, your basic weaning method involves lots of substitution and distractions. Keep tasty things to nibble on within easy reach. By frequently offering him drinks of water or, occasionally, unsweetened juice, during the day, his thirst will also be quenched, often before he even realizes he's thirsty and asks to nurse. Chunks of fresh fruit are good, too—oranges, melons, or peaches.

Go out of your way to make the time at which you are omitting the nursing warm and happy in other ways. Your baby's father can be a tremendous

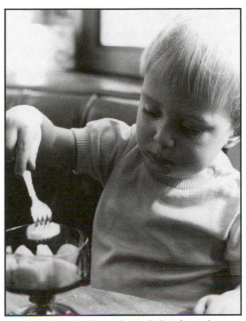

Sometimes a healthy snack can substitute for nursing.

help at this time, by taking the baby out for a stroll or putting him to bed at night, and perhaps by getting up with him if he wakes during the night.

Your toddler may be enthralled by your sudden interest in going for walks, visiting the playground, or doing puzzles. You may need to avoid the situations in which he is accustomed to nursing, such as in a favorite rocker or climbing into bed with you in the morning.

This method of weaning "gradually and with love" can be a lot of work. But abrupt weaning can be physically and emotionally traumatic and is never a good idea for you or your baby. By substituting lots of "other-mothering" you can help your little one come through the weaning process with his confidence and trust in you still intact. He may have a hard time understanding why he can no longer nurse, but at least he'll be reassured that his mother has not deserted him, she's still there with lots of love and understanding.

One mother from Missouri, Maggie Bryan, tells how the course of weaning took place with her son:

> While attending La Leche League meetings with my constant
> companion, Sean, I learned with great surprise about baby-led
> weaning and witnessed the wonderful closeness of mothers and nursing
> toddlers. The months slipped by; I was confident that he would
> eventually decide to stop nursing at his own pace, in his own time.

Imagine my dismay when I found myself becoming increasingly impatient with his continued nursing. I yearned to have a night free of bedtime nursing, to enjoy my bodily privacy once again, and a small thing, to read a few pages of the morning newspaper uninterrupted. It seemed to me that sometimes Sean was using nursing to trap my attention.

Whether or not my perceptions were accurate, my feelings were definitely a reality and had to be dealt with. So, with some trepidation, I decided to try to reduce the number of Sean's nursings and see if my impatience would lessen.

I began to ask him to wait a minute until I was finished with the morning paper, and, to my surprise, I found that he could cooperate for about five minutes. I found that delay also worked well in public situations. I found life with a nursing toddler becoming easier to manage. Sean nursed mainly at naptime, bedtime, and occasionally once at night.

As time passed, Sean began to give up naps and then stopped asking to nurse at night. On the rare occasions when he awakened, his Daddy held him close for a snuggle while he went back to sleep. Then to my astonishment Sean began to prefer to get up and have a bowl of cereal rather than stay in bed and nurse in the morning!

All of a sudden, it seemed, Sean was weaned! But actually the process had taken about six months. Sometimes I led, and sometimes Sean led. But his father and I only encouraged new behavior that he was ready and willing to learn. In this gentle way, I feel weaning was a maturing experience for both Sean and me.

Although our experience was not exactly the way I had imagined weaning would be, it did happen gradually and with love.

Toddler NURSING

Our culture today has geared us to thinking that all babies should be off the breast at an early age. But this is far from the custom that prevailed in centuries past. In biblical days weaning at age three was often mentioned, and still today in many parts of the world children wean themselves at ages up to three, four, or even older. The late Niles Newton, PhD, pointed out that in most periods of history and in most parts of the world babies have been breastfed for two to four years. She also observed that the changes in breastfeeding customs do not seem to have come alone, but in conjunction with a whole body of related customs. "La Leche League's repeated emphasis that breastfeeding is part of a whole philosophy of mothering is borne out by historical trends," she said.

Since cultural expectations about weaning vary, anthropologist Katherine Dettwyler decided to do research into the weaning ages of primates and other mammals to determine a "natural" weaning age for humans. She examined criteria such as length of gestation, age of eruption of permanent teeth, relationship of offspring to adult body size and made comparisons to average age of weaning in each species. Using these criteria, she determined that a "natural" weaning age for humans might be between three and seven years. Knowing this may not influence the decision you make about weaning your baby, but it can be reassuring if you and your baby are satisfied to follow a natural weaning but others are critical of this decision.

BENEFITS OF TODDLER NURSING

Fulfilling your child's individual needs is the key. From the moment he is born, a mother strives to respond to the needs of her child. As the child grows, if he continues to express a need to nurse, it is a natural response for a mother to continue to meet this need.

If your toddler continues to enjoy nursing, you may find there are many advantages that continue to go along with toddler nursing. It is so easy to help an overtired or fussy child calm down and often fall asleep through nursing. If he hurts himself there is no better way to soothe him. Because nursing eases frustration, many families find that it helps turn the "terrible twos" into the "terrific twos," minimizing the usual competitive behavior of the two-year-old. Sometimes behavior that is normal for a toddler is blamed on breastfeeding if the child is still nursing. Behavior such as clinging and demanding normally occur at this age, whether the child has weaned or not.

Traveling with a child is much easier when he is still nursing. Even though you are away from home, your little one can be kept happy with the familiar comfort of your breast.

Your milk continues to provide immunities, vitamins, and enzymes for as long as your child continues to nurse. In one study, mothers reported fewer instances of illness requiring medical care in toddlers sixteen to thirty months of age who were still breastfeeding. If your child does become ill, nursing will be a comfort to him. If he has an upset stomach, he may be unable to keep anything down but mother's milk.

You will probably find it convenient to encourage your child to use a special word for nursing. Choose carefully so that the word can contribute to discreet toddler nursing. One family uses "num num"; another calls nursing "mama." When the child shouts out, "I want mama!" in a restaurant, no one even turns around.

There will be occasions when it would be very inconvenient to nurse a toddler. If your two-month-old infant had begun to scream in a long check-out line at the supermarket, you might have pushed the basket to one side and gone out to the car for a few minutes to feed him. When he is older and has demonstrated the ability to wait and understand the concept of time, you may offer him a nutritious snack and ask him to wait until you get to the car to nurse. If you are about to visit someone you know would be extremely upset to see your child nurse, you might encourage him to nurse before you go, in the hope that he would then not need to nurse during the visit.

NURSING TOO MUCH?

Many little nursing persons nurse only occasionally, such as to fall asleep or for comfort when they hurt themselves. Sometimes however, a small child nurses much more avidly. If you feel your little one wants to nurse "too much" for his age, take a close look at what is happening in his—or your—life right now. Make sure he has lots and lots of other kinds of attention from you, and provide him with a nutritious snack or story before he asks to nurse. You can talk with him, sing, read, play games, or explore the outdoors together. Let him be a part of the jobs you do. He can wash pan lids while you do the dishes; he can carry socks to the clothes washer and push the vacuum cleaner around.

Is he away from you more than is comfortable for him? Are you home with him but busy with other projects? Are you spending lots of time on the phone? Are you going through a time of emotional upset? Moving? Is he making great strides in some other area of growth? Does he have an ear infection, allergies, or other illness? You can probably add your own ideas of things that might cause a child to want the extra reassurance of increased nursing.

When your child asks to nurse, if you are unsure that he really needs to nurse, you may choose to offer him an apple and a story instead of nursing. If the child is happy with this, fine, but if he asks repeatedly or cries to nurse, this would indicate that he feels a real need. You can respect the laws of inner growth and individuality, nursing him with the confidence that he will grow away from this kind of closeness at his own pace.

Some little ones continue to want to nurse several times a night as well as during the day. When your little one wakes up during the night, pick him up, cuddle him, take him into bed with you, and nurse him if he wants it. Then, if he's willing, put him back into his own bed. However, he may sleep better and wake less often if you keep him in bed with you. There are a number of reasons why toddlers want to nurse often at night. He could be teething, which is a common cause for little ones to fret. Perhaps he's hungry or thirsty during the night and needs a nutritious bedtime snack. Or it could be that he's been so busy all day he hasn't had his share of hugging and cuddling and just needs time to be close to you.

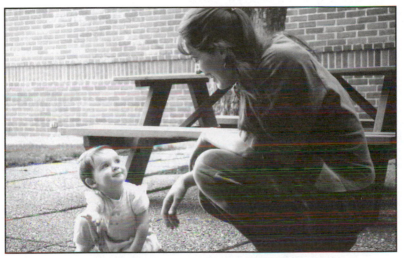

Toddlers need to explore and experience all the new and exciting aspects of their world.

WHAT DO YOU DO WHEN THERE'S NOTHING TO DO?

Sometimes a mother needs to evaluate the nursing relationship she has with her toddler and consider whether things are really going well. In some situations, nursing can become the easy way out, substituting for other kinds of attention the toddler really needs.

An older baby or toddler may want to nurse simply because he has nothing more interesting to do, or because it is the only way to get mother's attention. As your little one is growing out of the infant stage, his need for mother does not really lessen. It changes, certainly, and mothering a toddler requires a great deal of ingenuity and even physical dexterity. His whole being is growing. His mind as well as his body needs stimulation. He needs conversation and a companion to explore and experience all the new and exciting things his broadening horizons have brought into focus.

No one can better share these things with him than you, his very own teacher, guide, protector, and special person. No one knows his "language" as well as you do, nor understands so well his interests and needs. You know best when he's hungry and needs a snack to tide him over until dinnertime. You know when he's over-tired and needs to wind down in your arms.

One mother tells this story about how she realized her daughter needed more kinds of loving attention besides just nursing. Freda Main from Arizona writes:

> *A month ago Celeste was a two-and-a-half-year-old nursing child who had become increasingly demanding of me. She seemed discontented and often angry at everything and everyone including herself and me. This is not unusual, I know, for a child whose baby sister had come into the family five months ago. I had always assumed Celeste would eventually stop nursing when she was ready, with no part played by me.*

> *One day the light dawned. I had been thinking, "This child does nothing but nurse!" Then I realized this was precisely the case. I had not stopped thinking that nursing met all of Celeste's needs—as indeed it had for a long time. I had not observed until then that I was not giving Celeste the attention she deserved at times when she was not nursing.*

> *For me nursing had become so easy and effortless that I had fallen into the trap of not growing in my relationship with my daughter. What had always worked so well before was not meeting her needs now.*

> *I began to change my complacent ways. I began faithfully spending time with Celeste each day and giving her my undivided attention. We did many things together: making playdough, collecting Popsicle sticks and gluing them together, and reading many stories. I would sit and hold her and hug her and kiss her even without "nursies." We talked. When my five-month-old slept, I spent the time with Celeste instead of crossing off items from my list of things to be done. We started having regular mealtimes, reading bedtime stories, and following daily routines. I started to be conscientious about eye contact and really made an effort to do less talking and more listening.*

*To my amazement, in a matter of days the little girl whose nursing
I had once seen no end to, was hardly nursing at all. I was becoming
more attuned to what she really needed and was giving more of
myself to meet her needs.*

*It was hard for me to change. In weaning myself, Celeste weaned also.
Now I no longer think of baby-led weaning as "mother doing
nothing." As in everything else, experience is the best teacher.*

Pregnant and NURSING?

If you find that you are pregnant, there is no sudden need to wean.
Your child may wean himself early in the pregnancy when a few little
ones notice a taste change in the milk, or he may stop nursing around
the fourth month when some women notice a reduction in the milk
supply. He may even wean toward the end of pregnancy when the milk
changes to colostrum, or after the birth because of the separation if you
are in the hospital for several days or because the increase in your milk
supply does not suit his taste. If he seems to have a strong desire to
nurse in spite of the changes that occur during pregnancy, feel free to
continue if you wish.

You may have some concerns about continuing to nurse while you
are pregnant. If you are eating a well-balanced diet including a variety
of nutritious foods there should be no cause to worry about either baby
being harmed. Some mothers may worry that nursing through pregnancy will cause a miscarriage. There is no evidence that breastfeeding
will cause a miscarriage and some mothers who have previously miscar-
ried have not done so while nursing a toddler.

During your pregnancy, you may find that you are just not happy
about continuing to nurse your toddler. In this case, we suggest you
consider following the recommendations that are given for weaning
"gradually and with love." It is up to you to make the decisions that
will work best in your own family.

In a study of 503 La Leche League members who became pregnant while still nursing, researchers found that 69% of their babies
weaned at some time during the pregnancy. Of course, there was no
way to know how many of these little ones would have weaned if their
mothers had not been pregnant.

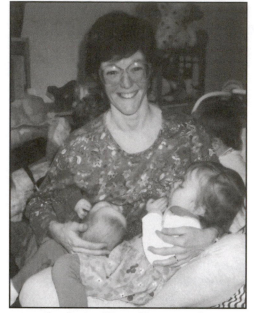

Sometimes a toddler continues to nurse after the new baby is born.

TANDEM NURSING

If you nurse through your pregnancy, you will probably find yourself in a situation called "nursing siblings who are not twins" or more simply, "tandem nursing." If nursing is still an important part of your older baby's life, it would not be fair (or wise) to cut him off abruptly when the new baby is born. Mothers find there are advantages as well as disadvantages to this somewhat unique situation.

It can be reassuring to the older child to continue nursing and sharing these special times with his new sibling can help to avoid feelings of jealousy. You may worry, however, that your new baby will be somewhat deprived of milk or of the intimate one-to-one relationship with just you. Some mothers are surprised by the intensity of their feelings toward protecting the newborn which can cause resentment when their toddler wants to nurse. You may want to restrict your toddler's nursing to only certain times of the day, or establish a rule that he only nurses after the new baby is finished. Most mothers, however, find these things work out and the new baby gets plenty of milk without any problem. It helps to talk with other mothers who have gone through this experience.

One mother, Brenda May from California, tells how nursing two worked out in her family:

When I became pregnant with our fourth child, my son Jon was a very active toddler who still enjoyed his frequent nursings. I soon realized he was not ready to wean himself, and I did not feel it was necessary to encourage him.

By the sixth month of my pregnancy, my lap seemed to completely disappear. This made our nursings somewhat awkward, but with the help of a pillow under his head, Jon continued. As my birthing time grew nearer, my milk supply decreased, and I thought Jon might decide to wean. However, he still continued, seemingly content with whatever he received at the breast.

On the morning of what was to be our fourth child's birthday, Jon and I lay in bed together nursing. It helped me to relax, as my labor had already begun. Six hours later, Jacob Allen was born at home with his family all sharing the experience. That day we began tandem nursing. Jon was twenty-one months old.

For the next three weeks, we spent most of our days nursing. Jon had increased his nursings, and Jake was nursing every hour or so. Soon after, my toddler went back to his regular routine but clearly enjoyed the abundant supply of milk now available.

I didn't know anyone who had tandem nursed; no one in our LLL Group had done it. So I felt unsure at times, but I just trusted my mothering instincts that told me what I was doing was right for myself and my children.

Occasionally, after apparently completely weaning himself, a toddler might suddenly ask to nurse again. (This sometimes happens when the new baby arrives.) Don't be afraid to let him try it. Most likely, instead of nursing he will giggle and slide off your lap, reassured by your willingness to go along with his request. A mother from Ohio, Mary Beard, recalls:

After Julian was born, Elliott asked once if he could nurse. I said, "Yes," and he said, "Oh," and walked away. Apparently he only wanted to make sure he could. Once he was reassured, we never heard anything more about it.

If, on the other hand, your toddler reacts with enthusiasm and delight at the discovery of this bounty, relax and let him nurse. The more ambivalent your feelings about it, the less sure he is that you still love him, or even want him around. Many little ones still need lots of this kind of reassurance. Jan Wilcke of Kansas writes about her experience:

When Ardith was twenty-eight months old, Carrie was born and I weaned Ardith. The weaning would have been too abrupt by itself without the added burden of a new sister contending for mommy's affection. Ardith seemed more tense, and I was unhappy about the situation. So, after two months, Ardith began nursing again.

For about six months after that, Ardith nursed twice a day. She now nurses once every few weeks. I believe this occasional nursing is important to her in a way different than it is for Carrie. Her need to nurse occurs quite often when she's had a bad morning, and we're both "nearing the end of our rope." It's as if she's asking, "Do you love me as much as Carrie? Do you love me enough to let me nurse?" I think tandem nursing, while difficult at times, is a wonderful way to reassure a toddler when a new sibling arrives. And a warm lap with some mommy's milk is a safe retreat for the child when the demands of his enlarging world are too much for him.

All aspects of nursing a toddler past a year or so are discussed in Norma Jane Bumgarner's book, MOTHERING YOUR NURSING TODDLER. Norma Jane, a long-time La Leche League Leader, shares the experiences of other mothers as well as advice from experts. It is an excellent resource for mothers who are nursing toddlers, considering weaning, nursing while pregnant, or tandem nursing. You can order a copy from La Leche League International or your local LLL Group. For details, see the Appendix.

15

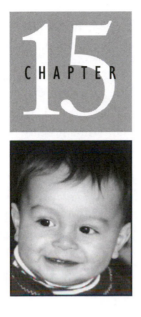

Discipline Is Loving Guidance

As parents, our goal is to have the wisdom to guide our child's growth so that he can become an independent, mature, loving person, with his talents and abilities developed to their fullest.

Our first job is to meet his physical and emotional needs as fully as we can, so that a secure foundation is laid for his advance to maturity. Through breastfeeding we are getting him off to the right start. The breastfeeding relationship itself makes us more sensitive to his needs, so we are quicker and surer in devising ways of meeting them. As our child grows, his needs change. We must progressively let go of him as he assumes the direction of his own life. This process will not be complete until he is fully grown, but it starts in babyhood. This book, therefore, would be incomplete if we did not look into the beginnings of independence.

Before your baby enters the toddler years, it is important for you and your husband to share your feelings and ideas about discipline with each other as you develop your own style of parenting.

Setting the STAGE

Discipline is an integral part of everything we do for and with our children. Having developed a philosophy of mothering our babies and toddlers through breastfeeding and weaning, we are now ready to go on to develop other aspects of mothering our young child. "If you have been doing a good job of mothering, you are already doing a good job of disciplining," says Dr. Hugh Riordan, psychiatrist and LLL father.

In his book, BECOMING A FATHER, Dr. William Sears tells how parents begin the process of disciplining their child:

> *By being available and responsive to your baby during the first year you learn to read your baby's cries. You learn to anticipate the behavior that will follow certain cues. You learn to interpret what your baby is feeling by watching how he is acting. Learning to read the feelings behind a baby's actions sets the stage for a very important part of discipline in the older child; determining the feelings behind a child's actions.*

A NEED FOR GUIDANCE

As the baby-child grows, he will need guidance, instruction, and sometimes correction to learn the ways of our world. If the foundation of secure love was laid when he was a baby, and if he sees his parents as kind, polite, and considerate people, he will try to imitate them, because he wants to act in ways that will please them (most of the time). We still have to respect his growth patterns and not ask of him more than he is capable of giving at his stage of development, but we can and should give some direction to his inexperience. How to do this is where the difficulty often lies. Before we can successfully begin to discipline our little ones we must have a clear idea of why we are doing what we are doing and how we should go about doing it. There should be no sharp break in our ways of guiding our child's development. From infancy on, children need loving guidance which reflects acceptance of their capabilities and sensitivity to their feelings.

Elizabeth Hormann, an experienced mother and La Leche League Leader, wrote this about toddlers' needs:

> *We would like to think that children learn the civilizing virtues— caring, compassion, consideration—simply by our good example, but most children need a little more than that. A clear definition of acceptable behavior, our expectation that they can meet that standard, and periodic guidance when they stray—all of these are*

necessary. Sometimes we have to thwart our wee ones....We have to be alert so that they don't hurt other people or their possessions; we need to know the difference between the normal behavior of toddlers and small children and behavior that becomes disruptive and out of hand. It is not easy to guide a small child when she clearly wants to go in another direction, but she needs us to do that for her.

It is not really so very different from what we did when they were babies. We looked to their needs, met them, and tuned out the critics who said we were spoiling them or babying them or ignoring our own needs too much. We were confident we knew our babies and ourselves best—and for the most part, we did. That hasn't changed. We still know our children better than anyone else. Because we know them and love them dearly, we are better equipped than anyone else to guide them through the complex steps of growing up, of learning the rules, of developing character.

Guiding our children—lovingly—is an important part of caring for them and helping them be loving and lovable to people within our families and beyond. Next to breastfeeding, it is the best gift we can give a small child; and like breastfeeding, the benefits last a lifetime.

Discipline and PUNISHMENT

Discipline is a much maligned word, often associated with punishment and deprivation. Yet discipline actually refers to the guidance which we as parents lovingly give our children to help them do the right things for the right reasons—to help them grow into secure, happy, and loving persons able to step out into the world with confidence in their own ability to succeed in whatever they set out to do.

In *The Discipline Book* by William and Martha Sears, the authors explain their approach to discipline based on their professional knowledge and their personal experience raising eight children:

Discipline is grounded on a healthy relationship between parent and child. To know how to discipline your child you must first know your child.

They go on to explain:

Wise disciplinarians spend time and energy keeping one step ahead of their child and setting conditions that promote good behavior, leaving the child fewer opportunities to misbehave. Wise disciplinarians:

- *stay connected to their children*
- *develop a mutual sensitivity between parent and child*

Parents need to develop their own parenting style as their little one grows.

- *spend more time promoting desirable behavior, so they need less corrective discipline*
- *have a working understanding of age-appropriate behavior*
- *use humor to promote cooperation in the child*
- *are able to get behind the eyes of their child and redirect behavior.*

In discussing the role of punishment in discipline, the Sears' believe that it must be used wisely:

The child who is punished too much (or too severely) behaves more out of fear of punishment or the punisher than for the satisfaction of behaving right.

WHAT ABOUT SPANKING?

Outwitting a determined toddler is a challenge. His pranks and explorations are to him just innocent fun but they may be dangerous or destructive. It's our job to teach him and set limits for him. But we have found that in the long run, spanking a defiant toddler only leads to tears, resentment, and an uncontrollable (and understandable) urge to hit a baby brother or sister. Our children learn by examples they see, and parents are the ones they most desire to imitate. So we must ask ourselves what kind of example we want to set for them. Punishing young children by spanking and slapping frequently reflects the impatience and frustration of the parent. It is not the kind of behavior we want our children to imitate. Spanking does not help a child learn self-discipline.

As psychologist and popular columnist Eda LeShan writes in her book *When Your Child Drives You Crazy:*

Is spanking a helpful, constructive form of discipline? No, it is not. Unequivocally! It may relieve our anger and clear the air when the atmosphere has gotten pretty tense and wound up, but it does not teach any constructive lessons about human relations, and after all, that's what discipline is all about: the way in which we try to teach our children to live in a civilized fashion with themselves and others....

Even when we think we are being rational about spanking, we're still not teaching any terribly valuable lessons. We say, for example, "I have to give you a spanking in order to make you remember how dangerous it is to run across the road." The lesson there is: "Here I am, a grown-up—a college graduate, even—and the only resource I have at my disposal to teach you the dangers of traffic is physical violence!" What a discouraging picture of human potential!

Of course, there are other things parents do that can be harmful to a child. Physical punishment is only one aspect. Parents can undermine a child's self-esteem in other ways, too. Nancy Samalin, author of *Loving Your Child Is Not Enough,* explains:

Children take criticism from a parent very personally. They feel attacked by someone whose admiration they crave.... Children need appreciation and praise, not indifference and criticism.

No child ever has too much self-esteem. If you take every opportunity to point out what children do well, praise them descriptively for it, and express appreciation, your child will become more cooperative, competent, and confident.

Normal Toddler TRAITS

Parents sometimes find it difficult to make the changeover from the total giving that a baby needs to the more active role of meeting the needs of a toddler. Over the years many of us had to unlearn some of the attitudes about discipline we had been raised with. We learned to relax a little, laugh a lot, and be incredibly quick on our feet.

A large part of mothering a toddler is helping him through the transition from babyhood, when his every wish was a real need, to later on, when he becomes an outward-looking youngster just starting to become aware of the needs of others. In the process he needs help in

Nursing your toddler can provide a few moments of relaxation for both of you.

learning that not all of his wishes are needs, and in fact, some of them, if granted, would most surely not be good for him at all.

While most people tend to respect the growth pattern of the infant, the eighteen-month-old or two-year-old is another story. When little fingers reach for electrical outlets, coins go into mouths, and lamps are toppled over, parents face a new challenge. Of course, we can't permit utter chaos in our home, or unrestricted freedom. But we need to recognize that another stage of growth is taking place. The toddler is discovering the world around him, as he wants to touch, feel, and take apart everything he sees. He is an inquisitive two-year-old private eye, investigating everything. This is normal behavior for his age; punishing him is entirely out of place and will only frustrate him. That doesn't mean that you should do nothing at all. What's needed here is distraction and firm but gentle steering in another direction.

Not all children are alike; with some it is only necessary to caution them a few times about a forbidden object. If a child can learn to respect a few taboos without being nagged or scolded and without frustration on his part, then this method is fine. Usually it is wiser to remove dangerous or breakable objects from sight.

If your explorer discovers a "forbidden" object, one good way to satisfy his curiosity is to sit down with him and let him touch, feel, and even hold it himself. Show him how the electric hair dryer works, and explain in simple language, with lots of gestures, that we must be careful because it can be dangerous, break, or come apart. Give him plenty of time to explore it with your guidance. Than change the subject, distract him, and put the forbidden article away—out of sight or reach or, better yet, both. (Remember that toddlers are great climbers.)

AN OUNCE OF PREVENTION

The time-honored adage, "An ounce of prevention is worth a pound of cure" can be most important in avoiding upsets with our busy little toddler. "It makes good practical sense," says Nancy Stanton of Florida, "to baby-proof your house as much as possible, because otherwise you'll spend your entire day battling with your child. It's hard enough to protect your child against the things you have no direct control over (such as cars on the street), so, especially if you have several preschoolers, keep your home environment as simple as possible. One mother even suspended her kitchen garbage can from the ceiling.

Nancy continues: "With very active toddlers, extreme measures are sometimes necessary to preserve your sanity. Someday you can put the knobs back on your kitchen cabinets. Most likely you have already given up at least one lower cupboard to your toddler anyway. Be sure to fill it with real utensils—an old coffee pot, plastic bowls, and spatulas."

DANGEROUS SITUATIONS

In the case of a really dangerous situation, such as chewing on an electric cord or running out in the street, mother should allow herself the full emotional expression of her fears; the child will gradually adopt these justifiable fears of real dangers and avoid them. A sudden shriek of alarm, accompanied by some fast footwork gets the message across pretty well when your little one reaches for the electric plug or runs toward the street.

In any case, always keep an eye on your toddler, for his own safety. Pediatric experts who have carefully studied accident patterns in the very young child state that it is only when a child has reached the age of approximately three that you can begin to teach him how to protect himself. Until that age he can only be protected by the watchful eye of his caretakers, and it's up to you to make sure the eyes are there.

LOOK TO THE CAUSE

When your little one is crabby and uncooperative, there may be a variety of reasons. Is he tired? Bored? Hungry? Over-stimulated? Sometimes figuring out the cause of misbehavior is a good way to avoid future problems.

Little children (like grown-ups) are often at their worst if they are over-tired or hungry. Nancy Stanton observes: "Toddlers usually need some extra sleep in the daytime, but they don't want to miss anything. If your child is really tired, stop everything—close the drapes, turn off the TV, don't do anything yourself—put a pillow on the floor and both of you lie down."

Or maybe his behavior is a signal to mother, telling her it's time to stop talking on the telephone or visiting with the neighbors, or whatever it is she is doing that takes her away from her little one, mentally if not physically. It's time to get back down on his level and notice him.

SAY WHAT YOU MEAN

"Come in the house right now, Kate," you call for the fifth time. Kate, still ignoring your summons, goes right on playing. Do you really want her to come in "right now" or don't you care? If you don't care, then don't call her until you do. Then, call her once. Wait a couple of minutes and call again. If she doesn't respond, go out, scoop her up, and carry her cheerfully and speedily into the house. She will soon learn that you mean what you say.

"To a two-year-old child, a call to stop playing and come in for lunch may on certain days be too much," says Edwina Froehlich, one of LLL's co-Founders. "Try going out there ten minutes in advance with a nutritious snack you know he'll like, and when that's finished start the getting-in process."

LIMIT TELEVISION TIME

Television programs can be a tremendous influence on young children's behavior. You need to monitor the kinds of programs your children watch as well as how much time they spend watching TV. A young child needs to learn from a variety of activities and interactions. Television does not offer the opportunity for these types of learning. What children do learn from TV may not be in keeping with your family's values. Preschoolers often cannot distinguish fantasy from reality and programs depicting violence can be particularly upsetting and frightening for them.

But often, it's not so much what's happening on the television screen that causes the biggest problem—it's what's not happening that matters most. Too much television interferes with active communication among family members.

There are, of course, educational programs directed toward young children which you may find of value. As a parent, you have the responsibility to make informed judgments. Even so, you need to be aware of the hazards of commercials. A child can be enticed into wanting expensive toys and non-nutritious food products simply because he is bombarded with advertising campaigns.

TEMPER TANTRUMS

On the subject of toddlers and tantrums, Edwina Froehlich recalls her own experiences:

Temper tantrums can be devastating to both mother and child. Having had to cope with two children who had tantrums, I did learn a little. I followed the usual suggestions with the first boy—a spank on the bottom made him scream harder, of course; trying to firmly take him to his room was hard on my shins; a stern reprimand couldn't be heard over his screaming. Ignoring him was the best of the lot, since at least it didn't add to the child's hysteria. Still, this neither solved anything, nor prevented future tantrums. As I became better informed about our nutritional needs, I became aware that the timing of the tantrums often coincided with periods of hunger. They seldom occurred immediately after a meal. Once in progress, you can't stop a full-blown tantrum by offering food, but understanding the cause at least enables you to cope better. Better still, it can perhaps show you the way to help prevent or at least lessen future tantrums.

When our youngest was about two and a half, a friend had come for lunch, and Peter was for the most part amusing himself. But late in the afternoon, when I told him to stop something he was doing, his tolerance level burst and he had his first tantrum! I went over and sat on the floor beside him and reached over to pat him gently. At first he rejected my hand and literally threw it back at me. So I just sat by him and waited, whispering, "I love you Petey." He quieted very quickly and rolled himself over to me, burying his face in my lap, and finally sobbing in comfort. When the storm was over he had forgotten what started it and we trotted immediately to the kitchen. While I was happy and relieved to know that I had been able to calm him, I girded myself for repeat performances. To my surprise, he had only two or three more tantrums, and they were mild and quickly over.

If your child has tantrums often, try to determine if there is a pattern. Do the tantrums occur at the same time each day? Only with certain people? What seems to be the source of the frustration? Can you possibly remove the source? Do what you can to avoid the frustrating situations that cause him to explode.

If your child does have a tantrum, he'll calm down sooner if you remain calm and nonthreatening. As soon as the child will permit it, touch him gently and try to help him recover. When the sobbing has stopped you can offer him a nutritious snack if you suspect he is hungry, but be sure it is not a sweet, or he may react with another tantrum soon afterward.

The tantrum a child throws in public is no harder on him than if he were at home, but it is agonizing for the parent. Onlookers are quick to show their disapproval of your "naughty" child. Embarrassing though it is, the basic approach to handling the tantrum is the same—the parent cannot react in anger, but must remain calm and speak in quiet, soothing tones. Both mother and child are in a state of distress in this situation, but the child is the more helpless of the two. He cannot just turn off his rage on command. If it is at all possible, pick the child up and move to a more secluded spot where he will bother fewer people. Any attempt to reason with him in this highly emotional state will be wasted. It may be that the only thing you can do is stand by quietly and wait it out.

THE BITING CHILD

What about the child who bites or hits? This seems to be a rather common problem, and a difficult one, especially when other children are around. Norma Jane Bumgarner, author of MOTHERING YOUR NURSING TODDLER, tells this story:

About two years ago (at an LLL meeting), my beautiful, superbly mothered, absolutely perfect toddler was bitten by somebody's rotten, neglected, little monster—or so it appeared to me at the time. As I comforted my baby I shot reproachful glances in the direction of the little culprit's mother, making no attempt to hide the feelings we all have when somebody hurts our child.

As proof that there is justice in the world, our next child turned out to be not only a biter, but the most determined, dangerous biter I have ever seen. This is one of the most difficult things I have ever dealt with in my life, and it was made even harder for me by those few mothers who reacted the way I did two years ago.

Naturally, when we realize this is going to be a problem with our youngster, it behooves us to be ever watchful and intervene by removing him from the scene with great dispatch and firmness. Speed is of the essence. Yelling, spanking, or biting the child back doesn't solve the problem. Diane Kramer of New Mexico writes, "Young children are usually very oral in reaction. They use their mouths to feel, to love, to test, and to argue, and it takes time and maturity for them to realize that not all these reactions are acceptable. Meanwhile, love them, cuddle them, help them through their frustrations, and recognize that this too shall pass."

If your child seems to resort to biting when confronted with groups of children, you may need to avoid these situations for a while. Help him learn to get along with just one other child at a time, with careful vigilance as he does so.

THE SANDMAN COMETH NOT

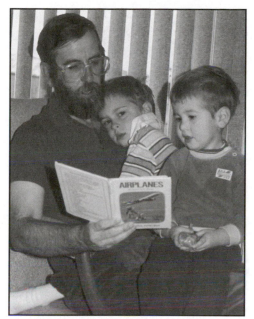

Reading a bedtime story can become part of your family's nighttime ritual.

In some families, bedtime is a source of frustration, with everyone ending up exhausted and exasperated before finally getting to sleep. Planning a course of action ahead of time may help to avoid disaster! While it may not matter whether or not your preschooler goes to bed at a predetermined time every night since he doesn't have to get up early the next morning, some bedtime regularity is a good idea.

Don't set bedtime too early though, or he just won't be sleepy. Children can only sleep a certain number of hours, and if your child goes to bed at seven, he may be up bright-eyed at five in the morning. You can't have it both ways.

When bedtime comes, make it a cozy, quiet time, with no rush or hurry. A warm bath with time to play in the tub, a nutritious snack such as an apple, with tooth brushing afterwards, and a quiet story while you snuggle together under the covers, all lead to a relaxed little person, ready and willing to go to sleep. He may want you to stay with him for a while, and of course, you should. It's scary all by himself.

A Look AHEAD

As your children get older, discipline becomes even more of a challenge. Children will keep pressuring you, testing the limits, on into their teens. If they know that you are and always have been firm and consistent and loving, and that you trust them, it will be easier.

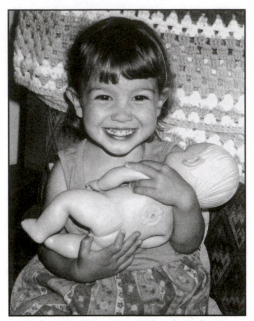
Your little one will learn about gentle mothering from you.

As you set limits for your older child you may find that at times he may be really angry with you, but he'll get over it soon as long as he knows that you really love him. Show him you love him by your actions, even when you have to say "no." As Dr. Ross Campbell reminds us: "The first fact we must understand in order to have a well-disciplined child is that making a child feel loved is the most important part of good discipline."

Whatever happens, remember that each child is an individual, and you can't lay down hard and fast rules that will be appropriate for all children. In this matter of discipline, if you have the intimate understanding of your little one that the breastfeeding relationship fosters, and if you are clear in your mind about the real nature of discipline, you can safely follow your own instincts as parents. "It's not our job as parents simply to take care of our children, but to help them learn how to take care of themselves," says Norma Jane Bumgarner. Jalelah Fraley, a mother from California, once remarked: "Out of all this will come sons and daughters well on the road to meeting the needs of our grandchildren in a wholesome, happy way—we shall see an era of 'gently nurtured' loving human beings."

When your child is born, you devote yourself to meeting all of his needs; you nurse him when he is hungry and hold him close as long as he needs and likes it. As he grows, he wants less snuggling and more sociability; you prop him up in the midst of the family from time to time. As the days and weeks and months go by, he becomes more independent in other ways; he starts eating solid foods and does not nurse so long or so often. Soon he picks up bits of food to bring them to his mouth himself. And one day, he is feeding himself, handling a spoon with dignity and aplomb, albeit with occasional spectacular messes. Now he is drinking from a cup, and as the months speed by, taking no more than a friendly nightcap from the breast. You are still there when he needs you. There is never an abrupt withdrawal of your love as expressed first through the warmth and closeness of breastfeeding and later in other ways. Secure in knowing that he can retreat for a bit into babyhood if he wants to, he ventures further and further into childhood, and finally (all to soon, it seems in retrospect), he isn't a baby anymore. Before you know it, he will be on his way to school, with a cheerful wave good-bye as off he goes.

The years go by, and though parenting does get somewhat easier, it is always challenging and interesting. Our children will never stop needing us in one way or another, thank goodness! But we have to learn when to stand back and when to offer our help. And someday, your little boy may be standing over his own wife as she happily nurses their baby, or your daughter, looking so like her mother at that age, may be proudly nursing hers. All the work and worry, the time and the endless patience, will have paid off. It was all very much worthwhile.

With your understanding guidance, your child will grow from dependence to independence gradually, and always with the love that is his birthright, and the great need of our world.

PART SIX | *Special Situations*

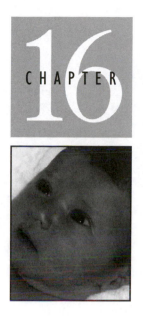

Problems at the Beginning

Breastfeeding in special situations often requires patience and commitment, but mothers have continued breastfeeding in almost every situation imaginable. They have discovered that when the circumstances surrounding breastfeeding are less than ideal, the special benefits of breastfeeding become even more important.

New babies and mothers struggling with special problems after birth appreciate the emotional closeness and reassurance of their unique breastfeeding relationship. Breastfeeding helps them get to know one another despite the complications. In addition, human milk's nutritional and immunological benefits are especially important for the baby at risk.

The circumstances that might temporarily prevent you from nursing your baby are extremely rare. If you or your baby become ill, make it clear to your physician or health care provider that you want to breastfeed your baby in spite of the special circumstances, and ask for his or her cooperation in bringing this about. Your positive

Parents are understandably distraught to find out their newborn has a serious problem.

attitude toward breastfeeding is a most important factor and one your doctor will take into consideration. Be confident that your milk is the best possible nourishment for your baby if he can have any liquid or food by mouth (or even by nasogastric tube inserted through the baby's nose and into his stomach). Not only is breastfeeding safe for the sick baby, it is one of the best medicines for him. Doctors have often commented on how quickly a breastfed baby seems to recover. Your insistence on continuing to breastfeed whenever possible during a period of medical treatment can make a difference in the type of treatment the doctor may suggest.

In the case of an unusual breastfeeding situation, your doctor can contact La Leche League International's Center for Breastfeeding Information (CBI) for additional information; encourage him or her to do so. See the Appendix for further information abut the CBI. Many doctors and nurses take advantage of La Leche League's information and experience with mothers breastfeeding in unusual situations.

You'll also appreciate the support of your local La Leche League Leader. She may be able to put you in touch with another mother who has breastfed in a situation similar to yours. If your doctor is unwilling or unable to take positive steps to keep your baby nursing, you have a right to seek other medical advice and assistance. Your baby's welfare comes first.

Breastfeeding After a CESAREAN BIRTH

Of course you can breastfeed your baby despite a cesarean birth. You will probably get off to a somewhat slower start, however, as a cesarean section is major abdominal surgery, and it will take time to recover. If you know you are going to be having a cesarean, you'll want to find out in advance as much as possible about cesarean births. Many mothers who have previously had cesarean deliveries have been able to deliver subsequent babies vaginally. But if it is necessary for you to deliver your baby by cesarean, or if you are reading this after you've had a cesarean birth, you can be confident that a cesarean birth need not be a deterrent to a happy breastfeeding experience.

Babies born by cesarean may be more lethargic than those born without the aftereffects of anesthetics. It may take a few days for these to wear off, and your baby may temporarily have a weak sucking reflex. Be sure to discuss the choice of anesthetics with your doctor ahead of time. While a general anesthetic may be the easiest to administer and may be necessary in an emergency situation, it will make you unconscious for the birth and drowsy for some time afterwards. Your baby may also be sleepy at first. This may postpone your first contact with the baby you have waited so long to hold and nurse. A regional (spinal or epidural) anesthetic allows you to be conscious so you can hold and nurse your baby soon after he is born. However, some reports show that a baby's sucking can also be affected by these anesthetics.

It is important to breastfeed your baby as soon as possible not only because of the importance of early contact and bonding, but also because breastfeeding helps the uterus to contract and return to its normal size more quickly. This also aids healing.

Breastfeeding can begin on the delivery table in the operating room, although you will need help in positioning and holding the baby. Because you will still have an IV in one arm, and the other arm may be strapped down while the doctors finish stitching the incision, it will be difficult for you to maneuver the baby. The baby's father or a nurse can help you place the baby tummy down on your chest to nurse, moving him gently toward your nipple.

If you are breastfeeding for the first time in the recovery room, position baby so he can reach your nipple easily. You may have to lie flat on your back due to the anesthesia, so make sure he is well supported and close enough to you to easily latch on. You should be fairly comfortable, if the anesthesia is still in effect. Again, feel free to ask for assistance in positioning the baby.

THE EARLY DAYS

Rooming-in is a wonderful way to get to know your baby and get nursing off to a good start. Some hospitals do not allow rooming-in for cesarean mothers for the first twenty-four hours, but most are becoming more flexible about this. Mothers find it comforting to have their babies with them all the time. Plan on having your baby's father, another family member, or a friend with you to help with the baby.

For the first few days after giving birth your abdomen will be sore and tender. Most medications that are given for pain will not affect your baby through your milk, so do not feel that you must endure discomfort. You and your baby will get off to a better start if you are comfortable.

Pay special attention to the baby's sucking patterns and how he latches on to your breast. Studies have shown that some anesthetics used during a cesarean birth can have an effect on baby's suck. It is especially important to avoid the use of artificial nipples which can cause nipple confusion. If baby is showing any signs of difficulty in sucking effectively, check to see if the hospital has a lactation consultant on staff who can assist you. Or contact your La Leche League Leader for further help.

POSITIONING WHILE LYING DOWN

It may be easiest to nurse while lying down for the first day or so. You and your baby can nap together, enabling you to spend more time with him without becoming fatigued.

With the bed in a flat position, have a helper place the side rails of your bed in the "up" position and use extra pillows behind your back for additional support. Carefully roll to one side while grasping the side rail and relaxing your abdominal muscles. Move slowly to avoid any strain. Cover your abdomen with a towel or rolled-up blanket to protect you from baby's kicking. Flex your legs and place a pillow between them for more support and less strain on your stomach muscles. Lean back into the pillows behind your back.

Ask your helper or a nurse to place the baby on his side facing you so you are positioned chest to chest. His head may need to rest on your arm or a rolled-up blanket to bring his mouth up to the level of your nipple. In this position, the baby should be able to latch on well.

It is important to nurse on both breasts at each feeding in the early days, which means you will have to roll over. Turn your hips a little at a time with your feet positioned flat on the bed. Move slowly, being careful not to pull suddenly on your incision. Again, use the side rails to help. Reposition the pillows and have a nurse help you ease the baby onto the other breast.

A baby born by cesarean may need extra help getting started breastfeeding.

Once your incision is less tender, you can roll over in bed by yourself while holding the baby on your chest. Use the technique described above while securely grasping the baby.

POSITIONING WHILE SITTING UP

It is wise to use several different nursing positions in the early days in order to speed your recovery. Some women, despite a tender incision, prefer to nurse while sitting up in bed or in a chair.

Place the head of your bed upright while elevating your legs slightly. Flex your legs from time to time to help circulation. Prop a pillow (or rolled-up blanket) under one arm while placing baby on a pillow over your incision. This not only raises him to your nipple, but also protects your sore abdomen. Hold baby very close, with his whole body facing yours, resting his head on your arm for support. This allows your free hand to support your breast.

FOOTBALL HOLD POSITION

This is a good way to avoid direct pressure on your incision as baby is lying beside you, not on your lap. While sitting in an upright position, tuck a pillow under one arm. Place baby's head close to your breast, facing toward you, with his body tucked under your arm. His body should be bent at the hips, with his bottom against the back of the chair or bed you are leaning against. Support the back of his neck with your hand. Be sure he is up at the level of your nipple so you are not straining forward to reach him.

WHEN YOU GET HOME

Because you have had major abdominal surgery, as well as having given birth, you will need plenty of rest when you go home. Put the baby in a cradle next to your bed or right in bed with you so you don't have to get up and down. With plenty of diapers, a pitcher of juice or water, and a snack, you'll be set for several hours. You'll both get lots of rest while getting to know one another.

If at all possible, find someone to come and help out with cooking and household tasks while you rest in bed. Ask friends to bring meals, entertain toddlers, or do laundry.

Some women have trouble adjusting to a cesarean birth when they had envisioned themselves giving birth vaginally. Major surgery, especially when unexpected, can be upsetting when other plans had been made for the birth experience. Mothers who have had cesarean births may want to get in touch with a support group to share their common problems and experiences. For further information, see the Appendix. La Leche League can also help you through your local Leader, who can provide suggestions, support, and more information about breastfeeding and mothering after a cesarean birth.

Ann Hague, a mother from Georgia, writes:

After a cesarean, a mother and baby may have to be more patient and persistent, but the rewards are well worth it. My surgery healed nicely, and my baby and I are experiencing a beautiful relationship through breastfeeding. A cesarean birth can be an apprehensive time, but it should not rob you of the remarkably loving experience of breastfeeding.

What If Your Baby Is JAUNDICED?

Your baby may be only hours old, but more likely he is two or three days old. You notice that the whites of his eyes as well as his skin have a yellow cast. Or maybe he looks as though he's been to the tropics and acquired a golden tan. The doctor informs you that the baby is jaundiced and may refer to the bilirubin level in the baby's blood.

Jaundice is common in babies during the first weeks after birth and tends to occur more often in breastfed babies. In almost all cases, it is harmless and no treatment is necessary. The jaundice disappears, and the baby is none the worse for the experience. You can continue to nurse your baby, and both of you can be assured of receiving breastfeeding's ongoing benefits. In fact, nursing your baby soon after he is born and frequently thereafter is an excellent way to keep jaundice from becoming a problem. Even when treatment is necessary, there are a number of ways to avoid any separation between mother and baby. Knowing more about jaundice will help you understand what is happening so that you don't have to feel anxious about your baby's welfare. Understanding jaundice will also help you communicate with health care providers.

NORMAL OR PHYSIOLOGIC JAUNDICE

Jaundice in the newborn is a common and usually harmless condition. Nearly half of all newborns appear jaundiced in the days after birth to a mild or moderate degree with no ill effects. In most cases the jaundice will disappear by itself in two to three weeks.

Normal newborn jaundice is called "physiologic jaundice." This means the jaundice occurs as part of a normal physiologic process. Jaundice itself refers to an excess of bilirubin being temporarily stored in the baby's blood and tissues. The bilirubin is an orange-yellow pigment which gives the baby's skin the yellowish cast that is characteristic of jaundice. Bilirubin comes from the normal process of breaking down extra red blood cells, part of baby's adjustment to life outside the womb.

In the normal course of events, new blood cells are continually being produced and old ones broken down. Newborns have an excess of red blood cells because the oxygen supply in utero is limited and the baby needs the extra red blood cells to carry oxygen. After birth, the baby's lungs supply plenty of oxygen and the extra cells are no longer needed. The breakdown of these old cells frees iron and bilirubin. The iron is stored in the liver and other tissues to be used later in the manufacture of new blood cells.

Bilirubin is simply a residual product of this process, which must be disposed of by the liver. When a newborn's immature liver cannot eliminate the bilirubin as fast as it is produced, the excess is stored in the tissues and the result is jaundice. To determine if treatment is needed, the bilirubin level is measured with a blood test. If the baby has an abnormally high level of bilirubin, or if levels are rising rapidly, these blood tests may be repeated several times a day in the first week in order to monitor the changes in the bilirubin level.

Physiologic jaundice usually appears on the second to fourth day in normal, full-term babies. In most cases, it gradually disappears by itself, although this may take several weeks in some babies. Normal jaundice is not a disease; it is a harmless condition that has no aftereffects. In fact, because physiologic jaundice appears more often in breastfed babies, some experts believe that higher bilirubin levels may be nature's norm for newborns; they actually may have a beneficial effect.

JAUNDICE STARTING ON THE FIRST DAY

Pathologic jaundice in a newborn is caused by an abnormal breakdown of red blood cells or any other cause of increased bilirubin production or reduced excretion by the liver. This situation is most commonly caused by Rh or ABO blood incompatibilities. While Rh incompatibility is becoming relatively rare, ABO incompatibility, a much milder condition, is still quite common. Your doctor will know whether he needs to watch for either of these conditions by checking your blood type before your baby is born. Other causes of pathologic jaundice include infection, metabolic problems, or gastrointestinal obstruction.

Pathologic or abnormal jaundice is often visible at birth or within the first 24 hours and the bilirubin level may rise quite rapidly. Medical treatment is usually necessary in cases of pathologic jaundice, but breastfeeding can continue during treatment and often helps to reduce the jaundice. The reason for concern about very high bilirubin levels is that bilirubin can damage brain cells. A level of 20mg/dl or above is considered to be a high level in the first forty-eight hours; after that 25 mg/dl or above is considered a high level in an otherwise healthy, full-term baby. Problems can occur at lower levels in premies. Kernicterus, the medical term for the brain damage that can be caused by excessively high concentrations of bilirubin, is quite rare, and is of greater concern in the premature or sick baby with pathologic jaundice.

WHY JAUNDICE CAUSES PROBLEMS FOR NEWBORNS

When parents are told that their baby's bilirubin level is elevated, that the baby needs more blood tests, or that their baby's jaundice needs treatment, they may become very worried. Their precious newborn, who was fine yesterday, suddenly seems to have a frightening and complicated condition. Parents may have lots of questions, and the answers may be confusing.

Some mothers may even be told that their baby's jaundice is caused by human milk. At one time it was thought that high bilirubin levels that persisted past the first few days in breastfed babies were a special kind of jaundice called "breast milk jaundice." Many physicians suggested feeding the baby formula for 24 to 48 hours as the best way to bring down bilirubin levels. Unfortunately, even if this weaning was meant to be "temporary," for many mothers it was the beginning of the end of breastfeeding. Mothers of jaundiced babies, in general, tend to wean earlier—not because jaundice interferes with breastfeeding, but because the treatment often does.

It is important for parents to remember that complications or damage from high bilirubin levels are very rare. Decisions about treatment will depend on how old the baby is, whether there are other health problems, and how quickly bilirubin levels are rising. Parents have input into treatment decisions, and you should let your doctor know how important it is to you to continue breastfeeding and not be separated from your baby. Your feelings will influence your doctor's recommendation. Frequent breastfeeding itself will help lower bilirubin levels and should be considered an important part of the treatment plan. Continued monitoring of the baby's condition along with efforts to encourage the baby to nurse often and effectively may be all that is needed. While some physicians may still recommend a day or two without human milk to bring down the bilirubin level, many have come to recognize that this advice is not in the best interest of either a breastfeeding mother or her baby. Instead they may suggest the use of phototherapy along with continued breastfeeding, if the jaundice needs to be treated at all.

PHOTOTHERAPY AS TREATMENT

If your doctor feels that your baby's jaundice requires treatment, he or she will probably prescribe phototherapy. "Bili-lights" are used to speed up the elimination of bilirubin. The baby is placed under the lights, wearing only a diaper, with protective patches covering his eyes.

This treatment is designed to keep the bilirubin from approaching critical levels at which, in extreme cases, an exchange transfusion may be necessary.

Generally speaking, the earlier and more rapid the rise in the bilirubin level, the sooner phototherapy will be started. It might be started at 18 mg/dl in a full-term baby who is two to three days old, or at 20 mg/dl in a baby more than 72 hours old. Sick or premature infants who are jaundiced present special problems, and medical treatment is often necessary at lower bilirubin levels.

Even if your baby needs to spend time under the bili-lights, frequent breastfeeding is important in helping the baby get rid of excess bilirubin. You'll want to be sure he nurses approximately every two hours, or ten to twelve times per day. This will also help him avoid dehydration.

Light therapy does not have to be continuous to be effective. When you nurse your baby, remove his eye patches, cuddle him close, and look into his eyes. Holding and stroking him even when he is under the lights will be reassuring for both of you.

In some cases, you may be able to have the baby and the bili-lights moved into your room. You'll feel better with the baby close by, and keeping up frequent nursings will be that much easier. Light therapy

A baby who is receiving phototherapy needs to breastfeed often.

can also be done at home with a rented light unit, so that baby does not have to remain in the hospital after mother is discharged. The newest option is the Wallaby unit, a fiberoptic blanket that wraps around the baby's trunk. The baby doesn't need eye patches and mother can hold the baby and breastfeed without interrupting the treatment. You will probably need to return to the hospital for blood tests to monitor the baby's bilirubin level. See Appendix for information on the Wallaby unit.

"FLUSHING OUT" JAUNDICE

At one time, it was thought that giving a baby bottles of water would help to "flush out" the jaundice. But research has shown that water supplements given to newborns in the first few days do not help to reduce jaundice. In fact, one study showed that the more water the baby received the higher the level of bilirubin reported.

Bottles of water may reduce the amount of nursing the baby does and cause nipple confusion. Anything that makes the baby less interested in the breast or interferes with nursing at least ten to twelve times per day can increase jaundice in the breastfed baby. Since bilirubin is eliminated in the baby's stools, frequent nursing is one of the best ways to help the baby get rid of the excess bilirubin.

Hypoglycemia in NEWBORNS

Newborns are often tested to determine their blood glucose levels and parents are sometimes told that their baby has hypoglycemia—or low blood sugar—and needs to be treated with a glucose supplement. Babies at greater risk for hypoglycemia include those who are premature or postmature, those who are small or large for gestational age, and those who have been deprived of oxygen. Hypoglycemia can also indicate infection or a metabolic disorder.

The most common cause of hypoglycemia is delayed or inadequate feedings. A baby who is put to the breast soon after birth and kept near the mother so he can nurse freely will be much less likely to show signs of hypoglycemia. In adults, treatment for low blood sugar includes small, frequent, high protein meals which is exactly what the newborn receives when he nurses often.

Giving glucose water feedings instead of nursing causes a sudden rise in blood glucose levels and then a sudden drop. Glucose water feedings in the early days have also been associated with greater weight loss and higher bilirubin levels.

In some hospitals, glucose feedings are given to all babies whose birth weight falls above or below certain standards. It's a good idea to discuss this with your health care provider before the baby is born and request that routine glucose supplements not be given. If a blood test indicates a glucose supplement is necessary, artificial nipples can be avoided by giving the glucose by spoon, cup, or eyedropper. Sometimes the glucose is given by IV. Nursing at least ten to twelve times per day is the best way to stabilize a baby's glucose levels.

If Your Baby Is PREMATURE

Premature babies come in many sizes. Some may weigh two pounds or less; other premies may be fully developed and weigh close to five pounds. Some will be able to nurse soon after birth, while others will have to be kept warm and protected in an isolette and will not be ready to nurse at the breast for several weeks. If your baby is very small, he may have to stay in the hospital for a month or more and may at first be fed through a tube inserted through his nose to his stomach. Pumping milk for your baby is something only you can do, and it will help you overcome the worry and fear you feel about his condition. Kathie Patten of South Dakota writes:

> It was a good feeling knowing that I was able to do something for my baby. Giving birth prematurely had left me with subtle feelings of guilt. Even though I could not give our baby the warm, loving feelings of motherly touch and sounds, I knew I was the only one who could provide him with superior nourishment.

Later on, breastfeeding helps make up for the separation you and your baby have experienced. Rebecca Strasser from Tennessee was happy that she persevered in her efforts to breastfeed her son Jonathan

Research has shown that breastfeeding is less stressful for a premature baby than bottle-feeding.

who was born twelve weeks early weighing just under three pounds. She explains, "Nursing Jonathan has soothed the pain of our early separation....I am forever grateful to all who encouraged me to persevere so that I could know the precious joy of nursing."

HUMAN MILK IS BEST

Your baby benefits in many ways when he receives your milk. Research shows that milk from mothers who deliver prematurely contains greater amounts of antibodies and of some nutrients than does the milk of mothers delivering at term. It has been found that some of these differences are evident for as long as six months. The immunities in your milk protect your baby from illnesses to which premature infants are especially vulnerable. Human milk is easy for your baby to digest; babies use the fats and proteins in human milk more efficiently than those in formulas. Human milk may also enhance brain development in premies; one study that compared premies fed human milk with those given formula showed higher IQ scores at ages 7½ to 8 in the human milk group. When you provide your own milk for your baby you are making a critical contribution to his care. Medical technology cannot duplicate mother's milk, the perfect food for your baby.

A very tiny premie, born more than two months before his due date, may require a vitamin and mineral supplement in addition to mother's milk. If your doctor finds your baby needs this type of supplement, don't think that something is wrong with your milk. It's just that such very tiny premature babies may need more of certain nutrients to grow and develop properly. Your milk still provides the basis of the special nutrition your premature baby needs.

If your premie is unable to nurse directly from the breast at first, you'll want to start pumping or expressing your milk as soon as possible. Colostrum is especially important for him because of the immunities it provides. You'll want to freeze the milk you pump so it can be given to your baby later on. As soon as he is able to take anything by mouth (or nasogastric tube), your milk is best for him.

It will take time to learn how to pump or hand-express your milk. Thinking about your baby, looking at his picture, and calling the hospital for a report on his progress will help bring in more milk. Don't despair if the supply decreases somewhat as time goes by. Your body doesn't respond to a pump the way it would to a cuddly baby. Your supply will go up again when you begin to nurse your baby directly. (More information on pumping and storing your milk is found in Chapter 7.)

Start out by pumping or hand-expressing from both breasts at least five times a day for a total of 100 minutes or more of pumping. You do not need to pump as often as your baby would be nursing, unless you find you are not pumping enough to provide the milk he needs. Renting a hospital-quality pump that can pump both breasts at the same time will make it much easier to pump your milk.

Ideally, your milk should be stored in a refrigerator and fed to your baby within five to eight days of collection without any kind of processing. Heating the milk to high temperatures destroys many of its protective qualities. If your milk cannot be fed to your baby within five to eight days, it should be frozen.

A mother can talk to her baby and offer a comforting touch even when baby is hooked up to monitoring equipment.

The hospital may provide you with containers for collecting your milk. If not, any sterilized container may be used. Be sure your hands are scrupulously clean when you pump your milk. However, your daily shower is enough to keep your nipples clean, and it is not necessary (or even desirable) to clean them with soap, since nature has provided its own cleansing secretions.

The appearance of your milk may surprise you. It is generally thin and bluish-looking; yet, if you let it stand awhile, you will find that cream rises to the top. From one pumping session to the next, the amount of cream will differ—and this is as it should be. Pumping longer, from ten to fifteen minutes at each breast, tends to produce milk with a higher fat concentration.

Although the benefits of mother's milk for premature babies are becoming more widely recognized, there may be some reason why your milk cannot be given to your baby for a while. If this is the case, keep up your supply by pumping regularly. You can freeze the milk for later use.

A NEED FOR SUPPORT

Hospitals vary in the amount of support and cooperation they extend to mothers of premature infants. It is a real asset when the doctors and nurses caring for your infant encourage and support you in your efforts to provide human milk and realize that you alone are able to provide the perfect nourishment for him. They can help build your confidence in your ability to nurse your baby.

If, however, the hospital staff is less supportive than you'd hoped, you can still be successful. If you find you are having problems, try to discover why. Sometimes a nurse who cares for prematures isn't fully aware of how to help with breastfeeding, and it's difficult for her to assist you. Knowing that many other mothers have nursed premature babies is bound to increase your self-confidence. A supportive La Leche League Leader or experienced lactation consultant can help at times like these.

Be persistent about keeping in touch with the hospital and doctor about the baby's progress. Most professionals are very understanding about the parent's need to know what is happening to their baby. They will also encourage you to come in and give your baby as much personal care and attention as possible. Even when the baby is in an isolette, he needs human contact, and you need to be with him, too.

KANGAROO CARE

Ask the nurses about "kangaroo care" for your baby. This means placing the premature infant skin-to-skin on mother's chest under a loose-fitting shirt or gown covering them both. Research has shown that this has almost magical effects. Babies spend more time in quiet alertness and peaceful sleep. As a result, mothers feel more confident and more connected to their babies. After spending time with their babies skin-to-skin, mothers even find their pumping efforts produce more milk. Kangaroo care may be possible even for very tiny babies, and fathers can participate, too.

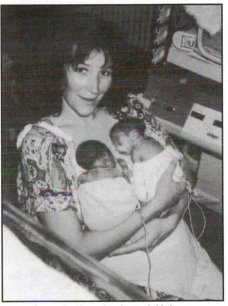

Two-week-old premie twins are held close to their mother in "kangaroo care."

THE FIRST TIME BABY NURSES

Depending on his size and gestational age it may be days or weeks before your baby is finally ready to suck. A pacifier or a "premie" nipple may be used initially to stimulate his interest in sucking, but, whenever possible, mother's breast is always best. If a premie nipple or pacifier is used, it should be used only briefly and efforts should be made to put the baby to the breast as soon as possible.

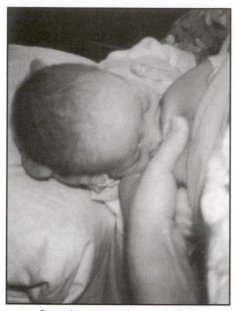

Even a tiny premie can learn to breastfeed.

Research has shown that nursing at the breast is actually less stressful to a tiny baby than bottle-feedings. Some doctors suggest that a baby get cup feedings or tube feedings when mother is not available to feed him at the breast, in order to avoid nipple confusion while baby is learning to breastfeed.

Getting a premature baby to latch on and nurse for the first time often requires patience and persistence. Ask for a comfortable chair, preferably in a private area, and lots of pillows. Both the new mother and the nurse, who may not have had a great deal of experience with helping premature infants breastfeed, may easily become frustrated at the slow progress the baby seems to make.

Keep in mind that he isn't really very strong and will need much cuddling, coaxing, and patience. He may not be able to suck well for more than a few seconds at a time. You need to be as relaxed and comfortable as possible, which sometimes isn't easy. Use pillows under your arm and in your lap, and settle your baby and yourself in a comfortable position. Be calm, gentle, patient, and observant. Initially, he may or may not show interest in the milk-giving breast. Since he has received other types of feedings, he may become confused. Reassure him with calm, gentle handling.

He may latch right on and start nursing, or he may just play around and do some half-hearted sucking, or even merely lick the nipple. This will be a learning experience for both of you. Remember that a baby may not nurse very well during the first several attempts. Often these first nursings are made up of more loving and cuddling than actual nursing. Both of you are benefiting from the close contact. Gently try to place your nipple in his mouth, but if he doesn't suck or seem interested this time, he will probably do better the next time—or the next. Remember your first attempts at feeding will take time. If he seems to be getting tired or stressed, take a break and just hold him skin-to-skin. Premature babies tire easily.

The usual positions for feeding a large, healthy infant may not work well for the small premature infant. This baby needs more support. Try supporting the baby's head with your left hand if you are nursing on the right breast. Your arm extends along the length of the baby's body which is supported with pillows in your lap. Your hand grasps his head to help hold him at the breast. Use your right hand to support your breast. You will have a good view of what is going on and good control over your baby's movements. Be sure that your back and arms are well supported with pillows, and try to relax your back and shoulders.

The nurses may want to monitor your baby's condition closely during these first feedings at the breast. After your baby has learned to latch on and actually suck for a few minutes at a feeding, he may be weighed on a very precise electronic scale to determine how much milk he has taken. Be sure to congratulate yourself for every single gram! Focus on the positive and use the scale results to help yourself learn what effective breastfeeding looks and feels like.

TAKING YOUR BABY HOME

The long-awaited day will finally come when you can take your tiny baby home from the hospital. You'll probably find yourself feeling somewhat unsure of your ability to care for your baby, since up until now his life has been so dependent on technical knowledge and complex medical equipment.

Be assured that your loving arms, careful attention, and warm milk are what he needs most at this point. Prematures babies have a lot of loving and nursing to catch up on, and they need all the time and closeness you can offer. Sleep with him, carry him in your arms or in a baby carrier or sling, let him feel the nearness of you in every way. This will help you get to know him better, so that you will be able to tell when he is hungry or when he needs rest. Give him lots of skin-to-skin contact, with only his diaper between you and him. Keep your breast readily available to him.

If he has been on supplements (either formula or pumped human milk), ask your doctor for guidelines on how much supplement to give until your baby makes the transition to total breastfeeding. It's normal during these first days at home to be concerned about whether your baby is getting enough milk at each feeding. For some mothers, renting an electronic scale, like the ones used in the hospital, and weighing the baby before and after feedings may ease these worries and make it easier to gradually discontinue the supplements. As breastfeeding becomes established, the mother may weigh the baby only once a day until she feels fully confident that he will grow and thrive on her milk alone. You can also tell that your baby is getting enough milk by counting the number of wet and soiled diapers. As usual, six to eight wet cloth diapers (five to six disposable diapers) and three to five bowel movements per day are good indications that he's getting plenty of milk.

If it is necessary to continue supplementing your premature baby, you can pump your milk after he nurses to have extra hindmilk to use as a supplement. Continuing to pump will keep up your milk supply until your baby learns to suck effectively. Try using a nursing supplementer at the breast. Check the information in Chapter 7 for tips on increasing your milk supply.

With lots of closeness and loving care your premature baby will grow and thrive. Is it worth the trouble to keep up your milk supply in order to breastfeed your premie? Jo-Anne Montgomery of Manitoba, Canada thinks so. Her daughter, Shannon, was born nine weeks early. She says, "Nursing my baby daughter has been and still is one of the greatest pleasures of my life. I encourage any mother who wants to nurse her premature baby not to give up."

A Baby with SPECIAL NEEDS

The baby born with a handicap or medical problem needs breastfeeding even more than a healthy baby does. The baby with special needs benefits particularly from the stimulation, attention, and reassurance that go with nursing at the breast. Baby's mother benefits, too, since breastfeeding helps her to focus on her baby as a baby first and foremost. If your baby has a health problem that complicates nursing, remember that breastfeeding is nearly always possible and should be encouraged. If your baby has a problem, contact your local La Leche League Leader or LLLI for information and help with breastfeeding.

The Baby with DOWN SYNDROME

For the baby with Down syndrome, a loving home environment with maximum interaction between baby and the rest of the family will help to develop his capabilities to the fullest.

Breastfeeding demonstrates to your baby your love and affection in a very special way. Breastfeeding is especially important for Down syndrome babies because they have a greater susceptibility to infections than normal infants do, so the immunity factors found in colostrum and human milk are especially valuable. And mother will find joy and delight in breastfeeding her baby and meeting his special needs.

Breastfeeding is especially important for a baby with Down syndrome

The baby with Down syndrome responds readily to love and returns it enthusiastically to those around him. He is often a delight to the whole family. Lucille Clancy says this about her son, "My heart said 'I love him,' my head said 'I wish it didn't have to be this way,' but soon Chad's big, happy smile thanked me a million times for the extra love I had given him."

Many mothers have said how important the emotional support they received from their husbands was in helping them adjust to having a handicapped baby. As Louise Wills puts it, "I cannot underestimate my husband's help with Erika. Because of him, I have been more able to think of Erika first as a child, and second as a child with a disability." Remember that by drawing on each other for support and understanding, you and your husband will both grow stronger in the process.

A baby with Down syndrome is often sleepy during the first few weeks and may have a poor sucking reflex, so extra help and patience with breastfeeding are in order. Be calm and patient as he learns to latch on, suck, and swallow. You may need to pump after feedings in the early days to stimulate your milk supply. If your baby needs supplements at first, you can offer this high-calorie hindmilk in a cup, eye dropper, feeding syringe, or nursing supplementer. The rewards of nursing your baby are well worth the extra effort, so don't be discouraged if you encounter problems. With your loving help your baby will catch on.

Above all, remember that this special baby who has been placed in your care will give as much as he receives. As Lucille Clancy explains, "Loving Chad is a continually growing experience which teaches us love, acceptance, patience, and humor. The added dimension that Chad has given our family will continue to enrich us as we live and grow together."

These two babies with bilateral cleft lip and palate are able to breastfeed effectively.

A Baby with a CLEFT LIP or PALATE

Cleft lip and cleft palate often occur together, although a cleft palate is somewhat more common. The baby with a cleft lip can usually nurse at the breast even before surgery to close the cleft. With a cleft palate, an opening in the baby's palate (the roof of his mouth) makes it difficult for him to maintain the suction that helps him nurse. But unless the cleft is extremely severe, you and your baby can probably discover a way for him to breastfeed.

This does not mean breastfeeding will always be easy. It may in some cases be very difficult, and in others, impossible. But even if your baby is unable to nurse at the breast, your milk is still very important to him. One mother used an electric pump for eight months to express milk for her child, giving it to her baby in a special bottle. As a result, the baby was in the best of health before undergoing the necessary surgery, and recovery was quick. By holding your baby close to your breast as you feed him, you will be able to give him the warm closeness of breastfeeding.

Edith Grady, a La Leche League Leader from Indiana, found that if she held her breast in baby Andrea's mouth, Andrea, who had a cleft of the soft palate, could "milk" the breast with her gums and tongue. It is mainly the baby's jaws, tongue, cheeks, and gums that work to draw the milk from the breast. Edith managed to keep her breast in Andrea's mouth by shaping her breast tissue with her fingers to make it firm enough for Andrea to grasp and keeping the baby's head very close to the breast throughout the feeding.

At first she also pumped her milk and gave it to Andrea in a bottle after nursing her. By four months, Andrea was strong enough to get all of her milk at her mother's breast.

This technique and other information about breastfeeding a cleft-palate baby are explained in La Leche League's pamphlet titled,

"Nursing a Baby with a Cleft Lip or Cleft Palate." This is available from your local La Leche League Group or LLLI.

If the baby is bothered by milk running into his nose during nursing you may have to stop from time to time for a breathing spell. These babies often nurse better sitting up, or in the football hold. Experiment in your first weeks of nursing with different positions. Be patient with this special baby of yours, as it will probably take him longer to learn to nurse.

Cleft palate repair usually comes between one and two years of age. Your nursing toddler may not want to suck immediately after the operation because the roof of his mouth will be sore. He may want to lie at your breast or simply hold your nipple in his mouth without actually nursing. But as he recovers—in a week or so—he'll return to nursing, maybe with more enthusiasm than ever since the repair surgery makes it so much easier to breastfeed.

If your baby has a cleft lip, he will probably be able to breastfeed with some adjustments to help him keep the nipple in his mouth. Your doctor may want to perform some type of repair surgery while he is still nursing. Lip-repair surgery is often performed while the baby is still quite young and receiving only human milk. Tammy Shaw from Illinois persuaded her doctor to allow her son Peter to nurse immediately after his lip-repair surgery. She writes:

My husband and I showed Dr. Johnson the information about nursing. He enthusiastically agreed to allow me to breastfeed soon after surgery. He understood my wish to nurse Peter right away. He assured me that if any stitches pulled out after nursing, it would not harm Peter in any way to have him quickly replace a stitch. He agreed it was important that Peter be comforted. After surgery when Dr. Johnson appeared and saw that Peter was nursing happily, he commented that it was nice to see him calm and not crying so soon after surgery.

Another mother, Valerie Hawkes-Howat from Massachusetts, learned that it was not easy to find a doctor who was willing to allow her son to nurse immediately after lip-repair surgery. In the end, Valerie was able to nurse her son Willie immediately after his surgery. The repair healed beautifully and the scar is barely noticeable. Valerie writes about Willie's first nursing after his surgery:

When Willie was brought down from surgery, his bright eyes looked up at me and his little mouth opened into a wide, sleepy smile. I could have wept with relief. The only bandage on his face was a trio of narrow "steri-strips" across the upper lip. The nurse helped me take him into my arms and get him settled in my lap without disturbing the IV in his foot. I snuggled him and he began to root at my breast, so I immediately began to nurse him. He showed only profound pleasure to be back at my breast again—no signs of discomfort whatsoever. I noted the way his upper lip lay over the top of my areola, completely free of stress. There was no swelling or bruising around the sutures.

So Willie finished his first postoperative nursing by falling peacefully asleep in my arms, completely and blissfully ignorant of how hard both his parents had worked to make this possible.

In recent years, the idea that babies can breastfeed immediately after cleft lip repair has become more widely accepted, and articles on this subject have been published in medical journals. Still, some doctors may be reluctant to change their usual procedures, so be prepared to seek a second opinion, if necessary.

Cystic Fibrosis and METABOLIC DISEASES

Babies with cystic fibrosis, celiac disease, or other malabsorption problems do very well on mother's milk. In fact, the point at which symptoms appear is often delayed if baby is breastfed. Later, when baby is older and the disease does begin to manifest itself, it is far easier to treat and manage.

Kathleen Winterer's son, Ben, gained weight steadily on human milk despite cystic fibrosis; Ben was much healthier because he was breastfed:

At the time of Ben's hospitalization we were told we could expect one or two bouts with pneumonia his first year, and I am very happy to say Ben just turned two last month and hasn't had any yet. Of course, I like to think that colostrum's benefits in the beginning helped him through that first crucial year.

METABOLIC DISORDERS

In the United States, almost all newborns are tested routinely for PKU (phenylketonuria), a rare metabolic disorder which interferes with normal brain development if left untreated. It was once thought that babies with PKU could not be breastfed. However, since human milk is lower in phenylalinine than cow's milk formula, a baby with PKU can continue to be partially breastfeed and also given supplements of a special low-phenylalinine formula.

One study found that babies who had been breastfed before their PKU diagnosis scored an average of 14 points higher on IQ tests during elementary school than those who had been formula-fed from birth.

False positives can occur on PKU tests, so it's important to know that breastfeeding can continue while re-testing is done to confirm the diagnosis.

Galactosemia is another rare metabolic disorder in which a baby is unable to tolerate lactose. Unfortunately, in most cases, babies with galactosemia cannot be breastfed and must be given lactose-free formula.

When a BABY DIES

The death of a baby, whether through miscarriage, stillbirth, shortly after birth, or later through illness or accident, is an experience most of us shudder to think about. Sadly, the lives of many families are touched by such tragedies. Parents who suffer this terrible loss are usually shocked and grieved to find themselves also coping with the fact that the mother's body doesn't immediately realize what has happened; milk will begin, or continue, to be made.

Mothers whose infant dies at birth or shortly after or who miscarry in the second trimester of pregnancy or later, are often discharged early from the hospital. So the process of the milk coming in will take place at home. It helps to be prepared for what will happen, but often mothers are shocked to experience engorgement—hard, painful swollen breasts.

A mother whose baby dies when the milk supply is well established will also experience engorgement, and will need to seek relief. Check into the treatments suggested for engorgement in Chapter 4.

Women are often afraid to relieve their discomfort by expressing milk for fear of encouraging their breasts to make more milk. However, expressing enough milk to relieve discomfort is probably the most useful thing to do. Even a few drops may be enough to help you feel more comfortable. A hot shower or a hot bath is a good preliminary to expressing some milk. Not only will the warmth enable you to handle your painful breasts, but the warm water often helps the milk to be released. At first, you may need to express a small amount of milk several times a day, and at night too, if you wake in discomfort. The point of expressing a little milk is first to alleviate discomfort, and secondly to prevent undue accumulation of milk in the ducts, which could lead to a breast infection. You may also find it helpful to wear a firm bra for support and comfort. One size larger than usual may be necessary for a few days.

When the milk supply is already fully established, some mothers report that expressing milk and donating it to a local milk bank helps them feel they are doing something positive to help another baby. If you choose to do this, you will be able to cut back gradually and decrease your milk supply more comfortably.

Many mothers are taken aback by the way the let-down reflex can be triggered just by thinking about the baby. Comforting hugs from friends may also make the milk let down. Wearing bra pads, loose and patterned clothing, even taking a change of clothing with you on outings all help.

HOW CAN FRIENDS HELP?

Support from friends, family, and involved health professionals is vital. Celia Waterhouse, from Great Britain, whose baby Leo died at three months, offers this suggestion to friends. "Say simply how sad you are to hear about it. Your saying so will not make the mother any sadder for being reminded of her baby—as if she could ever forget! Even if nothing further is said between you, your acknowledgment of her sorrow will have helped."

Certainly practical help will be welcome—help with meals, laundry, or the older children—but having friends willing to talk, cry, and listen is wonderful in itself.

Whatever your feelings are, accept them as normal. Grief can continue for a very long time indeed. Remembering the baby's birthday and the anniversary of the funeral, sharing photographs, naming the baby, even if he was stillborn, all can help. Couples need to support each other and understand that grief may affect husband and wife in different ways, at different times. Often there is a lot of help provided initially, but after a few weeks people may expect parents to "get over it." This is a vulnerable time for bereaved parents, who may find grief welling up repeatedly. Dr. Penny Stanway, a British physician whose third baby was stillborn, says: "Most women find that they want to go over the circumstances of their baby's death time and time again with whoever will listen. A mother will have to have time to incorporate her loss, and the best way of doing this is by repetition of the event in her mind or by talking, as if 'to learn,' to stamp on her mind, what has happened."

There are several support groups for parents who have lost a child. They offer a chance to share feelings and experiences with other parents. See the Appendix.

17

When Extra Care Is Needed

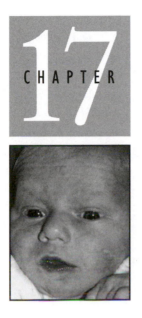

In certain circumstances, additional information on specialized techniques may be needed in order for breastfeeding to proceed smoothly. After reading this chapter, you may still have questions and concerns. Remember that your La Leche League Leader is available to provide information and encouragement. Don't hesitate to call on her for help.

Multiple Births— MULTIPLE BLESSINGS

Can a mother breastfeed twins? Of course she can. In fact mothers who breastfeed their twins find that the benefits of breastfeeding are multiplied when they have two babies to love. Because twins sometimes come in smaller packages, they need the protection of mother's milk even more than single babies.

In her book, MOTHERING MULTIPLES, Karen Gromada, a La Leche League Leader and mother of twins herself, writes about the benefits of breastfeeding twins:

The advantages of breastfeeding one baby are even more important and intense for multiples. How nice to save twice the money and twice the preparation time. And it is twice as nice to curl up at night for feedings in bed, rather than awaken to crying babies who must wait for you to warm their meals....One advantage is particularly important.... Breastfeeding ensures maximum skin contact with each baby.

There's something very special about having two pairs of eyes gazing up at you as they nurse.

PLENTY OF MILK

All of the doubly blessed mothers agree that having enough milk is no problem. The tried and true maxim for breastfeeding holds for multiples as well as for one baby—the more you nurse, the more your milk supply builds up. A mother who lived in Illinois, Lee Mueller, had twins who each weighed eight pounds at birth, yet she found no need to resort to supplementary formula or to start solids earlier than usual. A Wisconsin mother of twins, Judy Latka, commented, "I've taken breastfeeding a baby so much for granted that it surprises me when people are amazed that the twins are nursing. That part is easy—it's the extra set of loving arms that I need." Judy was aware of the importance of nursing the babies soon and often, and she adds, "I had discussed my desires many times with my doctors, and it was well worth the effort. My hospital stay was brief. We went home when the babies were twenty-eight hours old."

In planning for two or more (and we hope you have prior notice so you can plan), take the hints for easy housekeeping and relaxed mothering and multiply them to fit your needs. Cut your housework to a minimum. Your babies need the same loving attention that every baby deserves, and a tired mother is hard pressed to give this. If you possibly can, get help with the house for the first few months. Your spare minutes should be spent resting and relaxing, not catching up on laundry.

With two babies on the way, a Massachusetts couple, Marge and Jon Saphier, outlined a plan of action. Marge explains:

We decided to try to relieve me as much as possible from the housework so I could dedicate my time to the twins and our four-year-old daughter. Fortunately, we were able to have a graduate student live with us. She was given room and board for making two meals a day, cleaning up the kitchen, and cleaning up the general clutter of the house. We also decided to buy food in bulk; our cellar now looks like a supermarket. I only had to buy fresh produce weekly. This not only cut down on my time in the supermarket but also reduced our food bill.

Twins can be positioned with their bodies criss-crossed.

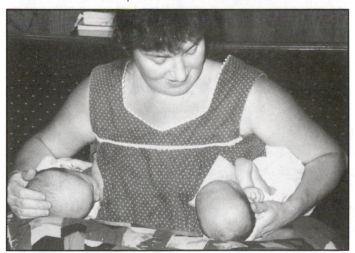

Using a nursing pillow can help you position both twins in the football hold.

Marge offers the following five hints for functioning effectively as a nursing mother of twins: "(1) Get as much rest as possible. (2) Drink plenty of liquids. (3) Eat good, nutritious meals and snacks. (4) Have help with meals and household tasks. (5) Last, but certainly not least, contact LLL. Although I am a La Leche League Leader myself, I cannot tell you how much I needed and appreciated the support the other mothers gave me."

A question that was uppermost in Paula Johnson's mind as a new mother of twins was how to feed both babies when they decided to nurse at the same time. This Missouri mother tells of her experience:

The first try was hilarious! If you're holding a baby in each arm, what do you do when a newborn loses the nipple? Wish for a third hand, that's what! I soon discovered pillows, and we've got the system down pat now. For a couple of frantic weeks, they refused to nurse at the same time. But with practice and the aid of pillows we finally discovered a lying-down position that is comfortable for all three of us. The nicest part is that now I can doze off while nursing, whereas before I sat upright until both were finished. That made for short nights!

Looking back now, I realize I did little else but nurse the babies in those first couple of months. But now, here we are at four-and-a-half months, the girls are both completely breastfed, and believe it or not, things are going pretty smoothly for us (well, most of the time). I have a fantastic husband who helps by preparing breakfast and by accepting my relaxed housekeeping. You can't be too hung up on those little details when there are twins to nurse. Our son, Aaron, who is two and a half, gets in on the act by finding a vacant place and just snuggling in. He sometimes gets out his babies to nurse while I'm nursing mine. He's sure babies only come in twos!

From Texas, Patti Lemberg reflects on the trying times and also the rewards she found in breastfeeding two:

They nursed every two hours for twenty minutes at a time and slept one four- or five-hour stretch a day. The hardest time for me was the six-week growth spurt when each of them nursed every forty-five minutes. It was a bit much, but I just took the same attitude I had taken during the last weeks of pregnancy: "Next year at this time they'll be toddling around, so cute—I won't even remember this day."

The most important advantage I have gleaned from the whole nursing experience is confidence. I know my way of mothering is good, and that makes me happy. This in turn relaxes me into a patient frame of mind.

In discussing how to position the twins for simultaneous nursings, Patti goes on to say:

When they were tiny, each rested in the crook of an arm, bottom at my hand, legs extended along my thigh. If one wiggled out of place I caught the back of the diaper and pulled him back. In fact, I still use this position if they both want to rock and nurse at the same time. Another good position is sitting on the couch with heads in my lap and bodies extended under my arms onto the couch. This one is great because both hands are free to hold a book and sip a beverage. When they are still tiny it's best to put a pillow under each for height and comfort. These days, we prefer to nurse lying down on their bed (a mattress on the floor), with David on the left in the standard nursing position for lying down and Alan on the right across my chest. That may sound awkward, but any position that is comfortable to all is fine. You need to work with the furniture and pillows until you find what's best for you.

The most valuable piece of furniture I owned during the first six months was a big overstuffed rocking chair my dad bought at a garage sale.

A New York mother, Patricia Berg, explains how the relationship with each baby developed at its own pace:

I got to know baby Megan very quickly since she slept little and needed a great deal of nursing and contact. My relationship with Joelle was a little slower in forming as she was quieter and it seemed we had less time together in the beginning. I realize now that I often hesitated to nurse the girls simultaneously during those early weeks. However, when I did nurse them together (their feet toward my back, heads on a pillow), I found that the rush of good feelings so familiar to the nursing mother came even more easily. There's just something about four little eyes looking up at you so absorbingly! I also found that nursing the babies together would bring on a very strong let-down whenever I felt my supply a little low, usually in the late afternoon.

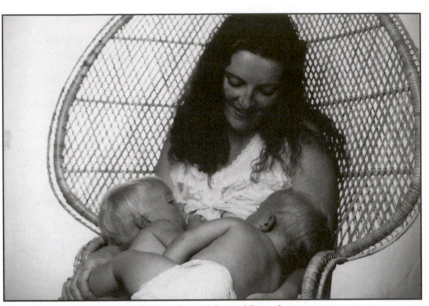

Nursing twins can bring special rewards.

Whether to nurse the babies together or separately is one of those things that mothers work out quickly to suit themselves and their babies. Another La Leche League Leader and twin mother, Carolyn Johnson of Illinois, described her method of satisfying two babies:

When time was a factor, I nursed the twins together, sitting in a rocker, with Jill on Judy's lap. Otherwise, I found it much easier to nurse the babies separately. I would awaken one about half an hour before the other was "due" to get up so as to avoid nursing them together. Of course, I alternated so that one twin wouldn't always have "first pickings."

If one was still hungry after nursing on one side, I would offer the other breast. Then the next one would begin on the breast last nursed by the other. Usually, the last to be nursed would be the first to wake up hungry. There were times when they would want to nurse again after only one and a half to two hours, and this served to increase my milk supply to meet their demands. Usually it would take two days of very frequent nursing and they would again be satisfied with a less demanding schedule.

I always made sure the twins were nursed at least every three hours and would awaken them if necessary. At night I didn't watch the clock, but kept them alongside our bed in a bassinet and buggy, and all I had to do was scoop the hungry one into bed, doze and nurse until the other one awakened, and then switch. This was a marvelous system for me because it gave me the sleep I needed. I also didn't change them at night unless they had soaked through everything. They never got diaper rash and didn't seem to mind not being changed.

Almost all mothers who nurse more than one baby comment on their hearty appetite and increased thirst. Some make a practice of eating an extra meal before going to bed. Carolyn Johnson says:

I noticed my appetite and thirst increased quite a bit during the first few weeks (I think I ate about six times a day), which is probably nature's way of providing the extra fluid and food for nursing two. I lost twenty pounds when they were born and an additional seven pounds in the next two weeks, which put me a little underweight. However, these pounds gradually came back so that by the time the twins were six weeks old we were all in fine shape.

Regarding the work of managing more than one baby, one mother of twins commented, "The rewards are great, but during the first three months you won't have time to think about them."

With more than one baby, your attention is focused on the babies in a special way. Just watching them—noticing their differences, their different growth patterns, their inherent temperamental leanings—is an ever-interesting, ever-changing spectacle. It can give you insight and knowledge that add greatly to your competence as a mother, as well as your enjoyment of your babies. As one twin mother puts it, "I'm afraid having one baby will be rather dull after watching two bloom and grow!"

Nursing More than TWO

If nursing twins sounds like an amazing accomplishment, it may astonish you to know that mothers have also been able to fully breastfeed triplets, and even quadruplets! Supplements may be needed at first, but once the babies are breastfeeding well, a healthy milk supply is usually no problem.

One mother of triplets pumped her milk for many weeks while her premature babies were in the hospital. After all three babies came home, she had no trouble nursing the two boys, but her daughter had become nipple confused and continued to prefer the bottle.

The mother was so determined to provide the benefits of human milk for all three babies that she continued to pump her milk for her daughter while fully breastfeeding the two boys.

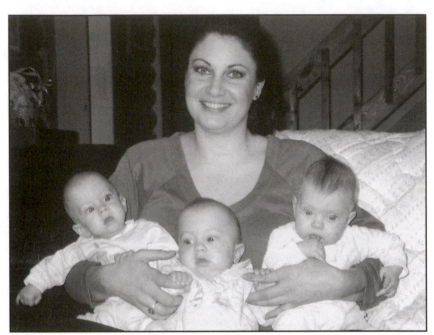

Breastfeeding triplets is quite an accomplishment.

With three or four babies to feed and care for, mothers often find it helpful to keep track of feedings as well as wet and soiled diapers to be sure each baby is nursing often enough and getting plenty to eat.

If you are expecting multiples (or have them already), you'll find additional information on breastfeeding and caring for more than one baby in MOTHERING MULTIPLES, a book that's available from La Leche League Groups or La Leche League International. See the Appendix for details.

Relactation and Induced LACTATION

In the usual course of events, a mother's body prepares for lactation during pregnancy, and the birth of the baby signals the mother's breasts to begin producing milk. With the baby's eager sucking, the milk continues to be produced. If the baby is not put to the breast after birth, or if breastfeeding ceases soon afterward, the milk "dries up." Relactation is the process by which a mother is able to re-establish her milk supply several weeks or months after lactation has stopped. It is a difficult and time-consuming process, but it can be done. This is possible because the sucking of the baby stimulates milk production. In fact, some mothers have been able to establish a milk supply for an adopted baby without the impetus of pregnancy and birth. This is called induced lactation.

Often mothers who have attempted relactation have been those whose babies could not tolerate any artificial formula and needed human milk to survive. Beth Robertson from Tennessee tells of her experience with relactation:

I started breastfeeding my son Zachary in the hospital. My pediatrician was not supportive of breastfeeding and told me I should give it up. I followed his advice and quit breastfeeding after only seven days. I felt miserable about it but thought that the doctor must know what was best.

When Zachary was seven weeks old, he developed severe diarrhea and diaper rash. After almost four weeks of trying different formulas and medicines, his new doctor said we had gone as far as we could go with different formulas and human milk was probably the only solution. He suggested that I find out about relactation.

I contacted Marty Wilson of La Leche League, and she assured me it could be done, but would require time and patience. She also found some mothers who were willing to give us milk until mine came in. I used a nursing supplementer to give Zac the donated milk.

The first day I gave Zac the donor milk the diarrhea stopped entirely. It was a miracle! During the second week I began to express a few drops of milk and was delighted. I continued giving the donated breast milk at every feeding until Carol Blanton, another Leader, suggested I try cutting off the donor milk entirely for a day or two, with permission from the baby's doctor, and just nurse Zac more often to see if my milk increased. The doctor agreed. The next few days were rough going, to say the least, but things began to improve. By the next week Zac had gained seven ounces, and at the end of another week the doctor had me stop all supplements. I was finally on my own!

Relactation was a difficult process, harder than I had anticipated. I got discouraged many times, but I did make it at last. Zac is now thriving and gaining weight and is quite a happy and contented baby. We are both very grateful to La Leche League and everyone involved in helping us.

Another mother, Kimberly Fradejas from Florida, was understandably concerned when her daughter Brandy didn't seem able to tolerate any of the formulas they had tried. When the baby was three weeks old, they took her to see a nurse practitioner at the clinic. Kimberly tells what happened next:

> *I asked if it was too late for me to breastfeed. I had taken dry-up pills for ten days after Brandy was born. The nurse said it might not be too late. She showed me how to guide the baby to the breast, and Brandy took right to it. She nursed for the first time right there in the office. I never will forget the look on her cute little face. It was as if that was what she had wanted and needed all along. The nurse then advised me to let Brandy nurse first whenever she was hungry, then to supplement her afterward with a small amount of formula. As my milk supply increased, I decreased the amount of formula Brandy was taking until she no longer needed a supplement.*

> *The nurse arranged for me to talk with a La Leche League Leader, who gave me information on increasing my milk supply and books on breastfeeding. Since I knew nothing about nursing a baby, she invited me to come to La Leche League meetings where I could meet other nursing mothers.*

> *Brandy is four-and-a-half months old now and weighs nearly twenty pounds. She is a very healthy and happy baby. I am proud to be doing the best I can for her. My only regret is that I didn't begin nursing her the minute she was born.*

NURSING ADOPTED BABIES

After hearing stories of mothers who had successfully re-established their milk supplies for their allergic babies, mothers who were planning to adopt babies began to wonder if they could also provide mother's milk for their babies. The first few adoptive mothers who were in touch with LLL were nursing their toddlers when they adopted their new babies. By putting the young baby to their breast often, they were able to increase their milk supply to meet some or all of the infant's needs.

Carol Marino from Connecticut tells about her experience when she adopted a baby girl from Korea:

> *When Carol Ann Ree Ja, just four months old, arrived to join her homemade sister, Judea Vera, she was tired and hungry. I put her to my breast and she nursed beautifully. It was surprising to me that she took to nursing so readily, since she had been bottle-fed from the time she was born until she came home to us.*

Judea was seventeen months old when Carol Ann Ree Ja arrived. She had been gradually weaning herself and was only nursing occasionally—maybe once every week or so. I realized that I'd have to build up my milk supply, and I started pumping a month ahead of time—five minutes on each breast four times a day the first week, eight times a day the second week, and from then on each hour during the day, until the last three days, when I pumped five minutes on each breast every two

Using a nursing supplementer allows an adoptive mother to breastfeed even if she does not have a full milk supply.

hours around the clock. This pumping brought in plenty of milk so I had a good supply when Carol Ann Ree Ja arrived.

Judea stepped up her nursing when the baby came home, and during the first month I often nursed two children at the same time, one on each breast. Finally one day Judea pointed authoritatively to my breast and announced, "Baby's!" She never nursed again.

Encouraged by these success stories, other mothers planning to adopt babies became interested in nursing them. Even mothers who had never been pregnant were able to establish at least a partial milk supply so that their babies were receiving some human milk even though they also received formula or other supplements. By giving these supplements at the breast with a nursing supplementer, these mothers and babies enjoy the closeness of breastfeeding.

Jo Young, from England, who had never been pregnant, was able to bring in her milk for her adopted son, Peter. She began when he was three weeks old and explains it this way:

With great effort and sacrifice from a small handful of people I succeeded in my effort to induce lactation, and incredibly, Peter was completely nourished and sustained at my breast by the time he was three and a half months old. He remained solely breastfed from then until he began to experiment with solids at about six months. During the early months when he was basically dependent on formula, Peter looked rather fragile and unwell, suffering from constant colds. I am convinced that the breast milk he has had is responsible for the marvelous changes in his looks. His skin has cleared and he is now a large, bouncy, blooming, typical breastfed baby.

I can never hope to convey totally the depth of my gratitude to the friends who helped us. I think they realize the wealth of the gift they have given Peter and me.

The practice of nursing adopted babies has become so well accepted that some adoption agencies hold meetings for the mothers who plan to breastfeed. Mothers report that the extra effort required in building a milk supply for their adopted babies is well worth it. The closeness and intimacy of the breastfeeding relationship is what matters most to these adoptive mothers, more than how much milk they produce. From Arizona, Anne Sanger writes:

It seems like such a short time since we took Lisa from the adoption agency into our family. She was four days old then and seemed so small. Now she is a happy, beautiful one-year-old.

I was able to nurse Lisa with the help of a nursing supplementer. I did a lot of preparation prior to her arrival. When Lisa was ten months old, we were able to discontinue using the supplementer. We are still a happy nursing couple.

It is difficult for me to explain what it means to me to be able to nurse Lisa. I wanted to give her the gift of love and the wonderful way of communicating that the nursing relationship opens to mothers.

I know that breastfeeding my adopted child was not the easiest thing I ever did in my life, but it has been one of the most rewarding. We feel very fortunate to be the parents of such a happy child.

The Basic TECHNIQUE

The basic technique for relactation or induced lactation is to encourage the baby to nurse as often as possible. This is how you stimulate the breasts to produce milk. Adoptive mothers can often begin establishing a milk supply before they have their babies. It helps, of course, to know when you'll get the baby. Use a pump or hand-express for three to five minutes on each breast several times a day, gradually increasing the number of times per day. If this is kept up faithfully, the breast will begin to produce milk—usually in two to six weeks. It may only be a few drops at first, but this will increase once your baby starts to nurse.

One of the most difficult aspects of relactation is getting the baby interested in sucking at the breast if he has been used to bottles and artificial nipples for several weeks or months. This requires a great deal of patience and determination. The mother who is attempting to relactate needs a generous amount of support and encouragement. It's a good idea to be in touch with a La Leche League Leader who can provide further information.

You will need to continue giving the baby some formula or donated human milk. You should nurse the baby first, for as long as he is willing, before you offer the supplement. Many mothers avoid bottles and artificial nipples completely and use a spoon, cup, small flexible bowl, or feeding syringe. If a nursing supplementer is used, the baby can receive his supplement as he nurses at the breast. (See the Appendix.)

If you are putting the baby to the breast as often as possible and giving the supplement only during or after a feeding, you may be able to gradually cut back on the total amount of supplement you give the baby as your milk supply increases. If you write down the amount of supplement he takes each day, and you see the total decreasing slowly, you'll know your milk supply is increasing. You'll need to watch the baby's wet diapers and bowel movements to be sure he is still getting plenty to eat.

While you are establishing a milk supply, it is very important to keep in touch with the baby's doctor and check the baby's weight on a weekly basis to be sure he continues to gain weight.

Many adoptive mothers continue using a nursing supplementer to give their babies formula at every feeding until the baby starts taking large amounts of solid foods. Even though they continue using a supplement, they find that feeding their babies at the breast provides a wonderful closeness that both mother and baby enjoy.

The mother who is relactating finds that for a time she is working almost around the clock feeding her baby as often as she can. Of course, the more often the baby nurses the more milk there will be waiting for him the next time.

Further information from mothers who have nursed adopted babies including details on establishing a milk supply, on having realistic expectations, and keeping your perspective about the situation can be found in other publications available from your local La Leche League Group or LLLI. See the Appendix for details.

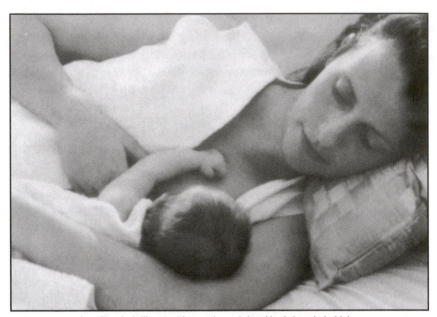

A mother who is ill can get the rest she needs by taking baby to bed with her.

What If Mother Is ILL?

"How can I take care of my baby if I get sick?" This is a common question of anxious mothers. Of course, caring for an active, healthy baby is a demanding job at any time, but when mother is ill it can be of real concern. It is reassuring to know that nursing your baby makes caring for him so much easier. For minor illnesses, such as a cold or the flu, you needn't even consider interrupting breastfeeding. The germs are not transmitted through your milk, and the baby has no doubt been exposed to the illness for at least as long as you have, and certainly was exposed to it before you knew you had it.

Your milk can actually protect your baby from getting sick when you have a cold or the flu. A nursing mother produces antibodies to the specific germs her baby has been exposed to. These antibodies are transmitted to the baby through her milk. Continuing to breastfeed also helps you get the extra rest you need when you aren't feeling well. Sudden weaning would not be good for either you or your baby.

If your illness is more serious—for example, if you have pneumonia, hepatitis, or tuberculosis—doctors on our Health Advisory Council still advise continued breastfeeding. Breastfeeding requires a minimum of effort for you, giving you the most rest. In addition, your milk provides special protection for your baby against the virus or bacteria causing your illness.

If you become seriously ill and your doctor suggests weaning the baby, explain how important breastfeeding is to both of you. If your doctor still insists that weaning is necessary, you may find talking to your baby's doctor may help you sort out your options and find a way to avoid weaning your baby. It would be a good idea to discuss your situation with your local La Leche League Leader as she may know of other doctors who are more supportive of breastfeeding.

HOSPITALIZATION

Consider all options before being admitted to the hospital. It is much better if you can remain at home during your illness. Get help with the necessary housework, laundry, and meals, and caring for the older children. Tuck your little one in bed with you, where he will be close by all the time and able to nurse whenever he wants.

If a serious illness or an accident requires hospitalization, you will want to make arrangements to have your baby kept with you, or at least brought to you. Nursing mothers have found all kinds of ingenious ways to avoid being separated from their babies during hospital stays. Discuss your needs and those of your baby with your husband and your doctor. Your condition, the hospital's facilities, and your baby's age and usual nursing pattern will all influence the situation.

More and more surgery is being performed nowadays on an outpatient basis under local anesthesia. You can then return home to rest and nurse your baby without any prolonged separation. Procedures such as dental work can nearly always be carried out without interruption of breastfeeding. When the potential surgery is elective, your doctor may be willing to postpone it until the baby is older.

If you must stay in the hospital overnight or for several days, your husband or a friend or relative can bring the baby in to visit you and nurse. Some hospitals may be willing to admit the baby and allow him to room-in with you, though they may require that someone stay in the room with you to help care for the baby.

Be flexible and polite as you talk over your requests with the doctors and hospital. If you are willing to cooperate with hospital personnel, they will usually be cooperative, too. Let them see how much it means to you to keep your baby with you.

MAJOR SURGERY

Even when a mother is required to have major surgery, arrangements can often be made to allow her to continue breastfeeding. If some feedings must be missed, you can plan on using a breast pump so your breasts will not become engorged.

In some cases where a few days of separation are unavoidable, your little one will more than likely be willing and eager to return to nursing once you're are back together. Marilyn Mastro of Florida needed to have a hysterectomy when her daughter Frances was a year old and still nursing. She tells her story:

> *The surgery was successful. There were no postoperative complications, and my husband was allowed to bring the girls in to see me four days later. Frances was allowed to nurse (with a pillow under her to protect my stitches) for the first time in four and a half days. I had used a breast pump to relieve the engorgement and to keep up my milk supply. Pete said that after that short period of nursing, Franny slept better than she had during any of the other nights while I was away.*
>
> *My doctor discharged me the next day and I came home and resumed breastfeeding and mothering my family. I had presumed that "complete hysterectomy" would mean the end of the joys of nursing, and this thought was very depressing and frightening. As my daughter suckled my milk supply back to her satisfaction I realized how important motherhood and nursing had become to me. I'm glad my doctor hadn't convinced me to wean Franny completely because I need her closeness now almost as much as she needs me.*

MEDICATIONS FOR THE NURSING MOTHER

Be sure to check with your doctor before taking any medication while you are breastfeeding, even drugs that are available without a prescription. Usually the amount of the drug found in mother's milk is so small that it won't affect the baby at all, but you still want to avoid unnecessary drugs for your own sake while you are nursing your baby.

If any doctor is prescribing medication for you, be sure he or she is aware that you are breastfeeding your baby and knows how important it is for you to continue. There are three questions to consider when a breastfeeding mother needs medication: Will the drug harm the nursing baby? Will weaning harm the baby or the mother? What are the alternatives?

When prescribing a medication for a nursing mother, some physicians routinely insist on weaning as a precaution. In reality, few drugs have been proven to be harmful to the nursing infant. Abrupt weaning is traumatic for mother and baby. Mother may develop painfully engorged beasts, risking a breast infection and compounding the problems for which she was advised to take the medication in the first place. Also, the mother/baby relationship is affected. Caring for the baby and keeping him content becomes difficult or impossible; the baby is often utterly inconsolable.

There are other reasons to avoid even temporary weaning. A baby with a family history of allergy may develop asthma or eczema when exposed to cow's milk or formula. In addition, he no longer enjoys the benefits of the many immune factors known to be in human milk, including antibodies to a number of infections to which infants are particularly susceptible—antibodies which, in many cases, may protect him from his mother's illness as well.

Most doctors have found that if a particular drug poses a potential risk for the baby, usually it is possible to substitute another drug with lesser or no risk. When little is known about a drug's effect on a nursing baby, another drug about which there is more information can often be used instead. It may also be possible to alter or postpone treatment until the baby is older.

An increasing number of studies are being done on the subject of medications and their effects on breastfeeding. If there is any question about the safety of a drug for a nursing mother and her baby, it's a good idea to check with someone who is knowledgeable about medications as well as supportive of breastfeeding. Several reference books listed in the Appendix include information about the effects of medications on breastfeeding. A La Leche League Leader may be able to help, or guide you to someone who can give you accurate information.

If your doctor insists on prescribing a certain medication and advises you to wean the baby, it may be wise to check with the baby's doctor. A pediatrician may be more familiar with the effects of medication on a breastfed baby.

DRUGS THAT SHOULD BE AVOIDED WHILE NURSING

There are a small number of drugs that are contraindicated while you are breastfeeding. The American Academy of Pediatrics publishes a listing of drugs that are safe to take while breastfeeding along with those that are contraindicated.

If radioactive compounds are used for diagnostic tests it will be necessary to discontinue nursing temporarily as these materials can be excreted in your milk and are dangerous to your baby. There are varying lengths of time that weaning is necessary depending on the type of radioactive compound used. Discuss this with your doctor ahead of time and let him or her know you prefer using a material that will allow you to resume breastfeeding as quickly as possible. Your doctor or the radiologist supervising the treatment can advise you as to when it is safe to resume nursing. In the meantime, pumping your milk and discarding it will help clear the radioactive material more quickly.

Radioactive compounds used for treatment may require lengthy weaning; however, some mothers have pumped and discarded their milk, as necessary, for several months and then resumed nursing once their milk was free of radioactive material.

Chemotherapy, the use of strong anticancer drugs, is considered hazardous to the nursing baby. It is always necessary to wean if chemotherapy is required.

Illegal substances, such as heroin, cocaine, and marijuana, should be avoided. They are not only hazardous to the nursing baby because they are excreted in human milk, but also they interfere with a mother's ability to care for her baby. The use of marijuana has been found to cause a decrease in levels of prolactin, the "mothering" hormone that is especially important in assuring an adequate milk supply.

Be sure that anyone prescribing medication for you knows that you are breastfeeding. You may find that it helps to check with your baby's doctor if another doctor who is prescribing for you is concerned about the potential effect of a medication on your breastfed baby. If a drug is prescribed for you that may be of concern, the American Academy of Pediatrics suggests monitoring the baby's reaction rather than discontinuing breastfeeding.

IMMUNIZATIONS

If your blood is Rh-negative and your baby's is Rh-positive, you will probably receive an injection of Rh antibodies (RhoGAM) very soon after you deliver. RhoGAM is used widely to prevent Rh complications, and it is not harmful to your nursing infant.

Along with RhoGAM, many other vaccines do not affect the breastfed baby through his mother's milk. According to the United States Centers for Disease Control (1994): "Neither killed nor live vaccines affect the safety of breastfeeding for mothers and infants." Acceptable vaccines include: chicken pox, smallpox, typhus, typhoid, yellow fever, oral and injected polio, tetanus, diphtheria, pertussis, rabies, measles, rubella, cholera, and influenza. Hepatitis B vaccine is also safe for nursing mothers.

With regard to immunizations for your baby, the same schedule is followed for the breastfed baby as for formula-fed infants. There is no need to refrain from nursing the baby before or after administration of any vaccine, including the oral polio vaccine.

Mothers with
SPECIAL PROBLEMS

A mother who is disabled in any way will find it convenient to breastfeed her baby. This is true of blind mothers, hearing-impaired mothers, mothers who are confined to wheelchairs, and mothers who are recovering from illness or injuries. Breastfeeding requires less effort than bottle-feeding, and nourishing her baby with her own milk may be especially satisfying to a mother with a disability. Many LLL publications are available on cassette tape or in Braille for use by blind or handicapped parents. See the Appendix for details.

Mother and baby can continue to enjoy the benefits of breastfeeding even when one or the other is ill.

Mothers with chronic illnesses also benefit from the ease and satisfaction of breastfeeding their babies. Illnesses such as diabetes, lupus, arthritis, epilepsy, or multiple sclerosis need not interfere with a mother's decision to breastfeed her baby. Most medications taken for these conditions are compatible with breastfeeding. Breastfeeding makes life easier. One mother with diabetes says:

> When a mother breastfeeds, she doesn't waste her time sterilizing bottles and preparing formula. The mother only has to bring the baby to bed, relax, and enjoy. Probably the biggest advantage is that the baby is healthier. Breastfeeding saves many trips to the doctor's office with ear infections, digestive problems, and allergies.

Breastfed babies also tend to be less fussy because human milk is more easily digested than formula. If a breastfed baby is fussy, often just putting him to the breast is enough to calm him.

One physical advantage of breastfeeding is especially noteworthy. Many women with chronic illnesses find that the normal hormonal changes of pregnancy result in a temporary remission of their symptoms. When a woman breastfeeds, her hormonal levels do not revert back to their pre-pregnancy state right away; this happens gradually. If weaning occurs at a natural pace, her symptoms often return much later than if she were bottle-feeding, giving her better health when her tiny baby needs her most. Temporary remission during pregnancy and breastfeeding has been reported by mothers with rheumatoid arthritis, multiple sclerosis, lupus, and diabetes. Some diabetic mothers need only half as much insulin while nursing than they needed before they became pregnant, which makes the first months after birth easier.

Breastfeeding can contribute to a woman's self-esteem and self-confidence as a mother. These kinds of positive feelings also have a favorable effect on the course of an illness. One mother with epilepsy says:

> *Breastfeeding has been a salvation for me, especially on days when I knew there was very little I could do for my child. At least I was giving the very best of myself in extremely important areas—food, warmth, affection, touching, and caring. I could never have gathered the strength or had the energy to give bottles.*

There may be some things a mother can do, depending on her illness, to make nursing easier. For the mother with rheumatoid arthritis, it might help to set up a comfortable place to nurse with good support and extra pillows. An epileptic mother needs to have a safe place to lay the baby in the event of a seizure and to nurse in a chair that is well-padded or in a bed with guard rails or extra pillows.

Another benefit of breastfeeding for the chronically ill mother is the emotional closeness it adds to her relationship with her baby and the sense of normalcy that it brings to her situation.

Gail Stutler, who was recovering from brain surgery when her second child was born, recalls that she "couldn't even name a diaper." But she continues, "I could scoop up a tiny bundle, put her to my breast, and nurse her close to my heart. I could satisfy at least one of the desperate needs I had when deprived of all my capabilities."

DIABETES MELLITUS

In recent years medical science has made pregnancy and childbirth safer for diabetic women, and more and more of them are deciding to nurse their new babies. Breastfeeding offers special advantages for the diabetic mother. Studies indicate that breastfeeding may reduce the baby's risk of developing diabetes later in life. Since some forms of diabetes are inherited, this is particularly important for insulin-dependent diabetic mothers.

Many diabetic mothers find that nursing improves their condition. The natural hormonal transition from pregnancy to nursing makes an easier metabolic adjustment, because your body continues to support both your baby and yourself.

A diabetic mother will have to make adjustments in her diet depending on how often her baby nurses from day to day. If she takes insulin, she will have to regulate the dosage as carefully as she did while she was pregnant in order to keep her diabetes under control while nursing. The insulin itself will not hurt the baby because its molecules are too large to pass into the milk. La Leche League's information sheet, "The Diabetic Mother and Breastfeeding," provides further information. See the Appendix for details.

EPILEPSY OR SEIZURE DISORDER

Mothers with epilepsy or seizure disorder benefit from the nursing hormones and the relaxation engendered by natural mothering. If the mother must take medication to control her seizures, she should check with her doctor about the drug's effects on breastfeeding. Most drugs prescribed for epilepsy or seizure disorder won't harm the nursing baby. If your doctor is uncertain about the effects of a particular drug, perhaps one that is so new little is known about it, he or she may be able to prescribe another drug instead. Another option is to monitor the baby and watch for any signs that the drug is affecting his growth or development.

If you are a mother with a disability, or chronic illness, it would be helpful for you to be in touch with your local LLL Leader. She will be able to offer you additional information and encouragement and may be able to put you in touch with another mother who has nursed her baby in circumstances similar to yours. Contacting someone who has "been there" can help give you the confidence you need to feel that you can do it, too.

HUMAN IMMUNODEFICIENCY VIRUS (HIV)

A mother who is HIV-positive faces a difficult situation when she considers whether or not to breastfeed her baby. Human immunodeficiency virus (HIV) is the virus that causes AIDS. HIV can be transmitted from mother to baby during pregnancy or at birth. About one-third of infants born to mothers with HIV will become infected at this time. There is evidence that suggests that HIV can also be passed to the baby through breastfeeding. One study suggests that one in five breastfeeding infants will become infected through their mother's milk. Which babies become infected may be influenced by the stage of the mother's infection, the duration of breastfeeding, the mother's nutritional status, and other factors.

Whether or not an HIV-positive mother chooses to breastfeed will depend on her circumstances. In parts of the world where not breastfeeding puts a baby at serious risk of dying from infection or malnutrition, babies of HIV-positive mothers have a greater chance to survive if they are breastfed. In parts of the world where artificial feeding does not carry such monumental risks, mothers with HIV may well choose not to breastfeed. Both the World Health Organization and the United States Centers for Disease Control advise against breastfeeding in HIV-infected women where safe alternatives are available.

Research on HIV and breastfeeding continues and new and more effective treatments for HIV are becoming available. A pregnant woman who is HIV-positive may want to seek out the most recent information before making a decision about breastfeeding.

POSTPARTUM DEPRESSION

Many mothers experience a day or so of "baby blues" in the first week postpartum. They suddenly find themselves crying for no apparent reason, wondering how they can feel so sad when they're supposed to feel so happy. The great changes and responsibilities that come with a new baby may be the source of the sudden ups and downs, and the emotions are magnified by the shifting postpartum hormones. For most women this period of intense feeling passes quickly, but for others, anxiety, sadness, mood swings, and other symptoms persist for weeks or even reappear months after giving birth. This is no longer "baby blues"; this is postpartum depression.

Depression is not something you can just "snap out of," though there may be people who suggest that a mother should do just that. Mild depression may lift with time, especially if a mother makes a disciplined effort to take care of herself. She should eat nutritious meals and snacks, take a daily walk or try some other form of exercise, get help with household tasks, and sleep when the baby sleeps. Most importantly, she should find other women with babies to talk with, friends who can reassure her that she is doing a good job and that she is not alone in her feelings. A La Leche League Group can be a valuable source of support for a mother struggling with postpartum adjustments.

When a mother is anxious about her ability to care for her baby, or is just plain feeling "down," breastfeeding may become the focus of her worries. She may find it hard to trust that her body will make enough milk for her baby, or she may begin to feel that breastfeeding itself is the cause of her unhappiness. While difficulties with nursing can certainly be upsetting, many mothers find that getting some assistance in order to resolve the breastfeeding problems is a more positive course of action than deciding to wean. Ultimately, both mother and baby benefit. It's also important to remember that most of the challenges experienced by new mothers will still be there, even if the baby is switched to formula.

Sometimes postpartum depression needs the attention of a professional, a counselor or therapist, or a doctor. Be sure to look for someone who is supportive of breastfeeding and understands its importance to both mother and baby. Studies have shown that breastfeeding itself does not contribute to postpartum depression.

Depression is often treated with medication, and there may be some concerns about whether a particular drug is safe for the baby. This is a time to consider carefully the mother's need for the drug, the possible alternatives, and the latest information available about the medication. A mother who is seriously depressed may want to include her husband or a friend in these discussions with the doctor, to help make clear her desire to avoid weaning. Ending the breastfeeding relationship can be very difficult for a mother emotionally and sudden weaning may cause hormonal changes that intensify a mother's depression. Any decisions about how to treat postpartum depression should take this into account.

If Your Baby Gets SICK

Most of the time your breastfed baby will be happy and healthy. You will be pleased and proud to know that your milk is contributing to his good health. But what's best for your baby if he does develop an illness, such as a cold or ear infection, vomiting or diarrhea, or something more serious?

No matter how serious your baby's illness is, he can almost always continue breastfeeding. If a baby can take anything by mouth, your milk is the best food for him. Human milk provides perfect nutrition that is easily digested and also provides antibodies to help him fight his illness. And the comfort provided by breastfeeding is also important in recovering from an illness.

COLDS AND EAR INFECTIONS

Breastfed babies are statistically less likely to have respiratory infections and ear infections. But that doesn't mean your baby won't ever experience these problems. A baby with a cold, sore throat, or ear infection may find it difficult to nurse. These suggestions may help:

- Carry the baby in an upright position, such as a sling or baby carrier, for a short time before trying to nurse him. This may help to drain the mucus from his nose.
- Nurse the baby in a semi-upright position. This may help with an ear infection as lying down to nurse puts pressure on baby's ears.

- Use a cool-mist vaporizer in the room where baby sleeps and where you'll be nursing him.
- Clear baby's nose with a soft rubber suction bulb before feedings.

If baby is still too uncomfortable to nurse, pump or express your milk and offer it to him in a spoon, cup, or eyedropper. Of course, you will want to be in touch with your doctor if baby has a fever or is refusing to nurse for more than a few hours.

Diarrhea or Vomiting

If your baby is otherwise well and thriving, it really doesn't matter how loose his bowel movements are. Not all loose, frequent stools constitute diarrhea. In the breastfed infant it is quite normal for baby to have very loose, runny bowel movements. Many breastfed babies, especially in the early weeks, have as many as six or eight stools a day; some will soil a diaper every time they nurse. Later on, when they are more than six weeks old, they may have only one bowel movement a day or one a week or even less often. If a baby has infrequent bowel movements, they are usually quite profuse. All this is well within the realm of normalcy. Even the occasional green, watery stool in an otherwise healthy baby is nothing to worry about.

When a baby is not running a fever, it is wise to consider other possibilities before assuming that illness is the cause of diarrhea or vomiting. If vitamin, iron, or fluoride supplements have recently been started, or if the baby is taking an antibiotic, these could be the cause. Sometimes vitamin, iron, or other supplements taken by a nursing mother can cause digestive problems in her baby. An occasional bottle of formula could result in diarrhea or vomiting in a sensitive baby. Diarrhea is also a common side-effect of certain medications, such as antibiotics, taken by the mother. Another possibility is that the baby is sensitive to a new food that has been introduced. In some cases, a food eaten by the nursing mother may affect her baby.

Because of the immunological protection received through mother's milk, a breastfed baby is less likely to become ill when colds and flu are going around. When a nursing mother is sick, it is best for her baby to keep on breastfeeding. The baby has already been exposed to the germs causing the illness, and human milk will help protect the baby. In fact, the nursing mother produces antibodies on demand to the specific germs that challenge her baby. When the baby picks up a germ and passes it to the mother, her more experienced immune system begins to manufacture the necessary antibodies. Then she gives these back to the baby through her milk.

Even so, breastfed babies do sometimes get sick with diarrhea. If a baby is having twelve to sixteen stools a day, or if the stools have an offensive odor or contain flecks of blood, the baby most likely has diarrhea. Usually symptoms will improve in three to five days, but diarrhea occasionally causes more serious problems in babies and young children. The lining of the intestine is inflamed and irritated, and it tends to leak fluids and pass nutrients through the body too rapidly. The loss of water and salt can lead to dehydration and eventually to shock. Signs of dehydration

When a baby is sick, he needs the comfort of nursing and the protection that human milk provides.

include listlessness, lethargy, dry mouth, less than the usual amount of tears, minimal urine output, and fever. You should call your doctor if you suspect your sick baby is becoming dehydrated. You can help prevent dehydration by making sure that your baby gets plenty of fluids. The best way to do this in a breastfed baby is to offer small, frequent nursings. Even if an oral rehydration solution is recommended, breastfeeding can and should continue.

Some doctors still routinely advise that the baby or toddler who is vomiting or has diarrhea be taken off all milk products—including human milk. When confronted with this advice, a nursing mother would be wise to question it. Mothers with breastfeeding babies or toddlers know that abrupt—even if temporary—weaning can make life miserable. When the familiar source of solace is taken away, a sick baby becomes even more frustrated and upset. Meanwhile mother's breasts become fuller and more uncomfortable.

There are several options open to the nursing mother when her doctor's medical advice goes against her instincts and her other sources of information. Some mothers might seek out another, more likeminded doctor, one who is more knowledgeable about breastfeeding. The best answer is to work with your doctor to arrive at a solution acceptable to everyone—physician, mother, and baby.

Recent studies support the idea that a baby with diarrhea should continue to breastfeed. Much of the work on the subject comes from developing countries where diarrhea can be a serious, even life-threatening problem in infants and small children. Even breastfed babies may experience diarrhea in areas where sanitation and hygiene are poor. In this situation, taking babies off the breast for a few days with each episode of diarrhea risks malnutrition and premature weaning, and hence, more severe attacks of diarrhea. Research has shown that babies who continue to breastfeed recover more quickly from bouts of diarrhea.

The rule of thumb for the breastfeeding baby is: If a baby can take anything by mouth, it should be human milk. Human milk is digested so quickly that some nutrients and fluid will be absorbed even if it seems like the feeding comes right back up. As long as the baby is having at least two or three wet diapers per day during his illness, he is not in danger of dehydration. In more serious cases of diarrhea, the doctor may want you to give the baby supplementary feedings of an oral rehydration solution, but human milk should continue to be baby's main source of food and fluids.

For the baby who's vomiting, it will be best to take him off solid foods for the duration. If his stomach is very upset, it might help to hand-express most of your milk and let him nurse for comfort on a fairly empty breast. If he gets only a small amount of milk each nursing (while nursing fairly often), the baby may be less likely to lose it all again. After a few hours of tolerating these smaller feedings, the baby can begin to take more milk at each nursing. If even the smaller feedings quickly come back up for several hours, you should call your doctor and watch for signs of dehydration.

For the baby who is six months or older, or the toddler who is begging for something because he is thirsty, perhaps a few ice chips or water from a teaspoon will satisfy him for a while. Freeze some of the milk you are expressing to keep yourself comfortable and use frozen mother's milk to quench his thirst. The advantage of ice is that it goes down slowly and is an interesting distraction to boot. If you can hold him off with something like that, fine. If not, let him nurse on the emptied breast but don't give him anything else. In any case, weaning is not necessary or advisable.

Human milk is the best food there is for the sick baby, and as long as he can take anything by mouth it should be your milk. When a nursing baby is sick, the comfort he receives at the breast may be the most important benefit of all.

LACTOSE INTOLERANCE

Occasionally, when a baby has very frequent, loose stools it may be suggested that he has something called lactose intolerance, and you may be told to take the baby off the breast. There is no need to do that. True lactose intolerance is virtually unknown in babies and young children under weaning age. As children grow beyond weaning age, the enzyme lactase, with which they were all born and which is necessary to digest milk sugar (lactose), begins to disappear from their systems. This occurs because after weaning, milk is no longer a necessary part of the human diet.

Lactose intolerance is not a problem for the totally breastfed baby. On the other hand, cow's milk allergy (sensitivity to the protein in cow's milk) is frequently confused with lactose intolerance and should be ruled out as a possible cause of baby's diarrhea. Sensitive babies may react to cow's milk products in their mother's diet.

If baby is ill or has been given certain medications, such as antibiotics, he may develop something called "secondary lactose intolerance," which shows up as diarrhea. Dr. William Sears, in his book, SAFE AND HEALTHY, calls this "nuisance diarrhea." The lining of the baby's intestine is irritated, and it takes time to return to normal. The best thing to do in such situations is to take baby off everything by mouth except your milk. For the toddler who has been on lots of solids and other liquids, you may want to avoid foods that are difficult to digest. Offer bananas, rice, unsweetened applesauce, lean meat, or strips of whole wheat toast, along with frequent nursings and water in a cup. As the effects of the illness or the medication wear off, the stools will return to normal, although it may take two to four weeks before the baby's usual bowel pattern returns. In the meantime, because of the special closeness and comfort he derives from the breastfeeding relationship, as well as the physical benefits of your milk, he will recover much faster.

Regardless of the age of your nursling, whether he is a little newborn or a sturdy toddler, remember that if he develops diarrhea, don't panic. And whatever else you do, keep nursing.

GASTROESOPHAGEAL REFLUX

If your baby spits up after feedings, or even vomits frequently, he may be suspected of having gastroesophageal reflux (GER), a condition in which the stomach empties upward into the esophagus. Some babies with GER do not spit up at all but develop other symptoms. If your baby is suspected of having this condition, be assured that breastfeeding can and should continue. Breastfed babies with GER have been found to have fewer and less severe episodes of reflux than formula-fed babies. The digestibility of human milk is definitely an advantage. Ways to manage breastfeeding include feeding the baby in an upright position and keeping the baby upright in a carrier or sling after feedings. Short, frequent feedings are also suggested. Further information can be obtained from a group called PAGER, listed in the Appendix.

SURGERY ON A BREASTFED BABY

If a breastfed baby requires surgery, discuss with the doctor ahead of time how long the baby will need to fast prior to surgery and how soon afterwards the baby will be allowed to nurse. Guidelines for the time a breastfed baby needs to fast prior to surgery are in the process of changing. Current research supports the idea that the breastfed baby need only fast for two to three hours prior to surgery. You'll need to find ways to distract the baby during the time he is not allowed to nurse. After surgery, many mothers are able to join their babies in the recovery room and nurse the baby as soon as he awakens. Nursing can be comforting at this time for both mother and baby. Again, as soon as baby can have anything by mouth, human milk is the first choice.

Slow Weight GAIN

Slow weight gain in an otherwise healthy breastfed baby is a warning signal. It calls for a close look at baby, mother, and the nursing routine. If you find yourself in this situation, don't rush to replace human milk, the best food for babies, with an artificial substitute. Instead, take a closer look at the baby's breastfeeding patterns. With a few adjustments, breastfeeding, with its long-term benefits, can continue.

Why do some babies gain weight slowly? There may be one simple explanation or a combination of reasons. Could a minor illness be causing the problem? Often, a baby who is not feeling well does not nurse well. Of course, the baby's doctor will check him over thoroughly to be assured that illness is not the cause of the problem. And if the baby is sick, nursing is of even more value. An all-out effort to maintain breastfeeding, along with appropriate treatment for the illness, will speed recovery.

In all cases of slow weight gain, the baby should be under the care of a doctor. In the majority of these cases, the baby is doing well and the breastfeeding difficulties can be readily resolved. Look over the section in Chapter 7 called "Is Baby Getting Enough?" It explains many of the breastfeeding management techniques that help to increase a mother's milk supply and help baby gain weight.

Remember that some babies lose up to five to seven percent of their birth weight before they begin to gain weight. Baby's weight gain should be figured from the lowest point, not from his birth weight.

What is a good average weight gain? Normal weight gain for a breastfed baby is four to eight ounces (113-127 grams) a week in the first three to four months. From four to six months, a breastfed baby's weight gain may slow to three to five ounces (85-142 grams) per week. Increases in length, head, and chest circumference are also signs of growth. Alertness and good skin tone also indicate that baby is getting enough to eat. From six to twelve months, a healthy breastfed baby may gain only 1½ to 3 ounces (42-85 grams) per week.

Studies comparing growth in breastfed and formula-fed babies show that there are differences between the two groups. After three months of age, breastfed babies gain more slowly than artificially fed infants. While changes in length and head circumference are similar, the breastfed babies, on average, are leaner at one year of age. The growth charts used by most doctors are based on formula-fed infants, and may not be accurate for breastfed babies.

TIME AT THE BREAST

If a baby is not gaining well, the first question is how often is the baby being breastfed? Not nursing often enough is probably the most common cause of slow weight gain. Human milk is quickly digested, and frequent nursings are easier for the baby and provide him with a steady supply of nutrients. If slow weight gain is a problem, it's important that the baby nurse on both breasts at least every two hours, with perhaps one longer stretch of three to four hours at night if baby is asleep. If a feeding begins at eight o'clock, put the baby to the breast again at ten, regardless of how long the eight o'clock nursing lasted. Plan to nurse the baby ten to twelve times in each twenty-four-hour period.

"SWITCH NURSING"

If your baby is not gaining well because he is falling asleep at the breast, try "switch nursing" to keep him interested. This means that you'll nurse on one side for as long as baby is actively sucking and swallowing. When he slows down and begins to lose interest, switch to the other breast. For some babies, this can be as long as ten minutes on each breast; for others it will be only two or three minutes before you switch. Be sure to let the baby nurse from both breasts at least twice at each feeding. If baby tends to fall asleep, changing his diaper before switching sides can wake him up.

"Switch nursing" keeps a sleepy baby more interested in nursing and helps a baby get more milk because he sucks more actively. It also encourages more let-downs for the mother, which may bring down more of the high-fat hindmilk and give her breasts more stimulation so she will produce more milk. A few days of "switch nursing" can sometimes bring about a dramatic improvement in baby's weight gain.

GETTING ENOUGH HINDMILK

In some cases of slow weight gain, just the opposite of "switch nursing" is what's needed. Sometimes limiting a baby's time at each breast does not allow him to get the hindmilk which provides the fat and calories he needs to put on weight.

This situation is called a "foremilk-hindmilk" imbalance or an overabundant milk supply. The mother seems to have a good supply of milk but her baby is gaining slowly. He may be nursing often, but he is fussy, very gassy, and has loose greenish stools. He seems to be getting too much milk and may even spit up after feedings. A mother whose baby shows these symptoms may need to let the baby nurse his fill on the first breast, letting him pull away himself when he is satisfied before offering him the other side. It may help to offer only one breast per feeding for a while to see if baby shows signs of improvement. It may be that the baby is filling up on the thinner foremilk from both breasts and not getting enough of the rich hindmilk that comes later in a feeding.

NIPPLE CONFUSION

Using a pacifier, nipple shields, or supplemental bottles of water, formula, or juice can cause nipple confusion and interfere with baby's ability to suck effectively at the breast. Just one bottle is enough to confuse some babies, especially in the early weeks. A baby uses totally different techniques to remove milk from your breast than he uses to drink from a bottle. You'll want to be wary of bottles or pacifiers if your baby is gaining slowly as nipple confusion can add to rather than solve the problem. If a slow gaining baby needs to be supplemented, alternate feeding methods can be used in order to avoid artificial nipples.

THE EXTRA-PLACID BABY

The slow gainer may be a placid baby, a quiet infant who regularly sleeps for four or five hours at a time. This little sleeper isn't gaining well because he just isn't nursing as much as he should be. If your baby is one who sleeps a lot, you may be thinking, "Such a good baby." But don't be lulled by such placidness. Keep a careful check on the number of wet and soiled diapers. After the first few days, you should be getting at least six to eight really wet diapers a day. If you are using disposable diapers, they may not feel as wet but baby should be wetting five to six disposable diapers per day. A new baby, under six weeks, will usually have three to five bowel movements per day. As he gets older, the number may decrease and he may only have a bowel movement every three or four days, or sometimes even less often, but in these cases, the amount will be substantial.

With a sleeper, mother takes the initiative and actively encourages her baby to nurse more often. You have to become a clock-watcher. For a time, you are the gentle prod encouraging your baby to nurse. Handling baby and nursing him often helps to rouse him. He needs this stimulation as much as he needs your good milk. It all works together to get him going.

ENCOURAGING THE SLEEPY BABY

To wake a sleepy baby who needs to eat more often, strip him down to a diaper and hold him, skin-to-skin, next to you. (If you are chilly, throw a blanket loosely around the two of you.) Rub his back or feet. Talk or sing to him. One mother of a sleeper said that every time her baby opened his eyes during a nursing, she'd say loudly, "Yes! Good! You can do it!" Each time he responded to her words by nursing well for another minute or so. Whether it was mother's pep talks or her all-around attentive mothering we can't say, but baby's thinness was soon replaced by dimpled elbows and chunky legs.

If baby is still too drowsy to nurse, try sitting him in your lap with his chin in your hand and bend him forward at the hips. Or gently bring him from a horizontal to a vertical position with one hand supporting his head. Or try walking your fingers up and down his spine.

TINY AND FUSSY

Occasionally, a baby is wakeful—fussy even—and spends a considerable amount of time at the breast, but still lags in the weight department. The question then is—how well is the baby sucking? Is he taking the breast well? He should be getting a large portion of the areola, the dark area surrounding the nipple, into his mouth. The baby who sucks in a fluttery manner on the end of the nipple will get the milk that has already collected in the breast, but he will not take in the additional milk that comes when he draws the nipple far back into his mouth and sucks vigorously. He isn't getting as much milk as he should, nor is it the richest milk, with the highest fat content.

If you suspect that your baby has such a sucking habit, look carefully at how he is nursing and listen for his swallows. A baby who is sucking well will swallow often once your milk lets down.

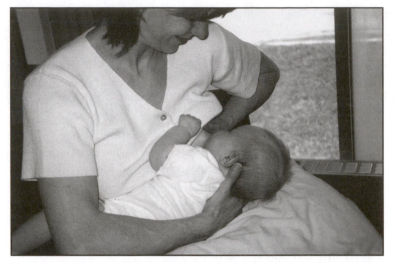

In the cross-cradle hold, the mother's right hand supports baby's head and her left hand supports the breast as baby nurses on the left breast.

In the football hold, the mother has a better view of how baby is latching on.

When there is concern about the baby's weight gain, his position at the breast and the way he latches on are very important.

Check over the section in Chapter 4 called "Breastfeeding in Slow Motion." Be sure baby is positioned so his whole body is facing you and he does not have to turn his head in order to reach your nipple. Be sure that baby opens his mouth wide as he latches on and that he gets a good-sized mouthful of breast, so that the nipple is positioned far back in his mouth.

You may want to try using the football-hold position or the cross cradle hold in order to support his head and have a better view of baby's position and sucking techniques. With the football hold, be sure his body is bent at the hips and he does not arch his back.

CHECKLIST FOR MOTHERS

If your baby is slow to put on weight, you'll want to take good care of yourself so you can build up your milk supply to meet baby's needs. Are you doing too much and not getting enough rest? One pediatrician's prescription for slow gainers is to put mother and baby to bed together for a few days. Try to reduce outside stress in your life. Make your baby your main concern for the time being.

Are you eating well? Think now—what did you have for breakfast today? Was lunch "on the run"? Are you drinking enough water or juice? Your liquid intake can include some coffee and tea, but keep in mind that excessive amounts of beverages containing caffeine have been known to adversely affect the weight gain of some babies. The same is true of smoking, especially if the mother is a heavy smoker.

Are you using hormonal contraceptives, especially those that contain estrogen? These have been found to affect a mother's milk supply. Could it be that you are anemic or have an underactive thyroid? Both of these conditions can affect a mother's milk supply if they are left untreated. Check with your doctor about these possibilities.

When a baby is not gaining as well as he should be, there is bound to be concern. But taking him off the breast is seldom, if ever, the answer to the problem. There is always the possibility that this will introduce a whole new set of problems.

TAKE SPECIAL NOTE

When babies do not gain well on mother's milk alone, everyone becomes concerned. The mother may feel frightened and inadequate. The doctor stresses that something needs to be done, but lack of knowledge about breastfeeding can lead to inappropriate interventions. The following points can be reasons for concern and indications that some changes, perhaps even supplemental feedings, may be needed for a time. Determining the cause of low weight gain and taking appropriate action can relieve everyone's concern and boost the baby's weight.

- If baby's weight gain is below four ounces a week or at least a pound a month in the first four months
- If baby has not regained his birth weight by two to three weeks of age

- If there are too few wet diapers or scanty bowel movements
- If the baby is not waking to nurse at night
- If the baby is nursing fewer than ten to twelve times a day
- If the baby has gotten into a habit of taking only the end of the mother's nipple or will only stay at the breast for a very short time, or refuses the breast
- If the baby nurses "all the time" but is mostly sleeping or "mouthing" the nipple, not actively sucking and swallowing
- If mother has persistent sore nipples in spite of treatment and correct positioning of baby

These situations may indicate the baby is not sucking effectively. A baby who is not sucking well cannot build up his mother's milk supply to meet his needs. The mother and baby require the help of someone familiar with sucking problems. In such cases, breastfeeding can and should continue but the baby may need to receive supplementary feedings for a while. Your local La Leche League Leader may have experience helping mothers with these kinds of problems, or she can refer you to another knowledgeable person.

Supplements do not have to be given with a bottle. In fact, using artificial nipples can make it harder for the baby to learn how to breastfeed effectively. As an alternative to bottles, consider using a cup, eyedropper, feeding syringe, spoon, or bowl. All of these work well when baby needs supplements temporarily, while you work on improving the breastfeeding situation.

To give the baby supplementary feedings with a cup or bowl, choose a small cup, for example, a shot glass, or a small flexible plastic bowl. Fill it about half full. Be sure the baby is awake and alert and swaddle him in a blanket so that his hands don't get in the way. Hold him upright in your lap. Rest the cup gently on his lower lip and tip it so that a small amount of milk touches his lips or goes into his mouth. Leave the cup in position as he swallows, then offer another sip. Let the baby set the pace.

Feeding with a spoon, an eyedropper, or a syringe is similar to cup feeding. Hold the baby in an upright position. Proceed slowly and patiently, and pay careful attention to baby's own feeding rhythm.

Supplements can also be given at the breast using a specially designed nursing supplementer. The baby receives the supplement through a tube while he nurses. This avoids any nipple confusion from artificial nipples and continues to provide the sucking stimulation that your breasts need in order to produce more milk.

First choice for supplementing the breastfed baby is the mother's own milk which she hand-expresses or pumps. Pumping after feedings will yield more of the high-fat hindmilk that helps babies grow. Pumping or hand-expressing provides your baby with all the benefits of human milk and also stimulates your breasts to continue producing lots of milk. When baby is able to suck more effectively, there will be plenty of milk there to reward his efforts.

If donated human milk is available from another nursing mother, this would be a better choice than formula. Do not give your baby formula or any other food without the advice of your doctor.

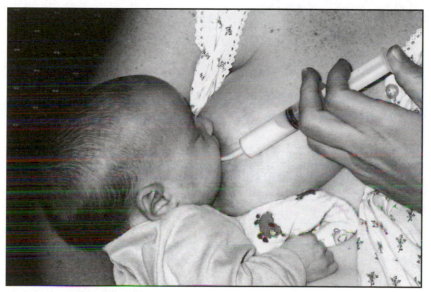

A feeding syringe can be used to provide supplement while baby nurses.

THE DOCTOR'S ADVICE

The doctor should be seeing the baby regularly to assess his weight gain and overall condition. If weight gain is very slow, and the doctor suggests a supplement, discuss the possibility of pumping or hand-expressing between feedings and supplementing with your own milk.

If the doctor insists on a supplement despite the fact that the baby is healthy and gaining at least four ounces per week, you may want to seek a second opinion. Improved weight gain may be possible with better breastfeeding techniques.

If the doctor finds that the baby's weight gain is seriously low, and believes it would be dangerous to delay while you attempt to build up your milk supply, it is important to give the supplement as recommended while taking steps to improve the breastfeeding situation. Use the alternate feeding methods described above in order to avoid using artificial nipples.

In all cases of slow weight gain, keep in touch with your doctor, watch the baby's progress carefully, be aware of the baby's wet and soiled diapers, and continue efforts to help the baby breastfeed more effectively.

Support and encouragement from a La Leche League Leader can be helpful any time a mother and baby are having a problem with breastfeeding.

FURTHER HELP

A mother whose baby is gaining weight slowly needs additional information along with lots of encouragement. Your La Leche League Leader can provide the support you need if your baby is not gaining well. She may be able to offer specific suggestions that can help you, or she may refer you to a more experienced Leader or a lactation consultant for help. Your baby may need special guidance in learning to suck effectively and there are experts available who can show you how this can be done.

In some very few cases a mother may not be able to increase her milk supply to fully meet her baby's needs. This could be caused by a variety of reasons—previous breast surgery, a pituitary deficiency, or inadequate breast development. Whatever the cause, a mother can continue to offer the breast while the baby receives whatever supplements are needed. She does not have to give up breastfeeding entirely.

Babies are meant to grow and thrive and everyone is happy when they do. If your baby is not gaining well, there may be reason for concern, but be assured that your milk is still the perfect food for him. Once he gets enough to eat, his glowing health and fat cheeks will be a source of pride and satisfaction for you in the months and years ahead.

CHAPTER 18

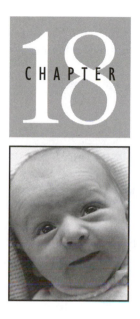

The Superior Infant Food

Human milk has long set the standard for infant feeding. After all, human breast milk is the only food uniquely designed by nature for the human baby. It contains all the nutrients babies need each day, plus many substances that help keep them healthy and promote optimal growth and development. Through the years, research has confirmed what common sense dictates: a mother's own milk is the best possible food for her infant. Artificial infant feeding products can't even come close to duplicating the rich mix of nutrients and biologically active substances manufactured in mothers' breasts.

Just consider what human milk feeding accomplishes in a newborn baby. The comment "My, how that baby has grown" is music to a nursing mother's ears. Your baby's rate of growth during the early months is far greater than at any other period of life. The human brain is one-third its adult size at birth and reaches the two-thirds mark by age one. Your baby's head grows about four and one-half inches (11.25 centimeters) during his first year to allow for the tremendous growth of his brain. Good muscle development and substantial increase in length are other significant signs of progress, along with baby's weight gain. Getting bigger is serious business for a baby, and mother's milk provides all that babies need to grow, until solids are started sometime in the middle of the first year. Even then, human milk remains baby's nutritional mainstay for most of his first year.

Human milk, custom-made for the human baby's digestive system, is more readily assimilated than artificial formulas. It also protects against disease and helps every system in baby's body develop in the way nature planned.

Your milk is uniquely suited to meet your baby's nutritional needs. No two mothers produce identical milk. Even the milk of an individual mother varies from day to day and during different times of the day— just as other fluids and systems in our bodies fluctuate. The colostrum your baby receives on the first day of his life is different from the colostrum on day two or three. The milk produced by mothers of premature babies is higher in certain nutrients to meet her baby's special needs. Even the taste of the milk changes with the diet of the mother. You could say that your milk is programming your baby's taste buds for the coming fare on the dinner table. One study showed that when mothers consumed garlic capsules, their milk had the odor of garlic, and their babies sucked more vigorously and took in more milk. During one feeding, your milk varies from skim to creamy, permitting your breastfed baby to enjoy a change of tastes that could be compared to a multi-course meal. Human milk will sustain, strengthen, protect, and fill out your baby's precious body, and put a recognizable bloom on his skin. Human milk is the food of choice for human infants; anything else is a distant second.

Designed for the HUMAN BABY

All mammals produce milk but milk differs from one species of mammal to another. All milk consists mainly of water, protein, fat, and lactose (a sugar), along with a generous dash of vitamins and minerals and traces of enzymes and hormones. However, the proportions of the various components of milk differ greatly from one species to another to accommodate different growth rates, different behavior, and different needs.

Cow's milk contains larger amounts of protein than human milk since calves need to grow rapidly to keep up with mother in the meadow. Whale's milk is high in fat, since the babies need a layer of blubber to keep them warm in cold seas. Human milk has higher levels of lactose and specific long chain fatty acids which are important to the development of humans' most distinguishing characteristic—the brain.

Most infant formula is made from cow's milk, but a lot has to happen to make it into even a rough imitation of human milk. In the preparation of infant formula, cow's milk is diluted with about an equal amount of water, and sugar must be added to recoup the lost calories. Both milks are more or less the expected white color, although human milk may sometimes look thin and blue compared to the grayish tint

A mother can take pride in the benefits she is giving her baby by breastfeeding.

of artificial formulas. Completely missing in artificial infant feeding products are the live cells that help protect baby from disease and the enzymes and hormones that support baby's physiological development. Infant formula cannot duplicate all the subtle ways in which human milk supports infant growth and health. Human milk is uniquely suitable for human infants because of the complex balance of ingredients.

PROTEINS ARE THE KEY TO GROWTH

Of all the substances that make up living things, proteins are the most distinctive, the most characteristic of the species. Proteins in your milk are as different from those in cow's milk as you are from a cow. The most notable distinction is the difference in relative amounts of casein and whey proteins. The large amount of casein protein in cow's milk forms large, tough, rubbery curds that are difficult for the human baby to digest. This explains why a formula-fed baby's tummy remains "full" longer than the breastfed baby's. Whey protein, which is more plentiful in mother's milk, is perfectly suited to the human baby's digestive system. It is higher in nutritive value than casein protein and makes for a softer, better-smelling stool.

AMINO ACIDS AND TAURINE

Proteins break down into amino acids, the building blocks of body tissue. Your milk contains essential amino acids in the proper proportions that your baby needs.

Taurine, for example, is an important amino acid found in high concentrations in human milk. It is virtually absent in cow's milk. Evidence is accumulating that taurine has an important biologic role in the development of brain tissue and of the retina of the eye. The human infant is unable to make taurine out of other nutrients, so he is completely dependent on his food to supply this amino acid. Because of its potential importance to brain development, it is currently being added to some prepared infant formulas, but taurine has always been available to the infant who receives his mother's milk.

FATS PROVIDE ENERGY AND MORE

The fat in your milk provides energy for growth and a reserve store of fuel. The resulting layer of fat tissue blankets a baby against heat loss. Along with his soft skin, it makes him especially nice to cuddle. A breastfed baby has firmer flesh and feels more solid than a formula-fed baby, probably because of the kind of fat in human milk.

Human milk averages approximately two to three percent fat. Fat accounts for 30 to 55 percent of the total calories in human milk. Mothers who are severely undernourished and have no fat reserves of their own to draw on tend to produce milk that is somewhat lower in fat than that of well-nourished mothers, though the protein and lactose content of their milk is still within the normal range. Also, the types or proportions of the various fats in human milk vary according to the mother's diet.

Unlike the predetermined constant fat content of infant formula, the amount of fat in a mother's milk varies from feeding to feeding and from week to week. The fat content of the milk changes even during a feeding; the amount of fat increases as the let-down reflex sends the higher fat milk down toward the nipple. This is why it's important to let a baby finish at the first breast before offering the second. He needs the high-fat milk that shows up late in the feeding from the first breast.

If fat cannot be absorbed, it is useless to the baby. Fat that is not absorbed may even act as a bandit, robbing the baby of calcium, since fat and calcium can form an insoluble "soap" which passes right through the baby's digestive system. The fat (or lipid) of human milk is absorbed and utilized by the baby with remarkable efficiency because the fat-digesting enzyme lipase is present in mother's milk.

This maternal lipase is active in the baby's intestine and aids in the efficient digestion of milk lipids.

Certain kinds of fat are important to the development of the brain and nervous system, and here again, research suggests there are important differences between human milk and artificial formulas. Human milk contains significant amounts of DHA and AA, which are long-chain polyunsaturated fatty acids derived from linoleic and linolenic acid. These fats are important to the process of myelination, the development of the sheath around nerve fibers that enables them to send messages. This process is critical during baby's first year and the presence of these particular fats in baby's diet may be important. In one study, higher blood levels of DHA and AA were associated with better visual and cognitive development in infants. In some parts of the world DHA is added to cow's milk formulas, though researchers are not certain whether adding this one component to infant formula will make a difference. Human milk is a complex substance and how everything in it works together is not fully understood.

Attention has focused in recent years on reducing the amount of cholesterol in adults' diets—but a baby in the first two years of life needs cholesterol. It is used to build tissue in the brain and nervous system. Research has also suggested that exposure to cholesterol in human milk may be advantageous in later life, enabling a person to better handle dietary cholesterol as an adult. Giving babies a physiologically sound start in life seems to be the best insurance against future disease.

LACTOSE IS ESSENTIAL

Sharing top nutritional billing with protein and fat is the sugar lactose. It is found only in milk and is frequently referred to as milk sugar. Among sugars, lactose has remarkable properties that benefit the newborn. In the familiar role of carbohydrate, it is a source of quick energy, but that is only one of its functions. Lactose may contribute to the optimal development of your baby's brain and central nervous system. In general, the bigger the brain of a species, the higher the percentage of lactose in the milk.

Mother's milk contains one and a half times as much lactose as is found in cow's milk—a fact that is readily verified by the sweet taste of human milk to the adult palate. The sugar content of cow's milk must be increased for use in infant feeding. If sucrose or other substitute sugars are used, they are not the equal of lactose. Lactose breaks down and releases its energy at a slow, steady pace, thus avoiding the highs and lows in blood sugar that are characteristic when sucrose is used.

This high level of lactose in mother's milk is related to a corresponding low level of minerals and salts in the milk, an arrangement that is ideal for the human infant. Lactose enhances the absorption of certain minerals, calcium in particular, that are necessary for good bone and tooth development.

One reason that the lactose in your milk is ideal for your baby is because of its special effect on the environment within the intestines. Milk sugar promotes the growth of a select group of bacteria, mainly *Lactobacillus bifidus*, in the infant gut. This thwarts the growth of undesirable bacteria that can cause diarrhea in the young. Aiding the growth of these good bacteria is a substance called the bifidus factor. Mother's milk contains much more bifidus factor than does cow's milk or formula. Evidence of its effectiveness may be recognized by anyone who changes a breastfed baby's diaper. The bowel movements of the totally breastfed baby have a distinct, not unpleasant, buttermilk-like smell. This is proof that the small world within is populated by a preponderance of beneficial bacteria. The formula-fed baby's stools have a strong odor—very unbecoming to the baby.

VITAMINS AND MINERALS IN PERFECT BALANCE

Vitamins and minerals are essential to growth and health, and human milk is the best and most balanced source for infants. There is an ever-growing body of research on all these various nutrients, their presence in human milk, and their role in infant nutrition. This section contains only the highlights.

Even though human milk is recognized as the superior food for the infant, there seems to be no end to the promotions aimed at a mother to persuade her that her breastfed baby needs something in addition to her milk. The "something," it seems, is always for a price. Glossy advertisements will congratulate you on nursing your baby and then smoothly slip in a statement to the effect that some vitamin or other popular and important-sounding item is "borderline" in mother's milk. The ready solution, we are to believe, is to give the baby the commercial product. Nursing mothers should be aware that what is really "borderline" is the scientific background of such ads.

When it comes to vitamins and minerals for the baby, it is important to remember that more is not necessarily better. The workings of our bodies require a balance of nutrients. Dropping a supplemental dose of liquid vitamins or minerals into your baby's mouth "just in case" is not a good thing to do. Supplementary doses of iron are a case in point.

The iron in mother's milk, while low in quantity, is extremely well absorbed. Up to fifty percent of the iron in human milk can be

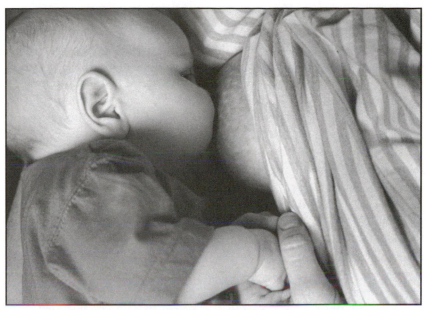

As he peacefully nurses at his mother's breast, a baby receives a complex array
of nutrients and protective substances.

absorbed by the infant, as compared to ten percent of the iron in cow's milk and four percent of the iron in iron-fortified formulas. A recent study showed that infants exclusively breastfed for seven months or longer were not anemic at their first birthday and had higher hemoglobin levels at one year and two years of age than breastfed babies given solids before seven months. Clearly, breastfed babies don't need iron supplements. They may even be harmful.

When iron supplements are given, the baby's delicately balanced use of iron may be put in jeopardy. Two specialized proteins in mother's milk, lactoferrin and transferrin, pick up and bind iron in the infant's intestinal tract. This deprives harmful bacteria of the iron needed for growth. When iron supplements are given to the breastfed baby, the iron-binding abilities of lactoferrin and transferrin are overwhelmed, and the harmful bacteria are allowed to thrive.

CALCIUM, PHOSPHORUS, AND VITAMIN D

Calcium and phosphorus are two major minerals found in milk that are generally thought of in tandem. Calcium, in particular, is well known for its role in the formation of strong bones and teeth. Cow's milk has different proportions of calcium and phosphorus and they are found at much higher levels than those in human milk. This is necessary in cow's milk because the calf starts walking from birth. Despite the large supply of calcium in cow's milk, rickets, a disease of young children caused by lack of calcium, was rampant in the United States in the early 1900s as populations shifted to the cities and artificial infant feeding replaced breastfeeding. The sight of older children with abnormally bowed legs was all too common until it was learned that a high concentration of calcium in the blood means nothing if there isn't sufficient vitamin D to activate it. So the essential vitamin D was added to the cow's milk sold for human consumption. Calcium in human milk is well-absorbed, and rickets is not found in breastfed infants of well-nourished mothers who receive some exposure to sunlight.

Some doctors have expressed concern about the low levels of vitamin D found in human milk. A 1989 study in the *Journal of Pediatrics* reported that "unsupplemented human milk-fed infants had no evidence of vitamin D deficiency during the first six months." Of course, you will want to take your baby outdoors, weather permitting, so that he benefits from the natural sunlight, which activates the formation of vitamin D. A few minutes a day of sun on your baby's cheeks is all that is needed. Being sure that you yourself get adequate amounts of vitamin D will ensure that there is enough in your milk. This may be especially important for dark-skinned individuals, those who wear traditional clothing that leaves little skin exposed, and those who live in colder climates where there is less exposure to sunlight.

ZINC

The zinc in human milk is better absorbed by your baby than the zinc in infant formula. In fact, human milk is a specific treatment for a rare, inherited metabolic disease called *acrodermatitis enteropathica* (AE). Infants with this condition suffer a zinc deficiency brought about by a reduced ability to absorb zinc. Babies who develop the disease are cured when their feedings are switched from formula to human milk. Cow's milk formulas actually contain more zinc than human milk, but the zinc in human milk is absorbed more easily. In the rare case that a mother herself was deficient in zinc, her milk could be affected. The solution is to give a zinc supplement to the mother.

Other minerals, such as copper and manganese, have been found to have a significantly better biological availability in human milk than in cow's milk or formula.

VITAMIN C

The milk of an adequately nourished mother contains all the vitamin C her baby needs. Scurvy, a disease caused by lack of vitamin C, is virtually never seen in the breastfed infant.

Keep in mind that this important vitamin is not stored in the body and mothers must therefore replenish their own supply each day, more or less. This is seldom a problem since a wide variety of fruits and vegetables contain vitamin C. Giving vitamin C supplements directly to the baby is inadvisable. If there is a question of vitamin C adequacy, a supplemental dose can be taken by the mother. She not only benefits herself, but dispenses the vitamin in the proper form and amount to her baby through her milk.

FLUORIDE

Over the years, fluoride supplements have received a great deal of attention, linked as they are to sound teeth and decreased dental caries. Mother's milk contains some fluoride, and while the amount is small, it seems to be perfectly suited to the baby's need. The American Academy of Pediatrics no longer recommends fluoride supplements for babies under six months. Some mothers who have used fluoride supplements have found they cause their babies to be fussy.

ENZYMES AND HORMONES

Human milk contains many other substances whose role in infant physiology is yet to be determined. Enzymes present in human milk include the fat-digesting lipase described above, amylase which helps break down carbohydrates, and protease which works on proteins; these help make the nutrients in human milk more available to the baby. Hormones in human milk may influence how infant physiology responds to feedings as well and may guide other aspects of early development. Human milk contains high levels of a hormone called epidermal growth factor which may affect growth and development of the intestinal tract.

Mother's milk is a unique and unmatched commodity. In their definitive book, *Human Milk in the Modern World,* Jelliffe and Jelliffe state, "There is no possibility of cow's milk being humanized biologically. The two products are much too complex and dissimilar."

Much remains to be learned about the subtle effects of human milk on infant growth and development, but the more science learns about differences between formula-feeding and breastfeeding, the more compelling the argument in favor of breastfeeding. A system this complex cannot be duplicated in the laboratory.

In a 1989 article titled "Science and Politics of Breastfeeding," T. B. Mepham states:

> *Not only are attempts to mimic breast milk by modifying cow's milk increasingly revealed as inadequate, but the non-nutritive advantages of breastfeeding, such as in disease prevention and through its contraceptive properties, are assuming greater human and economic significance.*

Human Milk—an Arsenal against ILLNESS

Mothers who breastfeed their babies have often noticed that when the rest of the family comes down with a cold or flu, the baby remains free of it or has only a mild case. Breastfeeding is important to infant health. Even in parts of the world where overall infant mortality is low, breastfed infants are likely to be sick less often and less severely than their formula-fed counterparts. In developing countries, breastfeeding is critical to infant survival.

Studies confirm the beneficial effects of breastfeeding for babies living in poverty. In a 1996 study of infants in the Philippines, deaths from respiratory infection and diarrhea were 8-10 times higher in babies who were artificially fed than in those who were even partially breastfed for six months. The risk was even greater for low birth weight babies. A study of infant deaths in metropolitan areas of Brazil found that the risk of death from diarrhea was 14.2 times higher in infants who were weaned from the breast than in fully breastfed babies; the risk of death from respiratory infection was 3.6 times greater. Infants who were partially breastfed were at greater risk than those who were fully breastfed, but were better off than those who were fully formula-fed. In Bangladesh, breastfeeding was associated with a 70 percent reduction in the risk of contracting severe cholera; breastfed children up to 30 months of age were less likely to become ill, despite cholera epidemics. Another study done in Bangaladesh showed that breast-feeding in the first six months reduced the mortality rate from diarrhea by 24-27% and that non-breastfed children had a 4.2 times greater risk of death from diarrhea before age five.

These are only a few examples of the dramatic effect breastfeeding has on infant health in parts of the world where poor sanitation, unsafe water supplies, poverty, and lack of medical care contribute to enormous public health problems. Mother's milk is the first line of defense for the community's smallest, most vulnerable members. But even in affluent areas of the United States, Canada, New Zealand, and Western Europe breastfeeding improves infant health.

STATISTICS TELL THE STORY

Over the years, a variety of studies have been done that show breastfed babies are heathier. One classic study followed over 20,000 babies in Chicago in the 1920s and 30s. Mothers regularly brought their babies to the Chicago Infant Welfare Society for checkups, and the young-sters in the study were followed for at least nine months. Grulee and his associates divided the babies into three groups, based on how they were fed: breastfed, almost half of the babies, 9,747; those who were partially breastfed, 8,605 babies; and totally artificially fed, 1,707 babies. A record was kept of deaths from all causes and illnesses due to infections.

In all of the babies, respiratory infections were by far the most common cause of illness. A noticeable difference in the three groups was found in the ages at which the babies came down with respiratory illness. Once past five months, only a small number of breastfed babies developed respiratory infections, while such illness among the artificially fed group remained

Studies continue to show that breastfed babies are healthier.

high. An even more telling difference among the three groups was the number of deaths from respiratory infections—four of the more than 9,700 breastfed babies, 44 of the 8,600 partially breastfed babies, and 82 of the 1,700 babies of the artificially fed group died of respiratory illness. Deaths from respiratory infections in artificially fed infants were 120 times greater than among breastfed babies.

The second biggest problem for these babies was gastrointestinal infections such as diarrheal diseases. The breastfeeding babies had fewer intestinal infections compared with both partially breastfed and artificially fed babies, fewer even than respiratory problems. When figures were compiled on the total number of deaths from infections of all kinds, it was found that in all, 129 of the artificially fed babies and 75 of the partially breastfed group died of infections. If the rate of deaths among the totally artificially fed infants were applied to the completely breastfed group in the study, it could be expected that there would be over 730 deaths in this large number of infants. But the records show that only 13 of the 9,700 breastfed babies died from infection. Even in the light of today's modern medical advances, the low mortality rate in breastfed infants as recorded by Grulee from the Infant Welfare Society reports stands out as an enviable record.

A comparison of illness among breastfed and bottle-fed infants was made in 1977 in the United States. The babies in the study were from middle-class families who enjoyed a high level of medical care, education, and housing. Dr. Allan S. Cunningham found that episodes of significant illness in the 164 breastfed babies were uncommon, and when there was an illness, it occurred at a later age than in the artificially fed babies.

FEWER DOCTOR VISITS

A 1982 study done in a rural community in the United States reviewed illness in babies as measured by visits to the doctor. Records were compared on 66 formula-fed and 40 breastfed babies. Only 25 percent of the breastfed babies had to be seen by the doctor even once in their first three months because of illness. For the formula-fed babies, this figure was 94 percent. A study from 1980 reports that formula-fed infants were hospitalized for infections three times more frequently during the first three months of life than breastfed babies.

Research that was done in 1995 by a health insurance company in the United States showed that infants who were breastfed for six months saved the company an average of $200 each for doctor visits, prescription drugs, and hospitalizations compared to formula-fed babies. In the Colorado USA WIC program (a supplemental food program), it was estimated that a total savings of $478 per infant was realized when a baby was breastfed for six months. This total reflected medical and prescription costs for formula-fed infants.

In another large study of babies from affluent, well educated families, there were significantly fewer episodes of diarrhea and *otitis media* in those who were breastfed. Even in the best of living conditions, breastfeeding makes a significant contribution to infant health. Another study found that babies who were exclusively breastfed for four months or longer had, on average, half the number of acute ear infections as those who were not breastfed at all, and 40% fewer ear infections than infants who were breastfed and given supplements.

Over the years, research in industrialized nations has found that many specific kinds of infectious diseases are less likely to occur in breastfed babies; these include respiratory infections, ear infections, urinary tract infections, *haemophilus influenzae* type B (HiB), pneumonia, and meningitis. Breastfeeding's protective effect is especially significant in gastrointestinal illness. One study reported in the *American Journal of Public Health* in 1985 found that "the risk of acute gastrointestinal illness in infants receiving formula was six times greater than in infants receiving breast milk and 2.5 times greater than in infants receiving cow's milk." A study done in Israel reported that babies less than twelve months of age had a lower incidence of acute diarrhea during the months they were breastfed than formula-fed babies during those same months. An American study found the incidence of diarrhea among formula-fed babies to be twice that of breastfed babies. Even in developed countries, diarrhea can be dangerous in infants; worldwide it's a leading killer of babies and small children.

Studies also show that breastfeeding has a protective effect against chronic health problems, such as allergy. Breastfeeding has been associated with lower rates of juvenile diabetes, celiac disease, childhood cancer, rheumatoid arthritis, urinary tract infection, multiple sclerosis, dental caries, severe liver disease, and even acute appendicitis. In recent years, researchers have also found substantial evidence that breastfeeding lowers the risk of a baby dying of Sudden Infant Death Syndrome (SIDS). Large studies of SIDS in the United States, New Zealand, and England have shown that infants who were not breastfed had a two to three times greater risk than breastfed infants.

The resistance to disease that human milk affords a baby cannot be duplicated. Even when babies have every other possible advantage, breastfeeding gives them an extra boost on the way to good health. Human milk is the very best infant food available, and it's free. If more babies were breastfed, infant mortality rates would drop, even in affluent countries, and health costs would also decrease. Breastfeeding is best for babies, no matter where they live.

Colostrum has been called "nature's vaccine for the newborn."

Nature's Vaccine for the NEWBORN

La Leche League's long time medical advisor, Dr. Herbert Ratner, coined a phrase that aptly describes human milk's unique anti-infective qualities—"nature's vaccine for the newborn." Your milk contains unique substances that help to explain why breastfed babies are healthier. Thirty years of research on the immunology of breastfeeding has revealed a rich array of protective substances that fight bacteria and viruses and keep baby from getting seriously sick.

Your infant arrives in the world with a supply of protective proteins called antibodies that come to him from your blood via the placenta. The antibodies, which are also known as immunoglobulins, have been manufactured by your immune system in response to infections that you have been exposed to. These include some of the common contagious diseases of childhood and the everyday household germs found in your environment. While the immunity you have to these diseases is lifelong, the immunity which is passed on to your unborn baby in the form of immunoglobulins, known as IgG, gives him only temporary protection until his own immune system begins to develop.

The first milk from your breast, which is called colostrum, is low in fat and carbohydrates, and high in protein. It is exceptionally easy to digest, and it contains many living cells that defend the newborn against a number of potentially harmful agents. The immunoglobulins and other substances in colostrum take over from the placenta and continue on with the job of protecting the baby.

THE PROTECTIVE SHIELD—HOW IT WORKS

Colostrum has an abundance of an antibody that is new to the baby, secretory immunoglobulin A (IgA). Secretory IgA acts as a first line of defense in the body. Whereas IgG, the main antibody coming to the baby through the placenta, is a blood-circulating or humoral antibody, IgA exerts its protective effect directly at those points where germs are most likely to arrive on the scene, on the mucous membranes that line the portals of entry to the body, such as the throat, lungs, and intestines. The antibody's construction allows it to resist the processes of digestion. Secretory IgA stands as a sentry along the frontier that is the lining of the gastrointestinal tract. It prevents germs or foreign proteins from penetrating the membranes and causing allergies or illness. Colostrum is also alive with protective white cells called leukocytes. These white cells, which are also found in blood, have the ability to destroy or thwart the bacteria and viruses that can cause serious disease.

The presence of live white cells in milk means that milk is a living tissue, very much like blood. In fact, there are about as many white cells in milk as there are in blood. Even before scientists knew about these live white cells, human milk was referred to by some doctors as "white blood," precisely because of its life-giving properties. Some of these white cells, the type called lymphocytes, manufacture IgA. Other leukocytes in mother's milk react to the presence of a virus by producing interferon, a protein that warns the surrounding cells of impending danger. The interferon manufactured by human milk leukocytes closely resembles that produced by blood leukocytes and is added protection for the infant against a variety of viral diseases.

Researchers have found that the presence of IgA in human milk stimulates the infant's own gastrointestinal production of IgA. The early stimulation of the immune system may have far-reaching effects in protecting infants from disease in later life.

A leading type of leukocyte in human milk is the macrophage. Macrophages are capable of engulfing troublesome organisms. They swallow the germs, and with the help of a protein enzyme, lysozyme, destroy them. (Lysozyme is also in good supply in mother's milk.)

The concentration of immune factors in human milk is at its highest in colostrum, the first milk. This provides yet another reason for putting baby to your breast as soon as possible after birth. No other fluid—glucose, water, tea, formula—comes close to being as good for your baby in the early days as colostrum.

As the days of breastfeeding go by, and colostrum gives way to mature milk, the concentration of antibodies in your milk decreases. Although fewer of these immunities are found in each milliliter of milk, the amount of milk your baby takes is increasing, so he is still getting plenty of immunological protection against many organisms, both viral and bacterial. Even past your baby's first birthday, there are significant amounts of protective factors in your milk. Their concentration actually increases during weaning.

SPECIALIZED PROGRAMMING AGAINST ILLNESS

Another fascinating finding related to human milk's immune properties was the discovery that the breast can deliver a particular antibody in response to a new germ in baby's environment. A chain of events begins when the fully breastfed baby is beset with a new germ. As he continues to nurse, perhaps even more often than usual because he is not feeling well, the offending organism is passed from baby to mother. The breast produces the needed immunoglobulin on site, locally, and sends the protective element along to the baby in the milk. This is a system of "specialized programming," with the nursing mother making antibodies on demand to germs that challenge her baby. The baby places the order, and mother programs the cells and delivers the appropriate antibody.

Human milk's direct dynamic role in preventing illness helps to explain how babies, as long as they are breastfed, can survive in a highly infected environment. Even before their own immune systems can protect them, this is an advantage of breastfeeding that cannot be duplicated by artificial formula.

WHAT ABOUT CHEMICAL CONTAMINANTS?

Chemical contaminants in the environment have become an inescapable fact of modern life. Traces of environmental contaminants are found in milk, both human milk and cow's milk. The situation can become intensely personal for a breastfeeding mother when large amounts of a contaminant are discovered in the area in which she lives and the media calls attention to high levels found in human milk. What are the implications for her and her baby? Should she have her milk tested? Should she continue to breastfeed?

Our advice is to use common sense. Put the matter of contaminants in perspective. First of all, there is no evidence to date of any harm coming to a breastfed baby because of the presence of these substances in his mother's milk. Only a small percentage of contaminants present in a mother's body are released into her milk. One study that examined a possible correlation between levels of contaminants in human milk and infant development found higher cognitive scores in the children who were breastfed, compared to those given formula. Another study published in 1996 in *Pediatrics* found that infants exposed to PCB and dioxin through human milk scored significantly higher on mental and motor tests than artificially fed infants. The benefits of breastfeeding clearly outweighed any possible effects of exposure to environmental contaminants through human milk.

Contaminants are not to be taken lightly, of course. They pose a risk to all of us, and research must continue to determine the overall extent of this risk. Publicity is sometimes focused on the amounts of contaminants found in human milk, mainly because human milk sampling provides an indication of the levels of contaminants in the general population.

When mother's milk is analyzed, it is not unusual to find that levels of one or more of the contaminants exceed the currently established limit for commercial foods. Dr. Edward Kendrick of the University of Wisconsin spoke to this issue in *Pediatrics:* "It should be clear to all that risk/benefit analysis leads to different conclusions for commercial milk as compared to human milk.... The application of particular contaminant limits to commercial cow's milk does not lead to the use of a substitute food but rather to the use of cow's milk with a lower contaminant level. However, the application of these limits to human milk leads to the use of a substitute and possibly inadequate food for the infant, namely infant formulas."

In addition to levels of contaminants in cow's milk, a baby being fed formula is exposed to other contaminants related to artificial feeding, such as lead and contaminants in the water used to prepare the formula. There is even concern about exposure to latex used in artificial nipples.

Analysis of human milk shows variability on a day-to-day and even a morning-to-evening basis, so testing a single milk sample cannot give a true picture of what the baby is actually getting. A study in Norway on insecticides in human milk showed a dramatic variance in the same mother's milk at different times. Repeated testing and careful analysis would be required to give meaningful results, and even then, safety levels have not been clearly defined.

Dr. Kendrick speaks for many other authorities when he explains: "To ask mothers to have their milk sampled voluntarily when neither the experts nor local physicians can decipher the results not only wastes health-care dollars but generates maternal anxiety with no useful outcome. We must await the clear demonstration of risks associated with breastfeeding before making such suggestions. At present, it is a balance of potential risks against known benefits, and the known benefits must take precedence."

What can you do to lower the amount of contamination you, your baby, and the rest of your family receive? Give serious thought to what you eat and the products you use in your home. Discontinue the use of pesticides and other sprays in your home or on your lawn or garden. As much as possible, try to avoid eating foods with pesticide residues. Fruits and vegetables should be peeled or thoroughly washed under running water. When you are pregnant and nursing, freshwater fish from waters that are known to be contaminated should be avoided. You can reduce your intake of red meat and dairy products and cut fat from meat and poultry, since most of the contaminants are concentrated in the fat.

Avoiding ALLERGIES

Protection against allergy is another of the many advantages a baby receives from breastfeeding. Your baby will not be allergic to your milk; you can count on this with certainty. It is a law of nature that infants never become sensitized to their natural food.

Proteins make the critical difference. The protein in human milk is totally compatible with human babies, but the proteins in cow's milk and in formulas based on cow's milk are potential troublemakers for the human infant. Some babies, when first exposed to these foreign proteins, become sensitized. When they are again fed cow's milk or cow's milk formula, they react with a variety of symptoms: stomach upsets, vomiting, diarrhea, stuffy nose, rashes, general crankiness. Even one bottle of formula, fed during the night in the hospital nursery while mother "gets her rest," is enough to sensitize some babies to cow's milk proteins and produce allergic symptoms months later.

Not only will a baby never be allergic to his mother's milk, but breastfeeding can be a factor in protecting the baby from future allergies. Many studies have found that babies who were exclusively breastfed for several months or more had fewer allergic symptoms later in childhood.

A 1988 study reported in *Annals of Allergy* found that allergies were less likely to occur among breastfed infants and that breastfeeding, even for a short period, was clearly associated with a lower incidence of wheeze, prolonged colds, diarrhea, and vomiting. More recently, a 1995 study published in *Lancet* followed children from infancy through adolescence (seventeen years of age) and found that breastfeeding provided long-term protection from eczema, food allergy, and respiratory allergy.

A MIRACLE CURE

For some infants, breastfeeding serves as both a preventive measure and a cure for allergic disease. One of the most dramatic cases of an extremely ill baby getting well on mother's milk came early in La Leche League's history. Lorraine and Emil Bormet's two-and-one-half-month-old David, formula-fed since birth, had been suffering from almost continuous diarrhea, breathing difficulties, and eczema. Different formulas had been tried, including soybean and meat-based varieties, with no improvement in David's condition. As a last resort, the doctor suggested that human milk was probably the only thing David could tolerate.

Lorraine located a nursing mother several miles from their Illinois farm home, and the mother agreed to help. Following David's first feeding of human milk late one evening, his astonished mother reported that, "he fell asleep and slept through the night for the first time in his life."

Convinced of the value of human milk, the Bormets wondered if Lorraine could bring in her own milk, even though it had been almost three months since the baby's birth. They contacted La Leche League for information. Milk production, we could assure her, is stimulated by the baby's sucking, and so she began the painstaking work of encouraging David to take the breast. Lorraine stayed in close touch with Marian Tompson, one of La Leche League's co-Founders, and David continued to receive human milk from generous donor mothers. Eight days after she began her efforts to breastfeed, drops of milk appeared. Some weeks later, Lorraine Bormet was completely nursing her baby, who by then was symptom-free, healthy, and content.

In the years since the Bormet story unfolded, other mothers with similarly allergic babies have contacted La Leche League, and many have found that, despite a late start, they could provide their own milk for their babies.

A BREASTFED BABY CAN STILL BE ALLERGIC

Even with exclusive breastfeeding, some babies still develop allergies. A baby may react to foods other than cow's milk or soy formula—early solids, for instance, or even vitamin or fluoride drops. You'll do your baby a favor if you're careful to limit what goes into his tummy to what is compatible with his young system. Your milk alone is your best bet for about six months. While your baby remains on mother's milk, his intestinal tract is protected and given time to mature. Potentially allergenic foods, which might cause problems even at six months of age, may be better tolerated later on, especially if baby continues to nurse. Be especially careful about offering foods with a high potential for causing allergic reactions. These include: egg white, citrus fruits, corn, wheat, fish, tomatoes, chocolate, cabbage, berries, and nuts, especially peanuts. If your baby shows signs of a reaction to a new food or if there is a history of allergy

We had experienced a series of problems with our first child, Jennifer, who was formula-fed. She vomited after almost every feeding until she was nearly six months old. This was followed by chronic diarrhea until she was past two. Her pediatrician changed the formula numerous times, but to no avail. He finally concluded that it was an inherited allergy.

Needless to say, I was eager to avoid this nightmare with Michael. Some of my friends had tried to encourage me to breastfeed, but frankly, it scared me to death. Coming from a large, close-knit, strictly bottle-feeding family, I had visions of my relatives shaking their heads in pity at my poor starving baby. Finally, after much debate, my husband and I decided the best thing for Michael would be to give breastfeeding a try for a week or two. Now, fourteen months later, I have to look back and laugh, for Michael turned out to be the chubbiest, healthiest child I could have imagined. Needless to say digestive problems were nonexistent (he rarely even spit up). Nursing my son has been an experience I wouldn't have missed for anything.

Kathy Driskell
Illinois, USA

Protection from allergies is especially important in some families.

in your family, you may want to ask your doctor about postponing solids until eight or nine months. Be sure to read Chapter 13 on starting solids before introducing your baby to other foods.

Jani Howd of South Dakota did not think allergies would be a problem in her family, but she later found out her daughter was highly allergic:

Avoiding allergies was not one of my primary reasons in deciding to breastfeed our first child. Now, two years later, I definitely know that it is an advantage that should not be taken lightly.

During her first year, Angie was a perfect example of a contented, healthy breastfed baby. Her only problem seemed to be a supersensitive skin. When I began introducing table food to her at about five and a half months, she ate willingly with a good appetite. At twelve months any attempt to feed Angie cow's milk or eggs resulted in a reaction. By eighteen months, eggs were no longer a problem, and at twenty-one months she seemed to tolerate milk.

Shortly after this, Angie developed eczema. We immediately took cow's milk away, but the eczema did not disappear completely until I put Angie on a strict elimination diet to determine exactly which foods she was allergic to. Then the fading eczema wasn't the only change noticeable in Angie. Starting about the age of eighteen months, temper tantrums and sleepless nights had become a matter of course, along with a loss of appetite. John and I attributed it to her growing independence and tried to handle her with love and patience.

Now that she is eating foods that agree with her, it is a rare sight for her to have a temper tantrum. She is our happy, contented, breastfed toddler. Her appetite has returned and the change in her disposition is almost unbelievable. Breastfeeding does not entirely prevent allergies, especially with a very allergic individual like Angie, but it was reassuring to hear the dermatologist tell me that had she not been breastfed, her allergies would be more severe, in greater number, and that she would have had food-related skin problems sooner, and have kept them longer.

If there is a history of allergies in your family it is generally a good idea to avoid eating an excessive amount of any one food during pregnancy, particularly cow's milk. There is evidence that a baby can become sensitized before birth to a food that his mother eats.

CAN BABY REACT TO SOMETHING MOTHER EATS?

In some instances, a food that a breastfeeding mother eats will cause a reaction in her baby. The protein from cow's milk, eggs, or some other food in the mother's diet may penetrate her gastrointestinal tract. These "stray" proteins in her blood can find their way into her milk. If her baby reacts to these foreign proteins, it's an indication of a pronounced sensitivity to that food, and very likely the baby has a strong tendency toward developing allergies. Eliminating that food from the mother's diet will clear the baby's symptoms. Keep in mind that the mother's milk itself is fine; the stray protein riding along is what's causing the problem. Switching the baby from human milk to an artificial infant food would overwhelm him with a large dose of potential allergens and more than likely make the problem worse.

When a baby is unusually fussy, has a rash or diarrhea, or develops other symptoms, it may not be caused by something in your milk. The reason for the problem could be something quite simple, so consider the most common possibilities first. Is the baby receiving any supplemental bottles of formula or juice? Vitamins or medication? He may be crying because he's coming down with an illness. A baby who is nursing very frequently may be going through a growth spurt. Consider your own situation. If you're continually tired or rushed, make life easier for yourself and your baby by slowing down. Are you taking any medication or food supplements? Are you consuming large amounts of caffeine or smoking cigarettes? One of these could be causing the problem. Something that the baby comes in contact with could be causing a rash. A few common possibilities include detergents, soaps, fabric softeners, dyes (colored sheets), wool, feathers, lotions, spray deodorants, and hair sprays (place a towel around your shoulders when you spray your hair or do without).

If the rash, fussiness, or whatever persists, your totally breastfed baby may indeed be reacting to something you are eating. Fortunately, there is a relatively simple and cost-free method of finding out if your diet is involved. Start by eliminating a particular food for a week or two and see if there's a difference in the baby. Since cow's milk is one of the most troublesome foods in this regard, you might want to try eliminating milk first. Be sure you also exclude other dairy products and all foods that are made with milk or dried milk solids. You'll have to read the labels of any prepared foods to be sure you are avoiding milk products completely. It may take ten days to two weeks to get the food out of your system, so don't expect your baby's reaction to clear up immediately.

If there's no change in your baby when you avoid dairy products, you might want to try eliminating other foods one at a time (or several at once) for a week or so to see if baby's symptoms disappear. Other common allergens are eggs, wheat, citrus fruits, corn, onions, fish, peanuts, cabbage, chocolate, and other nuts. If baby seems to improve when you eliminate a group of foods, try reintroducing them one at a time in order to identify the source of the problem.

Occasionally, a mother can eat a small portion of a food as part of a meal with no reaction on the baby's part, but a large amount taken alone at one time will spell trouble. If you have a highly allergic child, a little detective work may be necessary on your part, but you're already ahead of the situation by breastfeeding.

If you have a baby who is sensitive to the foods you eat, you'll want to be especially careful to delay the introduction of solid foods and be cautious about which foods you offer.

Dental CARIES

Studies have shown that breastfeeding itself does not cause tooth decay. In a traditional Eskimo society, Dr. Otto Schaefer, Director of the Northern Medical Research Unit of the Canadian Department of Health and Welfare, reports that his personal experience with several thousand Eskimo children who were breastfed for two to three-and-a-half years shows no evidence of rampant tooth decay.

A more recent study (1993) of dental caries in South African children showed no differences between children breastfed for one year and children formula-fed for one year in the incidence of dental caries up to age four. However, in the group that did experience dental caries, those who were breastfed had lower levels of decay.

Some studies show that defects in tooth enamel formed during pregnancy can predispose a child to tooth decay. Also, certain bacteria found in the mouth may contribute to tooth decay in some individuals.

Those breastfed toddlers who do develop tooth decay do so in spite of breastfeeding, not because of it. Often improvements are needed in dental hygiene and careful monitoring of sweets and snacks. When a toddler already shows signs of tooth decay, some dentists recommend tooth brushing after every nursing. It is not usually necessary to do so after nighttime nursings.

Renee Cox, a mother from Michigan, tells the story of her toddler's experience with tooth decay:

My daughter, Katherine, who is four now, had numerous cavities and even has one crown, so I was sure to bring William in for his first checkup as soon as his first few teeth appeared at about one year. At that point I heard the bad news: four cavities in the top front four teeth.

William's having so many cavities was somewhat surprising. William had very few sweets and very little juice (mostly water, instead). He did nurse on demand and William slept in our bed and nursed through the night.

I was later to learn that some believe frequent night nursing may contribute to dental caries in susceptible individuals even though milk doesn't leak from the breast as it does from a bottle. It is believed that mother's milk may still coat the teeth because the flow of saliva in the baby's mouth, which helps to clean the teeth, is lower at night. The PH of the mouth lowers and high-acid-producing bacteria can flourish. The percentage of nursing mothers and babies affected by this is very small, but our family ended up being one.

With a clear understanding that William was going to continue to nurse on demand day and night, my dentist suggested a routine in which we would try to keep his teeth immaculately clean, wipe them with a cloth after every breastfeeding, brush his teeth three to four times a day, and apply a small amount of topical fluoride (being sure to wipe off the excess fluoride). This was a solution that would allow us to continue breastfeeding as much as we needed to and have healthy teeth for William as well.

So we started on this experimental program—wake up, brush his teeth, apply topical fluoride, nurse throughout the day, keep a dry cloth handy, wipe his teeth after every nursing (which he didn't like), go to sleep, nurse at night. I must confess that I did not wake up at night to wipe his teeth with a dry cloth. One of the reasons William is in bed with us is so he can nurse and I don't even have to wake up.

We continued this routine for three months, had a checkup and no cavities. Then another three-month checkup and no cavities. Six months with no cavities! Everyone in the office was happy for us and even William managed a smile. I was pleased to know that continued nighttime nursing had not caused further decay.

William still protests through every brushing, but at 21 months old he still nurses on demand, is cavity-free, and oh, he has the sweetest smile.

Jaw, Teeth, and SPEECH DEVELOPMENT

The fitness enthusiast working out in a gym and the little one at your breast—his fists tightly closed, drops of perspiration on his brow, and his jaws working vigorously—are both engaged in body shaping routines. The body-builder's exercise may result in developing big muscles; your baby's exercise in eating may affect the shape of his face, his smile, and his ability to speak clearly.

Of course heredity lays the foundation for facial structure. A square jaw or a narrow chin, for example, may be a family trait. But whatever your child's potential, it is enhanced by the simple, repeated motions of sucking at mother's breast. Breastfeeding encourages proper facial development and may indeed spare your child dental or speech problems in future years.

A baby sucks differently on an artificial nipple than he does at his mother's breast. The sucking techniques used in bottle-feeding may lead to underdeveloped facial structure and may also encourage baby's tongue to thrust forward, causing the baby to develop an incorrect way of swallowing. If this habit persists beyond bottle-feeding days, there's the possibility that the alignment of permanent teeth will be affected. An artificial nipple, a pacifier, or baby's thumb may also press against the roof of his mouth, narrowing the upper dental arch and limiting the amount of room for teeth. Researchers from Johns Hopkins School of Public Health reported on a study of nearly 10,000 children in which they found that the longer the duration of breastfeeding, the lower the incidence of malocclusion. Children who were breastfed for a year or more required 40% less orthodontia than those who were bottle-fed.

Facial DEVELOPMENT

When your baby nurses at your breast, your nipple responds by shaping itself to his mouth in a way that no artificial nipple can. A mother's nipple is soft and flexible. Your baby moves your nipple back into his mouth and up against the hard palate with his tongue, elongating the nipple and bringing his gums and lips around the areola (dark area).

His cheek muscles are extremely active, enhancing facial development.

Two speech surveys in New Zealand, one in 1971 and the other in 1973, tested whether "factors influencing the development of the sucking response could have an effect on improving the muscles required for speech." Frances E. Broad, who conducted the survey, looked for "any differences in speech between breastfed and bottle-fed children." She also examined "influences likely to affect early reading ability," because, she explained, "it has

The interaction between mother and baby contributes to his social development.

always been thought amongst speech teachers that if a child could speak clearly he had a very good chance of being able to read well." Her study covered 319 children, ages five and six. Dr. Broad writes, "The surveys show that improved speech and reading ability coincide with breastfeeding and that the improvement is dramatically seen in the case of the male child."

Clear speech also depends on good hearing. Repeated ear infections early in life can make it difficult for a young child to hear the fine differences in sounds. Breastfeeding's protection against infection is an added bonus. Ear infections occur more frequently in bottle-fed babies.

The good effect breastfeeding has on a baby's ability to speak is, of course, enhanced when his mother and father talk to him and respond to the first attempts at speech from their budding linguist.

Social, Motor, and MENTAL DEVELOPMENT

All parents take pride in their baby's development and carefully watch his progress as he learns to roll over, sit, crawl, stand, walk, and talk. You watch his social development, too, as he responds with smiles and coos and learns to play peek-a-boo and patty-cake. Every baby is an individual and develops these skills at his own pace, and this development, of course, is influenced by many factors in a baby's environment besides breastfeeding. Nevertheless, studies show that breastfeeding does make a difference in infant development. In two recent studies, breastfed infants were ahead of their formula-fed peers in visual development. A 1984 study indicated that breastfed babies have a significant advantage over their bottle-fed peers in psychomotor and social development in the first twelve months. Breastfeeding has also been associated with optimal physiological organization and increased responsiveness. A 1987 study suggests that the tendency of breastfed babies to cry more often for feedings during periods of wakefulness serves to stimulate an increase in mother-infant interaction which has positive results in terms of the infant's development.

A study that was done in 1988 showed a small but significant relationship between the duration of breastfeeding and scores on the Mental Development Index of the Bayley Scales at one and two years of age. A study of low birthweight infants found the ones who were breastfed had an 8 point advantage in mean scores on the Bayley Mental Development Index over infants who had not been breastfed. Recent studies of possible effects on infant development from environmental contaminants in human milk found that breastfed babies scored higher on the various tests than infants fed formula which did not contain potentially harmful PCBs or dioxin.

More recent studies provide even stronger evidence that breastfeeding enhances cognitive development. One fascinating study compared premature infants who had received human milk in the hospital neonatal unit with those who had not. Children who were fed human milk had significantly higher IQs at 7½ to 8 years of age when compared with those who had not received human milk. The children's cognitive scores were directly related to the amount of their mother's milk they received. When the children whose mothers had provided their own milk were compared to children of mothers who had intended to provide milk but were unsuccessful in doing so, the higher IQ scores were still apparent, suggesting that development could not be attributed to having the kind of mother who was willing to make the extra effort to pump. The researchers concluded that there is something in human milk that enhances brain development, at least in premature babies.

Every year professional journals publish hundreds of articles reporting on research related to lactation. La Leche League International's Center for Breastfeeding Information (CBI) maintains an extensive database along with a collection of more than 12,000 full length articles from 1,300 professional journals. See the Appendix for information on requesting a free brochure describing the services available from the CBI.

How Breastfeeding Affects a Mother

Lactation is the natural follow-up to pregnancy and childbirth. A mother's body makes milk for her newborn baby whether she chooses to breastfeed or not. Actually, what is best for baby also turns out to be best for mother's body. While making milk for the baby, the lactation process causes changes in the mother's body that benefit her directly. At the same time, however, she must remember that during breastfeeding, anything that affects her may also affect her baby.

How the Breast GIVES MILK

Breast changes are an early sign of pregnancy. You may have had trouble buttoning the buttons on a favorite shirt even before you found it difficult to zip your jeans. This increase in breast size comes as estrogen and progesterone stimulate the duct system within your breasts to grow and prepare to deliver milk to your infant. Although colostrum is present in the breasts during pregnancy, the hormonal changes that follow birth are what kick milk production into high gear. As estrogen and progesterone levels fall, prolactin, the milk-making hormone, takes over. A mother's milk supply increases rapidly or "comes in" and her breasts feel full with milk.

A mother's breast is a superior food source. The way in which it supplies milk for the baby is as remarkable as the milk itself. In a bottle-feeding culture, a person may think of the breast in terms of a bottle and transfer some characteristics of the bottle to the breast. Mothers may be told to wait until the breast feels full before offering it to the baby, just as a bottle is filled before giving it to the baby. Mothers may have heard that "the breast must fill before the milk will flow."

Not so. Your breast may feel empty, but as your baby nurses, milk will be there. While an infant feeding bottle is a container and nothing more, a nursing mother's breast is the manufacturing site. It is never totally empty and is always capable of producing more milk.

Your baby's eager sucking is the key to continued milk production. While the making of milk is usually associated with the birth of a baby, there have been instances throughout history of women bringing in a milk supply for a baby not biologically their own by encouraging the baby to suck frequently at the breast. A member of La Leche League tells of having been breastfed by her grandmother following the death of her own mother. Her grandmother had nursed all of her children and felt that this was the least she could do for this motherless child.

A picture of the inner structure of the breast could remind one of branches of a tree. The top branches are deep in the breast, coming together at the trunk, leading to the nipple. Small buds represent the milk-producing cells, known as the alveoli, which select and manufacture the nutrients and protective agents needed to make the milk. Droplets of milk pass through the small ducts and are stored in reservoirs just behind the nipple.

There is a continuous build-up of milk that collects in these reservoirs between feedings. Over a period of time, this supply can make the breast feel quite full, but it is only a fraction of the milk the baby receives. The milk that collects between feedings, known as the foremilk, usually accounts for about one-third of a baby's intake at a feeding. The remainder and greater portion of milk comes directly "off the production line" as your baby nurses. This manufacturing process begins as his strong sucking action makes contact with the nerves in your nipple. Impulses from these nerves travel to the pituitary, the master gland in the brain, by way of the hypothalamus, which is near the pleasure center of the brain. Nature intends mothers to enjoy breastfeeding their babies.

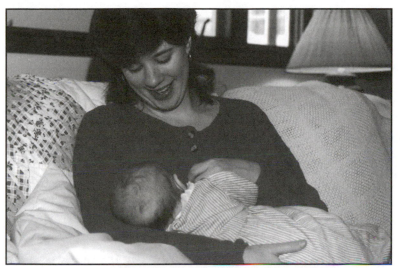

Just settle in and relax, allowing your baby to decide when he's finished nursing.

Two hormones, prolactin and oxytocin, are then released. Prolactin tells the cells to make milk, while oxytocin moves it from the alveoli into the ducts. When oxytocin is released, band-like cells around the alveoli constrict and squeeze out larger, more concentrated fatty globules and proteins than are found in the foremilk. This is the milk ejection reflex that some mothers experience as a tingling, cramping, or pins-and-needles sensation in the breast. Others notice only a change in the baby's sucking rhythm. The milk-ejection reflex releases the hindmilk. It is a tasty reward for baby's continued nursing and for your patience in keeping him at the breast. It's also the milk that puts weight on your baby, which is the reason babies need to suck well and long enough in order to gain well. The milk ejection reflex (or "letdown") occurs several times during a feeding. Since babies themselves regulate the release of the hindmilk, it is not a good idea to set a time limit on how many minutes a baby should nurse.

BREASTFEEDING HORMONES

The late Niles Newton, PhD, former professor of behavioral sciences at Northwestern University, had a special interest in oxytocin, which she described as "the hormone of love." According to Dr. Newton, the presence of oxytocin is one reason a breastfeeding mother is physically different from a mother who does not nurse her baby. Oxytocin triggers nurturing behavior, which in Dr. Newton's words, is "an essential ingredient in the success of reproduction." Both prolactin and oxytocin may help to produce the feeling of relaxation that mothers come to associate with nursing sessions. Many women recognize that they feel calmer during the months they are nursing their babies and better able to cope with whatever comes along. A recent study showed that lactation suppresses the nervous system's hormonal response to stress.

Niles Newton's research years ago showed that the release of oxytocin is a conditioned response. A mother's body can produce oxytocin in response to familiar sights, sounds, and activities associated with breastfeeding, not just from the direct stimulation of the baby's suck. More recent research found that oxytocin levels increased in 30% of the mothers when their babies became restless and in 20% as they were preparing to nurse. Prolactin levels were found to increase only when the baby actually sucked at the breast.

Niles Newton also showed that the let-down reflex could be inhibited by stress—in her research, the subject (herself) was made to do complex math problems in her head while breastfeeding. This resulted in less milk being available for the baby.

The let-down reflex is especially sensitive in the early days of nursing. This may give a mother the impression that she has "lost" her milk. Milk is still there, and more will come, once mother and baby relax. Scientists believe that this interesting phenomenon in milk letting down developed in the early periods of the human race. When a wild creature or some danger threatened a mother and her baby it was time for mother and baby to flee, not sit and nurse.

There are no longer wild animals at our doors, so even when you feel anxious there's no reason to flee. Just snuggle down with your baby and imagine your milk pouring out to him in all the profusion of a glorious Milky Way. A sixteenth century artist, Tintoretto, portrayed what has been identified as the milk let-down in a painting, appropriately titled, "The Origin of the Milky Way." It shows Hercules nursing at Juno's breast as her milk ejects in a spray of stars.

Breastfeeding and Your REPRODUCTIVE CYCLE

If your baby nurses often, day and night, you probably won't ovulate or have menstrual periods for several months. The time when you can again conceive is postponed. While eventually you may be able to become pregnant while still nursing, it will not be as soon as it would be if you were not a breastfeeding mother. Other than milk production, this is the most noticeable effect of breastfeeding on a mother's body.

Many mothers find that their periods do not return until the baby is a year old or older. By this time, he is nursing less often and eating a variety of foods. Dr. Herbert Ratner notes: "It is the baby's sucking that controls the mother's ovulation. The more the baby has a need to suck, the less ready he is to be displaced by another. The less the baby has a need to suck, the more ready and able he is to cope with a new sister or brother."

Almost all mothers who are fully breastfeeding their babies are free of menstrual periods for the first three to six months or longer. This is called lactational amenorrhea. Fully breastfeeding means the baby relies completely on mother for nourishment and for all of his sucking needs. Your baby's frequent nursing inhibits the release of hormones that cause your body to begin the monthly preparations for a new pregnancy. Ovulation does not take place, and you do not have menstrual periods.

Lactational amenorrhea is a normal, healthy part of the female reproductive cycle. Women who bear only two or three children during their reproductive years come to think of their monthly menstrual cycle as normal and the period of lactational amenorrhea as a departure from the norm. However, going for years without having a period is probably what women's bodies were meant to do. When women have large families, and nurse each baby for a year or more, they experience fewer menstrual periods in their lifetime. Periods of lactational amenorrhea may help to explain the lower rates of ovarian, endometrial, and breast cancer found in women who breastfeed.

When your menstrual cycle is in the resting state, you are less likely to have problems with anemia and the fatigue that goes with it, since there is no monthly loss of blood. Also, you will not have the tension or other mood swings that often precede menstruation. One husband listed this as an added advantage of breastfeeding because he found that "living was easy" during the months his wife was breastfeeding.

BREASTFEEDING'S CONTRACEPTIVE EFFECT

Numerous studies over many years have confirmed that breastfeeding reduces fertility. We learned this, too, from our own experience and the experience of the thousands of breastfeeding mothers who have been associated with La Leche League. John and Sheila Kippley, founders of the Couple to Couple League, gathered data on American women who practiced total breastfeeding for the first six months and then introduced solids gradually. They found there was an average of 14.6 months without periods following childbirth. LLL Leader Sheila Kippley writes in her book, *Breastfeeding and Natural Child Spacing*, "This is only average. Some, an exceptional few, will experience a return before 6.0 months postpartum. Others will go as long as 2.5 years without menses while nursing."

More recently, scientists specializing in the study of lactational infertility have developed the Lactational Amenorrhea Method of contraception (LAM), based on research done in a variety of cultures

Breastfeeding's effect on your fertility may space your babies about two years apart without any other form of family planning.

around the world. LAM has a 98 percent effectiveness rating in the first six months after birth, which compares well to other contraceptive methods.

LAM will reduce your chances of becoming pregnant in the same way that it has worked for the women in the studies. Using LAM for contraception is safe, simple, cheap, and effective. Knowing exactly what conditions make it likely that you will remain infertile can help you use breastfeeding's effect on your reproductive cycle to your advantage. You are unlikely to become pregnant if you can answer "no" to all three of the following questions:

1. Have your menses returned?

2. Are you supplementing regularly or allowing long periods without breastfeeding, either during the day (more than four hours) or at night (more than six hours)?

3. Is your baby more than six months old?

If your answer to any of these questions is "yes," the chances of becoming pregnant increase. A recent study of employed mothers in Chile suggests that hand-expressing milk at work at regular intervals was also effective in delaying a return of fertility.

WHEN YOUR PERIODS DO RETURN

Fully breastfeeding will always delay ovulation for a time, but the resumption of regular periods is usually an indication that ovulation is occurring. For some women, especially those who are still exclusively breastfeeding, the first one or two menstrual periods may occur without previous ovulation. But a mother who has regular periods should consider herself able to conceive again. When menstruation does return, there is no reason to stop nursing the baby. Breastfeeding can and should continue.

When baby gets older, is nursing less, and eating a variety of other foods, a mother who has not been having periods is more likely to resume ovulation without a prior menstrual period and conception can take place before menstruation resumes. Ovulation may also resume if a mother returns to work and is separated from her baby for several hours each day and is not pumping her milk, or if a baby who was nursing often suddenly starts to sleep through the night.

Any time the amount of baby's sucking at the breast is reduced, a mother should realize that her hormone level could be affected and her menstrual cycle may resume. More importantly, if this change in nursing patterns has happened suddenly, ovulation is more likely to occur before the first menstrual period.

Early periods may be less regular than they were before you became pregnant, since it takes a while for the menstrual cycle to settle into a predictable schedule after childbirth, whether a mother is breastfeeding or not. You can find a more detailed and thorough explanation of the physical changes in your reproductive cycle while breastfeeding, and how you can become more aware of them, in Sheila Kippley's book, *Breastfeeding and Natural Child Spacing* and in *Your Fertility Signals: Using Them to Achieve or Avoid Pregnancy, Naturally* by Merryl Winstein. See the Appendix for details.

Since certain patterns of breastfeeding have been shown to significantly delay the return of fertility, you may not need to consider other methods of family planning in the early months. However, as your natural period of infertility is ending, you may want to think about family planning options. Cultural, religious, and family values will certainly influence the choices you make, as will the fact that you are breastfeeding.

If a breastfeeding mother chooses to use any type of artificial contraception, her first choice should be one of the non-hormonal methods. Hormonal contraceptives that contain estrogen have been shown to decrease milk supply in some mothers as well as result in changes in milk composition. They are not usually recommended by most health professionals knowledgeable about breastfeeding for use during lactation. Hormonal contraceptives that contain progesterone, while widely prescribed for lactating women, may have negative effects on milk supply if introduced too early in the course of lactation. Also, since the composition of progestin-only pills continues to change as new varieties appear, there are still no conclusive studies on long-term effects on mother or baby. For this reason some health professionals advise that hormonal contraceptives be avoided by nursing mothers.

The baby who is under six months of age or the older baby who is still primarily breastfeeding is especially at risk when his mother is taking oral contraceptives.

Other Changes in YOUR BODY

Your baby adapts to milk-making in many ways that are unseen. Just as with pregnancy, this is a time to marvel at how your body knows just what to do to nourish your baby. It is also a time to take special care of yourself—not because lactation is exhausting or a drain on your body, but because having a new baby is stressful. You will weather the challenges better if you are well-nourished, reasonably well-rested, and relaxed enough to concentrate on what's important.

One thing you don't have to worry about is your milk. How much milk you make is controlled by how much your baby nurses, and studies of breastfeeding babies show that they have a remarkable ability to regulate their own milk intake. Breastfed babies may consume less milk than artificially fed infants. From four to twelve months they grow more slowly and are leaner than their formula-fed counterparts. But they are healthy and thriving—not hungry.

The quality of mother's milk—the nutrients in it—is also something you can depend on. You would have to be severely malnourished before there would be reason to worry abut whether your milk is meeting your baby's nutritional needs. The survival of the young of the species is so important that nature has made special provisions to ensure the quality of your milk.

One such provision is the extra fat you put on during pregnancy to fuel the milk-making process after baby's birth. Your body's metabolism becomes more efficient during lactation, another energy safeguard. Blood flow to the breasts increases, carrying needed nutrients. The calming effect of breastfeeding hormones is also in your baby's best interest.

Does a mother's body rob itself of nutrients to make milk? There is no simple answer to the question of where all the good things in human milk come from, but concerns raised about nursing mothers being deficient in particular nutrients have proven to be unfounded.

Much of the dietary caution leveled at breastfeeding women is about calcium. Calcium, of course, is needed for strong bones, and calcium deficiencies may contribute to osteoporosis, or bone degeneration as women age. The news that a lactating woman's body uses calcium from her bones to make milk thus raises some alarms. Do women who nurse their babies, especially for a long time, place themselves at risk for bone problems later in life? The answer is no, because here again, the body makes special allowances for lactation.

Calcium is absorbed more efficiently from the intestines during lactation and for a time after weaning. Researchers have discovered that while mothers' bones may lose a small amount of calcium during lactation, as determined by measurements of bone mineral density, bones are built up again within six months of weaning.

In studies of postmenopausal women, those who breastfed for extended periods of time had comparable or higher bone mineral densities than women who had never breastfed and actually had a lower risk of hip fracture. Rather than being a cause for concern about osteoporosis, breastfeeding may actually offer some protection against it.

Mothers do, of course, need plenty of calcium in their diets. Milk and dairy products, including cheese and yogurt, are good sources. If you find you must avoid dairy products because of allergies or because they bother your baby you can get calcium from other foods. A cup of cooked bok choy (a type of cabbage) provides almost as much calcium as a cup of milk. Half a cup of ground sesame seeds has twice as much calcium as a cup of milk. Other calcium-rich foods to include in your diet are blackstrap molasses, calcium-enriched tofu, collards, spinach, broccoli, turnip greens, kale, liver, almonds, Brazil nuts, and canned salmon and sardines, which are normally eaten with the soft bones.

Some Special PRECAUTIONS

Part of taking care of your baby is taking care of yourself, baby's food source. While your body is doing the amazing work of nourishing your baby, you'll want to be careful about certain substances that may not be good for either you or your infant.

SMOKING

You probably know some of the disturbing statistics on the effects of smoking. The potential hazards of smoking during pregnancy may have been incentive enough for you to quit or cut down. However, despite your best intentions you may find yourself still smoking when your baby is born, and you wonder how this will affect breastfeeding.

The fewer cigarettes smoked, the less chance there is that difficulties will arise. By keeping smoking to a minimum, a mother can decrease the risk. In general, if a mother smokes less than a pack (twenty cigarettes) a day, the amount of nicotine in her milk is not usually enough to cause any problem for the baby. Nicotine is not readily absorbed by the baby's intestinal tract and is rather quickly metabolized.

When a nursing mother smokes heavily (more than twenty cigarettes a day), the risks increase. Heavy smoking can reduce a mother's milk supply and on rare occasions has caused symptoms in the nursing baby such as nausea, vomiting, abdominal cramps, and diarrhea.

One study found that smoking lowers prolactin levels in nursing mothers. In other studies, smoking has been shown to interfere with the let-down reflex. If a mother smokes, she should do so away from the baby, in a separate room or outdoors.

Many studies have shown that second-hand, or "side-stream" smoke, is harmful for babies and young children. One study featured in *Lancet,* a British medical journal, found a significant correlation between parents' smoking habits and the incidence of pneumonia, bronchitis, and SIDS during their babies' first year of life.

Since there are legitimate concerns about the effects of smoking on a breastfeeding mother and her baby, the ideal solution is to avoid smoking. For those who can't seem to quit, cutting down is another option that might seem more within reach.

ALCOHOL

The effects of alcohol on the breastfeeding baby are directly related to the amount the mother ingests. When the breastfeeding mother drinks occasionally and limits her consumption to two drinks or less per day, the amount of alcohol her baby receives has not been proven to be harmful. It is generally recommended that alcohol be avoided entirely during pregnancy.

Alcohol passes freely into a mother's milk and has been found to peak at 30 to 90 minutes after consumption of one alcoholic drink. Once the mother's body metabolizes the alcohol, the alcohol is eliminated from her system and from her milk. The more alcohol that is consumed, the longer it takes to be eliminated.

Two studies were done that showed babies nursed more frequently but consumed less milk when their mothers had been given an alcoholic drink. Regular abuse of alcohol by a breastfeeding mother could result in slow weight gain or failure-to-thrive in her baby.

At times, the use of alcohol has been suggested as a way to encourage a mother's let-down reflex. However, large amounts of alcohol can actually inhibit milk ejection.

An anxious, overtired mother may sometimes find that an occasional glass of wine or beer helps her to feel relaxed. Of course, as mother becomes less tense so does her baby. Many mothers who choose not to drink alcohol find that tension drains away with a cup of hot or iced tea, or another favorite beverage. Lying down can do wonders, and listening to music is soothing. Especially nice is having your husband's reassuring arms around you when you're feeling stressed by your new responsibilities.

DRUGS AND MEDICATIONS

You should make it a practice not to take any medication whatsoever unless it is definitely necessary and has been prescribed or approved by a physician. In general, there are relatively few medications that must be totally avoided by a nursing mother. This topic is discussed more thoroughly in Chapter 17.

As for so-called "recreational drugs," these should be totally avoided by a breastfeeding mother. Research shows they can have harmful effects on the nursing baby and they can also be detrimental to a mother's ability to care for her baby. The use of marijuana, for example, has been found to cause significantly lower levels of prolactin, the "mothering" hormone that is important not only to an adequate milk supply but to the whole mother-baby relationship. THC, the active chemical in marijuana, is concentrated in human milk and appears in a baby's urine after a breastfeeding mother has used it. Why take the chance of exposing your baby to potential harm?

Cocaine and heroin pass into a mother's milk in significant amounts and can cause intoxication and addiction in the breastfed baby. Nursing mothers should avoid these substances.

Taking good care of yourself and taking good care of your baby go hand in hand. The better you feel yourself, the better you will feel about your baby.

Benefits of BREASTFEEDING

Throughout this book we have pointed out many advantages of breastfeeding for you and your baby. This next section highlights a few of them and gives more detail.

PROTECTION AGAINST BREAST CANCER

Are women who breastfeed their babies less likely to develop breast cancer than those who do not? Numerous studies have suggested that breastfeeding does indeed offer mothers protection against breast cancer. The effect is strongest for premenopausal breast cancer, although some studies show that breastfeeding lowers the risk of breast cancer after menopause as well. Protection against breast cancer is related to duration of breastfeeding, with the greatest risk reduction seen in women whose total amount of breastfeeding, for one or more children, totals several years.

One study reported in the *American Journal of Epidemiology* showed that the risk of breast cancer decreased among both premenopausal and postmenopausal women with increasing duration of lifetime breastfeeding experience, although the effect was consistently stronger for premenopausal women. In 1989, the *Journal of Clinical Epidemiology* reported a study which included 4,599 women, 20-55 years of age, identified as having an initial diagnosis of breast cancer. The same number of women of similar ages were selected at random from the same geographic areas to be a control group. After age at first full-term pregnancy had been factored out, number of pregnancies and duration of breastfeeding were shown to have a strong influence on the risk of breast cancer. Compared with women who had given birth but had never breastfed, women who had breastfed for 25 months or more were one-third less likely to develop breast cancer.

In 1995, a study published in Japan showed that there was a significant protective effect that lowered the risk of premenopausal breast cancer among women who had breastfed for more than 6 months. And another 1995 study showed a 10% reduction in breast cancer risk when a woman had breastfed for any length of time.

One factor that seems to be closely related to the low incidence of breast cancer in women who have nursed their babies is the total number of anovulatory months during the reproductive years. Decades of repeated menstrual cycles may make breast tissue more vulnerable to cancer. In support of this thinking is the fact that women who have no children have one of the highest incidences of breast cancer. Among Canadian Eskimos studied by Dr. Otto Schaefer, mothers commonly breastfed their babies for three years or longer. Another pregnancy followed, with more years of nursing. Dr. Schaefer found only one case of breast cancer in the fifteen-year period from 1954 to 1969, even though the population grew from 9,000 to 13,000. As the traditional Eskimos were assimilated into Western culture and the length of time that a mother nursed her baby decreased (or the bottle replaced the breast altogether), the incidence of breast cancer increased.

One significant finding about breast cancer rates was reported in *Epidemiology* in 1994. The study shows that women who were breastfed themselves had significantly less risk of developing breast cancer. Both premenopausal and postmenopausal breast cancer were decreased by 26-31% in women who had been breastfed. Interestingly, this study points out that women who had been breastfed were more likely to breastfeed their own children, but this was not taken into consideration as a factor for the decreased risk shown in this research.

Even though statistical reports show that breastfeeding decreases a woman's chances of breast cancer, a mother should not ignore a lump in her breast that stays constant in size or enlarges. Most lumps in the lactating breast are milk-filled cysts (galactoceles), inflammation (mastitis or plugged ducts), or benign tumors (fibromas). However, in rare cases, a breastfeeding mother can develop breast cancer. If testing needs to be done, try to find a doctor who is familiar with breastfeeding and can evaluate the situation without insisting that you wean your baby.

Without spending extra money, mothers provide their babies with the very best when they breastfeed.

ECONOMY, ECOLOGY, CONVENIENCE, AND ENJOYMENT

"As a mother who has done both, I can tell you that nothing is more convenient than breastfeeding," states Katie Hartsell from Kansas. "When the baby begins to cry, the mother has a readily available supply of milk at the right temperature. There is no waiting for the bottle to be warmed. There is quite a savings to the family budget and no waste."

The savings with breastfeeding are considerable, especially compared to premixed formulas and disposable bottles. One young couple, trying to budget for their new baby and their first apartment, were shocked by the "substantial sum" that would be added to their weekly food bill with the regular purchase of formula.

Viola Lennon, one of La Leche League's co-Founders, suggests that the money you save by breastfeeding might be used to purchase a major appliance. A father from New Zealand, Harry Parke of Cambridge, told a group of fathers, "My wife and I figured that by nursing our first son, Christopher, we saved considerably in the first year by not using formula, sterilizers, early solids, electricity, birth control means, etc. Raewyn immediately decided that the money saved was to be a deposit on a freezer, and it now stands in the hall!"

At one point, in the United States, formula costs increased at such a rapid pace that the entire industry was investigated by the Federal Trade Commission. The price of infant formula increased six times faster than the price of cow's milk. The current price of premixed formula on supermarket shelves in the United States means that a formula-feeding family may spend up to $30 per week or $1500 per year, to feed the baby.

Low income mothers in the United States can receive food supplements for themselves, their babies, and their young children through the WIC (Women, Infants, and Children) program developed by the federal government. Formula prices have escalated the cost of this program. In 1986, only 38% of WIC mothers were breastfeeding their babies at hospital discharge. In a 1987 Summary Report from the US Department of Agriculture, it was estimated that 29 million dollars could be saved annually if mothers in the WIC program breastfed their babies for just one month.

In 1996, the Colorado WIC program determined that they could save $74,000 per month if only 50% of the new mothers in their program breastfed for five to six months. They estimated that a nationwide savings of 9.3 million dollars a month could be realized if 50% of all the mothers in the WIC program across the country breastfed for five to six months.

WORLDWIDE IMPLICATIONS

In Third World or developing countries, the impact on the economy is devastating when mothers choose to abandon breastfeeding. Gabrielle Palmer, a nutritionist and breastfeeding counselor from Great Britain, writes in *The Politics of Breastfeeding*:

> *Human milk is a commodity which is ignored in national inventories and disregarded in food consumption surveys, yet it does actually save a country millions of dollars in imports and health costs. The Mozambiquan Ministry of Health calculated in 1982 that if there were a mere twenty percent rise in bottle feeding, in just two years this would cost the country (the equivalent of) 10 million US dollars, and this did not include fuel, distribution, or health costs. They also calculated the fuel required for boiling the water would use the entire resources from one of the major forestry projects. Inventors of fuel-saving cars are rewarded, why not energy-sparing women? For every three million bottle-fed babies, 450 million tins of formula are used. The resulting 70,000 tons of metal in the form of discarded tins are not recycled in the developed countries.*

Once you become an experienced nursing mother, you will probably spend two or three hours a day relaxing in your favorite chair, casually offering your baby the emotional, nutritional, and immunological benefits of breastfeeding. You will take this for granted as part of your daily routine. You may pause for a moment to reflect on the fact that you're giving your little one the very best start in life—but you may never stop to realize the global implications of what you are doing. You may not be aware that a mother's decision to breastfeed has economic, ecological, and political significance.

Worldwide trends toward artificial feeding have drastic consequences in terms of maternal and infant health. We can be proud of the involvement of La Leche League in efforts to reverse this trend. Forty years ago, the seven Founders wanted to help their friends and neighbors experience the benefits of breastfeeding their babies. Now the organization's outreach extends to mothers in every part of the world who need that same kind of mother-to-mother support and encouragement. La Leche League also works with UNICEF, the World Health Organization, and local governments to help provide mothers with breastfeeding information and support. Becoming a member of La Leche League and contributing to the organization are positive ways to convey a message of support to mothers all over the world who want to give their babies the best start in life.

Women who choose to breastfeed their babies are making a difference in the world. They are preserving the environment, improving infant health, and saving precious resources. And their loving, generous example models a caring way of life for their families and communities.

YOUR MILK IS ALWAYS AVAILABLE

As a nursing mother, you can take off on short notice for a family excursion, a long trip, or a full-day picnic—situations in which formula can spoil. You can make your plans and pack your bags without worrying about having an adequate supply of formula for the baby—a formula that may not be available everywhere. You won't even have to be concerned that a strange water supply will make your baby ill, since a breastfed baby does not need extra water.

Wherever you and baby are, so is your milk. It's a most reassuring thought, particularly in the rare, but always stressful time when the usual, normal supplies of food are cut off. This doesn't happen too often, but we do hear from mothers who have had such experiences and are most grateful that their little ones were spared the brunt of this disturbing situation.

In the Midwest, an unexpected and severe snowstorm stranded a family in their car. While the husband went for help, his wife snuggled the baby under her coat, keeping them both warm, and the baby nursed and slept. The young mother found the feeling of normalcy associated with feeding the baby helped to keep her own fears in check until a rescue crew came for them.

EMERGENCY SITUATIONS

Another family unexpectedly spent a night in the mountains. The four Walkers of Ohio—mom, dad, five-year-old Scott, and one-year-old Adam, in a backpack atop his father's shoulders—set out for an afternoon's hike and didn't make it back to their camper for twenty-one hours. "We had hiked these trails so often we thought we knew them all thoroughly," Judy Walker wrote. But when the Walkers started down the trail they thought led back to their car, they inadvertently went down another trail, which they learned later, "went right off the map." The night spent in the isolated area was cold, rainy, and so dark "we couldn't see each other." Judy concludes her story: "My husband kept scooping leaves over us trying to keep us dry, and all night, at least once an hour, Adam woke, hungry, wet, screaming. Each time I nursed him, as it was the only thing that calmed him. I thank God that throughout that cold, wet night I had warm milk to fill my baby's tummy and to comfort him."

Kay Troisi from Alabama tells of her family's experience:

A hurricane came roaring through our community with little advance warning of its nearness or intensity. A lot of damage resulted, including many fallen wires, and snapped pine trees perilously perched on power lines. Consequently, we were without electricity for two and a half days. During this time, I realized even more what an advantage breastfeeding is. Our daughter, Tamara, was only three weeks old and not having to worry about how to feed her was an immense relief. There was no concern over preparing formula, not to mention sterilizing, storing, or heating it without electricity. Not only did I have ready nutrition and reassurance for Tamara, but baby and mother were also consoled by our nursing session during the worst of the storm. We could be in our little world while nursing, oblivious to the external ragings. After the storm, continuous closeness ensured a peaceful baby, contented mother, and overall a happier family, during a time when other families might have been in chaos.

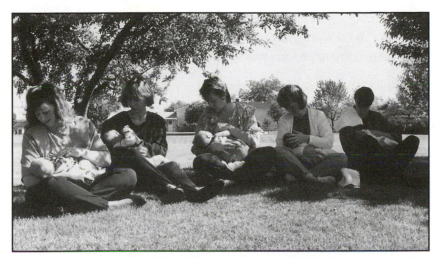

Mothers everywhere find an island of peace as they breastfeed their babies.

A PLEASURABLE EXPERIENCE

Breastfeeding is intended to be a pleasurable experience for a mother. A woman who breastfeeds with pride and satisfaction is aware that breastfeeding is a sensual experience. She also knows that this is a perfectly healthy and normal aspect of her sexuality. Dorothy V. Whipple, MD, wrote in the *Journal of the American Medical Women's Association*:

Suckling a baby, for the woman who accepts and enjoys her femininity, is a particularly moving experience. The physical sensation is pleasant, the guzzling eager mouth against the sensitive erectile tissue of the nipple is enjoyable in itself. It also brings peace, contentment, fulfillment to the whole body and personality. The sensation is not orgasmic; it is more like the peaceful afterglow of orgasm. It brings to the woman a deep and personal understanding of her role as a woman. It brings to her also a bond with women in distant times and cultures. The mature woman who carries out the totality of her feminine functions knows she has a niche in the ultimate scheme of things.

And Selma Fraiberg, in describing how a baby learns to love, tells about the mutual satisfaction of breastfeeding:

In breastfeeding, the infant is cradled in the mother's arms. Pleasure in sucking, the satisfaction of hunger, intimacy with the mother's body, are united with his recognition of her face. The baby learns to associate this face, his mother's face, with an enjoyable and comforting experience. As we watch the nursing baby we see how gradually the skin surface of the body is suffused with pinkness— a sensual glow of pleasure and well-being.

When the baby is held at his mother's breast the entire ventral surface of his body is in contact with her body. And this sensual pleasure heightens his awareness of his own body. Nursing mothers also experience sensual pleasure through the baby's sucking. This should lead to no embarrassment. It is simply one of the rewards, one of the ways in which mutual sensual pleasure binds the mother to her baby and the baby to her.

To the list of breastfeeding's unique characteristics, we add yet one more—its universality. The baby at the breast represents the common language of mothering. Babies have basic needs that do not change, regardless of when or where they are born. And the beautifully natural act of nursing your little one has this same timeless quality. It is a link to other mothers and a sign, even, of womanly power. The ability of a mother's body to nurture her child is a source of strength to her. And through breastfeeding's gentling effect, an island of peace is secured. It is a small miracle, belonging rightfully to mothers, babies, and families the world over.

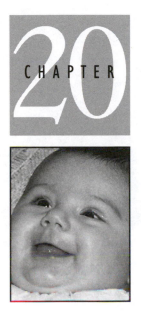

CHAPTER **20**

About La Leche League

La Leche League began with a wish—a dream, really—that all mothers who want to breastfeed their babies would be able to do so. The seven of us who founded La Leche League had overcome a variety of difficulties before we were able to breastfeed with ease and confidence, and we knew of too many mothers who were unable to breastfeed at all simply because they had no one to turn to for information and advice.

How It All BEGAN

It was at a church picnic that Mary White and Marian Tompson decided there had to be a way to help their friends who wanted to breastfeed their babies but found only frustration and failure when they tried. With their own nursing babies cradled in their arms on that summer afternoon in 1956, Mary and Marian talked abut finding a way to help those women experience the joy and deep fulfillment of breastfeeding.

In the weeks that followed, Mary talked to Mary Ann Kerwin, her sister-in-law, and Mary Ann Cahill, who casually

LLLI's Founders continue to enjoy being involved with mothers and their children.

mentioned the idea to Betty Wagner. Marian contacted Edwina Froehlich, who got on the phone to call her good friend Viola Lennon. Each had nursed one or more babies. We had no grandiose plans about how to go about helping our friends, but we were willing to try. Two local physicians, Drs. Herbert Ratner and Gregory White, advised us on those aspects of breastfeeding that were commonly associated with the medical community, and gave us the benefit of their wisdom and insights into human nature.

Confident of our information, and enthusiastic about breastfeeding, we invited our pregnant friends to a meeting at Mary White's house one October evening in 1956. What we offered to interested neighborhood mothers then—and what the 32,000 La Leche League Leaders who have followed us continue to provide—was information, encouragement, and support. Personal mother-to-mother warmth and caring have been a cornerstone of our organization since its inception. Although La Leche League has grown into a worldwide organization with over 3,000 Groups in sixty-six countries (located in communities throughout the United States, Canada, New Zealand, Europe, Africa, Asia, and South America), our focus still remains on the personal one-to-one sharing of information and encouragement that provides a new mother with the confidence she needs to breastfeed her baby.

Today La Leche League stands as the internationally recognized authority on breastfeeding. La Leche League has been contacted by mothers, fathers, doctors, nurses, lactation consultants, and other professionals throughout the world for expertise on breastfeeding. La Leche League International serves as a Non-Governmental

Organization Consultant to UNICEF, an agency of the United Nations and the World Health Organization (WHO), acts as a registered Private Voluntary Organization for the US Agency of International Development, is an accredited member of the US Healthy Mothers, Healthy Babies National Coalition, and a founding member of the World Alliance for Breastfeeding Action (WABA).

La Leche League's Annual Seminars for Physicians, held in North America, attract doctors from all over the world. They are cosponsored by the American Academy of Pediatrics and the American College of Obstetricians and Gynecologists. These seminars are also accredited by the American Medical Association—Category 1 of the Physician's Recognition Award, the American Academy of Family Physicians, and the American Osteopathic Association.

Workshops for Lactation Specialists are scheduled each year in the spring and fall to meet the needs of the emerging health professional who specializes in caring for the breastfeeding dyad. Continuing education credits are available to International Board Certified Lactation Consultants and to registered nurses.

How LLL Can Help YOU

Over the years it has been La Leche League's privilege to help hundreds of thousands of mothers breastfeed their babies. La Leche League, to us, is simply a mother with a baby in her arms and a smile on her face, proud of herself and eager to share all that she has learned and experienced. Mothers, like you, who find fulfillment and delight in nurturing an infant are the heart and soul of La Leche League.

La Leche League Leaders everywhere rejoice in the knowledge that by helping mothers to breastfeed their babies, they are playing a part in strengthening and deepening the love ties formed in infancy that will last a lifetime.

OUR ORGANIZATION

Our name, La Leche, is Spanish and is pronounced la lay-chay. Simply translated, it means "the milk." The name of our organization was inspired by a shrine in St. Augustine, Florida, dedicated to the Mother of Christ under the title "Nuestra Senora de la Leche y Buen Parto," which translates freely, "Our Lady of Happy Delivery and Plentiful Milk."

Our international headquarters, located in Schaumburg, Illinois, USA, is staffed by 50 employees. Every year they respond to thousands of pieces of mail and answer countless phone calls from the many people throughout the world seeking breastfeeding help or information.

There are LLLI Affiliate organizations in Canada, French Canada, Great Britain, Switzerland, Germany (Deutschland), and New Zealand. La Leche League is a nonprofit, nonsectarian organization and is entirely supported by donations, memberships, and sales of materials.

PROFESSIONAL SUPPORT

La Leche League has a Health Advisory Council comprised of doctors and health professionals from all over the world. This council is consulted about medical situations and evaluation of new research. Members of the Health Advisory Council review La Leche League publications that include medical information. Complementing the Health Advisory Council are doctors throughout the world serving as Medical Associates of La Leche League.

A Legal Advisory Council and a Management Advisory Council complete the LLLI Professional Advisory Board.

PUBLICATIONS

La Leche League's basic manual, THE WOMANLY ART OF BREASTFEEDING, has sold more than 2.5 million copies and is available in nine languages, on audiotape, and in English Braille. Other LLLI publications are available in 27 languages.

La Leche League is the world's largest resource for breastfeeding information. Currently, we publish 25 books and 80 pamphlets and information sheets. A selection of more than 200 books, information sheets, and pamphlets are listed in the LLLI Catalogue along with breast pumps, audiotapes, videos, and other products of interest to breastfeeding families.

CONFERENCES

International and Area Conferences are held periodically for parents and professionals. Speakers include experts in breastfeeding, parenting, childbirth, nutrition, childcare, and related topics. Doctors, educators, researchers, authors, and parents represent a wide range of experiences and options.

MEMBERSHIP

Members of La Leche League care about giving their babies the best. As an LLL member, you will have the satisfaction of being part of a worldwide network of mothers with breastfeeding experience who share information, support, and encouragement.

Membership in La Leche League offers you these benefits:
- one-year subscription (six bimonthly issues) to
  NEW BEGINNINGS, a magazine filled with inspiration, practical

hints, photos, book reviews, and breastfeeding information.

- a 10% member's discount on most purchases from the LLLI Catalogue which features a wide variety of outstanding publications on breastfeeding, childbirth, nutrition, and parenting.
- the opportunity to share the companionship of other mothers of babies and young children at monthly meetings of your local LLL Group and learn even more from the carefully selected books in the Group's library.
- participation in LLL special events, including local and international conferences, with a special member's discount on registration fees.

When you become a La Leche League member you support the efforts of your local Group Leaders who are volunteers, and you join an international mother-to-mother helping network with over forty years of experience sharing practical mothering wisdom.

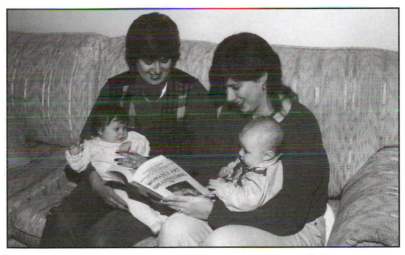

Mothers share information and support one another at LLL Group Meetings.

LA LECHE LEAGUE MEETINGS

LLL meetings are informal discussion groups often held in the homes of members or another easily accessible meeting location. Information is presented following a planned schedule of topics that cover the practical, physical, and psychological aspects of breastfeeding.

La Leche League meetings offer a wonderful source of information and encouragement, and a ready source of new friendships among mothers who have many things in common.

At these La Leche League meetings, the LLL Group Leader shares her knowledge about breastfeeding and related topics and encourages mothers to ask questions and share their own experiences. For every question or difficulty that might be brought up, there are usually several mothers at the meeting who are able to offer various solutions or suggestions. It is both exciting and reassuring to watch other babies in the Group thrive and grow. It is fun to see how unique each baby is, and the wonderful, warm way in which each mother and baby relate to each other. Babies are always welcome at LLL meetings.

Our Leaders are primarily mothers who have breastfed their own babies and are willing to share their knowledge and enthusiasm about breastfeeding with mothers who look to them for help. The personal experience and special training of each Leader prepares her for this role. Every LLL Leader has completed a specific application process before she is considered qualified to act as an official representative of La Leche League.

HOW TO FIND LA LECHE LEAGUE

With more than 3,000 La Leche League Groups meeting every month all around the world, the chances are excellent that there are one or more Groups in your community. Group Leaders make every effort to publicize their meetings so that mothers will be able to find the local LLL Group quickly and easily.

Nearly all Groups place meeting notices in the local newspapers. Watch your paper, or simply call the newspaper office and ask if they know how to get in touch with La Leche League Groups in the area. In some of the larger cities, you will find La Leche League listed in the white pages of the telephone directory. If there is not a listing, try calling the maternity wards of the larger hospitals or some of the obstetricians and pediatricians in your area. Childbirth instructors or your local library may have information about La Leche League Groups in the community.

Be sure to ask around among your friends and neighbors who are pregnant or have young children. You will more than likely find one or more of them have been to La Leche League meetings and would be delighted to put you in touch with a local Leader.

In the USA, we currently have a toll free number you can call for immediate answers to breastfeeding questions, a free copy of our Catalogue, or the name of a La Leche League Leader near you. Just call 1-800-LA LECHE. In Canada, the toll-free number is 1-800-665-4324. You can also visit La Leche League on the World Wide Web at http://www.lalecheleague.org/ where you will find an on-line catalogue, answers to frequently asked questions, and other current information.

For recorded information on specific breastfeeding problems, available 24 hours a day, you can call La Leche League's Helpline at 1-900-

448-7475 extension 93. You will be charged $1.99 per minute to hear the recorded messages.

Or you can write us at La Leche League International, 1400 N. Meacham Road, P. O. Box 4079, Schaumburg, Illinois, 60168-4079, USA. Our regular telephone number is 847-519-7730. The fax number is 847-519-0035. Business hours are from 9:00 AM to 5:00 PM, Central Time. At other times, a prerecorded message will refer you to another number for immediate breastfeeding help.

WOULD YOU LIKE TO HELP?

Perhaps you are not able to locate a La Leche League Group in your community and this book has been your only source of guidance for your breastfeeding experience. As the months go by and your baby grows and thrives on your milk, you may notice other mothers asking you questions about breastfeeding. We know, because that's how we got started! If you find this is something you enjoy, why not write to us for information on starting a La Leche League Group?

La Leche League needs mothers just like you who have read this book, followed its recommendations, and happily breastfed their babies. If there is no La Leche League Group in your area and you think you'd be interested in becoming a La Leche League Leader, write to LLLI Headquarters, c/o Leader Accreditation Department, and request a copy of our free brochure, "Becoming a La Leche League Leader."

If you are involved with an LLL Group, you can obtain more information about LLL leadership from the Leaders in your local LLL Group.

About This Book and Its AUTHORS

When the seven of us wrote the first edition of THE WOMANLY ART OF BREASTFEEDING in the 1950s, we were all mothers at home full-time. Writing was done in between other chores, while the baby napped or played nearby, perhaps with a preschool brother or sister. More often than not, the desk was the family dining table, and manuscript pages had to be hastily gathered up at mealtime.

We had mutually agreed that our families were our first priority. This understanding freed us to set aside LLL work when our families needed us. As our children grew and circumstances changed, some of us took on salaried jobs at La Leche League Headquarters. The interest that we shared more than forty years ago has not abated. All of us continue as members of the Founders' Advisory Council and Mary Ann Kerwin still serves as an active member of LLLI's Board of Directors.

When we started La Leche League, each of us knew one or more of the others, but some of us were getting acquainted for the first time. We were far from being carbon copies of each other. Some had bottle-fed older children; others had been fortunate enough to have breastfed their first babies. There is a span of sixteen years in our ages and great diversity among us. What solidly unites us is our belief in the importance of mothering and the value of breastfeeding.

Since our philosophy is based mainly on what we have found through experience to be the most valuable, we include some information about us as individuals.

Mary Ann Cahill, *McHenry, Illinois*: In 1956, the year La Leche League was founded, the Cahills of Franklin Park, Illinois, were wholeheartedly into "people building." "The more common term would be 'parenting,'" Mary Ann explains, "But we were idealists and dreamers, as are all parents of young children to some extent. For Chuck and me, it was a wonderfully exciting time."

The forty years since then saw the family grow from six to a total of nine children—Bob, Elizabeth, Tim, Teresa, Mary, Joe, Margaret, Charlene ("Charlie"), and Frannie, with room always at the table for Janet, a foster daughter who spent several of her grade-school years with her "Cahill family." There was also a move to a bigger house in Libertyville, and more recently, another to a smaller home that Mary Ann had built in McHenry, "overlooking a little pond and fields," where she now lives. Her husband, Chuck, died in 1978. "I will never forget the outpouring of love and sympathy from LLL people, their many kindnesses to me and my family at that time."

The days of intense parenting are now in the past, and the Cahill children have moved to different parts of Illinois and to Missouri, Wisconsin, and Colorado. They're mothers and fathers, and they work in maintenance, social work, designing, postal services, as a doctor, pharmacist, sign interpreter to the hearing impaired, librarian, and teacher. There are seventeen grandchildren. "When we're all together, we have a grand time," Mary Ann says. "The hopes and dreams, the prayers and hard work of 'people building' are well worth the effort. I can't imagine a more satisfying life." Mary Ann left the LLLI Headquarters staff in 1995 and now works part time at a local hospital. "But I still don't have enough time to do all that I'd like to do," she says. A favorite activity remains her work with the other Founders on the Founders' Advisory Council.

Edwina Froehlich, *Franklin Park, Illinois:* Edwina was one of the few women in the 1950s who devoted considerable time to a career and married late. She was thirty-six years old when she and John began their family. There were dire warnings from all sides about the perils of having a baby at such an "advanced" age. And certainly, it was said, the breasts of a woman over thirty could never produce milk. However, those aged mammary glands did her proud and produced plenty of milk for her three sons.

The Froehlich family now includes three daughters-in-law married to Paul, David, and Peter in that order. They are Marilyn, Sharon, and Paula—all outstanding young women, devoted wives, and very nurturing mothers; each has had three breastfed children. Marilyn became a La Leche League Leader. Edwina remains active as a member of the Founders' Advisory Council. As the designated Founders' Advisory Council facilitator, she sets up their meetings, takes notes, and distributes the minutes. Edwina loves best her role as Grandma to Leanne, Kristin, Laura, Steven, Michael, Colleen, Katrina, Jenna Marie, and Christian. All live within an hour's drive from Franklin Park which John and Edwina consider a real blessing since it allows for the frequent visits they enjoy so much.

Mary Ann Kerwin, *Denver, Colorado:* When Mary Ann and Tom Kerwin became parents for the first time in 1955, Mary Ann was eager to breastfeed even though not one of her friends was breastfeeding. The combination of her inexperience and a sleepy baby made it difficult to get started. Helpful advice and support were forthcoming from Greg and Mary White (Mary is Tom Kerwin's sister). Soon, Mary Ann and her first baby were a contented nursing couple. Mary Ann's major regret regarding her first breastfeeding experience is that she weaned at nine months. It was a painful and upsetting time for both mother and baby, but Mary Ann learned from this experience. All of the other babies were allowed to wean at their own pace. The Kerwins have eight children: Tom, Ed, Greg, Mary, Anne, Katie, John, and Mike. A ninth child, Joseph, born in 1959, died at six weeks of age—a victim of Sudden Infant Death Syndrome.

After serving as Chairman of LLLI's Board of Directors from 1980-83, Mary Ann returned to school and received her law degree in

1986. The education she received from her children gave her the necessary determination and self-discipline to achieve this goal. She continues as an active member of LLLI's Board of Directors and is currently practicing law in Colorado.

Mary Ann now has eight grandchildren. Her first two grandchildren were born prematurely to her daughter, Mary. Although Michael was two months premature and was a sick baby initially, Mary was able to breastfeed him completely within a few weeks. The hospital staff was very supportive and knowledgeable. Ben was born five weeks early but he began breastfeeding in a few days. They are thriving, due in large part to successful breastfeeding. The next six grandchildren, Lewis, Cecilia, Catriona, Clara, Mariana, and Avery, were healthy full-term babies. All breastfed shortly after birth. Mary Ann believes her children and their spouses are doing a better job with breastfeeding and parenting than she did. Now she is looking forward with her daughter Katie, and her husband, Cyrus, to the birth of their first baby.

Being a breastfeeding mother and a parent is never easy, but Mary Ann believes her children have a head start in that regard, thanks to the influence of La Leche League International. She says, "Whatever I might have done to help others has come back to me a thousandfold."

Viola Lennon, *Park Ridge, Illinois:* Vi's ten little Lennons came in all sizes, and just to prove that no challenge was too much for her, she even produced a set of twins in 1961. It was considered quite an accomplishment to nurse even one baby in those days, so Vi caused quite a stir in the neighborhood when she calmly proceeded to totally breastfeed both Catherine and Charlotte. Cathy was wakeful as an infant, nursing at least every two hours, while sleepy Charlotte nursed much less often, but gained more rapidly than her sister. She also weaned five months later than Cathy. The twins were sixth and seventh in the lineup, with Elizabeth, Mark, Mimi, Rebecca, and Matthew preceding them, and Martin, Maureen, and Gina following. Mimi was colicky as a baby, and Vi assumed that indicated a high-strung personality, but Mimi has grown into an easygoing, serene young lady. Vi is currently aiding the growth of La Leche League's Alumnae Association and helping to secure outside funds to finance La Leche League's ever-expanding work. Viola was the last of the Founders to become a grandmother, but currently she has thirteen grandchildren. Vi is a member of the Founders' Advisory Council.

Marian Tompson, *Evanston, Illinois:* Even though she switched to a new doctor with each of her first three babies, six months was the longest Marian was able to breastfeed. Each doctor gave her advice that was standard for the time—nurse no more than every four hours, give supplementary bottles to ensure the baby was getting enough, and start solids at six weeks. When the third baby arrived, that doctor told Marian she had lost her milk, a common occurrence in mothers caring for several small children. It was with the birth of their fourth baby, at home, in 1955 that Marian and her husband, Tom, found the supportive help they needed from Dr. Gregory White and his wife, Mary. Baby Laurel was nursed until she weaned herself as was true for the three succeeding babies. The seven Tompson children, Melanie, Deborah, Allison, Laurel, Sheila, Brian, and Philip are grown up now. Tom, "who was truly my partner and constant support of anything I was able to accomplish in LLLI" died in 1981. Their five daughters are married and all twelve grandchildren have been breastfed. Marian considers herself particularly blessed to have been present at most of their births.

Marian was La Leche League's first and only president. During the twenty-four years of her presidency she spoke out clearly and with love in many parts of the world for breastfeeding mothers. Her enthusiasm is still evident today as she continues to speak at La Leche League conferences. In 1995 she was part of a group of breastfeeding supporters who attended the Fifth UN Conference on Women in Beijing, China to ensure that breastfeeding was recognized as part of the solution to many of the issues being discussed. She continues to serve on LLLI's Founders' Advisory Council and serves on the International Advisory Council for WABA (World Alliance for Breastfeeding Action) and on the advisory boards of a number of other organizations concerned with childbirth and family life.

Betty Wagner Spandikow, *Springfield, Tennessee:* Betty breastfed all of her children, beginning back in 1943, thanks in large part to her mother, who was able to give her the practical help she needed. It was baby number six who presented Betty with new challenges. Dorothea cried a good deal and wasn't happy anywhere but in her mother's arms. Betty found it necessary to curtail all outside activities and rearrange her life around this little one who needed her so intensely. Dorothea was past her third birthday before she would venture very far from her mother, but about the time she was three and a half, she blossomed into a very self-confident, outgoing little girl. The Wagners had seven children—Gail, Robert, Wayne, Mary, Peggy, Dorothea, and Helen. Betty's daughter, Mary, was the first of the Founders' daughters to become a La Leche League Leader.

Betty Wagner was the Executive Director of LLLI for 19 years. She has retired from that position but continues to serve on the Founders' Advisory Council. Betty has twenty-four grandchildren and four great-grandchildren; all have been happily breastfed.

Betty's husband died in 1979. In 1991 she married Paul Spandikow, the father of seven (4 boys and 3 girls) and grandfather of fifteen. They now reside most of the time in Springville, Tennessee with lots of travel to parts of the country where their children, grandchildren, and great-grandchildren live.

Mary White, *River Forest, Illinois:* Mary's first attempt at breastfeeding was just like that of most mothers in the 1940s—disastrous! In a short time, baby Joseph was a bottle-fed baby. When their second baby was born, her doctor husband, Greg, was home from the Army, and she had the support that a nursing mother needs. Bill, Peggy, Katie, Anne, Jeannie, Mike, Mary, Clare, Molly, and Liz were all happily breastfed with never a bottle in the house. Only the first three were hospital births; the others were born at home and arrived at intervals of two to five years due solely to the most natural family planning of all, breastfeeding.

Their eldest daughter Peggy died of cancer in 1968 at the age of 18. Now nine children are married and their 46th grandchild has just arrived. All of the grandchildren have been breastfed, and all but three were born at home. Liz was born when her mother was forty-seven, and Mary recalls, "It was the shortest pregnancy I ever had because for the first three months I thought I was in the menopause!" Mary and Greg are now proud and happy great-grandparents of Kevin Francis Thornton and two more great-grandbabies are on the way.

Mary still attends La Leche League Area conferences and loves to talk on her favorite topic—moms and babies together. Mary's devotion to the special kind of mothering that is so much a part of breastfeeding has always been a guiding influence in La Leche League. If you were to ask Mary, she would tell you that she believes her most important job as a mother is to instill in her children a love and trust in God for all of their lives.

THOSE WHO HELPED

A dedicated office staff and many professional consultants worked long hours to prepare the manuscript for the third edition of this book in 1981. Mary Ann Cahill did most of the writing with lots of help from the other Founders. The fourth revised edition, published in 1987, was compiled and edited by Judy Torgus, long-time La Leche League Leader and Executive Editor of LLLI's Publications Department. Judy had worked on the 1981 edition, and she was able to pull together the needed information from a variety of sources in order to make the fourth edition as complete and up-to-date as possible. The Founders carefully reviewed the final manuscript, along with Sally Murphy and Gwen Gotsch. Last minute typing needed to get the book out on time was done in the evenings and on weekends by Joyce Kasheimer.

The fifth edition was published to commemorate La Leche League's Thirty-Fifth Anniversary in 1991. A chapter was added that reflected on the organization's history and its future. This information was compiled by Marlene Sweeney. Other changes were made where newer recommendations replaced the previous information. Ongoing research continues to disclose new benefits of human milk and substantiate the benefits already recognized.

Revising and editing the fifth edition was handled again by Judy Torgus, assisted by Elayne Shpak and other members of LLLI's Headquarters Staff.

This current edition is published to celebrate LLLI's 40th Anniversary. It has been updated again by Judy Torgus, now Director of LLLI's Publications Department, assisted by Gwen Gotsch, editor of BREASTFEEDING ABSTRACTS and author of BREASTFEEDING PURE AND SIMPLE. Betty Crase, Director of LLLI's Center for Breastfeeding Information, provided valuable information about current research. Before editing, it was necessary to input the whole book onto a computer, a task capably handled by Joyce Kashe.

Most of the personal stories that are included came from the pages of NEW BEGINNINGS, our bimonthly members' publication. We want to thank the parents who shared their experiences with us, as well as those who posed for photographs.

We are deeply grateful to each of the above and to many others—too numerous to mention—who have helped to make THE WOMANLY ART OF BREASTFEEDING the classic that it is.

CHAPTER

21

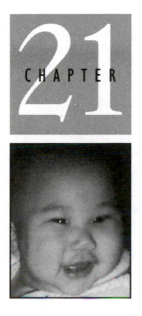

La Leche League's Influence

Many of the changes that have occurred in infant-care practices over the past 40 years have been attributed to La Leche League's influence.

In 1956 babies were routinely introduced to solids between one and three months. Based on valid medical research as well as their success in keeping up their milk supply by delaying solids, the Founders of La Leche League recommended postponing the introduction of solids for four to six months. Today the American Academy of Pediatrics agrees with delaying the start of solid foods, and few mothers are told to give solid foods in the early months.

When La Leche League began, babies were routinely separated from their mothers following birth for as long as twenty-four hours. La Leche League spoke out—babies need their mothers, and mothers benefit, too, by early nursing and uninterrupted bonding. Today women expect to hold their newborn baby immediately after birth. What was unheard of forty years ago is common practice now, and LLL helped mothers achieve this.

La Leche League's Founders hope that all mothers everywhere will be able to enjoy breastfeeding their babies.

Dr. Ruth Lawrence, author of *Breastfeeding: A Guide for the Medical Profession,* collects historical data about breastfeeding. Quoting from magazines and advertisements dating from the 1940s and '50s, Dr. Lawrence points out that considerable doubt was posed in the mind of the average mother at that time. She was led to believe she should rear her child according to the advice of "experts."

The women of the fifties came to La Leche League with very basic questions. How do I know if I have enough milk? How do I know when the baby is hungry? When will my child sleep through the night? Today's women still come to LLL in search of answers, encouragement, and the mother-to-mother support that we have become known for. The most common reason still given by mothers who stop nursing in the early weeks is that they didn't think they had enough milk.

Lynn Weiner, a historian and lecturer with the Women's Studies at Northwestern University, believes La Leche League's empowerment of women was the precursor of self-help groups and women's renewed control over family health-care issues. Seven women set out to give the baby back to the mother at a time when male experts dominated the child care field.

From its small beginning, La Leche League has grown into an international organization, recognized worldwide as an authority on breastfeeding. Today there are more than 3,000 Groups in 66 countries. La Leche League has matured into an experienced, well-seasoned, vital women's group making an impact on the world in which we live. La Leche League International is accredited by medical associations to present annual Seminars for Physicians. These are attended by doctors and other health care professionals from all over the world. A series of Lactation Specialist Workshops, accredited for lactation consultants and nurses, is presented each year.

One doctor who spoke at an LLLI Seminar for Physicians, Method A. Duchon, MD, a perinatologist from Ohio, pointed out that obstetricians and pediatricians are often unable to provide much information and support to nursing mothers because their education, background, and experience with breastfeeding have been so limited. In reviewing leading obstetrical and pediatric journals, current textbooks, and continuing medical education offerings, he found that breastfeeding was minimally represented, and the information he did find emphasized disease, problems, and suppression of lactation. "What I know of breastfeeding, I learned from my wife," he said, urging other health professionals to learn from the mothers they help.

La Leche League was represented at the United Nations when heads of government met at the World Summit for Children in 1990. La Leche League remains in the forefront of placing the needs of the nursing baby on the world agenda, acting as a non-governmental consultant to UNICEF, the United Nations agency concerned with the welfare of the world's children and La Leche League is also a non-governmental consultant to the World Health Organization (WHO). La Leche League is directly involved in a variety of programs around the world to promote and support breastfeeding.

In 1991, La Leche League participated in the formation of the World Alliance for Breastfeeding Action (WABA), a global network of organizations and individuals that is dedicated to protecting, promoting, and supporting breastfeeding. La Leche League also participates in the United States Healthy Mothers/Healthy Babies Coalition.

In the United States, a La Leche League program was developed to encourage breastfeeding among low-income minority mothers which has since spread to other countries. LLLI's Breastfeeding Peer Counselor Program works in cooperation with local community health care agencies, including WIC clinics in the USA, to offer accurate breastfeeding information along with mother-to-mother support.

What the FUTURE HOLDS

When the Founders of La Leche League were asked to share their views about La Leche League's future, here's what they said:

Today practically all reputable sources agree that breastfeeding is best for mothers and babies. Why is La Leche League still needed? Betty Wagner Spandikow responds: "Reputable sources may agree and the medical community may give lip service to the superiority of breastfeeding, but our current culture in the United States is definitely a bottle-feeding culture." Since health-care professionals often lack the practical know-how, our mother-to-mother support is unique and valuable in today's world.

Mary Ann Cahill, another of LLL's Founders, suggests, "Breastfeeding is a long-term commitment. In order to succeed, a mother needs the encouragement and companionship of other mothers. La Leche League succeeded in the beginning and continues to work well because it meets the dual need for sound, practical information and loving support. Babies don't change and neither do mothers, though the circumstances in which they find themselves differ from one generation to the next."

Mary Ann Kerwin adds: "Breastfeeding is a gift from the past that was in the process of being abandoned when we started LLLI. The incidence of breastfeeding in the United States decreased from 60% in the 1940s to less than 20% in the 1960s, probably the lowest in the history of the world. No previous culture dared to discard such a valuable resource. Mothers have always needed support in breastfeeding their babies, but the support system had broken down. We began to revive the womanly art of breastfeeding simply by providing a mother-to-mother support system. In an increasingly fragmented society that too often separates mothers and babies, LLLI is not only still needed but more needed now than ever."

Is the breastfeeding mother of today different from her counterpart of 1956? Marian Tompson responds, "Breastfeeding was simpler in some ways in the 1950s and 60s. Most mothers of small children stayed home to care for them." The mother of today has more demands on her time, more pressures to be "all things to all people." The nursing mother feels many outside forces pulling on her to place things and other people before her baby.

According to Mary Ann Kerwin, "Breastfeeding mothers today are pulled in far more directions than their counterparts of 1956. Life is much more complex. The new opportunities for young women are also creating enormous pressures. The attitude of the 1950s included the belief that women, children, and babies inevitably would be taken care of whereas mothers no longer have that sense of security."

How has the influence of La Leche League affected your family? There is no doubt that this question affirmed what every young mother wants to know—Yes, there are long-term benefits to your mothering style. All of La Leche League's Founders are now grandmothers, and each one of them attests to the influence La Leche League has had on the next generation. Edwina Froehlich explains: "There is no doubt that our three sons have somehow absorbed what I learned through La Leche League: the importance of the early mother-baby relationship, being aware of the emotional needs of infants and children, the importance of feelings in a one-to-one relationship, as in marriage. I believe it is no coincidence that they chose women who join them in these beliefs to be their wives. All three of these young mothers seem to have started their motherhood way ahead of where I was when I started. They already have so much of the knowledge that I had to struggle to get. As a grandmother it delights me to observe my grandchildren being nurtured in such a loving way."

In what direction do you see La Leche League heading as we approach the 21st century? Our influence in the world is definitely being felt. Founders envision La Leche League becoming a spokesperson for breastfeeding mothers worldwide. They see LLLI continuing to network with, collaborate with, and assist world organizations in maternal and child health issues.

Mary Ann Kerwin says, "We are joining hands all over the world to focus on breastfeeding as a world health issue and to help mothers everywhere realize the joys of breastfeeding their babies."

Betty Wagner Spandikow adds, "Our work is needed worldwide and mothers are answering that need and becoming volunteer accredited Leaders. In order for the rate of breastfeeding to increase, mothers need to know the benefits to their babies and themselves. A successful breastfeeding mother, more than anyone, understands the major benefits of breastfeeding. She is the one who is best able to spread the word to her sisters. La Leche League will continue to grow. La Leche League mothers know breastfeeding is so much more than giving milk to their baby."

Mary White summarized all of this by saying, "Our purpose is and always has been to foster good mothering through breastfeeding, and by so doing, to encourage good physical and emotional growth for the child and the development of closer and happier family relationships. That's the way we put it back in the beginning, and that's the way we see it today!"

Mothers Express Their APPRECIATION

Perhaps the basic story of La Leche League's forty-year history is best told by the mothers themselves who have found the support and encouragement they needed to breastfeed their babies—and sometimes to change their lives.

A mother from Colorado tells what happened in her life that led to an appreciation of La Leche League:

I have been a member of La Leche League for almost nine years, and have often wanted to write and express my appreciation and thanks for the encouragement, support, and nurturing I've received.

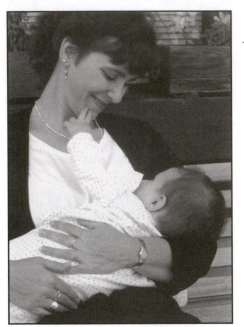

Breastfeeding does make a difference—
to mothers and babies all over the world.

I have three boys, ages eight, five, and two years. Nursing them has brought us all untold benefits—love, closeness, health, understanding, nurturing, and so much more.

I'm writing now because, for the past several months, I've been confronting pain from my own childhood. The realization that I grew up in a family where emotional needs were not met—creating a co-dependent situation. I'm having to face my childhood and learn that I can let go and learn healthier patterns for myself.

Most information on co-dependence and dysfunctional families says that you can't give what you didn't get. Well, I have given my children lots of love and nurturing and acceptance of them at every stage of development, and I have to give a lot of credit to La Leche League. From the birth of my first son, nursing has been the foundation of all I've done. Learning to answer their needs as infants has created a very nurturing way to parent. And we have three bright, happy, secure children.

Thank you, La Leche League, for helping me to give my children what they needed most! And in the process, I'm learning how to model healthy adult behavior, too. We're a healthy, happy, growing family and I'm very thankful for La Leche League.

And another mother, Kristine Williford, who lives in Venezuela, agrees that finding La Leche League made a big difference in her life:

I want to thank you for being there for so many of us. LLL has made a world of difference in our lives. I joined LLL when my son was two months old and going through a growth spurt. After trying my pediatrician's advice and making my son wait an hour and a half between feedings, I called the LLL number in the phone book. Talking with an LLL Leader solved my problems and lifted my self-confidence. I went to my first meeting two weeks later and was convinced of the wisdom in listening to our children. I'm blessed with a very supportive husband who has been enthusiastic about breastfeeding.

Since our son was born twenty months ago in California, we have lived in Texas, the Bahamas, and now Venezuela with month long stopovers in California in between. We're convinced that breastfeeding has provided stability and health in Sam's life. He's a great toddler and is comfortable meeting new people and seeing new places. At twenty months, he is beginning to wean during the day, but still loves nighttime snacks snuggled in between Mama and Papa.

I've never written letters to organizations before, but I wanted you to know that LLLI is important. Never doubt the effect you have on people's lives.

Susan Doran of Tennessee relied on THE WOMANLY ART OF BREASTFEEDING to give her the help she needed while she was breast-feeding her sons:

In 1978 my first son was born. We moved three times during his first year and had three pediatricians, each giving me conflicting advice. When I was told to start solids at two months of age, I resisted as a direct result of reading THE WOMANLY ART OF BREASTFEEDING. Another time, the day before we took to the road for a 700-mile interstate move, I was told to stop breastfeeding my five-month-old because he was vomiting. The next day, driving behind the moving van and listening to my baby cry, I finally pulled off the road, dug out my copy of THE WOMANLY ART OF BREASTFEEDING and read that it was certainly okay to breastfeed an ill baby. I immediately breastfed my son and the rest of the trip was a much more contented one. I am convinced that THE WOMANLY ART OF BREASTFEEDING made our nursing relationship a positive one.

I now have two more sons who were both breastfed. We have moved into nine different localities with the consequences of encountering a variety of different medical professionals. But all the revised editions of THE WOMANLY ART OF BREASTFEEDING were my continuing source of reliable breastfeeding information.

April Meyer from South Dakota agrees. She writes:

Just wanted to drop you a note to thank you for all the support over the last thirteen months. Since we don't have a La Leche League Group nearby that I could attend, your book THE WOMANLY ART OF BREASTFEEDING has been a lifesaver! I doubt I would have continued this long without it.

Breastfeeding for me has truly been a wonderful experience. I had many doubts over the months, due mostly to the fact that I'm the first in our family in generations to nurse, but it's been the best way to nurture and feed our baby. I'm thankful for all the support from your organization.

Joyce Bermes from Indiana attributes much of what she has learned about babies and mothering to her involvement with La Leche League:

This is my long overdue thank you to the Founders, and the second, third, and fourth generation of La Leche League Leaders.

My life has been so improved by the growth I have experienced from La Leche League. Not only have I learned how to breastfeed my children, I have become a very good cook, interested in better health through nutrition, able to organize a meeting, study with children all about, meet countless wonderful people, attend conferences, become a professional in an area unheard of 20 years ago, and most of all appreciate my career as a mother as being the single most important accomplishment I could possibly have done with my life.

Thank you for giving me support to really love my babies and children, to sleep with them, to hold them close, to cry when it is time to let go, to take them with me everywhere, when other experts tell me to "get away from them."

Thank you for seeing mothers through babies' eyes and letting me know that it is okay for my baby to prefer that I hold him, that it is normal for him to want to eat at night, that it empowers his independence when I meet his needs.

All of these seeds are in the hearts of mothers, but La Leche League nurtures, waters, fertilizes, and weeds them so that the wonderful world of mothering can mature and produce new nurturing parents who are not afraid to truly love their children.

Many health professionals turn to La Leche League's mother-to-mother support and find it invaluable when the time comes that they are breastfeeding their own baby. Dr. Eloise Skelton-Forrest, a prominent obstetrician/gynecologist from California and Director of the Alhambra Women's Medical Group, wrote the following to congratulate La Leche League on its anniversary:

How special you are! It is exciting to know that you have been helping families for so many years. I always smile when I think that my initial encounter with La Leche League was as a nursing mother with a hungry newborn. My training in obstetrics and gynecology prepared me for many things, but it was La Leche League that gave me the practical skills I needed to make my relationship with my daughter most rewarding.

I encourage mothers to seek assistance from La Leche League on a regular basis. THE WOMANLY ART OF BREASTFEEDING and EL ARTE FEMININO DE AMAMANTAR are well used in the lending library we have for our patients. The world looks forward to many more years of your watchful and loving support.

Others Add CONGRATULATIONS

Congratulations on your 40th Anniversary!

The celebration of this important landmark for La Leche League gives me the opportunity once again to say thanks to all of you in "the League" for all that you have taught me over my many years of wonderful association with you. You have opened my eyes, ears, and mind to the world of breastfeeding and to a broadened view of mothers and children, and fathers too, that every pediatrician should have. And, I have enjoyed every minute of it.

I wish you the greatest success in your next 40 years and in the next century. You have set forth an agenda for the world that is desperately needed and you should feel very proud of the enormous success you have achieved. There is much more yet to do and I look forward to working with all of you in these future years.

Lawrence M. Gartner, MD

Professor of Pediatrics, Obstetrics and Gynecology, The University of Chicago – Department of Pediatrics, Wyler Children's Hospital, Chicago, Illinois

I am pleased to extend congratulations to La Leche League International in celebration of your forty years as a supporter and promoter of breastfeeding.

As a former US Surgeon General, as a pediatrician, and as a woman, I wholeheartedly endorse breastfeeding. In today's modern world, breastfeeding is all too frequently circumvented when extraneous demands confront mothers. Yet, the many benefits of breastfeeding to infants and mothers are well documented.

In this country, promotion and development of successful breastfeeding plays a key role in our Government's major initiative to achieve healthy children. Internationally, breastfeeding serves as a healthful means to the survival and well-being of mothers and their children, particularly in developing countries.

La Leche League's history of support to mothers is commendable and most valuable. Again, I offer congratulations on your past accomplishments and wish you success with your future endeavors.

Antonia C. Novello, MD, MPH
Former Surgeon General of the United States

I wish to congratulate LLL International on this, the occasion of their fortieth anniversary. La Leche League has done more than any other organization to help mothers, babies, and fathers appreciate and live the benefits and wonders of breastfeeding. The health and psychological benefits have been incalculable.

From a more personal point of view, I can say that much of what I know about breastfeeding, much of the information and skills I use to help mothers and babies breastfeed, I learned from La Leche League and its dedicated members.

I wish La Leche League continued success, and cannot express the thanks I owe it.

Jack Newman, MD, FRCPC
Toronto, Ontario

On behalf of the Board of Directors of the International Lactation Consultant Association (ILCA) I would like to congratulate La Leche League International on celebrating its 40th year anniversary.

LLLI has undertaken and supported one of the most vitally important areas and times in a woman's life with mother-to-mother support. ILCA has enjoyed an ongoing relationship with LLLI and looks forward to its continuation.

Amy Spangler
President of International Lactation Consultant Association
Chicago, Illinois

Congratulations on your staying power. You were right to be outspoken, honest, scientific, and determined.

When I went to medical school a half-century ago, I believed everything I was told. The professors of pediatrics tried to be as scientific as possible. How can a doctor be scientific if the amount of ounces the baby is getting from the mother's breasts cannot be measured? One doctor said that breastfeeding would become acceptable to the medical profession if a flow-meter could be attached to the breasts. So we learned how to mix up formulas, and discouraged nursing. What a waste! We then created our own problems for ourselves as pediatricians.

Bottle-fed babies had more allergies, ear infections, anemia, rashes, gastrointestinal infections, needed more house calls, and I discovered later, had more trouble with malocclusion when they grew up. I did not discover the wonders and benefits of breastfeeding until La Leche League International got through my prejudices.

Congratulations! You have found out that what is best for the baby is breastfeeding and love. Our bodies were designed for this. Science cannot improve on what is the infant's birthright.

Lendon Smith, MD
Pediatrician and Author

It gives me great pleasure to convey to you warm congratulations from the World Health Organization (WHO) on the occasion of the fortieth anniversary of La Leche League International.

WHO is pleased that La Leche League, in the best of self-help traditions, remains true to its Founders' dedication to aiding mothers support each other in breastfeeding. In an increasingly complex world, yours is a message for all people everywhere. We wish you, and the organization's more than 30,000 members in some 60 countries, continued success in the sharing of information and encouragement that helps mothers breastfeed successfully, even as you strive to promote a better understanding of breastfeeding as an important element in the healthy development of babies and mothers.

As the fiftieth anniversary of WHO draws near, we are especially conscious of the indispensable contribution to carrying out international health work made by the nearly 200 international non-governmental organizations with which WHO enjoys official relations. WHO is fortunate to count La Leche League among its staunchest allies, and we look forward to our continued close collaboration for many years to come.

Hiroshi Nakajima, MD, PhD
Director-General
World Health Organization

The notion that a tiny group of women (not that they were tiny women) meeting in association with a church picnic could by pooling ideas, enthusiasm, and commitment radically change breastfeeding practices is breathtaking!

It has certainly made me much more circumspect when I see groups of women gathered together in earnest conversation at what is supposed to be a picnic.

In saluting the vision of La Leche League's Founding Mothers and their impact on child health internationally, I wish to also include that provocative gadfly who settled amongst them in the shape of Herb Ratner.

May the wisdom of the seven continue to flourish and expand.

Leo Buchanan
Paediatrics, Wellington, New Zealand

LLL is 40 years old! How wonderful! It wasn't in time for my mother when I was born, but when I think of the millions of mothers and babies who have benefited from your work over these years, I am truly moved.

Personally, LLLI has played a major role in my career. When I was a medical student, floundering about looking for an area where I might contribute to the public's health, LLLI recognized my senior thesis work with the Paul Gyorgy Award (albeit Second Prize!). A small gesture of this sort made one student feel important and useful. As I entered full time breastfeeding support work in the late 1980s, it became clear to me that LLLI had always been there, quietly reminding practitioners that there are women who care about other women and the childcare choices presented to them.

Congratulations and best wishes on your 40th Anniversary. As we enter the next millennium, I can only wish LLLI 40 times 40 more years of successful support of women in their choice to do what is best for them and their children.

Miriam H. Labbok, MD, MPH, IBCLC
Associate Professor, Director, Breastfeeding and MCH
Institute for Reproductive Health, Georgetown University, Washington, DC

We wish to add our voice to the chorus of congratulations coming your way as you reach your 40th milestone on the pathway of service to the world's children. It is surely gratifying to know that from your first moments of existence you were "on to something important."

I remember that time when the babes of our land were deprived of mothers' nurturing milk. Now, as if showering from the seven stars of the "Big Dipper" of Ursa Major, legions quaff their sustenance from the enduring source painstakingly restored in the face of overwhelming odds by La Leche League's seven founding "stars."

Our tardy science repeatedly confirms what those visionary women knew from the start.

May those stars burn ever brighter to perpetually provide that fount of life indeed to all the world's sweet babes.

Rick Czerniejewski, MD
Chairman, Board of Directors, Health for Humanity, Glencoe, Illinois

I am delighted to see that La Leche League International has celebrated 40 years of mother-to-mother support. I am delighted, as well, to have worked with Rebecca Magalhaes and other LLLI Leaders over the years on child survival. Other PVOs will partner with La Leche League International because your organization has so much to teach others.

Dory Storms, MPS, ScD
Director, School of Hygiene and Public Health
John Hopkins University, Baltimore, Maryland

Forty years ago all I knew about breastfeeding was "breast is best" but an article in the Chicago Tribune prompted me with several carloads of patients to attend a series of La Leche League meetings at Roberta Johnson's apartment on the south side of Chicago. How excited and enthusiastic we were and still are. We felt that we had stumbled into the pot of gold at the end of the rainbow.

I was delighted and impressed when Dr. and Mrs. White attended the final session. I remember asking, "What must we do to incorporate this service into my practice?" His answer, "Just start it." Now, you know that had to have been a long time ago! Within two years I had become an authority, an expert, because of putting into practice every jot and tittle of information as it became available from LLL's research department. Our association has kept my medical practice as fluid as mother's own milk, constantly changing to meet the patient's need. How's that for a simile?

So I thank you, La Leche League, and especially the Founders, for the privilege to stand with you as we are all meek to learn, flexible to try, wise to discern, and gutsy enough to help every baby "get some" from his own motherly mother.

PS: Thanks to LLL, most of my 16,000 babies were best fed!

Dr. Carolyn Rawlins
Retired Obstetrician, Rome City, Indiana

Congratulations to the Founders of La Leche League for positively impacting the lives of literally millions of mothers, their children, and extended families worldwide. Those Founders are, in my opinion, true modern day heroines who by their uncountable unselfish acts began and nurtured what has become the most potent women's self-help organization in the world.

The Founders and the subsequent thousands and thousands of Leaders who have modeled their awareness and behavior have literally given babies back to their mothers. I personally have been proud to have been associated with the Founders and La Leche for almost four decades. Our entire family, including six children and eight grandchildren, have benefited from the La Leche League approach. It is my hope and wish that La Leche League will remain strong, so mothers and children everywhere can experience the multiple benefits of mother's milk and all that goes with skin to skin contact, including personal empowerment, higher IQs, and less illness.

Hugh D. Riordan, MD, President,
The Center for the Improvement of Human Functioning International, Inc.,
Wichita, Kansas

La Leche League International is to be congratulated on its tremendous achievements these past forty years. I personally am grateful for the development of the program in the late 50s. I had been working endlessly in the breastfeeding vineyard since my residency at Yale with Dr. Edith Jackson in 1950. I found myself spending many, many hours on the phone with mothers, anxious to maintain breastfeeding but concerned about day-to-day problems. When La Leche League was formed and mothers in our area joined and began a mother-to-mother program throughout our region, it provided a remarkable service for women that we in the health care profession could not do as well. La Leche League has been a valuable partner in encouraging the initiation and continuation of breastfeeding for many, many mothers.

Never underestimate the power of a small group of women!

Ruth A. Lawrence, MD
Professor of Pediatrics, Obstetrics & Gynecology
University of Rochester Medical Center, Rochester, New York

Greetings to all of you on this very special anniversary from the tiny island of Yap, Federated States of Micronesia!

I simply had to write to tell you how very close to all of you I felt today, although geographically, I have never been farther away!

I have only been in Micronesia for a year, and, of course, I've been working hard on breastfeeding promotion since I arrived. Prior to my arrival I had been an LLL Leader in Oregon, USA, for 12 years.

But what a thrill to be asked to help with a National Workshop here introducing the mother-to-mother support concept.

And would you believe that there are SEVEN Headstart mothers from various local communities attending our conference with the intention of starting local groups?!! (Is that a coincidence or what?!)

It's all a very new concept here but folks are incredibly enthusiastic. I'm delighted! Many women from Yap are still bare-breasted, and many men and boys wear loincloths, but there's formula in the shops, misinformation everywhere, and lots of work to be done.

So—at this special Anniversary time, I wanted you to know that your hard work and dedication—and especially heartfelt warmth—have traveled to Micronesia! Please pat yourselves on the back—and give each other hugs from me. I will be forever grateful for that first meeting 40 years ago.

Judy Mieger
La Leche League Leader, Micronesia

The work of the Founding Mothers, and all who have followed in La Leche League, provides immeasurable inspiration and support to thousands of new mothers annually. The optimal health of innumerable infants and children, and the current worldwide promotion of breastfeeding can be traced back to the tireless efforts of La Leche League. LLL remains the standard of true compassion and commitment to improving the health and happiness of babies worldwide.

We, at Happy Child Foundation, drew our initial inspiration from La Leche League when we were new mothers nourishing our infants.

Now we spread LLL's philosophy worldwide through our foundation's work as we train midwives and promote maternal-child health in rural villages in Bali, Indonesia, and Guatemala.

Thank you, La Leche League, for all that you offer. May the next forty years bring even further growth to the organization and ideal infant nutrition to all babies on Earth.

Gina M. Farber
Yayasan Anak Bahagia, Bali, Indonesia

It is not surprising that there exists a broad base of support for breastfeeding in Israel, a country committed to the basic principles of public health and social welfare and challenged with the need to integrate a large number of new immigrants from a variety of cultures and countries into the existing community.

Most importantly, Israel as a society understands that its most valuable natural asset is its children and that its future as a country is dependent on the health and developmental well-being of its next generation. As such, breastfeeding is conceptualized as the ultimate value. In turn, the positive principles of breastfeeding are a given, all hospitals are essentially baby friendly, paid maternity leave is national policy, and as a result, well over 95% of mothers leave the hospital successfully breastfeeding their newborn infant irrespective of the country of origin of the mother, her social status, or her religious beliefs.

Critical to sustaining the success of breastfeeding beyond the neonatal and early infancy period is the Israeli network of devoted breastfeeding counselors and La Leche League support programs and publications such as THE WOMANLY ART OF BREASTFEEDING. As is well known, the Art of Nursing has to be combined with the Science of Human Milk and implemented through the respective and complementary roles of medical and nursing professionals and educated lay volunteers if the "Blessings of the Breast and the Womb" can be bestowed on all God's children wherever they may be.

Professor Arthur I. Eidelman
Director, Department of Neonatology, Shaare Zedek Medical Center, Hebrew University-Hadassah Medical School

A FINAL WORD—FROM THE FOUNDERS

On this occasion of La Leche League's 40th Anniversary, we seven women wish to acknowledge and express heartfelt thanks to those who have made important contributions to the development of La Leche League

The first is that of two physicians, Dr. Herbert Ratner and Dr. Gregory White, both of whom, as the fathers of breastfed children, were a rarity in 1956. Without their unfailing support and guidance, who knows how different the LLL scenario may have been? By being there for us, we could benefit from their knowledge and experience. Without this, it is almost certain that we who began La Leche League would have found it extremely difficult to face the criticisms and sometimes hostility of the medical community toward two basic womanly functions—natural childbirth and breastfeeding. Our own enthusiasm and appreciation of these two functions survived because of the solid backing of those two physicians. We are eternally grateful to them, and we thank them also on behalf of the breastfeeding mothers to whom we have passed on what we learned. Over time, many other courageous physicians have also openly supported our efforts and generously shared their knowledge with us, and we are well aware of and grateful for their help. But it was Dr. Ratner and Dr. White who spoke out clearly and consistently at a time when their voices were most needed. With deep affection, we thank them and rejoice that they are still with us 40 years later.

Another integral part of the past 40 years that we wish to fully recognize and gratefully acknowledge is the daily efforts of the thousands of generous women volunteers who have become La Leche League Leaders. It is LLL Leaders, many of whom spend countless hours administering to other Leaders in the field, and the Group workers who support them, who have built La Leche League. Without their continuing efforts over the years, we would not be celebrating today.

A wide variety of books are available to help you learn more about breastfeeding, childbirth, parenting, and nutrition. We are proud of the books that are published by La Leche League International because they reflect the same philosophy you have found in the pages of this book. All of the books we publish can be ordered by mail and shipped directly to your home. Local La Leche League Groups also have these books available for purchase and/or loan, and some of them can be found in your local bookstore or public library.

We encourage you to read and learn as much as you can about your role as parents. Follow your instincts and natural inclinations in choosing the advice and information that seems right to you. The basic philosophy of La Leche League encourages you to learn about babies' and children's needs so you can understand and respond to those needs from earliest infancy and throughout the years as your child grows. And always remember, babies and children need lots and lots of love.

Books That We PUBLISH

MOTHERWISE: 101 Tips for a New Mother
by Alice Bolster

This concise book offers practical, nurturing wisdom in a format that is easily accessible to busy new mothers. It presents the principles of La Leche League philosophy in succinct, concrete tips that affirm the value of motherhood, breastfeeding, and sensitivity to baby's needs. Written by a La Leche League Leader, this book captures the conversational mother-to-mother support offered in a Group meeting, and reassures mothers that they know what is best for their babies.
No. 255, $7.50

BREASTFEEDING PURE & SIMPLE
by Gwen Gotsch

Provides new mothers with a basic introduction that will guide them through the early months of their nursing relationship. Clear, straightforward text combined with lots of photos makes this book inviting and easy-to-read.
No. 251, $8.95

GROWING TOGETHER: A Parent's Guide to Baby's First Year
by William Sears, MD

Over 150 black and white photographs and 16 pages of color photos illustrate the growth of motor, language, social, and cognitive skills from birth to one year. Dr. Sears, the author of LLLI's GROWING FAMILY SERIES, advocates attachment parenting, and tells how parents can enhance their baby's development by their responsiveness. Includes tips on parenting, breastfeeding, and infant stimulation.
No. 273, $14.50

BECOMING A FATHER: How to Nurture and Enjoy Your Family
by William Sears, MD

Addresses the joys and problems of parenthood from the male perspective—everything from how to hold a tiny baby to sibling rivalry and organized sports. Dr. Sears, a pediatrician and father of eight, writes from personal experience and promises that becoming a father will bring rewards, among them love, a better marriage, and maturity.
No. 266, $8.95

NIGHTTIME PARENTING: How to Get Your Baby and Child to Sleep
by William Sears, MD

Explains how babies sleep differently than adults, how sharing sleep can help the whole family sleep better, and how a particular style of nighttime parenting can lower the risk of Sudden Infant Death Syndrome. Helps to reassure parents that meeting nighttime needs is important to their baby's well-being.
No. 276, $8.95

THE FUSSY BABY: How to Bring Out the Best in Your High-Need Child
by William Sears, MD

Assures parents that meeting the needs of a fussy baby does not cause baby to be "spoiled." Suggestions include "back to the womb" security tips and a guide to interpreting a baby's cries. Chapters on coping with colic, feeding, fathering, soothing, and avoiding maternal burnout include plenty of support, reassurance, and day-to-day survival tips.
No. 289, $4.99

MOTHERING MULTIPLES: Breastfeeding and Caring for Twins
by Karen Gromada

Full of practical tips from experienced mothers of twins. The author, herself a mother of twins, includes hints on streamlined housekeeping, baby equipment, family adjustments, and ways to comfort two fussy babies. Everything mothers need to know to cope with the challenge of more than one baby.
No. 267, $7.95

MOTHERING YOUR NURSING TODDLER
by Norma Jane Bumgarner

Warmth, wisdom, and wit illuminate a lively discussion of breastfeeding past the age of one. Besides exploring the "why" of nursing a toddler, this book helps a mother cope with the challenges: getting enough rest, dealing with criticism from friends and family, nursing (or avoiding nursing) in public places, communicating with her husband, and finally, weaning.
No. 268, $8.95

A SPECIAL KIND OF PARENTING: Meeting the Needs of
Handicapped Children
by Julia Darnell Good and Joyce Good Reis
Children with disabilities challenge their parents' emotional and physical resources. This book can guide parents through the problems and help them discover their disabled child as an individual. The authors cover both facts and feelings about handicaps, parents' reactions to the initial diagnosis, the grieving process, and effects on the marriage and the rest of the family.
No. 280, $8.95 (sale price - $7.50)

LEARNING A LOVING WAY OF LIFE
compiled and edited by Virginia Sutton Halonen and Nancy Mohrbacher
A collection of stories, photos, and poems that reflect La Leche League's philosophy told by parents themselves. Tells of the joys found in building strong family relationships. This book will help you understand and enjoy your own family more.
No. 275, $7.95 (sale price - $5.00)

SAFE AND HEALTHY: A Parent's Guide to Children's
Illnesses and Accidents
by William Sears, MD
Dr. Sears guides parents through some of the most stressful episodes of parenting by answering the most frequently asked questions about childhood illnesses. Tells when you should call the doctor and how to handle situations that don't require a doctor's advice. Written by a pediatrician, this book is an essential guide to caring for your child.
No. 281, $10.95 (sale price - $8.95)

OF CRADLES AND CAREERS: A Guide to Reshaping Your Job to
Include a Baby in Your Life
by Kaye Lowman
Examines the family vs. career dilemma, with stories from mothers who have found ways to combine their working lives with mothering. Tips on breastfeeding and working, job-sharing, and maternity leave round out a book that encourages women to explore a variety of options and helps them choose what works best for themselves and their families.
No. 278, $7.95 (sale price - $5.00)

WHOLE FOODS FOR THE WHOLE FAMILY: La Leche League International Cookbook
edited by Roberta Johnson

Complete nutrition-conscious cookbook contains over 900 kitchen-tested recipes. Filled with time-saving make-ahead meals, ideas for using leftovers, special diet and allergy recipes, suggestions for baby's first foods, and last-minute dinner menus. Uses only whole unprocessed foods and minimal amounts of salt and sweeteners. Complete with protein and calorie counts, recipes include meat and meatless dishes, ethnic foods, wholegrain breads, desserts, snacks, and sandwiches—a wondrous variety of wholesome, delicious eating.
No. 263, spiral-bound, $16.95

WHOLE FOODS FROM THE WHOLE WORLD
edited by Virginia Sutton Halonen

This cookbook combines the goodness of whole foods with the variety of ethnic dishes from around the world.
No. 264, spiral-bound, $14.50

WHOLE FOODS FOR KIDS TO COOK

This children's cookbook includes recipes that are simple enough for preschoolers, with a little help from Mom and Dad. Others are meant for older children who have already developed simple cooking skills. These recipes will encourage children to develop an understanding and appreciation for great food.
No. 261, spiral-bound, $9.95

PLAYFUL LEARNING: An Alternative Approach to Preschool
by Anne Englehardt and Cheryl Sullivan

This book offers a workable and enjoyable alternative to traditional preschools: the at-home cooperative preschool. You and other parents can provide a learning environment while you share in your children's emotional, intellectual, and social development. PLAYFUL LEARNING is designed to be a multi-purpose guide for adults who work with young children and includes a wide variety of craft projects, simple recipes, science experiments, plans for field trips, music activities, and much, much more.
No. 279, spiral-bound, $16.95

The Womanly Art of Breastfeeding: an Audio Guide

An exclusive audio edition of LLLI's best-selling manual offers a basic guide to breastfeeding in two 90-minute tapes. Information is excerpted from the fourth edition of THE WOMANLY ART OF BREASTFEEDING.
No. 663, $8.95

Other Helpful BOOKS

In addition to the books we publish, La Leche League International distributes a wide selection of books that offer helpful information to parents and professionals. Some of these are listed here. For a complete, up-to-date listing plus ordering information, call 1-800-LA LECHE for a free copy of the LLLI Catalogue, or call the Order Department at 847-519-9585.

BREASTFEEDING

**Breastfeeding and Natural Child Spacing:
How Ecological Breastfeeding Spaces Babies**
by Sheila Kippley
No. 320, $8.95

Breastfeeding: Biocultural Perspectives
edited by Patricia Stuart-Macadam and Katherine A. Dettwyler
No. 334, $31.95

Breastfeeding the Adopted Baby
by Debra Stewart Peterson
No. 355, $8.95

Eat Well, Lose Weight While Breastfeeding: The Complete Nutrition Book for Nursing Mothers
by Eileen Behan
No. 348, $11.00

The Nursing Mother's Guide to Weaning
by Kathleen Huggins and Linda Ziedrich
No. 361, $9.95

So That's What They're For! Breastfeeding Basics
by Janet Tamaro
No. 385, $10.95

Milk, Money, and Madness: The Culture and Politics of Breastfeeding
by Naomi Baumslag and Dia L. Michels
No. 328, $26.95

Nursing Your Baby
by Karen and Gale Pryor
No. 329, $6.95

PREGNANCY, CHILDBIRTH, AND POSTPARTUM

The Birth Book: Everything You Need to Know to Have a Safe and Satisfying Birth
by William and Martha Sears
No. 309, $12.95

Eating Expectantly: A Practical and Tasty Guide to Prenatal Nutrition
by Bridget Swinney
No. 3341, $12.00

Immaculate Deception II: Myth, Magic and Birth
by Suzanne Arms
No. 364, $16.95

Natural Childbirth After Cesarean: A Practical Guide
by Karis Crawford and Johanne Walters
No. 324, $14.95

Postpartum Survival Guide
by Ann Dunnewold and Diane G. Sanford
No. 341, $13.95

Your Fertility Signals: Using Them to Achieve or Avoid Pregnancy Naturally
by Merryl Winstein
No. 376, $12.95

A Good Birth, A Safe Birth: Choosing and Having the Childbirth Experience You Want
by Diana Korte and Roberta Scaer
No. 325, $16.50

MOTHERS' CHOICES

Mother in the Middle: Searching for Peace in the Mommy Wars
by Deborah Shaw Lewis and Chamaine Crouse Yoest
No. 3471, $12.99

Sequencing: The Groundbreaking Book on Having It All But Not
All At Once
by Arlene Rossen Cardozo
No. 347, $13.95

What's a Smart Woman Like You Doing at Home?
by Linda Burton, Janet Dittmer, and Cheri Loveless
No. 386, $8.95

Confessions of an Organized Homemaker: The Secrets of
Uncluttering Your Home and Taking Control of Your Life
by Deniece Schofield
No. 302, $10.95

CHILD REARING

The Discipline Book: Everything You Need to Know to Have a
Better-Behaved Child—From Birth to Age Ten
by William and Martha Sears
No. 332, $12.95

The Winning Family: Increasing Self-Esteem in Your Children
and Yourself
by Louise Hart
No. 388, $12.95

The Baby Book: Everything You Need to Know About Your
Baby from Birth to Age Two
by William and Martha Sears
No. 381, $21.45

Crying Baby, Sleepless Nights: Why Your Baby is Crying and
What You Can Do About It
by Sandy Jones
No. 326, $11.50

The Family Bed: An Age Old Concept in Child Rearing
by Tine Thevenin
No. 345, $9.95

Loving Your Child Is Not Enough: Positive Discipline
That Works
by Nancy Samalin
No. 359, $11.00

How to Talk So Kids Will Listen and Listen So Kids Will Talk
by Adele Faber and Elaine Mazlish
No. 353, $12.00

The Natural Baby Food Cookbook
by Margaret Kenda and Phyllis Williams
No. 365, $7.95

SPECIAL SITUATIONS

Empty Cradle, Broken Heart: Surviving the
Death of Your Baby
by Deborah L. Davis
No. 356, $15.95

Kangaroo Care: The Best You Can Do to Help
Your Preterm Infant
by Susan M. Ludington-Hoe with Susan K. Golant
No. 358, $10.95

SIDS: A Parent's Guide to Understanding and Preventing Sudden
Infant Death Syndrome
by William Sears
No. 313, $19.95

Professional BOOKS

THE BREASTFEEDING ANSWER BOOK
by Nancy Mohrbacher and Julie Stock
Revised edition.
Published by La Leche League International, this comprehensive
resource has an easy-to-use format designed for those who counsel
breastfeeding mothers.
No. 480, $52.00

An Overview of Solutions to Breastfeeding and
Sucking Problems
by Susan Meintz Maher, IBCLC
Outlines the steps needed to assess and solve the more challenging
cases of nipple soreness, breast problems, and ineffective suck.
Published by La Leche League International.
No. 67, $6.50

Breastfeeding: A Guide for the Medical Profession, 4th edition
by Ruth A. Lawrence, MD
This authoritative reference on nearly every aspect of breastfeeding is
a valuable resource for physicians, nurses, lactation consultants, and
League Leaders. It applies recent research to practical situations and
provides guidelines for the management of breastfeeding.
No. 307, $64.95

Breastfeeding and Human Lactation
by Jan Riordan, EdD, RN, IBCLC, and Kathleen Auerbach, PhD, IBCLC
A skillful blend of clinical experience, research documentation, and
technical know-how. Includes fully referenced studies, conversion
tables, and glossary of terms.
No. 337, $82.95

Booklets and Information SHEETS

Various booklets, pamphlets, and information sheets on specialized
topics are available from local La Leche League Groups and from La
Leche League International. For an up-to-date listing plus complete
ordering information, send for a copy of the LLLI Catalogue. Here is
just a sampling of the items:

Nursing a Baby with a Cleft Lip or Cleft Palate. No. 122
The Diabetic Mother and Breastfeeding. No. 17
Breastfeeding a Baby with Down Syndrome. No. 23
Breastfeeding Your Premature Baby. No. 13
Legal Rights of Breastfeeding Mothers, USA Scene. No. 59
Nursing Your Adopted Baby. No. 55
Breastfeeding Twins. No. 52
Breastfeeding After a Cesarean Birth. No. 80

Breastfeeding Rights Packet

Resource material for mothers involved in divorce, custody, employment, or other legal controversies that threaten their continued breastfeeding.
No. 78

Visually Impaired Resource List from LLLI

Provides current list of breastfeeding materials available in Braille and on cassette tapes. For more information send for free brochure.
No. 560

Center for Breastfeeding Information

A reliable source for health professionals, researchers, breastfeeding counselors, and medical students seeking breastfeeding literature, current references, bibliographic lists, and general information. For more information send for a free brochure.
No. 471

Breastfeeding-Aid PRODUCTS

Most breastfeeding mothers and their babies get along just fine without specialized equipment or products. However, in cases where some assistance is necessary to ensure continued breastfeeding success, La Leche League has certain products available that can be of help. Some of these items are available through local LLL Groups, or you can order directly from La Leche League International.

Medela Manualectric Breastpump/Feeding System

Engineered to operate with the same suck-release-relax cycle characteristic of a baby's nursing action, the Medela Manualectric Breastpump operates with a piston-type action. A special adapter fits inside the shield to adapt the pump to smaller breasts. Can also be used with the Medela Electric Breastpump.
No. 421, $31.50

Pump In Style

Double-pumping system designed for the active working mother; combines the performance of a fully automatic pump with a stylish tote bag for carrying everything you need. Powered by AC adapter or optional battery pack.
No. 424. $208.00

Nurture III Electric Double Breast Pump

An electric double pump that offers three adjustable speeds to provide maximum comfort and effectiveness.
No. 427, $110.00

Egnell One-Handed Breast Pump

This easy-to-use hand pump is small and convenient yet provides safe, effective suction.
No. 419, $30.95

Medela Supplemental Nutrition System

A thin tube taped to each breast carries supplement to the nursing baby from a plastic bottle hanging on a cord around the mother's neck. A valve in the bottle cap prevents the milk from flowing until the baby sucks; the two tubes make it easy to switch sides while breastfeeding. Helpful for mothers who are relactating or nursing a baby with a sucking problem.
No. 416, $36.95

Medela Hand Expression Funnel

The Medela Hand Expression Funnel is a specially designed plastic funnel that fits onto an ordinary baby bottle and allows a mother to collect her hand-expressed breast milk without spills or splashes.
No. 423, $7.95

Medela Breast Shell Kit

Medela breast shells allow air to circulate around nipples to correct inverted nipples and protect sore nipples.
No. 422, $13.95

Breast Shells

Two-piece breast shells recommended for use during pregnancy to correct inverted nipples.
No. 402, $6.00

Additional Items of INTEREST

Breastfeeding Your Baby: A Mother's Guide

One-hour video produced by Medela, Inc., in cooperation with La Leche League International. Families tell of the advantages of breastfeeding and experts give guidance on techniques. Celebrities like Linda Kelsey, Katharine Ross, and Cathy Rigby tell of their own breastfeeding experiences.
No. 601, VHS, $19.95

Baby Cuddler Baby Sling

A sling has been found to be the ideal way to carry a baby from birth to three years. Comfortable and adjustable, a sling distributes the child's weight over shoulders and hip to avoid back strain.
No. 401, $39.95

Lansinoh® for Breastfeeding Mothers

Created especially for nursing mothers, using a patented process that removes allergens and impurities, Lansinoh® is the world's purest lanolin. Does not have to be removed prior to nursing and can be used with complete confidence of safety for mother and baby.
No. 581, $9.95

Wallaby Phototherapy Unit

Allows baby to be treated for jaundice at home. Available from:
> **Fiberoptic Medical Products**
> Suite 300, Commerce Plaza, 5100 Tilghman St.
> Allentown PA 18104 USA

Organizations That Offer SUPPORT

Many of these organizations have local chapters. Check your phone directory or contact their headquarters at these addresses:

The American Academy of Husband-Coached Childbirth— The Bradley Method

Box 5224 Department CB, Sherman Oaks CA 91413-5224
800-423-2397 or 800-4ABIRTH www.bradleybirth.com
> Founded by Robert Bradley, MD and Jay and Marjie Hathaway for the purpose of making childbirth information available through films, classes, lectures, and workshops.

American College of Nurse Midwives

818 Connecticut Avenue NW, Suite 900, Washington DC 20006
202-728-9860
> Health care providers who offer a natural approach to birth.

American Society for Psychoprophylaxis in Obstetrics, Inc.— ASPO/Lamaze

1200 19th Street NW, Suite 300, Washington DC 20036
800-368-4404 or 202-857-1100
> Training and certification in the psychoprophylactic method of childbirth preparation.

Association for Breastfeeding Fashions
Post Office Box 4378, Sunland CA 91041
 Offers information on companies that design fashionable clothing for breastfeeding women. Please send S.A.S.E. for more information.

Association for the Care of Children's Health
7910 Woodmont Avenue, Suite 300, Bethesda MD 20814
800-808-2224 or 301-654-6549
 Partnership of parents and professionals dedicated to improving the newborn intensive care experience and future for babies, families, and caregivers.

Children in Hospitals, Inc.
31 Wilshire Park, Needham MA 02192
 Parents and health-care professionals concerned about the need for ample contact between children and parents when either is hospitalized.

Cesareans/Support, Education, and Concern, Inc.—C/SEC
22 Forest Road, Framingham MA 01701
508-877-8266
 Provides information on many aspects of cesarean childbirth in order to make couples more aware of their options.

The Couple-to-Couple League
Post Office Box 111184, Cincinnati OH 45211
513-471-2000
 An interfaith organization offering couples help with the practice of natural family planning. CCL teaches ecological breastfeeding and the full sympto-thermal method of predicting ovulation.

ICAN (International Cesarean Awareness Network)
1304 Kingsdale Avenue, Redondo Beach CA 90278
310-542-6400

International Childbirth Education Association—ICEA
Post Office Box 20048, Minneapolis MN 55420
612-854-8660
 A volunteer organization which brings together persons interested in family-centered maternity and infant care.

International Lactation Consultant Association
4101 Lake Boone Trail, Suite 201, Raleigh NC 27607-6518
919-787-5181

Can refer you to a lactation consultant who has been board certified as a health care provider.

InterNational Association of Parents and Professionals for Safe Alternatives in Childbirth—NAPSAC
Route 1 Box 646, Marble Hill MO 63764
573-238-2010

Parents, medical professionals, and childbirth educators who promote education enabling parents to assume more responsibility for pregnancy and childbirth.

Mothers at Home
8310 A Old Courthouse Road, Vienna VA 22182
703-827-5903 or 800-783-4MOM

An organization for the woman who has chosen to stay home and devote her skills to the nurturing of her family. Also publishes a monthly newsletter, "Welcome Home."

PAGER Association
P. O. Box 1153, Germantown MD 20875-1153
301-601-9541

A national organization that provides information and support to parents whose children have reflux.

Vaginal Birth after Cesarean—VBAC
10 Great Plain Terrace, Needham MA 02192
617-449-2490

Provides classes, lectures, and seminars for couples interested in learning about vaginal delivery after a previous cesarean or cesarean prevention.

World Alliance for Breastfeeding Action—WABA
26 N. Jalan Mesjid, Negeri, Penang, 11600 Malaysia

The World Alliance for Breastfeeding Action sponsors World Breastfeeding Week (August 1-7) and other projects that promote and support breastfeeding.

**P H O T O
C R E D I T S**

Chapter 10

Page 187, Judy Torgus; page 188, Rae Cassin; page 191, Paula Froehlich; page 193, Bill Sears; page 194, Betsy Liotus; page 196, © Jean Hoelscher.

Chapter 11

Page 199, JJ Anderson; pages 200, 207, 209, David Arendt; page 201, Trisha Noack.

Chapter 12

Pages 213, 224, Margarita Guarin, LLL Colombia; page 216, Mrs. Clarence Torkelson; page 220, Darrell Rideout.

Part 5, page 229, Mary Kolar

Chapter 13

Page 231, Cecelia Magalhaes; page 233, Darrell Rideout; page 235, Margarita Guarin, LLL Colombia; page 239, Judy Torgus.

Chapter 14

Page 241, Judy Torgus; page 242, JJ Anderson; page 247, Mrs. Clarence Torkelson; page 251, Betsy Liotus; page 254, Deborah Matthews.

Chapter 15

Page 257, David Arendt; page 260, JJ Anderson; page 262, Cindy Russell; page 267, © Jean Hoelscher; page 268, Susan Condon.

Part 6, page 271, © Harriette Hartigan/Artemis

Chapter 16

Page 273, Betsy Liotus; page 274, Peggy Eaton; page 277, Judy Torgus; page 284, Gene Cranston Anderson; page 285, John Roleson; page 287, © Mühlmann (Austria); pages 288, 292 (l & r), © Christa Herzog (LLL Switzerland); page 291, Debi Mitchell.

Chapter 17

Page 297, Peggy Eaton; page 298, Pam Shambaugh; page 299, Elaine Caper; page 302, Erin Rettig; page 304, Betsy Liotus; page 307, Linda Hardesty; page 310, © Andrea Leiber (LLL Germany); page 315, Rae Cassin; page 321, Bill Skees; page 328, Judy Torgus; page 331, Elaine Caper; page 332, Trisha Noack.

Part 7, page 333, Trisha Noack

Chapter 18

Page 335, © Harriette Hartigan/Artemis; pages 337, 345, 354, 359, David Arendt; page 341, © Fotoburo, Martin Droog (Netherlands); page 347, Betsy Liotus.

Chapter 19

Page 361, JJ Anderson; pages 363, 373, 377, David Arendt; page 366, Rae Cassin.

Part 8, page 379, Paula Froehlich

Chapter 20

Pages 381, 385, David Arendt; pages 382, 388, 389, 390, 391, 392, Rae Cassin.

Chapter 21

Page 396, David Arendt; page 400, © Jean Hoelscher.

Chapter 1—Why Choose Breastfeeding?

Overall benefits of breastfeeding.

Heinig, M. J. and Dewey, K. G. Health Advantages of breastfeeding for infants: a critical review. *Nutr Res Rev* 1996; 9:89-110.

Cunningham, A. S., Jelliffe, D. B., and Jelliffe, E. F. P. Breastfeeding and health in the 1980s: a global epidemiological review. *J Pediatr* 1991; 118(5):659-66.

Breastfeeding soon after birth causes uterus to contract.

Chua, S. et al. Influence of breastfeeding and nipple stimulation on postpartum uterine activity. *Br J Ob Gyn* 1994; 101:804-05.

Breastfeeding promotes jaw and facial development.

Labbok, M. H. and Hendershot, G. E. Does breastfeeding protect against malocclusion? *Am J Prev Med* 1987; 3:227-32.

Protection from obesity.

Kramer, M. S. Do breastfeeding and delayed introduction of solid foods protect against obesity. *J Pediatr* 1981; 98(6):883-87.

Protection from allergies.

Saarinen, U. M. et al. Breastfeeding as prophylaxis against atopic disease: prospective follow-up study until 17 years old. *Lancet* 1995; 346(8982):1065-69.

Wright, A. L. et al. Relationship of infant feeding to recurrent wheezing at age 6 years. *Arch Ped Adolesc Med* 1995; 149:758-63.

Wright, A. L. et al. Epidemiology of physician-diagnosed allergic rhinitis in childhood. *Pediatrics* 1994; 94(6)895-901.

Human milk inhibits the growth of harmful bacteria.

Goldman, A. S. et al. Anti-inflammatory properties of human milk. *Acta Paediatr Scand* 1986; 75:689-95.

Dewey, K. G. et al. Differences in morbidity between breastfed and formula-fed infants. *J Pediatr* 1995; 126(5) pt 1:696-702.

Enhanced development of baby's brain and nervous system.

Pollock, J. I. Long-term associations with infant feeding in a clinically advantaged population of babies. *Dev Med Child Neurol* 1994; 36(5): 429-40.

Premature infants have higher IQs if they had been fed human milk.

Lucas, A. et al. Breast milk and subsequent intelligence quotient in children born preterm. *Lancet* 1992; 33:261-62.

Breastfeeding delays menstruation and ovulation.

Lewis, P. et al. The resumption of ovulation and menstruation in a well-nourished population of women breastfeeding for an extended period of time. *Fertil Steril* 1991; 55(3):529-36.

Breastfeeding mothers lose weight gradually without restricting calories.

Dewey, K. et al. Maternal weight-loss patterns during prolonged lactation. *Am J Clin Nutr* 1993; 58:162-68.

Breastfeeding protects a mother from breast cancer.

Hirose, K. et al. A large-scale, hospital-based case-control study of risk factors of breast cancer according to menopausal status. *Jpn J Cancer Res* 1995; 86:146-54.

Breastfeeding protects a mother from ovarian cancer, urinary tract infections, and osteoporosis.

Schneider, A. P. Risk factor for ovarian cancer (letter). *N Engl J Med* 317:508-09.

Gwinn, M. L. et al. Pregnancy, breastfeeding, and oral contraceptives and the risk of epithelial ovarian cancer. *J Clin Epidemiol* 1990; 43(6): 559-68.

Coppa, G. V. et al. Preliminary study of breastfeeding and bacterial adhesion to uroepithelial cells. *Lancet* 1990; 335:569-71.

Sinigaglia, L. et al. Effect of lactation on post-menopausal bone mineral density of the lumbar spine. *J Reprod Med* 1996; 41(6):439-43.

Page 13   **Breastfeeding improves a mother's responsiveness to her baby.**

Sears, W. BECOMING A FATHER. Schaumburg IL: La Leche League International, 1986.

Breastfeeding enhances a woman's mothering role.

Virden, S. F. The relationship between infant feeding method and maternal role ajustment. *J Nurs Midwif* 1988; 33(1):31-35.

Chapter 2—Plans Are Underway

Page 18   **Feelings of self-esteem related to childbirth experience.** Korte, D. and Scaer, R. *A Good Birth, A Safe Birth*, 3rd ed. Boston: Harvard Common Press, 1992.

Page 19   **Effects of medication used in labor and birth.**

Crowell, M. K. et al. Relationship between obstetric analgesia and time of effective breastfeeding. *J Nurse Midwif* 1995; 39(3):150-56.

Righard, L. and Alade, M. Effects of delivery room routines on success of first breast-feed. *Lancet* 1990; 336:1105-07.

Sepkowski, C. et al. The effects of maternal epidural anesthesia on neonatal behavior during the first month. *Dev Med Child Neurol* 1992; 34:1072-80.

Page 20   **Nursing soon after birth encourages milk to come in.**

Yamauchi, Y. and Yamanouchi, H. Breastfeeding frequency during the first 24 hours after birth in full-term neonates. *Pediatrics* 1990; 86:171-75.

Separation of mother and baby may cause breastfeeding problems.

Righard, L. and Alade, M. Effects of delivery room routines on success of first breast-feed. *Lancet* 1990; 336:1105-07.

Page 21   **Cesarean birth rates in the USA; incidence of prematurity, respiratory distress, and other complications are higher with cesarean birth.**

Korte, D. and Scaer, R. *A Good Birth, A Safe Birth*, 3rd edition. Boston; Harvard Common Press, 1992.

Page 22   **Incidence of vaginal birth following a previous cesarean.**

Crawford, K. and Walters, J. N*atural Childbirth after Cesarean*. Cambridge, MA: Blackwell Science, Inc., 1996.

Page 23   **Choosing a health care professional.**

Freed, G. L. et al. National assessment of physicians' breastfeeding knowledge, attitudes, training, and experience. *JAMA* 1995; 273(6): 472-76.

Page 26   **Effect of positioning on sore nipples.**

Frantz, K. Baby's position at the breast and its relationship to sucking problems. LLLI Conference, 1983, 1985.

Montgomery glands cleanse and lubricate nipples.

Williams, J. Anatomy and physiology of breastfeeding. ILCA Conference, July 1992.

Page 28   **Treatment for inverted nipples.**

Main Trail Collaborative Group. Preparing for breastfeeding: treatment of inverted and non-protactile nipples during pregnancy. *Midwifery* 1994; 10:200-14.

Chapter 3—Your Network of Support

Page 36   **Effectiveness of mother-to-mother support.**

Rassin, D. K. Impact of maternal attitudes and social support on breast-feeding. *J Am Diet Assoc* 1991; Suppl:A-150.

WABA. *Mother-to-Mother Support for Breastfeeding*. 1993.

Breastfeeding mothers need support.

Lawrence, R. A. The management of lactation as a physiologic process. *Clin Perinatology* 1997; 14(1):1-10.

Lawrence, R. A. *Breastfeeding: a Guide for the Medical Profession,* 4th ed. St. Louis: Mosby, 1994.

Chapter 4—Your Baby Arrives

Page 45   **Newborn's capabilities.**

Klaus, M. T*he Amazing Newborn.* New York: Addison-Wesley, 1985.

The let-down or milk-ejection reflex.

Newton, M. and Newton, N. The let-down reflex in human lactation. *Pediatrics* 1948; 33:69-87.

Page 54   **Frequent nursing reduces engorgement.**

Moon, J. and Humenick, S. Breast engorgement: contributing variables and variables amenable to nursing intervention. *JOGNN* 1989; 18:309-15.

Hill, P. and Humenick, S. The occurrence of breast-engorgement. *J Hum Lact* 1994; 10:79-86.

Page 55   **Use of cabbage leaves to treat engorgement.**

Nikodem, V. et al. Do cabbage leaves prevent breast engorgement? A randomized, controlled study. *Birth* 1993; 20:61-64.

Page 56   **Frequent, unrestricted breastfeeding does not cause sore nipples.**

de Carvalho, M. et al. Does the duration and frequency of early breast-feeding affect nipple pain? *Birth* 1984; 11:81-84.

Allow baby to decide when to end the feeding.

Woolridge, M. and Fisher, C. Colic, "overfeeding," and symptoms of lac-tose malabsorption in the breastfed baby: a possible artifact of feed man-agement? *Lancet* 1988; 2(8605):382-84.

Page 57   **Using both breasts at each feeding.**

Woolridge, M. et al. Do changes in pattern of breast usage alter the baby's nutrient intake? *Lancet* 1990; 336:395-97.

Page 60   **Breastfeed often and avoid artificial nipples.**

Nylander, G. et al. Unsupplemented breastfeeding in the maternity ward. *Acta Obst Gyn Scand* 1991; 70:205-09.

Neifert, M. et al. Nipple confusion: toward a more formal definition. *J Pediatr* 1995; 126(6):S125-29.

Page 62   **Breast pumps and breastfeeding aid products.**

Frantz, K. *Breastfeeding Product Guide 1994.* Sunland, California: Geddes Productions, 1993.

Page 65   **Avoid hospital gift packs that include formula samples.**

Snell, B. T. et al. The association of formula samples given at hospital discharge with the early duration of breastfeeding. *J Hum Lact* 1991; 8:67-72.

Chapter 5—At Home with Your Baby

Page 70   Campbell, R. *How to Really Love Your Child.* New York: New American Library, 1982.

New Guinea infants nurse frequently.

Jelliffe, D. B. *Infant Nutrition in the Subtropics,* Geneva: World Health Organization 1968.

Page 71   Francis, B. Successful lactation and a woman's sexuality, *J Trop Ped Env Health* 1976; 22:4.

Page 74   **Pacifier use may lead to early weaning.**

Barros, F. C. et al. Use of pacifiers is associated with decreased breast-feeding duration. *Pediatrics* 1995; 95(4):497-99.

Page 74   **Normal weight gain for a breastfed baby.**

Dewey, K. et al. Growth of breastfed and formula-fed infants from 0 to 18 months. The DARLING study. *Pediatrics* 1992; 89(6):1035-41.

Page 80   **Carrying baby reduces crying.**

Hunziker, U. and Barr R. Increased carrying reduces infant crying: a randomized controlled trial. *Pediatrics* 1986; 77:641.

Page 90   **Even one bottle of formula can lead to allergies.**

Host, A. et al. A prospective study of cow's milk allergy in exclusively breastfed infants. *Acta Paediatr Scand* 1988; 77:663-70.

Chapter 6—A Time to Learn

Page 98   **Mother's diet may cause colic.**

Clyne, P. and Kluczycki, A. Human breast milk contains bovine IgG. Relationship to infant colic? *Pediatrics* 1991; 87(4):439-44.

Page 99   Sears, W. THE FUSSY BABY. Schaumburg IL: La Leche League International, 1985.

Pages 101, 109   Sears, W. NIGHTTIME PARENTING. Schaumburg IL: La Leche League International, 1985.

Page 102   Sears, W. *SIDS: A Parents' Guide to Understanding and Preventing Sudden Infant Death Syndrome.* Boston: Little, Brown and Company, 1995.

Wayne, NJ: Avery, 1987.

Page 105   Thevenin, T. *The Family Bed.*

Chapter 7—Common Concerns

Page 114   **Proper positioning prevents sore nipples.**

Frantz, K. *Baby's position at the breast and its relationship to sucking problems.* LLLI Conference, 1983, 1985.

Page 117   **Moist wound healing is effective in treating sore nipples.**

Huml, S. Cracked nipples in the breastfeeding mother. *Advance for Nurse Practitioners* 1995; 29-31.

Page 120   **Treatment for thrush.**

Amir, L. et al. *Candidiasis and Breastfeeding.* Lactation Consultant Series, Unit 18. Garden City Park, NY: Avery Publishing, 1995.

Page 125   **Breast pumps.**

Frantz, K. *Breastfeeding Product Guide* 1994, Sunland, CA: Geddes Productions, 1993.

Page 130   **Treatment of plugged ducts, breast infections.**

Lawrence, R. *Breastfeeding: A Guide for the Medical Profession*, 4th ed. St. Louis: Mosby, 1994.

Page 137   **No danger of breastfeeding with breast implants.**

Berlin, C. Silicone breast implants and breastfeeding. *Pediatrics* 1994; 94(4):547-49.

FDA. *Breast implants: an information update.* Rockville, MD: US FDA, March 1996.

Page 138   **Normal growth of breastfed babies.**

Dewey, K. et al. Growth of breastfed babies deviates from a pooled analysis of US, Canadian, and European data sets. *Pediatrics* 1995; 96(3):495-503.

Page 146   **Breastfeeding protects against later obesity.**

Kramer, M. Do breastfeeding and delayed introduction of solid foods protect against subsequent obesity? *J Pediatr* 1981; 98:883-87.

Chapter 8—Breastfeeding and Working

Page 155   **How employed mothers felt about their breastfeeding experiences.**

Auerbach, K. and Guss, E. Maternal employment and breastfeeding: a study of 567 women's experiences. *Am J Dis Child* 1984; 138:958-60.

Page 156   **Women who returned to work before their babies were two months old had more breastfeeding problems.**

Kearney, M. and Cronenwett, L. Breastfeeding and employment. *JOGNN* 1991; 20(6):471-80.

Page 157   **Giving bottles too soon can cause nipple confusion.**

Neifert, M. et al. Nipple confusion: toward a formal definition. *J Pediatr* 1995; 126(6):S125-S129.

Sears, W. and Sears, M. *The Baby Book.* Boston: Little, Brown Company, 1993.

Page 158   **Breastfeeding provides benefits to employers.**

Cohen, R. et al. Comparison of maternal absenteeism and infant illness rates among breastfeeding and formula-feeding women in two corporations. *Am J Health Promo* 1995; 10(2):148-53.

Storage guidelines for human milk.

Barger, J. and Bull, P. A comparison of the bacterial composition of breast milk stored at room temperature and stored in the refrigerator. *IJCE* 1987; 2:29-30

Pardou, A. Human milk banking: influence of storage processes and of bacterial contamination on some milk constituents. *Biol Neonate* 1994; 65:302-09.

Arnold, L. Storage containers for human milk: an issue revisited. *J Hum Lact* 1995; 11(4):325-28.

Page 162   **Previously frozen milk can be kept refrigerated for 24 hours.**

Human Milk Banking Association of North America. *Recommendations for Collection, Storage, and Handling of a Mother's Milk for Her Own Infant in the Hospital Setting.* West Hartford CT USA, 1993.

Studies show human milk retards the growth of bacteria.

Pardou, A. Human milk banking: influence of storage process and of bacterial contamination on some milk constituents. *Biol Neonate* 1994; 65:302-09.

Page 167   **Human milk provides protection for children in day care.**

Jones, E. et al. Relationship between infant feeding and exclusion rate from child care because of illness. *J Am Diet Assoc* 1993; 93(7):809-11.

Chapter 10—The Manly Art of Fathering

Pages 190,   **Fathers get involved.**
191,
192   Sears, W. BECOMING A FATHER. Schaumburg IL: La Leche League International, 1986.

Page 193   **Fathers provide a special touch.**

Kaplan, Louise. *Oneness and Separateness.* New York: Simon and Schuster, 1980.

Page 194   **Growth and development.**

Sears, W. GROWING TOGETHER. Schaumburg IL: La Leche League International, 1989.

Page 196   **Rewards of parenting.**

Stewart, D. *Fathering and Career: Keeping a Healthy Balance.* Marble Hill, MO: NAPSAC, Int'l, 1987.

Chapter 12—Nutritional Know-How

Page 223 **Nursing mothers' need for liquids.**

Dusdieker, L. et al. Effect of supplemental fluids on human milk production. *J Pediatr* 1985; 106(2):207-11.

Page 224 **Sources of calcium for nursing mothers.**

Behan, E. *Eat Well, Lose Weight while Breastfeeding.* New York: Villard Books, 1994.

Page 225 **Effects of caffeine on breastfed babies.**

Berlin, C. and Daniel C. Excretion of theobromine in human milk and saliva. *Pediatr Res* 1981; 15:492.

Nehlig, A. and Debry, G. Consequences on the newborn of chronic maternal consumption of coffee during gestation and lactation: a review. *J Am Coll Nutr* 1994; 13(1):6-21.

Page 226 **Mothers on vegan diets may need a supplement.**

Kuhne, T. et al. Maternal vegan diet causing a serious infantile neurological disorder due to Vitamin B_{12} deficiency. *Eur J Pediatr* 1991; 150: 205-08.

Page 226 **Breastfeeding mothers tend to lose weight without restricting calories.**

Dewey, K. et al. Maternal weight-loss patterns during prolonged lactation. *Am J Clin Nutr* 1993; 58:162-66.

Heinig, M. et al. Lactation and postpartum weight loss. *Mechanisms Regulating Lactation and Infant Nutrient Utilization* 1992; 30:397-400.

Page 227 **Studies show that breastfeeding mothers can safely exercise.**

Dewey, K. and McCrory, M. Effects of dieting and physical activity on pregnancy and lactation. *Am J Clin Nutr* 1994; 59(Suppl):446S-59S.

Dewey, K. et al. A randomized study of the effects of aerobic exercise by lactating women on breast milk volume and composition. *N Engl J Med* 1994; 330(7):449-53.

One study shows exercise may increase a mother's milk supply.

Lovelady, C. et al. Lactation performance of exercising women. *Am J Clin Nutr* 1990; 52:103-09.

Chapter 13—Ready for Solids

Page 231 **Pediatricians recommend only human milk for 4-6 months.**

Committee on Nutrition, American Academy of Pediatrics. On the feeding of supplemental foods to infants. *Pediatrics* 1980; 65:1178.

Page 232 **Solid foods displace human milk in a baby's diet.**

Cohen, R. et al. Effects of age of introduction of complementary foods on infant breast milk intake, total energy intake, and growth: a randomized intervention in Honduras. *Lancet* 1994; 344:288-93.

Starting solid foods early reduces protective antibodies baby receives.

Duncan, B. et al. Exclusive breastfeeding for at least 4 months protects against *otitis media*. *Pediatrics* 1993; 91(5):867-72.

Human milk protects against allergic reactions to other foods.

Taylor, B. et al. Transient IgA deficiency and pathogenesis of infantile atopy. *Lancet* 1973; ii:111-13.

Page 233   No need for vitamin supplements in breastfed babies.

Fluoride: American Academy of Pediatrics. Fluoride supplementation for children: interim policy recommendations. *Pediatrics* 1995; 95:777.

Vitamin D: Greer, F. R. and Marshall, S. Bone mineral content, serum, vitamin D metabolic concentrations, and ultraviolet B light exposure in infants fed human milk with and without vitamin D_2 supplements. *J Pediatr* 1989; 114(2):204-12.

Page 234   Allow baby to decide which foods and how much he wants.

Birch, L. et al. The variability of young children's energy intake. *N Eng J Med* 1991; 324(4):232-35.

Page 239   Too much fruit juice can interfere with child's appetite.
Smith, M. and Lifshitz, F. Excess fruit juice consumption as a contributing factor in nonorganic failure to thrive. *Pediatrics* 1994; 93(2):438-43.

Chapter 14—Weaning Gradually with Love

Page 242   Breastfeeding continues to offer immunity beyond the first year.

Prentice, A. Breastfeeding and the older infant. *Acta Paediatr Scand* 1991; 374:78-88.

Goldman, A. Immunologic components in human milk during the second year of lactation. *Acta Paediatr Scand* 1983; 72:461-62.

Van den Bogaard, C. et al. The relationship between breastfeeding and early childhood morbidity in a general population. *Family Medicine* 1991; 23:510-15.

Page 245   Bumgarner, N. J. MOTHERING YOUR NURSING TODDLER. Schaumburg IL: La Leche League International, 1982.

Page 248   Weaning ages in other cultures.

Mead, M. and Newton, N. Cultural patterns of perinatal behavior, in Childbearing: Its Social and Psychological Aspects, ed. S. Richardson and Guttmacher, A. Baltimore MD: Williams and Wilkins Company, 1967.

Dettwyler, K. A time to wean. BREASTFEEDING ABSTRACTS 1994; 14:3-4.

Page 249   Mothers reported fewer illnesses when toddlers were still nursing.

Gulick, E. The effects of breastfeeding on toddler health. *Pediatric Nurs* 1986; 12:51-54.

Page 253   **Continuing to nurse when mother is pregnant.**

Moscone, S. and Moore, J. Breastfeeding during pregnancy. *J Hum Lact* 1993; 9(2):83-88.

Newton, N. and Theotokatos, M. Breastfeeding during pregnancy in 503 women: does a psychobiological weaning mechanism exist in humans? *Emotion and Reproduction* 1979; 20B:845-49.

Page 254   **Nursing a toddler along with the new baby.**

Gromada, K. Breastfeeding more than one: multiples and tandem breast-feeding. *NAACOG* 1992; 3(4):656-66.

Berke, G. *Nursing Two: Is It for You?* Schaumburg IL: La Leche League International, 1989.

Chapter 15—Discipline Is Loving Guidance

Page 258   Sears, W. BECOMING A FATHER. Schaumburg IL: La Leche League International, 1986.

Page 259   Sears, W. and Sears, M. *The Discipline Book*. Boston: Little, Brown Company, 1995.

Page 261   LeShan, E. *When Your Child Drives You Crazy*. New York: St. Martin's Press, 1985.

Samalin, N. *Loving Your Child Is Not Enough*. New York: Penguin Books, 1987.

Page 264   **Influence of television on children's behavior.**

American Academy of Pediatrics, committee on communications. Children, adolescents, and television. *Pediatrics* 1995; 96(4):786-87.

Page 266   Bumgarner, N. J. MOTHERING YOUR NURSING TODDLER. Schaumburg IL: La Leche League International, 1982.

Chapter 16—Problems at the Beginning

Page 274   **Breastfeeding is less stressful than bottle-feeding for a sick baby.**

Marino, B. et al. Oxygen saturations during breast and bottle feedings in infants with congenital heart disease. *J Pediatr Nurs* 1995; 10(6):360-64.

Page 275   **Effects of anesthetics used for cesarean birth.**

Spigset, O. Anaesthetic agents and excretion in breast milk. *Acta Anaesthesiol Scand* 1994; 38:94-103.

Righard, L. and Alade, M. Effects of delivery room routines on success of first breast-feed. *Lancet* 1990; 336:1105-07.

Sepkowski, C. et al. The effects of maternal epidural anesthesia on neonatal behavior during the first month. *Dev Med Child Neurol* 1992; 34:1072-80.

Page 278   **Effects of cesarean birth on breastfeeding.**

Kearney, M. et al. Cesarean delivery and breastfeeding outcomes. *Birth* 1990; 17(2):97-103.

Full-term babies who are jaundiced suffer no long term adverse effects.

Newman, T. and Maisels, M. Evaluation and treatment of jaundice in the term newborn: a kinder, gentler approach. *Pediatrics* 1992; 89(5): 809-18.

Frequent breastfeeding keeps bilirubin levels within the normal range.

Gartner, L. Neonatal jaundice. *Pediatr Review* 1994; 15(11):422-32.

Page 279   **Higher bilirubin levels may be beneficial.**

Hegyi, T. et al. The protective role of bilirubin in oxygen-radical diseases of the preterm infant. *J Perinatol* 1994; 14(4):296-300.

Page 280   **Breastfeeding may be affected when parents worry about jaundice.**

Kemper, K. Neonatal jaundice in the development of the vulnerable child syndrome. Breastfeeding Abstracts 1990; 10:7.

Page 281   **Phototherapy can be used to lower bilirubin levels if necessary.**

Martinez, J. et al. Hyperbilirubinemia in the breastfed newborn: a controlled trial of four interventions. *Pediatrics* 1993; 91(2):470-73.

Page 283   **Early and frequent breastfeeding can stabilize blood glucose levels.**

Hawdon, J. et al. Prevention and treatment of neonatal hypoglycemia. *Arch Dis Child* 1994; 70:F60-F65.

Wang, Y. S. et al. Preliminary study on the blood glucose level in the exclusively breastfed newborn. *J Trop Pediatr* 1994; 40:187-88.

Page 284   **Human milk is best for preterm infants.**

Caplan, M. et al. Necrotizing enterocolitis: a review of pathogenic mechanisms and implications for prevention. *Pediatric Pathology* 1993; 13: 357-69.

Williams, A. Human milk and the preterm baby: mothers should breastfeed. *BMJ* 1993; 306:1428-29.

Schanler, R. and Hurst, N. Human milk for the hospitalized preterm infant. *Sem Perinatol* 1994; 18(6):476-84.

Improved IQ scores for preterm infants fed human milk.

Lucas, A. et al. Breast milk and subsequent intelligence quotient in children born preterm. *Lancet* 1992; 339:261-64.

Differences in milk of mothers who deliver prematurely.

Luukkainen, P. et al. Changes in fatty acid composition of preterm and term human milk from 1 week to 6 months of lactation. *J Ped Gastro Nutr* 1994; 18:355-60.

Lemons, J. et al. Differences in the composition of preterm and term human milk during early lactation. *Pediatr Res* 1982; 16:113-16.

Possible need for supplementing preterm infants.

Schanler, R. Suitability of human milk for the low-birthweight infant. *Clin Perinatol* 1995; 22(1):207-22.

Valentine, C. et al. Hindmilk improves weight gain in low birth weight infants fed human milk. *J Ped Gastro Nutr* 1994; 18:474-77.

Page 287   Kangaroo care for premies.

Anderson, G. Kangaroo care and breastfeeding for preterm infants. BREASTFEEDING ABSTRACTS 1989; 9:7-8.

Ludington-Hoe, S. with Golant, S. *Kangaroo Care: The Best You Can Do to Help Your Preterm Infant.* New York: Bantam Books, 1993.

Page 288   Cup feedings used for premature babies.

Armstrong, H. Breastfeeding low birthweight babies: advances in Kenya. *J Hum Lact* 1987; 3(2):34-37.

Breastfeeding less stressful for preterm infants than bottle-feeding.

Meier, P. Bottle and breastfeeding: effects on transcutaneous oxygen pressure and temperature in small preterm infants. *Nurs Res* 1988; 37:36-41.

Page 289   Use of an electronic scale to monitor baby's intake.

Meier, P. et al. The accuracy of test-weighing for preterm infants. *J Ped Gastro Nutr* 1990; 5:50-52.

Page 290   Breastfeeding a baby with Down syndrome.

Cooley, W. Supporting the family of a newborn with Down Syndrome. *Compreh Therapy* 1993; 19(3):111-15.

Timko, S. et al. *Breastfeeding the Baby with Down Syndrome.* Unit 9, La Leche League International Lactation Consultant Series. Wayne NJ: Avery Publishing, 1986.

Page 292   Breastfeeding a baby with a cleft lip or palate.

Danner, S. Breastfeeding the infant with a cleft defect. *NAACOG Clin Issues Perinat Women Health* 1992; 3(4):634-39.

Paradise, J. et al. Evidence in infants with cleft palate that breast milk protects against *otitis media. Pediatrics* 1994; 94(6):853-60.

Page 293   Surgery for cleft lip or palate.

Weatherly-White, R. et al. Early repair and breastfeeding for infants with cleft lip. *Plas Reconstruc Surg* 1987; 79:886-87.

Cohen, M. et al. Immediate unrestricted feeding of infants following cleft lip and palate repair. *J Craniofac Surg* 1992; 3(1):30-32.

Page 294   Symptoms of cystic fibrosis may be delayed if infant is breastfed.

Holliday, K. et al. Growth of human milk-fed and formula-fed infants with cystic fibrosis. *J Pediatr* 1991; 118:77-79.

Infants with PKU can be partially breastfed.

Greve, L. et al. Breastfeeding in the management of the newborn with phenylketonuria: a practical approach to dietary therapy. *J Am Diet Assoc* 1994; 94:305-09.

Page 295

Babies who had been breastfed prior to PKU testing scored higher on IQ tests at school age.

Riva, E. et al. Early breastfeeding is linked to higher intelligence quotient scores in dietary treated phenylketonuric children. *Acta Paediatr* 1996; 85:56-58.

Chapter 17—When Extra Care Is Needed

Page 298

Breastfeeding more than one baby saves time.

Sollid, D. T. et al. Breastfeeding multiples. *J Perin & Neo Nurs* 1989; 3(1):46-65.

Gromada, K. MOTHERING MULTIPLES. Schaumburg IL: La Leche League International, 1985.

Page 303

Breastfeeding triplets or quadruplets.

Mead, L. et al. Breastfeeding success with preterm quadruplets. *JOGNN* 1992; 21(3):221-27.

Duggin, J. Breastfeeding triplets—it can be done! *Breastfeed Rev* 1994; II(10):469-70.

Page 304

Relactation.

Auerbach, K. and Avery, J. Relactation: a study of 366 cases. *Pediatrics* 1980; 65:236-48.

Phillips, V. Relactation in mothers of children over 12 months. *J Trop Pediatr* 1993; 39:45-48.

Page 306

Nursing adopted babies.

Nemba, K. Induced lactation: a study of 37 non-puerperal mothers. *J Trop Pediatr* 1994; 40:240-42.

Peterson, D. *Breastfeeding the Adopted Baby.* San Antonio TX: Corona, 1994.

Page 310

Breastfeeding safe for a mother with hepatitis.

Ruff, A. Breast milk, breastfeeding, and transmission of viruses to the neonate. *Sem Perinatol* 1994; 18(6):510-16.

Fanous, E. and Balant, L. Recent developments in viral hepatitis. *Curr Opinion Gastroenterology.* 1994; 10:237-42.

Breastfeeding safe for a mother with tuberculosis.

Lawrence, R. *Breastfeeding: a Guide for the Medical Profession,* 4th edition. St. Louis: Mosby, 1994.

Mother's milk protects baby from illness.

Goldman, A. S. et al. Anti-inflammatory systems in human milk. *Adv Exp Med Biol* 1991; 262:69-76.

Page 311   **Hospitalization of nursing mother.**

Lawrence, R. *Breastfeeding: a Guide for the Medical Profession*, 4th edition. St. Louis: Mosby, 1994.

Spigset, O. Anaesthetic agents and excretion in breast milk. *Acta Anaesthesiol Scand* 1994; 38:94-103.

Page 313   **Most medications can be taken safely by the nursing mother.**

American Academy of Pediatrics Committee on Drugs. The transfer of drugs and other chemicals into human milk. *Pediatrics* 1994; 93(1): 137-50.

Anderson, P. Drug use during breastfeeding. *Clin Pharmach* 1991; 10: 594-623.

Temporary weaning necessary after radioactive testing.

Rose, M. et al. Excretion of iodine-123-hippuran, technetium-99m-red blood cells, and technetium-99m-macroaggregated albumin into breast milk. *J Nucl Med* 1990; 31:978-84.

Page 314   **Substances of abuse should be avoided.**

Wilton, J. Breastfeeding and the chemically dependent woman. *NAACOG Clin Issues Perinat Women Health Nurs* 1992; 3(4):667-82.

Vaccines safe for nursing mothers.

Centers for Disease Control. General recommendations on immunization. *MMWR* 1994; 43(RR-1):1-38.

Page 315   **Mothers with chronic illness or disabilities can breastfeed.**

Lawrence, R. *Breastfeeding: A Guide for the Medical Profession*, 4th edition. St. Louis: Mosby, 1994.

Page 316   **Mothers may experience temporary remission of symptoms while breastfeeding.**

Butte, N. et al. Milk composition of insulin-dependent diabetic women. *J Ped Gastro Nutr* 1987; 6:939.

Nelson, L. Risk of multiple sclerosis exacerbation during pregnancy and breastfeeding. *JAMA* 1988; 259:3441-43.

Mothers with diabetes can breastfeed.

Gagne, M. et al. The breastfeeding experience of women with type 1 diabetes. *Health Care Women Int* 1992; 13:249-60.

Breastfeeding may reduce baby's chances of developing diabetes.

Karjalainen, J. et al. A bovine albumin peptide as a possible trigger of insulin-dependent diabetes mellitus. *N Engl J Med* 1992; 327(5):302-07.

Page 317   **Mothers with epilepsy can breastfeed.**

Lawrence, R. *Breastfeeding: A Guide for the Medical Profession*, 4th ed. St. Louis: Mosby, 1994.

Breastfeeding and HIV.

Van de Perre, P. et al. Postnatal transmission of human immunodeficiency virus type 1: the breastfeeding dilemma. *Am J Obstet Gynecol* 1995; 173(3):483-87.

Page 318   **Postpartum depression in breastfeeding women.**

Astbury, J. et al. Birth events, birth experiences, and social differences in postpartum depression. *Aust J Public Health* 1994; 18(2):76-84.

Page 319   **Medications used for depression.**

Hatzopoulos, F. and Albrecht, L. Antidepressant use during breastfeeding. *J Hum Lact* 1996; 12(2):139-41.

Page 320   **Continuing to breastfeed if baby has diarrhea.**

Vonlanthen, M. Management of diarrhea: to continue to breastfeed or not? BREASTFEEDING ABSTRACTS 1995; 14:26-27.

Human milk inhibits the growth of harmful bacteria.

Goldman, A. S. et al. Anti-inflammatory properties of human milk. *Acta Paediatr Scand* 1986; 75:689-95.

Dewey, K. G. et al. Differences in morbidity between breastfed and formula-fed infants. *J Pediatr* 1995; 126(5) pt 1:696-702.

Enhanced development of baby's brain and nervous system.

Pollock, J. I. Long-term associations with infant feeding in a clinically advantaged population of babies. *Dev Med Child Neurol* 1994; 36(5): 429-40.

Baby is protected from many illnesses by breastfeeding.

Beaudry, M. et al. Relation between infant feeding and infections during the first six months of life. *J Pediatr* 1995; 126(2):191-97.

Page 321   **No need to avoid breastfeeding when baby has diarrhea or is vomiting.**

Brown, K. and Lake, A. Appropriate use of human and non-human milk for the dietary management of children with diarrhoea. *J Diarrhoeal Dis Res* 1991; 9(3):168-85.

Page 322   **If baby can take anything by mouth it should be his mother's milk.**

Russka, T. Occurrence of acute diarrhea in atopic and nonatopic infants: the role of prolonged breastfeeding. *J Ped Gastro Nutr* 1992; 14:27-33.

Page 323   Sears, W. SAFE AND HEALTHY. Schaumburg IL: La Leche League International, 1989.

Babies with gastroesophageal reflux.

Sutphen, J. Pediatric gastroesophageal reflux disease. *Gastro Clin N Amer* 1990; 19(3):617-29.

Page 324   **Surgery on a breastfeeding baby.**
Schreiner, M. Preoperative and postoperative fasting in children.
Ped Clinics N Amer 1994; 4(1):111-20.

Page 325   **Initial weight loss and regaining birth weight in breastfed babies.**
DeMarzo, S. et al. Initial weight loss and return to birth weight criteria
for breastfed infants: challenging the "rules of thumb." *Am J Dis Child*
1991; 145:402.

Possible illness as cause of slow weight gain.
Lukefahr, J. Underlying illness associated with failure to thrive in breastfed infants. *Clin Pediatr* 1990; 29:468-70.

Normal growth of breastfed babies.
Dewey, K. et al. Breastfed infants are leaner than formula-fed infants at
one year of age: The Darling study. *Am J Clin Nutr* 1993; 57:140-45.

Page 326   **Babies who get too much foremilk may gain slowly.**
Woolridge, M. and Fisher, C. Colic, "overfeeding," and symptoms of lactose malabsorption in the breastfed baby: a possible artifact of feed management? *Lancet* 1988; II(8605):382-84.

Artificial nipples may cause nipple confusion.
Neifert, M. et al. Nipple confusion: toward a more formal definition.
J Pediatr 1995; 126(6):S125-29.

Page 327   **Importance of correct sucking technique.**
Righard, L. and Alade, M. Sucking technique and its effect on success of
breastfeeding. *Birth* 1992; 19(4):185-89.
Marmet, C. and Shell, E. Training neonates to suck correctly. *MCN* 1984;
9:401-07.

Page 329   **Possible causes of slow weight gain: caffeine, nicotine, hormonal
contraceptives, mother's health.**
Nehlig, A. and Debry, G. Consequences on the newborn of chronic
maternal consumption of coffee during gestation and lactation: a review.
J Am Coll Nutr 1994; 13(1):6-21.

Dahlstrom, A. et al. Nicotine and cotinine concentrations in the nursing
mother and her infant. *Acta Paediatr Scand* 1990; 79:142-47.

Erwin, P. To use or not to use combined hormonal oral contraceptives
during lactation. *Fam Plan Perspect* 1994; 26(1):26-33.

Lawrence, R. *Breastfeeding: a Guide for the Medical Profession*, 4th edition.
St. Louis: Mosby, 1994.

Page 330   **Use of alternative feeding methods to avoid artificial nipples.**
Armstrong, H. Feeding low birthweight babies: advances in Kenya.
J Hum Lact 1987; 3:34-37.

Lang, S. et al. Cup feeding: an alternative method of infant feeding.
Arch Dis Child 1994; 71:365-69.

Page 331   **Supplementing with the mother's own milk.**

Valentine, C. et al. Hindmilk improves weight gain in low birth weight infants fed human milk. *J Ped Gastro Nutr* 1994; 18:474-77.

Page 332   **Mothers are more likely to breastfeed successfully when they have support.**

Hofmeyr, G. et al. Companionship to modify the clinical birth environment: Effects on progress and perceptions of labour and breastfeeding. *Br J Ob Gyn* 1991; 98:756-64.

Rarely, a mother may not be able to produce enough milk for her baby.

Neifert, M. and Seacat, J. Lactation insufficiency: a rational approach. *Birth* 1987; 14:182-88.

Willis, C. and Livingstone, V. Infant insufficient milk syndrome associated with maternal postpartum hemorrhage. *J Hum Lact* 1995; 11(2): 123-26.

Widdice, L. The effects of breast reduction and breast augmentation surgery on lactation: an annotated bibliography. *J Hum Lact* 1993; 9(3):161-67.

Chapter 18—The Superior Infant Food

Page 335   **A mother's own milk is the best possible food for her baby.**

Cunningham, A., Jelliffe, D., and Jelliffe, E. Breastfeeding and health in the 1980s: a global epidemiologic review. *J Pediatr* 1991; 118(5):659-66.

Page 336   **Nutritional and immunological components of human milk.**

Lawrence, R. *Breastfeeding: a Guide for the Medical Profession*, 4th edition. St. Louis: Mosby, 1994.

Mother's milk changes throughout the day.

Harzer, G. Changing patterns of human milk lipids in the course of lactation and during the day. *Am J Clin Nutr* 1983; 37:612-21.

Milk of mothers who give birth to preterm babies is more suited to the nutritional needs of the premie.

Lemons, J. et al. Differences in the composition of preterm and term human milk during early lactation. *Pediatr Res* 1982; 16:113-16.

Mother's milk changes according to her diet.

Sullivan, S. and Birch, L. Infant dietary experience and acceptance of solid foods. *Pediatrics* 1994; 93(2):271-77.

Infants sucked more vigorously after mothers consumed garlic capsules.

Menella, J. and Beauchamp, G. Maternal diet alters sensory qualities of human milk and the nursling's behavior. *Pediatrics* 1991; 88(4):737-44.

Page 337   **Proteins are distinctive in human milk.**

Hambraeus, B. et al. Nitrogen and protein components of human milk. *Acta Paediatr Scand* 1978; 67:561-65.

Page 338   **Amino acids and taurine in human milk.**

Rassin, D. K. et al. Taurine and other free amino acids in milk of man and other mammals. *Early Human Dev* 1978; 2(1):1-13.

Gaull, G. E. Taurine in the nutrition of the human infant. *Acta Paediatr Scand* 1982; 269(Suppl):38-40.

Severely undernourished mothers may have milk that is lower in fat than well-nourished mothers.

Smith, C. Effects of maternal undernutrition upon newborn infants in Holland (1944-1945). *J Pediatr* 1947; 30:229-43.

Page 339   **Importance of long-chain polyunsaturated fatty acids in human milk.**

Birch, E. E. et al. Breastfeeding and optimal visual development. *J Pediatr Ophthal Strab* 1993; 30:33-38.

Bjerve, K. S. et al. Omega-3 fatty acids: essential fatty acids with important biological effects, and serum phospholipid fatty acids as markers of dietary W-3 fatty acid intake. *Am J Clin Nutr* 1993; 57(Suppl):801S-95S.

Bergstrom, E. et al. Serum lipid values in adolescents are related to family history, infant feeding, and physical growth. *Atherosclerosis* 1995; 117:1-3.

Page 340   **Iron absorption from hum milk.**

Saarinen, U. et al. Iron absorption in infants: high bioavailability of breast milk iron as indicated by the extrinsic tag method of iron absorption and by the concentration of serum ferritin. *J Pediatr* 1977; 91:36-39.

Iron supplements may interfere with specialized proteins in mother's milk.

Bullen, J. J. et al. Iron-binding proteins in milk and resistance to *escherichia coli* infection in infants. *Br Med J* 1972; 1:69-75.

Page 342   **No evidence of vitamin D deficiency in breastfed babies.**

Greer, F. R. and Marshall, S. Bone mineral content, serum vitamin D metabolite concentrations, and ultraviolet B light exposure in infants fed human milk with and without vitamin D_2 supplements. *J Pediatr* 1989; 114(2):204-12.

Human milk prevents the occurrence of acrodermatitis enteropathica.

Sandstrom, B. et al. Zinc absorption from human milk, cow's milk, and infant formulas. *Am J Dis Child* 1983; 137:726-29.

Page 343   **Fluoride supplements no longer recommended.**

American Academy of Pediatrics. Fluoride supplementation of children: interim policy recommendations. *Pediatrics* 1995; 95(5):777.

Jelliffe, D. and Jelliffe, E. F. P. *Human Milk in the Modern World.* Oxford: Oxford University Press, 1978.

Mepham, T. B. Science and the politics of breastfeeding: birth right or birth rite? *SCI Public Policy* 1989; 16(3):181-91.

Page 344

Reduced morbidity and mortality in breastfed infants.

Yoon, P. W. et al. Effect of not breastfeeding on the risk of diarrheal and respiratory mortality in children under 2 years of age in Metro Cebu, the Philippines. *Am J Epidemiol* 1996; 143(11):1142-48.

Victora, C. G. et al. Evidence for protection by breastfeeding against infant deaths from infectious diseases in Brazil. *Lancet* 1987; 2:319-22.

Clemens, J. D. et al. Breastfeeding and the risk of severe cholera in rural Bangaladeshi children. *Am J Epidemiol* 1990; 131(3):400-11.

Teka, T. et al. Risk factors for deaths in under-age-five children attending a diarrhoea treatment centre. *Acta Paediatr* 1996; 85(9):1070-75.

Grulee, C. G. et al. Breast and artificial feeding: influence on morbidity and mortality of twenty thousand infants. *J Am Med Assoc* 1934; 103: 735-39.

Page 346

Fewer episodes of illness in breastfed babies.

Cunningham, A. S. Morbidity in breastfed and artificially fed infants. *J Pediatr* 1977; 90:726-29.

Paine, R. and Coble, R. J. Breastfeeding and infant health in a rural US community. *Am J Dis Child* 1982; 136:36-38.

Takala, A. K. et al. Risk factors of invasive *Haemophilus influenzae* type B a disease among children in Finland. *J Pediatr* 1989; 115(5p+1):694-701.

Koopman, J. S. et al. Infant formulas and gastrointestinal illness. *Am J Public Health* 1985; 75(5):477-80.

Dewey, K. G. et al. Differences in morbidity between breast-fed and formula-fed infants. *J Pediatr* 1995; 126(5) pt 1:696-702.

Lerman, Y. et al. Epidemiology of acute diarrheal diseases in children in a high standard of living in a rural settlement in Israel. *Pediatr Infect Dis J* 1994; 13(2)116-22.

Formula-fed infants were hospitalized more often.

Fallot, M. E. et al. Breastfeeding reduces incidence of hospital admissions for infection in infants. *Pediatrics* 1980; 65(6):1121-24.

Ware, J. and Hoey, C. Economic advantages of breastfeeding in an HMO setting. *ABM News & Views,* 1977; 3(1):3.

Page 348

Reduced incidence of infection.

Aniansson, G. et al. A prospective cohort study on breastfeeding and *otitis media* in Swedish infants. *Pediatr Infect Dis J* 1994; 13:183-88.

Beaudry, M. et al. Relation between infant feeding and infections during the first six months of life. *J Pediatr* 1995; 126(2):191-97.

Page 347   **Overall benefits of breastfeeding.**

Heinig, M. J. and Dewey, K. G. Health advantages of breastfeeding for infants: a critical review. *Nutr Res Rev* 1996; 9:89-110.

Cunningham, A. et al. Breastfeeding and health in the 1980s: a global epidemiological review. *J Pediatr* 1991; 118(5):659-66.

Breastfeeding protects against SIDS.

Hoffman, H. J. et al. Risk factors for SIDS: results of the National Institute of Child Health and Human Development SIDS Cooperative epidemiological study. *Ann N Y Acad Sci* 1988; 533:13-30.

Page 348   **How breastfeeding protects babies.**

Goldman, A. S. Immunologic system in human milk. *J Pediatr Gastroenterol Nutr* 1986; 5:343-45.

Goldman, A. S. et al. Anti-inflammatory properties of human milk. *Acta Paediatr Scand* 1986; 75:689-95.

Goldblum, R. M. et al. Antibody forming cells in human colostrum after oral immunization. *Nature* 1975; 257:797-99.

Page 349   **Immunities continue into second year of breastfeeding.**

Goldman, A. Immunologic components of human milk during the second year of lactation. *Acta Paediatr Scand* 1983; 72:461-62.

Koutra, A. K. et al. Fecal secretory immunoglobulin A in breast milk versus formula feeding in early infancy. *J Ped Gastro Nutr* 1989; 9(1):58-61.

Page 350   **Concerns about chemical contaminants.**

Koopman-Esseboom, C. et al. Effects of polychlorinated liphenyl/dioxin exposure and feeding type on infants' mental and psychomotor development. *Pediatrics* 1996; 97(5):700-06.

Huisman, M. et al. Neurological condition in 18-month-old children perinatally exposed to polychlorinated biphenyls and dioxins. *Early Human Dev* 1995; 43:165-76.

Kendrick, E. Testing for environmental contaminants in human milk. *Pediatrics* 1980; 66(3):470-72.

Rogan, W. J. and Gladen, B. C. Breastfeeding and cognitive development. *Early Hum Dev* 1993; 31:181-93.

Page 351   **Breastfeeding protects against allergies.**

Saarinen, U. M. et al. Breastfeeding as prophylaxis against atopic disease: prospective follow-up study until 17 years old. *Lancet* 1995; 346(8982):1065-69.

Wright, A. L. et al. Epidemiology of physician-diagnosed allergic rhinitis in childhood. *Pediatrics* 1994; 94(6):895-901.

Chandra, A. K. et al. Influence of maternal diet during lactation and use of formula feeds on development of atopic eczema in high risk infants. *Br Med J* 1989; 299(6693):228-30.

Gerrard, J. W. et al. Cow's milk allergy. *Acta Paediatr Scand* 1973; Suppl 234:1-21.

Merrett, T. G. et al. Infant feeding and allergy: 12-month prospective study of 500 babies born into allergic families. *Ann Allergy* 1988; 61:13-20.

Page 353   **A breastfed baby may still be allergic.**

Burr, M. L. Food allergy in childhood. *Hum Nutr Appl Nutr* 1985; 39A:277-93.

Heiner, D. C. Modern research relating to food allergy and its implications. *Clin Rev Allergy* 1984; 2:1-5.

Taylor, B. et al. Transient IgA deficiency and pathogenesis of infantile atopy. *Lancet* 1973:ii:111-13.

Page 355   Gerrard, J. W. Allergies in breastfed babies to foods ingested by the mother. *Clin Rev Allergy* 1985; 2-143-49.

Can baby react to something mother eats?

Jakobsson, I. And Lindberg, T. Cows' milk proteins cause colic in breast-fed babies: a double-blind crossover study. *Pediatrics* 1983; 71:268-71.

Lust, K. et al. Maternal intake of cruciferous vegetables and other foods and colic symptoms in exclusively breastfed infants. *J Am Diet Assoc* 1996; 96(1):46-48.

Clyne, P. and Kulczycki, A. Human breast milk contains bovine IgG: relationship to infant colic? *Pediatrics* 1991; 87(4):439-44.

Page 356   **Dental caries in breastfed children.**

Roberts, G. et al. Patterns of breast and bottle feeding and their association with dental caries in 1 to 4 year old South African children. *Comm Dent Hlth* 1993; 10:405-13.

Schaefer, O. *Personal communication,* 1978.

Page 357   Schneider, P. et al. Effects of caffeine intake during gestation and lactation on the acid solubility of enamel in weaning rats. *Caries Res* 1995; 29:285-90.

Wendt, L. K. et al. Analysis of caries-related factors in infants and toddlers living in Sweden. *Acta Odont Scand* 1996; 54(2):131-37.

Page 358   **Breastfeeding protects against malocclusion.**

Labbok, M. H. and Hendershot, G. E. Does breastfeeding protect against malocclusion? An Analysis of the 1981 Child Health Supplement to the National Health Interview Survey. *Am J Prev Med* 1987; 3:227-32.

Davis, D. et al. Infant feeding practices and occlusal outcomes: a longitudinal study. *J Can Dent Assoc* 1991; 57(7):593-94.

Page 359   **Speech development.**

Broad, F. Effects of breastfeeding on later speech development. *NZ Med J* 1972; 482:2831.

Broad, F. Further studies on the effects of infant feeding on speech quality. *NZ Med J* 1975; 82:373-76.

Fewer ear infections in breastfed babies.

Duncan, B. et al. Exclusive breastfeeding for at least 4 months protects against *otitis media*. *Pediatrics* 1993; 91(5):867-72.

Page 360   **Psychomotor and social development in first 12 months.**

Lucas, A. et al. Multicentre trial on feeding low birthweight infants: effect of diet on early growth. *Arch Dis Child* 1984; 59:722-30.

Morrow-Tlucak, M. et al. Breastfeeding and cognitive development in the first 2 years of life. *Soc Sci Med* 1988; 26:635-39.

Morley, R. et al. Mother's choice to provide breast milk and developmental outcome. *Arch Dis Child* 1988; 65:1382-85.

Lucas, A. et al. Breast milk and subsequent intelligence quotient in children born preterm. *Lancet* 1992; 339:261-64.

Rogan, W. et al. Breastfeeding and cognitive development. *Early Hum Dev* 1993; 31:181-93.

Birch, E. et al. Breastfeeding and optimal visual development. *J Pediatr Ophthal Strab* 1993; 30:33-38.

Baumgartner, C. Psychomotor and social development of breastfed and bottle-fed babies during their first year of life. *Acta Paediatrica Hungarica* 1984; 25(4):409-17.

DiPietro, J. A. et al. Behavioral and heart rate pattern differences between breastfed and bottle-fed neonates. *Dev Psych* 1987; 23(4): 467-74.

Chapter 19—How Breastfeeding Affects a Mother.

Milk production.

Page 361   Lawrence, R. *Breastfeeding: A Guide for the Medical Profession,* 4th edition. St. Louis: Mosby, 1994.

Page 364   Newton, M. and Newton, N. R. The let-down reflex in human lactation. *J Pediatr* 1948; 33:698-704.

Page 365   **Lactational amenorrhea.**

Campbell, O. et al. Characteristics and determinants of postpartum ovarian function in the United States. *Am J Obstet Gynecol* 1993; 169:55-60.

Gross, B. Is the lactational amenorrhea method a part of family planning? Biology and policy. Am J Obstet Gynecol 1991; 165(6):2014-19.

Kippley, S. *Breastfeeding and Natural Child Spacing.* Cincinnati OH: Couple-to-Couple League International, Inc., 1989.

Labbok, M. The lactational amenorrhea method (LAM): another choice for breastfeeding mothers. BREASTFEEDING ABSTRACTS 1993; 13:3-4.

Page 367   **Use of natural family planning while breastfeeding.**

Kennedy, K. et al. Breastfeeding and the Symptothermal Method. *Studies in Fam Plan* 1995; 26(2):107-15.

Kippley, J. and Kippley, S. *The Art of Natural Family Planning.* Cincinnati OH: Couple-to-Couple League International, Inc. 1979.

Winstein, M. *Your Fertility Signals: Using Them to Achieve or Avoid Pregnancy Naturally.* St. Louis MO: Smooth Stone Press, 1994.

Use of hormonal contraceptives.

World Health Organization (WHO) Task Force: Progestogen-only contraceptives during lactation: 1. Infant Growth; 2. Infant development. *Contraception* 1994; 50:35-68.

Madhavapeddi, R. and Ramachandran, P. Growth and morbidity of breastfed infants whose mothers were using combination pills. *Breastfeed Rev* 1990; 11(2):66-68.

Harlap, S. Exposure to contraceptive hormones through breast milk: are there long-term health and behavioral consequences? *Int J Gyn Ob* 1987; 25(Suppl):47-55.

Pardthaisong, T. et al. The long-term growth and development of children exposed to Depo-provera during pregnancy or lactation. *Contraception* 1992; 45:313-24.

Baby controls milk production.

Perez-Escamilla, R. et al. Maternal anthropometric status and lactation performance in a low-income Honduran population: evidence for the role of infants. *Am J Clin Nutr* 1995; 61(3):528-34.

Breastfeeding does not deplete a mother's energy.

Van Raaij, J. et al. Energy cost of lactation, and energy balances of well-nourished Dutch lactating women: reappraisal of the extra energy requirements of lactation. *Am J Clin Nutr* 1991; 53(3):612-19.

Breastfeeding helps a mother deal with stress.

Altemus, M. et al. Suppression of hypothalmic-pituitary-adrenal axis responses to stress in lactating women. *J Clin Endocrinol Metab* 1995; 80(9):2954-59.

Are breastfeeding mothers at risk for osteoporosis?

Kalkwarf, H. J. et al. Intestinal calcium absorption of women during lactation and after weaning. *Am J Clin Nutr* 1996; 63(4):526-31.

Sinigaglia, L. et al. Effect of lactation on postmenopausal bone mineral density of lumbar spine. *J Reprod Med* 1996; 41(6)439-43.

Kritz-Silverstein, D. et al. Pregnancy and lactation as determinants of bone mineral density in postmenopausal women. *Am J Epidemiol* 1992; 136(9):1052-59.

Fox, K. et al. Reproductive correlates of bone mass in elderly women. *J Bone & Min Res* 1993; 8(8):901-08.

Effects of smoking on breastfeeding.

Hill, P. D. et al. Smoking and breastfeeding status. *Res Nurs Health* 1996; 19(2):125-32.

Hopkinson, J. et al. Milk production by mothers of premature infants: influence of cigarette smoking. *Pediatrics* 1992; 90(6):934-38.

Matheson, I. And Rivrud, G. The effect of smoking on lactation and infantile colic. *JAMA* 1989; 261-42.

Colley, J. and Corkhill, R. Influence of passive smoking and parental phlegm on pneumonia and bronchitis in early childhood. *Lancet* 1974; 2:1031.

Page 370   **Use of alcohol while breastfeeding.**

Lawton, M. Alcohol in breast milk. *Aust NZ Obst Gyn* 1985; 25(1):71-73.

Mennella, J. and Beauchamp, G. The transfer of alcohol to human milk: effects on flavor and the infant's behavior. *New Engl J Med* 1991; 325(14):981-85.

Carlson, H. et al. Beer-induced prolactin secretion: clinical and laboratory study of the role of Salsolinol. *J Clin Endocrinol Metab* 1985; 60:673.

Mennella, J. and Beauchamp, G. Effect of beer on breastfed infants. *JAMA* 1993; 269(13):1637.

Page 371   **Drugs and medications used by a breastfeeding mother.**

American Academy of Pediatrics Committee on Drugs. The transfer of drugs and other chemicals into human milk. *Pediatrics* 1994; 93(1): 137-50.

Anderson, P. Drug use during breastfeeding. *Clin Pharmacy* 1991; 10: z594-623.

Wilton, J. Breastfeeding and the chemically dependent woman. *NAACOG Clin Issues Perinat Women Health Nurs* 1992; 3(4):667-82.

Page 372   **Breastfeeding protects against breast cancer.**

McTierman, A. and Thomas, D. B. Evidence for a protective effect of lactation on risk of breast cancer in young women. *Am J Epidemiol* 1986; 124:353-58.

Brinton, L. A. et al. Breastfeeding and breast cancer risk. *Cancer Causes and Control* 1995; 6:199-208.

Romieu, I. et al. Breast cancer and lactation history in Mexican women. *Am J Epidemiol* 1996; 143(6):543-52.

Yoo, K. et al. Independent protective effect of lactation against breast cancer: a case control study in Japan. *Am J Epidemiol* 1992; 135(7): 726-33.

Newcomb, P. et al. Lactation and a reduced risk of premenopausal breast cancer. *N Engl J Med* 1994; 330(2):81-87.

Freudenheim, J. et al. Exposure to breast milk in infancy and the risk of breast cancer. *Epidemiology* 1994; 5(3):324-31.

Layde, P. M. et al. The independent associates of parity, age at first full-term pregnancy, and duration of breastfeeding with the risk of breast cancer. *J Clin Epidemiol* 1989; 42(10):963-73.

Hirose, K. et al. A large scale, hospital-based case-control study of risk factors of breast cancer according to menopausal status. *Jpn J Cancer Res* 1995; 86:146-54.

Page 374 **Economic benefits of breastfeeding.**

Montgomery, D. L. and Splett, P. L. Economic benefit of breastfeeding infants enrolled in WIC. *J Am Diet Assoc* 1997; 97(4):379-85.

Palmer, G. *The Politics of Breastfeeding.* London: Pandora Press, 1993.

Page 377 Whipple, D. V. Breastfeeding in today's world. *Journal of the American Med Women's Association.* 1965; 10:936-37.

Fraiberg, S. How a baby learns to love. *Redbook* 1971.

INDEX

Would You Like to Know More?

As you read through this book, you find that La Leche League is mentioned over and over again as a source of information, support, and encouragement. La Leche League Groups meet monthly in communities all over the world to share breastfeeding and mothering experiences. Call 1-800-LA LECHE for a referral to a local LLL Group. Or visit LLL's Web Page at www.lalecheleague.org/

Perhaps you'd like to be a part of this mother-to-mother network. It is easy to become an LLL Member. Just return the coupon below along with your annual membership fee. You will receive six bimonthly issues of NEW BEGINNINGS, a magazine filled with personal stories, helpful hints, and up-to-date parenting information. Members automatically receive our LLLI Catalogues by mail and they are entitled to a 10% discount on most purchases. Term Life Insurance at special Group Rates is also available in some areas to LLL Members and their families. You don't need to attend Group meetings in order to join—though most members enjoy the interaction with other mothers that meetings provide.

Why should you join La Leche League? Because you care—about your own family and about mothers and babies all over the world!

Return this form to:
La Leche League International,
Post Office Box 4079, Schaumburg IL 60168-4079 USA.
In Canada, write to LLLC National Office,
18C Industrial Drive, Box 29, Chesterville, Ontario K0C 1H0

◻ I'd like to join La Leche League International. Enclosed is my annual membership of $30.

◻ In addition, I am enclosing a tax-deductible donation of $_____ to support the work of La Leche League.

◻ Please send me a copy of THE WOMANLY ART OF BREASTFEEDING, softcover $14.95 plus $4.25 for shipping and handling. (In California and Illinois, please add sales tax.)

◻ Please send me La Leche League's FREE Catalogue.

Name _____

Address _____

State/Province _____   Zip/Postal Code _____

Country _____